The STEP Test in Practical English Proficiency

【英検】
文で覚える
プラス
単熟語

1級

JN270865

Obunsha

英検とは

　文部科学省認定　実用英語技能検定（通称：英検）は、社会教育拡充政策の一環として文部省（現：文部科学省）後援のもと、1963年に第1回試験が実施されました。以来40年、社会教育的な役割という発足当初からの目的と日本社会の国際化が進展するに伴い、英語の四技能「読む・聞く・話す・書く」を総合的に測定する全国規模の試験としてその社会的評価は高まり、現在では年間300万人が受験しております。

　2002年7月に文部科学省の発表した『英語の使える日本人』の育成戦略構想では、中学卒業段階では英検3級、高校卒業段階では準2級から2級程度の英語力を目標とすると明言しております。また指導する英語教師も準1級程度の英語力を要すると謳っております。

　このように英検の資格はいつの時代も日本人の英語力を測るスケールとして生きており、最近、大学や高校の入学試験で優遇されたり、英語科目の単位として認定する学校が年々増えております。

　受験者の皆さんは自己の英語能力の評価基準として、また国際化時代を生きる"国際人"たり得る資格として、さらには生涯学習の目標として大いに英検にチャレンジしてください。

試験概要

(1) 実施機関
　　試験を実施しているのは、(財)日本英語検定協会です。ホームページ http://www.eiken.or.jp/ では、試験に関する情報・優遇校一覧などを公開しています。

(2) 試験日程
　　試験は年3回行なわれます。（二次試験は3級以上）
　　第1回検定：一次試験 ― 6月 ／ 二次試験 ― 7月
　　第2回検定：一次試験 ―10月 ／ 二次試験 ―11月
　　第3回検定：一次試験 ― 1月 ／ 二次試験 ― 2月

その後の5年間で借金を全額返済し、数億円の資産と毎月数百万円の収入を得て、いまでは働かなくても悠々自適の暮らしができるくらい裕福になりました。

つまり、お金に関して天国と地獄の両方を経験している特異な銀行員だということです。

この両極端の人生を体験したことにより、サラリーマンは金融知識だけではお金持ちになれないことを、身をもって知ることになりました。

では、どうすれば裕福になれるのか？

それをお話しするには、まずは私たちが信じ込まされてきた**「お金にまつわるウソ」**を話さなければなりません。

私たちは小さいころから、将来お金で苦労しないように「我慢してお金を貯めなさい」と親から教えられ、大人になってからは「金融商品を買ってお金を増やしなさい」と銀行などから教わって生きています。

でもじつは、これらがすべて根も葉もない真っ赤なウソだとしたら？

● プロローグ
どんなにお金の知識があっても裕福にはなれない

あなたはいま、将来に不安を感じないくらい裕福ですか？

20年以上も金融業界のど真ん中に身を置いて、私が悟ったことは、どんなにお金の知識があっても裕福にはなれないということでした。だから「お金のプロ」であるはずの銀行員でさえも将来に不安を感じ、給料をもらうため会社にしがみつきます。

私は、とあるメガバンクに勤める銀行員ですが、ある事情から普通の銀行員がしないような経験をしています。

20年以上にわたり個人や企業を相手にコンサルティングや資産運用のアドバイスをしてきたのですが、そうした自分の知識とスキルを過信した結果、**株で失敗し借金地獄に陥ってしまい、破産寸前にまで追い込まれた**のです。しかし、

例文の日本語訳	341
索引	446
More to Learn	89・228・340

品詞

v.t.	他動詞	*v.i.*	自動詞	*n.*	名詞
adj.	形容詞	*adv.*	副詞		

(「他動詞＋副詞」の熟語の場合，間に目的語が入ることがありますが，見出し語としてはすべて「他動詞＋副詞～」の形で代表しています)

関連情報

≒ 同義語または語句の定義　　⇔ 反意語

(同意語・反意語における用法の違いなどは，辞書などで確認してください)

発音記号

原則として『レクシス英和辞典』(旺文社)に準じています。例文中で用いられている品詞の発音を表示しています。

■装丁：銀月堂　　■本文デザイン：熊アート　　■編集協力：オリーブカンパニー

本書の利用法

本書は，例文を通して英検1級に出題される単熟語を効果的に学べるように構成されています。まずこのページを参照してから，学習を進めましょう。なお，本文の赤色部分は，巻末にある「暗記フィルター」を切り取ってのせると，隠れるようになっています。

共通

❶ **チェック欄**：有効に活用して，繰り返し語句を覚えるようにしましょう。
❷ **同義語・語句の定義**：ニュアンスを把握して，見出し語句に対する理解を深めましょう。ただし，ここで挙げる同義語は，必ずしも例文中の見出し語と入れ替え可能ではありません。

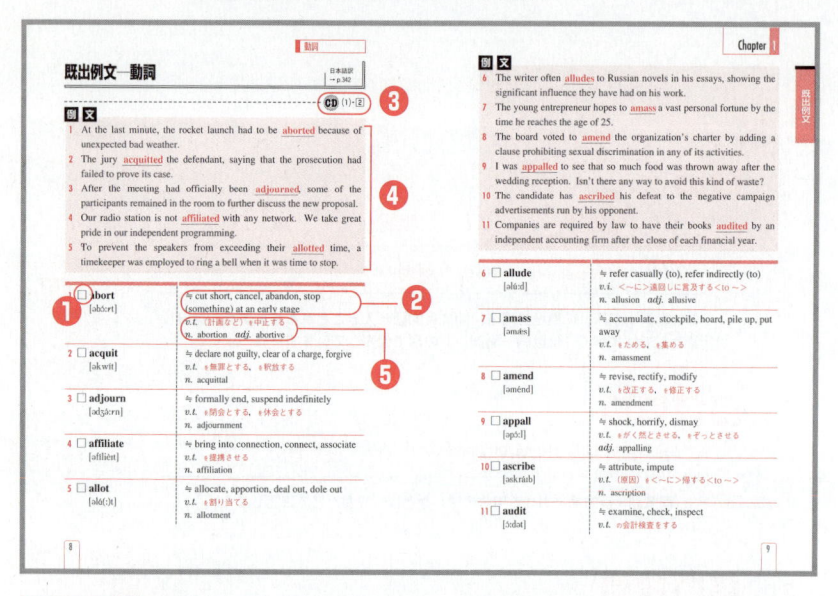

Chapter 1

❸ **CDマーク**：別売CDに収録されている箇所を示しています。詳しい収録内容はp.6を参照してください。
❹ **例文**：英検で実際に出題された「既出例文」と，今後出題が予想される「予想例文」の2つから成っています（日本語訳は巻末にまとめられています）。
❺ **語義・派生語・反意語**：英検1級合格に必須のものを挙げてあります。2つ以上の品詞を示す場合には，セミコロン（;）を用いて区別しています。

3 Bugs Fighting Back

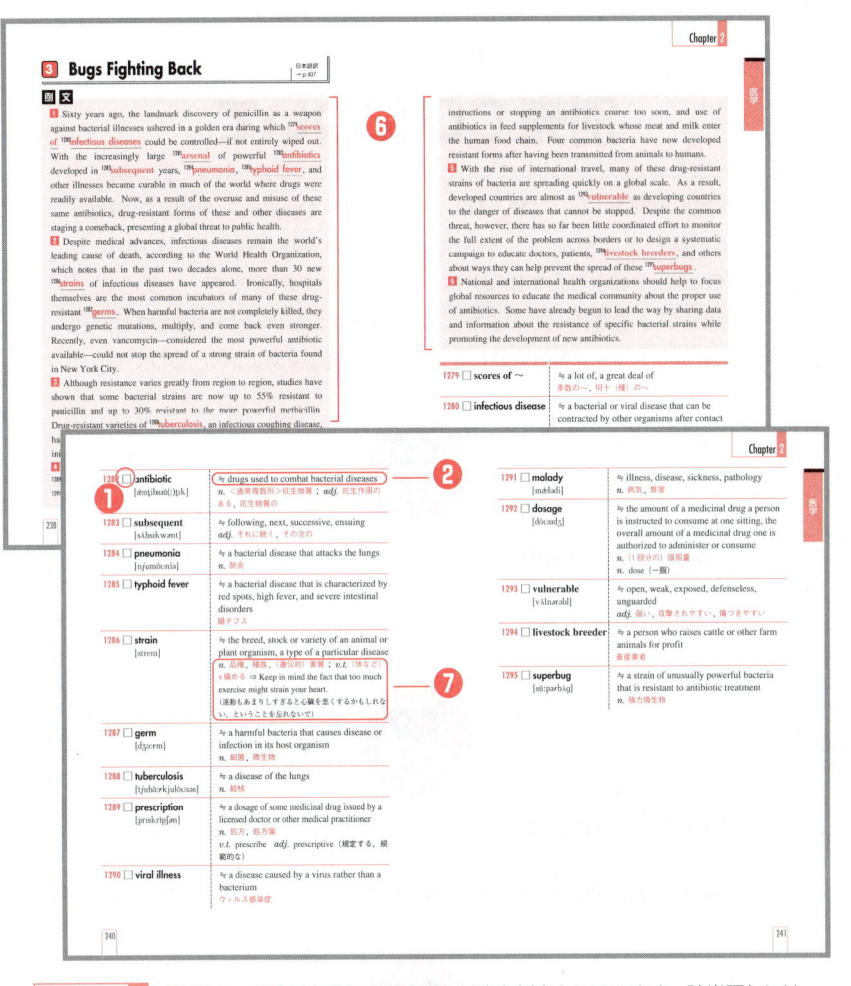

日本語訳 → p.407

原文

1 Sixty years ago, the landmark discovery of penicillin as a weapon against bacterial illnesses ushered in during which [1279]scores of [1280]infectious diseases could be controlled—if not entirely wiped out. With the increasingly large [1281]arsenal of powerful [1282]antibiotics developed in [1283]subsequent years, [1284]pneumonia, [1285]typhoid fever, and other illnesses became curable in much of the world where drugs were readily available. Now, as a result of the overuse and misuse of these same antibiotics, drug-resistant forms of these and other diseases are staging a comeback, presenting a global threat to public health.

2 Despite medical advances, infectious diseases remain the world's leading cause of death, according to the World Health Organization, which notes that in the past two decades alone, more than 30 new [1286]strains of infectious diseases have appeared. Ironically, hospitals themselves are the most common incubators of many of these drug-resistant [1287]germs. When harmful bacteria are not completely killed, they undergo genetic mutations, multiply, and come back even stronger. Recently, even vancomycin—considered the most powerful antibiotic available—could not stop the spread of a strong strain of bacteria found in New York City.

3 Although resistance varies greatly from region to region, studies have shown that some bacterial strains are now up to 55% resistant to penicillin and up to 30% resistant to the more powerful methicillin. Drug-resistant varieties of [1288]tuberculosis, an infectious coughing disease,

instructions or stopping an antibiotics course too soon, and use of antibiotics in feed supplements for livestock show meat and milk enter the human food chain. Four common bacteria have now developed resistant forms after having been transmitted from animals to humans.

5 With the rise of international travel, many of these drug-resistant strains of bacteria are spreading quickly on a global scale. As a result, developed countries are almost as [1293]vulnerable as developing countries to the danger of diseases that cannot be stopped. Despite the common threat, however, there has so far been little coordinated effort to monitor the full extent of the problem across borders or to design a systematic campaign to educate doctors, patients, [1294]livestock breeders, and others about ways they can help prevent the spread of these [1295]superbugs.

6 National and international health organizations should help to focus global resources to educate the medical community about the proper use of antibiotics. Some have already begun to lead the way by sharing data and information about the resistance of specific bacterial strains while promoting the development of new antibiotics.

| 1279 | scores of ~ | ≒ a lot of, a great deal of
多数の, 何十(幾)もの |
| 1280 | infectious disease | ≒ a bacterial or viral disease that can be contracted by other organisms after contact |

1282	antibiotic [æntɪbaɪɑ́(ː)tɪk]	≒ drugs used to combat bacterial diseases n.〈通例複数形〉抗生物質; adj. 抗生作用のある, 抗生物質の
1283	subsequent [sʌ́bsɪkwənt]	≒ following, next, successive, ensuing adj. それに続く, その次の
1284	pneumonia [njumóʊniə]	≒ a bacterial disease that attacks the lungs n. 肺炎
1285	typhoid fever	≒ a bacterial disease that is characterized by red spots, high fever, and severe intestinal disorders 腸チフス
1286	strain [streɪn]	≒ the breed, stock or variety of an animal or plant organism, a type of a particular disease n. 品種, 種族, 〈遺伝の〉素質; v.t.〈体など〉を痛める ⇒ Keep in mind the fact that too much exercise might strain your heart.（運動をあまりしすぎると心臓を悪くするかもしれない, ということを忘れないで）
1287	germ [dʒɜrm]	≒ a harmful bacteria that causes disease or infection in its host organism n. 細菌, 微生物
1288	tuberculosis [tjuːbɜrkjʊlóʊsəs]	≒ a disease of the lungs n. 結核
1289	prescription [prɪskrɪ́pʃən]	≒ a dosage of some medicinal drug issued by a licensed doctor or other medical practitioner n. 処方, 処方箋 v.t. prescribe adj. prescriptive (規定する, 規範的な)
1290	viral illness	≒ a disease caused by a virus rather than a bacterium ウイルス感染症

1291	malady [mǽlədi]	≒ illness, disease, sickness, pathology n. 病気, 弊害
1292	dosage [dóʊsɪdʒ]	≒ the amount of a medicinal drug a person is instructed to consume at one sitting, the overall amount of a medicinal drug one is authorized to administer or consume n.（1回分の）服用量 ≒ dose（一服）
1293	vulnerable [vʌ́lnərəbl]	≒ open, weak, exposed, defenseless, unguarded adj. 弱い, 攻撃されやすい, 傷つきやすい
1294	livestock breeder	≒ a person who raises cattle or other farm animals for profit 畜産業者
1295	superbug [súːpərbʌɡ]	≒ a strain of unusually powerful bacteria that is resistant to antibiotic treatment n. 強力微生物

別売CDについて

本書には別売CD（3枚入り）があります。Chapter 1 既出例文は見出し語とその例文が，予想例文は例文のみが収録されています（Chapter 2 および日本語部分はすべて割愛してあります）。本文の該当箇所には **CD** (1) - ② のように示してあり，(1) - ② という表示は CD の巻数とトラック番号を表しています。収録内容は以下のとおりです。

CD 第1巻

- このCDについての説明 ・・・・・・・・・・・・・・・・・・・・・・・・・・・・・・・ **1**
- Chapter **1** 既出例文 動詞〜副詞 ・・・・・・・・・・・・・・・・・・ **2** 〜 **34**

CD 第2巻

- このCDについての説明 ・・・・・・・・・・・・・・・・・・・・・・・・・・・・・・・ **1**
- Chapter **1** 既出例文 熟語・予想例文 No.449〜800 ・・・・・・・・・ **2** 〜 **40**

CD 第3巻

- このCDについての説明 ・・・・・・・・・・・・・・・・・・・・・・・・・・・・・・・ **1**
- Chapter **1** 予想例文 No.801〜1241 ・・・・・・・・・・・・・・・・・・ **2** 〜 **40**

Chapter 1

短文の空所補充問題に出題される単熟語

既出例文	
動詞	8
名詞	34
形容詞	52
副詞	69
熟語	72

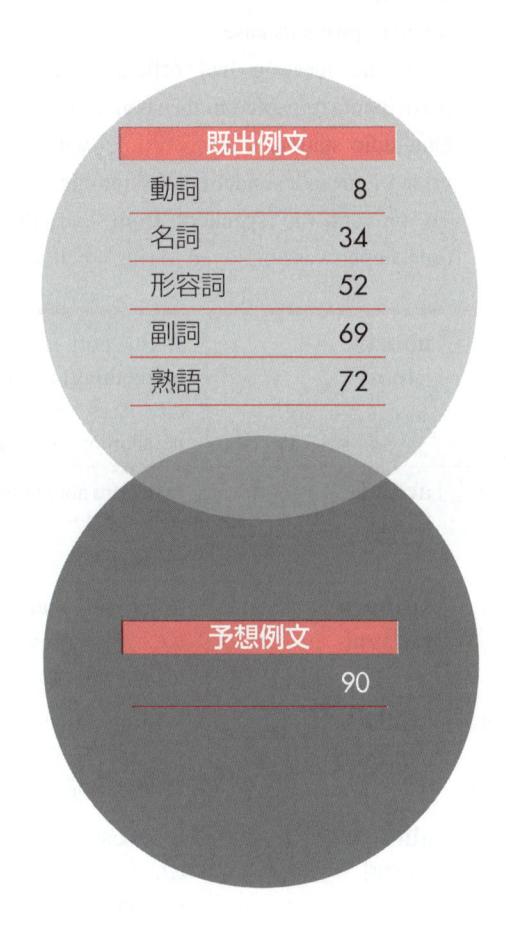

予想例文
90

動詞

既出例文—動詞

日本語訳 → p.342

例文

1. At the last minute, the rocket launch had to be **aborted** because of unexpected bad weather.
2. The jury **acquitted** the defendant, saying that the prosecution had failed to prove its case.
3. After the meeting had officially been **adjourned**, some of the participants remained in the room to further discuss the new proposal.
4. Our radio station is not **affiliated** with any network. We take great pride in our independent programming.
5. To prevent the speakers from exceeding their **allotted** time, a timekeeper was employed to ring a bell when it was time to stop.

---

1. **abort** [əbɔ́ːrt]
   ≒ cut short, cancel, abandon, stop (something) at an early stage
   v.t. (計画など)を中止する
   n. abortion   *adj.* abortive

2. **acquit** [əkwít]
   ≒ declare not guilty, clear of a charge, forgive
   v.t. を無罪とする、を釈放する
   n. acquittal

3. **adjourn** [ədʒə́ːrn]
   ≒ formally end, suspend indefinitely
   v.t. を閉会とする、を休会とする
   n. adjournment

4. **affiliate** [əfílièıt]
   ≒ bring into connection, connect, associate
   v.t. を提携させる
   n. affiliation

5. **allot** [əlá(ː)t]
   ≒ allocate, apportion, deal out, dole out
   v.t. を割り当てる
   n. allotment

Chapter 1

例文

6. The writer often **alludes** to Russian novels in his essays, showing the significant influence they have had on his work.
7. The young entrepreneur hopes to **amass** a vast personal fortune by the time he reaches the age of 25.
8. The board voted to **amend** the organization's charter by adding a clause prohibiting sexual discrimination in any of its activities.
9. I was **appalled** to see that so much food was thrown away after the wedding reception. Isn't there any way to avoid this kind of waste?
10. The candidate has **ascribed** his defeat to the negative campaign advertisements run by his opponent.
11. Companies are required by law to have their books **audited** by an independent accounting firm after the close of each financial year.

6 ☐ **allude** [əlúːd]	≒ refer casually (to), refer indirectly (to) *v.i.* <〜に>遠回しに言及する<to 〜> *n.* allusion *adj.* allusive
7 ☐ **amass** [əmǽs]	≒ accumulate, stockpile, hoard, pile up, put away *v.t.* をためる、を集める *n.* amassment
8 ☐ **amend** [əménd]	≒ revise, rectify, modify *v.t.* を改正する、を修正する *n.* amendment
9 ☐ **appall** [əpɔ́ːl]	≒ shock, horrify, dismay *v.t.* をがく然とさせる、をぞっとさせる *adj.* appalling
10 ☐ **ascribe** [əskráɪb]	≒ attribute, impute *v.t.* (原因)を<〜に>帰する<to 〜> *n.* ascription
11 ☐ **audit** [ɔ́ːdət]	≒ examine, check, inspect *v.t.* の会計検査をする

動詞

例文

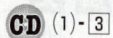

12 The hospital's doctors were **baffled** by the boy's disease and called in outside specialists to help diagnose it.
13 The buyers were very interested in our revolutionary product, but they **balked** at the high price. After careful consideration, we lowered it by 10%.
14 Spend your next vacation in style! The Tradewind Resort invites you to **bask** in the warm Caribbean sun on the white sand of our private beach.
15 My boss always laughs at my proposals in front of everybody. I think he's **belittling** me just because I'm a woman.
16 The success of the writer's first novel **bolstered** her confidence and inspired her to produce what became a series of award-winning books.

12 □ **baffle** [bǽfl]	≒ confuse, perplex *v.t.* を困惑させる、をまごつかせる *n.* bafflement *adj.* baffling
13 □ **balk** [bɔːk]	≒ hesitate, refuse abruptly *v.i.* ためらう、しり込みする、急にやめる
14 □ **bask** [bæsk]	≒ sit or lie back in warmth and light, warm oneself, repose *v.i.* 日光浴をする、＜恩恵などを＞享受する ＜in ～＞
15 □ **belittle** [bilítl]	≒ disparage, downgrade, deprecate, depreciate, put down *v.t.* を軽視する、を見くびる *n.* belittlement
16 □ **bolster** [bóulstər]	≒ strengthen, reinforce, buttress *v.t.* （士気・信頼など）を高める、（学説など）を支持する

Chapter 1

例文

17 You **botched** up the repair job on my engine so badly that the car broke down again within a week.
18 Press reports from the war zone are being heavily **censored** by military authorities.
19 The surgeon was officially **censured** by the hospital committee for performing a new surgical procedure without authorization.
20 Somehow, the company managed to **circumvent** the rules and place a bid for the contract even after the official deadline had passed.
21 The woman stood at the foot of the tree, trying to **coax** her beloved pet cat down from a high branch.
22 The defense lawyer maintained that his client had been **coerced** into signing a confession.

17 □ **botch** [bɑ(:)tʃ]	≒ do clumsily, screw up *v.t.* をやり損なう，を駄目にする
18 □ **censor** [sénsər]	≒ check to remove objectionable information (that might be useful to the enemy) *v.t.* （政府などが）を検閲する；*n.* 検閲官 *n.* censorship
19 □ **censure** [sénʃər]	≒ criticize severely, reprove, condemn, impugn *v.t.* を非難する，をとがめる；*n.* 非難
20 □ **circumvent** [sə̀ːrkəmvént]	≒ find a way round, evade, outwit *v.t.* の抜け道を見つける，の裏をかく *n.* circumvention
21 □ **coax** [koʊks]	≒ wheedle, cajole, beguile *v.t.* をなだめて～させる［～の状態にする］ ＜into ～, to *do*＞
22 □ **coerce** [koʊə́ːrs]	≒ make do, force *v.t.* を威圧して～させる＜into ～＞ *n.* coercion *adj.* coercive

動詞

例文

23 The firemen were **commended** by the mayor, and given medals for saving the children in the blaze.

24 Forced to **comply** with a growing list of costly environmental regulations, the company found it increasingly difficult to make a profit.

25 The special PTA committee, **comprising** 10 members, met each Saturday to discuss issues concerning local schools.

26 Though I strongly dislike her way of doing things, I will **concede** that she is an effective manager.

27 Several senior army officers were discovered to be **conspiring** to overthrow the government.

23 □ **commend** [kəménd]	≒ praise, extol, applaud *v.t.* を＜～のことで＞賞する，をほめる，を表彰する＜for ～＞ *adj.* commendable
24 □ **comply** [kəmplái]	≒ obey, submit to, conform to, act in accordance with *v.i.* ＜規則などに＞従う，応じて行動する＜with ～＞ *n.* compliance *adj.* compliant
25 □ **comprise** [kəmpráız]	≒ consist of, be composed of, include *v.t.* から成る，を含む
26 □ **concede** [kənsí:d]	≒ admit as true *v.t.* を（真実と）認める *n.* admission
27 □ **conspire** [kənspáıər]	≒ plot, scheme, machinate, collude, intrigue *v.i.* ＜…しようと＞陰謀を企てる，共謀する＜to do＞ *n.* conspiracy

例文

28 It is often difficult to determine legally what **constitutes** sexual harassment.

29 Two hours before the President's motorcade was to pass through the downtown area, police **cordoned** off several streets to keep traffic out.

30 Plumbers determined that an old section of iron pipe in the building's basement had **corroded** and caused the water leakage.

31 After two days of performances by local musicians, our annual music festival **culminated** in an appearance by a well-known country singer.

32 Senator Johnson's new bill is designed to **curtail** excessive spending by the military, thereby saving taxpayers millions of dollars.

28 □ **constitute** [ká(:)nstətjùːt]	≒ make up, be equivalent to, be tantamount to, establish by law *v.t.* を構成する、に等しい、を制定する *n.* constitution *adj.* constituent
29 □ **cordon** [kɔ́ːrdən]	≒ surround with a line of persons or objects *v.t.* に非常線を張る、を遮断する＜off＞
30 □ **corrode** [kəróʊd]	≒ wear away, rust, undermine *v.i.* 腐食する；*v.t.* を侵食する、をむしばむ *n.* corrosion *adj.* corrosive
31 □ **culminate** [kʌ́lmɪnèɪt]	≒ reach the highest point *v.i.* 最高点に達する *n.* culmination
32 □ **curtail** [kəːrtéɪl]	≒ reduce in extent, cut back *v.t.* を削減する、を切り詰める *n.* curtailment

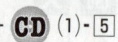

例文

33. George, you really need to learn how to **delegate** responsibility. You just can't do everything by yourself.
34. In his new book, the former police officer **denounces** as "unforgivable" the corruption he witnessed within the department.
35. Police have **detained** two men for questioning in connection with the bank robbery.
36. The reviewer **detested** everything about the movie, slamming the ridiculous plot and dreadful acting.
37. Though snakes are known to **devour** their prey whole, they are actually very particular about what they eat.

33 ☐ **delegate** [déligeɪt]	≒ hand over, assign, entrust, depute *v.t.* を (〜に) 任せる、を委任する；*n.* (会議などの) 代表、代議員 *n.* delegation (代表団；委任)
34 ☐ **denounce** [dɪnáʊns]	≒ criticize, attack, scold, malign *v.t.* を非難する、を告発する *n.* denouncement, denunciation
35 ☐ **detain** [dɪtéɪn]	≒ keep under restraint, keep in confinement *v.t.* を引き留める、を拘留する *n.* detainment
36 ☐ **detest** [dɪtést]	≒ hate, loathe, abhor *v.t.* をひどく嫌う *n.* detestation *adj.* detestable
37 ☐ **devour** [dɪváʊər]	≒ gulp down, gobble up, polish off *v.t.* をがつがつ食べる、をむさぼり食う

例文

38 Through community meetings, the government hopes to **dispel** the fears of the local populace concerning the toxic waste dump.

39 The journalist was given confidential information on the condition that he not **divulge** his sources under any circumstances.

40 The wealthy woman was **duped** into believing that the stranger was her long-lost nephew.

41 As the number of customers **dwindled**, management hurried to find a new strategy that would attract more people to the store.

42 Stephen was forced to give up his protest after he failed to **elicit** support from his co-workers.

43 Strange noises **emanated** from the robot before it started to smoke and then stopped.

38 ☐ dispel [dɪspél]	≒ drive away, disperse, dissipate *v.t.* （恐れ・疑念など）を払拭する
39 ☐ divulge [dəvʌ́ldʒ]	≒ tell what has been a secret, give away, disclose, reveal *v.t.* （秘密など）をもらす，を暴く
40 ☐ dupe [djuːp]	≒ trick, deceive, con *v.t.* をだます，をだまして〜させる＜into doing＞；*n.* だまされやすい人，カモ *n.* dupery
41 ☐ dwindle [dwíndl]	≒ decrease, diminish, decline, taper off *v.i.* だんだん減少する，衰える
42 ☐ elicit [ɪlísət]	≒ draw forth, evoke *v.t.* を引き出す *n.* elicitation
43 ☐ emanate [émənèɪt]	≒ come out, issue, emerge, radiate *v.i.* （期待・考え・光・音などが）出てくる，発する *n.* emanation

動詞

例文

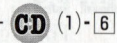

44 The politician's speech was **embellished** with fine-sounding phrases, but it contained very few concrete proposals.

45 The firefighters worked hard to save the people trapped in the building, which was already **engulfed** in flames.

46 Becoming a professional pianist **entails** countless hours of solitary practice, so make sure this is really what you want to do.

47 The young candidate **enthralled** voters with his fresh ideas and rousing speeches, but once elected, he failed to keep his campaign promises.

48 Your rent is several months overdue. If you do not pay by the end of this month, we will be forced to **evict** you from your apartment.

49 "If the coal mine is allowed to close, it will only **exacerbate** the problem of local unemployment," said the mine workers' union representative.

44 ☐ **embellish** [ɪmbélɪʃ]	≒ adorn, decorate, elaborate *v.t.* を飾る、(話など)を潤色する *n.* embellishment
45 ☐ **engulf** [ɪngʌ́lf]	≒ swallow up, overwhelm, swamp *v.t.* (波などが)を飲み込む *n.* engulfment
46 ☐ **entail** [ɪntéɪl]	≒ involve, require, necessitate, call for, include *v.t.* を伴う、を必要とする *n.* entailment
47 ☐ **enthrall** [ɪnθrɔ́ːl]	≒ captivate, entrance, fascinate *v.t.* (人の心)を夢中にさせる、を魅了する *n.* enthrallment *adj.* enthralling
48 ☐ **evict** [ɪvíkt]	≒ expel by legal process, oust, kick out *v.t.* を立ち退かせる
49 ☐ **exacerbate** [ɪgzǽsərbèɪt]	≒ make worse, worsen, aggravate *v.t.* を悪化させる

Chapter 1

例文

50. While conducting the dig, the archaeologists took great care to ensure that all **excavated** objects were properly identified and documented.
51. We need to complete this construction project by the end of the fiscal year, so do whatever is necessary to **expedite** it.
52. Although he **extolled** the joys of parenthood in his new book, the child psychologist also warned that child rearing is a serious social responsibility.
53. **Extrapolating** from past records of climatic change, experts predict an increase in global warming.
54. The researcher was fired from the lab when it became clear that he had **fabricated** the results of his experiments.

50 ☐ **excavate** [ékskəvèɪt]	≒ dig up, dig out *v.t.* を発掘する *n.* excavation
51 ☐ **expedite** [ékspədàɪt]	≒ hasten the progress of, facilitate, promote, advance *v.t.* をはかどらせる、を促進する *n.* expediency *adj.* expedient
52 ☐ **extol** [ɪkstóʊl]	≒ praise enthusiastically, applaud, acclaim, glorify *v.t.* を激賞する
53 ☐ **extrapolate** [ɪkstrǽpəlèɪt]	≒ calculate from known facts, infer *v.t., v.i.* (既知の事柄から) 推定する *n.* extrapolation
54 ☐ **fabricate** [fǽbrɪkèɪt]	≒ forge, concoct, counterfeit, assemble *v.t.* をねつ造する、を組み立てる *n.* fabrication (作り事、製作)、fabric (織物)

動詞

例文

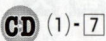

55. Parts of Asia are in trouble, with **faltering** economies and governments seemingly unable to find ways to recover.
56. Having **feigned** sickness as yesterday's excuse for not doing his assignment, the student wondered what reason he could give his teacher today.
57. The two brothers are now **feuding** about who will take over the family business.
58. Despite his strong academic background, the new recruit **floundered** when put in charge of the research project and thus had to be replaced.
59. The two countries **forged** a military alliance that resulted in better defense and reduced military expenditures.
60. In light of recent threats, security personnel now have the authority to **frisk** anyone who sets off the metal detector at the entrance.

55 ☐ **falter** [fɔ́:ltər]	≒ stumble, stagger *v.i.* 衰える，よろめく，つまづく，口ごもる
56 ☐ **feign** [feɪn]	≒ pretend, fake, simulate *v.t.* を装おう，のふりをする *adj.* feigned
57 ☐ **feud** [fju:d]	≒ quarrel, fight, be at odds *v.i.* 争う，反目する *adj.* feudal（封建的な）
58 ☐ **flounder** [fláundər]	≒ blunder, stumble, stagger *v.i.* まごつく，悪戦苦闘する，へまをする
59 ☐ **forge** [fɔ:rdʒ]	≒ form, make, counterfeit *v.t.* （関係など）を結ぶ，（文書など）を偽造する *n.* forgery（偽造）
60 ☐ **frisk** [frɪsk]	≒ search (a person) for a weapon, check, examine *v.t.* をボディチェックする，を調べる

Chapter 1

例文

61 My enjoyable experience as a volunteer at an overseas hospital **fueled** my enthusiasm for becoming a doctor.

62 New technologies are making it easier to **harness** the power of the sun and turn it into electricity for everyday use.

63 The old woman died in apparent poverty, but after her death it was discovered that she had **hoarded** thousands of dollars under her bed.

64 As the cold front moved in on the second night of our camping trip, we **huddled** around the fire to keep warm.

65 Visibility was severely **impaired** by the snowstorm, so the pilot chose to make an emergency landing at a nearby airstrip.

66 The deep snow and strong crosswinds severely **impeded** the progress of the mountaineers as they approached the Himalayan peak.

61 ☐ **fuel** [fjúːəl]	≒ stimulate, incite, inflame, provoke *v.t.* を刺激する、を燃え立たせる；*n.* 勢いを増加させるもの
62 ☐ **harness** [háːrnɪs]	≒ control to produce useful power, make use of, utilize *v.t.* （自然の力など）を利用する、を動力化する
63 ☐ **hoard** [hɔːrd]	≒ amass, put away, set aside, save, stash away *v.t.* （密かに金など）を蓄える；*n.* 蓄え
64 ☐ **huddle** [hʌ́dl]	≒ crowd together, gather, confer secretly *v.i.* 集まる、身を寄せ合う、談合をする
65 ☐ **impair** [ɪmpéər]	≒ ruin, spoil, deteriorate, debilitate *v.t.* （能力など）を弱める、（健康など）をそこなう *n.* impairment
66 ☐ **impede** [ɪmpíːd]	≒ obstruct, hinder, hamper *v.t.* を妨げる、を手間取らせる *n.* impediment

動詞

例文

67 Ladies and gentlemen, I <u>implore</u> you to vote for me! Together, we can make these changes!

68 Thanks to DNA evidence, the man was released after being wrongly <u>incarcerated</u> for 12 years for a crime he did not commit.

69 I'm <u>inclined</u> to support your analysis, but I need more information before coming to any conclusion.

70 Genetic tests can be used to identify people who may <u>incur</u> large medical expenses for hospitalization and treatment.

71 Although we know little about this newly-discovered dinosaur, we can <u>infer</u> from the shape of its teeth that it was a carnivore.

67 □ implore [ɪmplɔ́:r]	≒ entreat, beseech, beg, supplicate *v.t.* に懇願する *adj.* imploring
68 □ incarcerate [ɪnkɑ́:rsərèɪt]	≒ imprison, confine *v.t.* を投獄する、を閉じこめる *n.* incarceration
69 □ incline [ɪnkláɪn]	≒ lead, make, dispose, induce *v.t.* ＜通例受身形＞を…する気にさせる＜to *do*＞、を傾斜させる *n.* inclination
70 □ incur [ɪnkə́:r]	≒ bring upon *oneself*, become liable to *v.t.* （損害など）を被る、（危険など）を自ら招く *n.* incurrence
71 □ infer [ɪnfə́:r]	≒ surmise, deduce, conclude, gather *v.t.* ＜証拠・事実などから＞を推量する＜from ～＞ *n.* inference

Chapter 1

例文

72 Active participation by the audience **infused** the seminar with energy and made it a great success.

73 Already behind schedule, progress on the construction project was further **inhibited** by a shortage of materials.

74 The young recruit stormed out of the meeting after the manager **insinuated** that she had stolen his idea for the new project.

75 After peace talks failed, the U.N. **interceded** in an attempt to get the rebel groups and the government back to the negotiating table.

76 The political activist refused to be **intimidated** by police pressure and continued his protests against the government.

77 The driver was arrested after a blood-alcohol test revealed that she was **intoxicated** at the time of the accident.

---

72 ☐ **infuse** [ɪnfjúːz]	≒ fill, inspire, imbue *v.t.* <～を>に吹き込む<with ～>, を吹き込む *n.* infusion
73 ☐ **inhibit** [ɪnhíbət]	≒ hold back, hamper, restrain, impede, deter *v.t.* を阻止する, を抑える *n.* inhibition
74 ☐ **insinuate** [ɪnsínjuèɪt]	≒ imply, suggest, indicate, hint *v.t.* をほのめかす *n.* insinuation
75 ☐ **intercede** [ìntərsíːd]	≒ mediate, intervene on behalf of another *v.i.* 仲裁に入る, とりなす
76 ☐ **intimidate** [ɪntímɪdèɪt]	≒ make afraid with threats, scare, frighten, terrify, threaten *v.t.* を脅す, を脅して～させる<into ～> *n.* intimidation
77 ☐ **intoxicate** [ɪntá(ː)ksɪkèɪt]	≒ make drunk, inebriate *v.t.* <通例受身形>を酔わせる, を夢中にさせる

動詞

例文

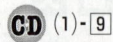

78 The airline was **inundated** with telephone calls from worried relatives after the plane was reported missing.
79 The banker assured us that a higher initial investment will be **justified** by greater earnings in the long run.
80 Results of a recent survey show that Britons **lag** far behind their fellow Europeans when it comes to pride in their national cuisine.
81 In his latest work, Dr. Albright **laments** society's increasing abandonment of what he calls "core spiritual values."
82 The prime minister is doing everything possible to **marshal** support for his new tax program.
83 The river **meanders** slowly through forests and fields on its way to the ocean.

78 ☐ **inundate** [ínʌndèit]	≒ flood, overwhelm, overflow *v.t.* に殺到する，に氾濫する *n.* inundation	
79 ☐ **justify** [dʒʌ́stɪfàɪ]	≒ vindicate, show to have a legal or moral basis *v.t.* を正しいとする，を正当化する *n.* justification	
80 ☐ **lag** [læg]	≒ move or act slowly *v.i.* 遅れる，のろのろ進む； *n.* 遅れ	
81 ☐ **lament** [ləmént]	≒ deplore, bewail, bemoan, mourn *v.t.* を嘆く *adj.* lamentable	
82 ☐ **marshal** [má:rʃəl]	≒ bring together, assemble *v.t.* （力など）を集結する，をまとめる	
83 ☐ **meander** [miændər]	≒ zigzag, turn, wind about, ramble *v.i.* 曲がりくねる，歩き回る	

Chapter 1

例文

84 The children sat motionless, completely **mesmerized** by the soothing voice of the storyteller.

85 The project became **mired** in controversy, so we decided to postpone funding until a consensus could be reached.

86 I thought that a surprise gift might **mollify** my wife, but it didn't make up for my suddenly canceling our anniversary dinner.

87 We'll need to **mull** the offer over before we make a final decision to take it or reject it.

88 Though weakened by hunger and thirst, the lost hiker somehow **mustered** the strength to continue walking.

89 Union leaders argued that the company's existing contract violated labor laws and demanded that it be **nullified**.

84 ☐ **mesmerize** [mézməràɪz]	≒ fascinate, spellbind *v.t.* ＜通例受身形＞を魅了する *n.* mesmerism（抗しがたい魅力，催眠術） *adj.* mesmeric（抗しがたい）
85 ☐ **mire** [maɪər]	≒ cause to get stuck, entangle, enmesh *v.t.* ＜通例受身形＞をぬかるみにはまらせる，を窮地に陥れる；*n.* 沼地，窮地
86 ☐ **mollify** [má(:)lɪfàɪ]	≒ calm, appease, pacify, assuage *v.t.* をなだめる *n.* mollification
87 ☐ **mull** [mʌl]	≒ think over, ponder, consider, study *v.t.* をじっくり考える
88 ☐ **muster** [mʌ́stər]	≒ summon up, collect *v.t.* （勇気・気力など）を奮い起こす，を呼び集める
89 ☐ **nullify** [nʌ́lɪfàɪ]	≒ make void, render invalid, annul *v.t.* を無効にする，を破棄する *adj.* null

既出例文

動詞

例文

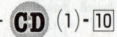

90 It is when someone becomes <u>ostracized</u> and is outside the group that bullying tends to take place.

91 The directors voted to <u>oust</u> the president and replace him with a company outsider.

92 After several weeks abroad, the Wilsons returned home to find their garden <u>overrun</u> with weeds.

93 Tests carried out by the government revealed that toxic waste had <u>permeated</u> the soil all around the factory.

94 The executive was deeply <u>perturbed</u> because her flight had been canceled, causing her to miss an important meeting.

90 □ **ostracize** [á(:)strəsàɪz]	≒ exclude, isolate, snub *v.t.* をのけ者にする *n.* ostracism（追放、つまはじき）
91 □ **oust** [aust]	≒ expel, remove, force out, drive out *v.t.* を＜場所・地位から＞追い出す＜from ～＞
92 □ **overrun** [òuvərrʌ́n]	≒ spread over, ravage, destroy *v.t.* （雑草などが）にはびこる、を荒らす
93 □ **permeate** [pə́:rmièit]	≒ spread through, pervade, penetrate *v.t.* （期待などが）に浸透する、（思想などが）に普及する *n.* permeation
94 □ **perturb** [pərtə́:rb]	≒ make uneasy, upset, worry, agitate, disturb *v.t.* を困惑させる、を不安にさせる *n.* perturbation

Chapter 1

例文

95 Her curiosity about the new student was **piqued** by the rumors that his father was a world-famous tennis player.

96 The store manager hoped to **placate** the angry shoppers by offering discount coupons in place of the sale items that never arrived.

97 After the bad news about the company's quarterly earnings, its stock price **plummeted** 49 percent, ending up at an all-time low for the year.

98 Stop **procrastinating**! We have to get those survey forms sent out today or we'll miss the deadline.

99 I don't mean to **pry**, but are you by any chance related to the Brickwell family that lives in Lancaster?

100 The government passed a new law against the possession of automatic weapons in an attempt to **quell** fears of increasing violence.

95 □ **pique** [piːk]	≒ arouse, excite, whet *v.t.* (興味など)を刺激する, をそそる
96 □ **placate** [pléɪkeɪt]	≒ pacify, conciliate, appease, mollify *v.t.* をなだめる, を慰める *n.* placation
97 □ **plummet** [plʌ́mɪt]	≒ plunge rapidly, drop sharply, fall straight downward *v.i.* 急速に下がる, 垂直に落ちる
98 □ **procrastinate** [prəkræstɪnèɪt]	≒ delay, dawdle, dilly-dally, put off *v.i.* 先延ばしにする, ぐずぐずする *n.* procrastination
99 □ **pry** [praɪ]	≒ nose (into), poke around, snoop *v.i.* ＜他人の私事などを＞詮索する＜into ～＞; *n.* 詮索
100 □ **quell** [kwel]	≒ alleviate, allay, mitigate, assuage *v.t.* を抑える, を和らげる

例文

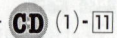

101 Nothing **quenches** the thirst in the hot summer months like an ice-cold glass of lemonade.
102 The mob **rampaged** through several blocks of the downtown area, damaging storefronts and overturning parked cars.
103 We came home from vacation to find the house **ransacked** and all our valuables missing.
104 I tried to get to know my new neighbor, but he **rebuffed** all my offers of friendship.
105 The other side has made concessions, and your side needs to **reciprocate** if these talks are to move forward.
106 Even though the stock market was down, James stayed in the market because he hoped to **recoup** some of his losses.

101	☐ **quench** [kwentʃ]	≒ satisfy, slake, sate, satiate, gratify, allay, appease *v.t.* （のどの渇き）をいやす，（欲望など）を押し殺す
102	☐ **rampage** [ræmpéɪdʒ]	≒ rush violently, storm *v.i.* 暴れ回る；*n.* 強暴な行動
103	☐ **ransack** [rǽnsæk]	≒ loot, pillage, plunder, maraud *v.t.* を荒らす，から略奪する，をくまなく捜す
104	☐ **rebuff** [rɪbʌ́f]	≒ reject, refuse, snub, spurn *v.t.* を拒絶する；*n.* 拒絶
105	☐ **reciprocate** [rɪsíprəkèɪt]	≒ return, repay, requite *v.i.* 報いる；*v.t.* に報いる，を交換する *n.* reciprocation
106	☐ **recoup** [rɪkúːp]	≒ recover, get back, make up for *v.t.* （損失など）を取り戻す，を埋め合わせる *n.* recoupment

Chapter 1

例文

107 Tips for careless husbands: Forget your wife's birthday? Then **redeem** yourself by bringing her a bouquet of flowers.

108 For weeks after the fire in the apartment building, the hallways **reeked** of burnt paint.

109 The old hotel was completely **refurbished** to mark its 70th anniversary, and soon regained its reputation as the premier hotel in the city.

110 Will your company **reimburse** us for all travel expenses during the entire period of our contract?

111 Even as government officials **reiterated** their position never to negotiate with terrorists, relatives of the hostages demanded a peaceful solution to the standoff.

107	☐ **redeem** [rɪdíːm]	≒ buy back, reinstate, restore, deliver *v.t.* の名誉をばん回する＜*oneself*＞，＜悪条件などから＞を救う＜from ～＞ *n.* redemption, Redeemer（救世主，キリスト）
108	☐ **reek** [riːk]	≒ smell, stink *v.i.* ＜～の＞強い悪臭を放つ＜of, with ～＞； *n.* 悪臭，湯気
109	☐ **refurbish** [riːfə́ːrbɪʃ]	≒ renew, renovate, polish *v.t.* を改装する，を一新する
110	☐ **reimburse** [rìːɪmbə́ːrs]	≒ repay, pay back *v.t.* に＜金，経費などを＞返済する＜for ～＞，を（人に）弁償する *n.* reimbursement
111	☐ **reiterate** [riː(ː)ítərèɪt]	≒ restate, repeat again and again *v.t.* を繰り返して言う *n.* reiteration

動詞

例文

112 The reunion was fun. It was nice to meet again after so many years and **reminisce** about old times.

113 "The new tax law is slowing down the economic recovery of this country," said the angry politician. "It must be **repealed** immediately."

114 Consumer groups, with support from the oil industry, demanded that the government **rescind** the new gasoline tax.

115 I recommend this applicant as a person who is very receptive to new ideas and **responds** well to criticism.

116 The foreign minister said his nation would **retaliate** in kind if trade sanctions were applied against it.

112	☐ **reminisce** [rèmɪnís]	≒ recollect or remember things (about) *v.i.* ＜〜の＞思い出にふける，＜〜を＞回顧する＜about 〜＞ *n.* reminiscence *adj.* reminiscent
113	☐ **repeal** [rɪpíːl]	≒ revoke, annul, nullify, rescind, reverse *v.t.* （法律など）を廃止する，を無効にする； *n.* 廃止，撤廃
114	☐ **rescind** [rɪsínd]	≒ cancel, void, abrogate *v.t.* を撤廃する，を廃止する
115	☐ **respond** [rɪspá(ː)nd]	≒ act in a corresponding manner *v.i.* ＜〜に＞対応する，反応する＜to 〜＞ *n.* response
116	☐ **retaliate** [rɪtǽlièɪt]	≒ take revenge, revenge *oneself*, pay back *v.i.* 仕返しをする *n.* retaliation

Chapter 1

例文

117 The instructions warned that although the sleeping bag's material would **retard** flames, it was not 100% fireproof.

118 If you don't follow the new state regulations, the authorities will be forced to **revoke** your company's business license.

119 The newly-elected congressman **savored** his victory over his long-time rival.

120 Unable to pinpoint the cause of the disease, the family doctor was forced to **solicit** the advice of a specialist.

121 My wife and I often **squabble** over things as trivial as who should check the mail or who should set the alarm clock.

122 Health officials instituted a program of mass vaccination to help **stem** the spread of the new and dangerous strain of influenza.

117	☐ **retard** [rɪtáːrd]	≒ delay, hold back, hinder, hold in check *v.t.* を遅らせる，を阻害する *adj.* retarded（知能・発達の遅れた）
118	☐ **revoke** [rɪvóuk]	≒ cancel, invalidate, nullify, rescind *v.t.* を取り消す，を無効にする *n.* revocation
119	☐ **savor** [séɪvər]	≒ relish, appreciate, enjoy, delight in *v.t.* を十分に味わう；*v.i.* （〜の）味がする *n.* 風味 *adj.* savory
120	☐ **solicit** [səlísət]	≒ ask for earnestly, supplicate, seek *v.t.* （援助など）を求める，を懇願する *n.* solicitation
121	☐ **squabble** [skwá(ː)bl]	≒ quarrel over a small matter *v.i.* つまらない言い争いをする
122	☐ **stem** [stem]	≒ stop, check, curb, arrest, quell, hinder *v.t.* を阻止する，をくい止める，を抑える

既出例文

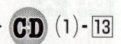

例文

123 Authoritarian governments have a variety of ways to **stifle** dissent, often resorting to military force.

124 Company regulations **stipulate** that all machine operators undergo a safety training program before starting on the job.

125 A: How much do you think we'll need for development of the new project?
B: Our forecast is that $10,000 should **suffice**.

126 After reconstructing the crime, the detective **surmised** that at least three people were involved in the burglary.

127 The dishonest investment advisor **swindled** several of his clients out of their life savings.

123	☐ **stifle** [stáɪfl]	≒ suppress, stop, smother, restrain, control, curb *v.t.* を抑圧する，をもみ消す，の息を止める
124	☐ **stipulate** [stípjulèɪt]	≒ state clearly, lay down, specify, designate *v.t.* を規定する，を明文化する *n.* stipulation
125	☐ **suffice** [səfáɪs]	≒ be enough, be adequate *v.i.* 十分である，足りる *adj.* sufficient
126	☐ **surmise** [sərmáɪz]	≒ assume, gather, conjecture, presume *v.t.* を＜…だと＞推測する＜that ...＞；*n.* 推測
127	☐ **swindle** [swíndl]	≒ take money from by deceit, defraud, fleece, cheat *v.t.* をだまして（財産を）奪う，を＜〜から＞だまし取る＜out of 〜＞，をだます

例文

128 The bicycle champion's victory was **tainted** by allegations of illegal drug use.

129 **Tampering** with smoke alarms in airplane lavatories is a serious offense punishable by law.

130 Reports of illegal campaign contributions have **tarnished** the candidate's reputation, despite his many accomplishments to date.

131 The electronics company is in deep financial trouble and is **teetering** on the edge of bankruptcy.

132 Taking responsibility for the team's poor showing, the basketball coach **tendered** his resignation to the team owner after the final game of the season.

133 After sinking the winning putt, the golfer **thrust** his fist into the air.

128	☐ **taint** [teɪnt]	≒ tarnish, stigmatize, sully, cloud *v.t.* <～に>毒される<with, by ～>、<通例受身形>を堕落させる；*n.* 汚染、腐敗
129	☐ **tamper** [tǽmpər]	≒ interfere with, tinker with, meddle with, monkey with *v.i.* <～を>いじくる、ひねくり回す<with ～>
130	☐ **tarnish** [tá:rnɪʃ]	≒ defame, damage, taint, blot, dull, besmirch *v.t.*（名声など）を損なう、を退色させる；*n.* 汚点、退色
131	☐ **teeter** [tí:tər]	≒ move unsteadily, sway, wobble, totter, waver *v.i.* よろめき進む、ふらふらする
132	☐ **tender** [téndər]	≒ offer, present, hand in, submit *v.t.* を申し出る、を提出する
133	☐ **thrust** [θrʌst]	≒ push, shove, stick *v.t.* を突く、を突き刺す、(仕事などを)に押しつける；*n.* 押すこと、前進、批判

動詞

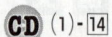

例文

134 High winds from the sudden storm caused the ship to **veer** off course.

135 I was **vexed** by my inability to get my point across when it was my turn to speak.

136 The scientist's controversial theory was finally **vindicated** when other researchers validated his test data.

137 Having been a colleague of Rachel's for many years, I can **vouch** for her honesty and diligence.

138 Due to **waning** interest in classical music, ticket sales for symphony performances have been on the decline.

139 To the whole staff's credit, this company has **weathered** four years of recession without losing any market share.

134	☐ **veer** [vɪər]	≒ turn, swerve, change direction *v.i.* <～から>それる<off ～>、方向を変える
135	☐ **vex** [veks]	≒ annoy, irritate, torment, afflict, disquiet *v.t.* を悩ませる、をいらいらさせる *n.* vexation *adj.* vexed（困難な）、vexatious（いらだたしい）
136	☐ **vindicate** [víndikèit]	≒ prove, support, uphold *v.t.* を立証する、の汚名を晴らす *n.* vindication
137	☐ **vouch** [vautʃ]	≒ guarantee, endorse, answer for, give a guarantee (for), give personal assurance (for) *v.i.* <人物・真実性などを>保証する<for ～> *n.* voucher
138	☐ **wane** [weɪn]	≒ shrink, weaken, fade, dwindle *v.i.* 衰える、弱くなる
139	☐ **weather** [wéðər]	≒ survive, withstand, ride out, bear up against *v.t.* （困難など）を無事に乗り切る

例文

140 As the hurricane moved closer to land, high winds and heavy rain threatened to **wreak** havoc on villages near the coast.

140 ☐ **wreak**
[riːk]

≒ inflict, unleash
v.t. <~に>（損害など）をもたらす<on, upon ~>；<人に>（怒りなど）をぶちまける

既出例文―名詞

例文

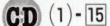

141 The **absurdity** of the senator's argument reflected his total lack of knowledge on the subject of tax reform.

142 The mayor was re-elected in spite of the smear campaign cleverly waged by his political **adversaries**.

143 The new restaurant had an art deco interior and a sophisticated **ambiance**, so we were pleasantly surprised at its reasonable prices.

144 The doctor explained that a local **anesthetic** would be administered, allowing the patient to stay awake during the procedure.

145 The two mayoral candidates exhibited **animosity** toward each other in their biting comments and hostile campaign ads.

141	☐ **absurdity** [əbsə́:rdəṭi]	≒ silliness, stupidity, ludicrousness ばからしさ、不合理 *adj.* absurd
142	☐ **adversary** [ǽdvərsèri]	≒ rival, challenger, opponent, contender, competitor 敵、敵対者
143	☐ **ambiance** [ǽmbiəns]	≒ atmosphere, milieu, environment 雰囲気、周囲のようす
144	☐ **anesthetic** [æ̀nəsθéṭɪk]	≒ removing the sensation of pain, anodyne, pain-killer 麻酔、麻酔剤
145	☐ **animosity** [æ̀nɪmá(:)səṭi]	≒ hostility, antagonism, enmity, ill will 敵意、憎悪

例文

146 Afraid he would be imprisoned for having spoken out against his country's human-rights abuses, the journalist sought political **asylum** in Sweden.

147 The senior members of the committee were outraged by the newcomer's **audacity** in suggesting an immediate change in leadership.

148 The public **backlash** against the proposed consumption-tax hike was so great that the government was forced to reconsider its plans.

149 This new translation software will be a **boon** to businesspeople who have difficulty understanding e-mail from foreign clients.

150 Players from both baseball teams were suspended for their involvement in a **brawl** that left several of them injured.

151 When the construction company failed to complete the bridge on time, the city sued it for **breach** of contract.

146	☐ **asylum** [əsáɪləm]	≒ refuge, sanctuary, safe haven 亡命、非難、避難所、保護施設
147	☐ **audacity** [ɔːdǽsəti]	≒ impudence, insolence, rudeness ずうずうしさ、厚かましさ *adj.* audacious
148	☐ **backlash** [bǽklæʃ]	≒ reaction, repercussion, retort 反発
149	☐ **boon** [buːn]	≒ blessing, asset, benefit, gift, advantage 恵み、利益、恩恵
150	☐ **brawl** [brɔːl]	≒ fight, fray, quarrel けんか、口論
151	☐ **breach** [briːtʃ]	≒ violation, infringement, rift 違反、不履行、不和

名詞

例文

152 The success of the new discount shopping mall drove several local stores to the **brink** of bankruptcy.
153 After his flight, Graham waited for 30 minutes at the baggage **carousel** but there was no sign of his suitcase.
154 The condemned man was executed after the governor rejected his final plea for **clemency**.
155 There was a great **commotion** among the soccer spectators when a fight suddenly broke out.
156 Police were charged with **complicity** in the smuggling operation after their involvement was exposed by an undercover agent.

152	☐ **brink** [brɪŋk]	≒ extreme edge, verge, border, rim 瀬戸際、ふち *n.* brinkmanship（瀬戸際政策）
153	☐ **carousel** [kæ̀rəsél]	≒ rotating conveyor system for passengers' luggage at an airport （空港で乗客の荷物を運ぶ）回転式コンベアー
154	☐ **clemency** [klémənsi]	≒ mercy, lenience, leniency 寛容性、寛大な態度、慈悲 *adj.* clement
155	☐ **commotion** [kəmóuʃən]	≒ tumult, confusion, disturbance, insurrection 大騒ぎ、混乱、騒動
156	☐ **complicity** [kəmplísəṭi]	≒ partnership in an improper or unlawful activity 共犯、共謀

Chapter 1

例文

157 The news of her friend's accident was so shocking that it took a while for Susan to recover her **composure**.

158 Military officials were told that rioting could break out at any time, and to prepare for any **contingency**.

159 "The **crux** of the matter is that we're going to have to close down all of our domestic plants if we can't reduce production costs dramatically," said the president.

160 At the conclusion of the divorce proceedings, the judge awarded **custody** of the couple's children to their mother.

161 The concert to promote the rock band's new CD turned into a complete **debacle** when two of the five members showed up drunk and barely able to play.

162 After the hurricane, it took several weeks to remove the **debris** left behind by the floodwaters.

157 ☐ **composure** [kəmpóuʒər]	≒ calmness, tranquillity 落ち着き、平静 *v.t.* compose ⇔ discomposure
158 ☐ **contingency** [kəntíndʒənsi]	≒ possibility of occurrence, future event 不測の事態、偶発性 *adj.* contingent
159 ☐ **crux** [krʌks]	≒ decisive point, essential point 核心、最重要点
160 ☐ **custody** [kʌ́stədi]	≒ guardianship, keeping, protection, captivity （子供の）保護、親権、監禁
161 ☐ **debacle** [deɪbáːkl]	≒ great disaster, fiasco 大失敗、崩壊
162 ☐ **debris** [dəbríː]	≒ remains, rubble, rubbish, waste, flotsam 残骸、瓦礫

名詞

例文

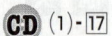

163 The girl's forceful manner in public contrasted sharply with her shy **demeanor** in private.

164 The **demise** of the region's coal industry plunged the local economy into recession.

165 Strict penalties for shoplifting may not be an effective **deterrent**, because few people believe they will be caught.

166 Against her doctor's orders, the woman continued to work overtime, to the **detriment** of her health.

167 The skies are so crowded these days that even a small **deviation** from an airplane's flight plan can be very dangerous.

168 We listened for what seemed like hours to the coach's angry **diatribe** on our recent lack of effort.

163	☐ **demeanor** [dɪmíːnər]	≒ behavior, conduct, deportment, bearing 振る舞い, 態度
164	☐ **demise** [dɪmáɪz]	≒ ceasing to exist, termination, decease, death 終り, 消滅, 死去
165	☐ **deterrent** [dɪtə́ːrənt]	≒ disincentive, hindrance, discouragement 抑止策, 抑止力 ; *adj.* 抑止する *v.t.* deter
166	☐ **detriment** [détrɪmənt]	≒ impairment, drawback, damage, injury 損なうこと, 損害, 損失 *adj.* detrimental
167	☐ **deviation** [dìːviéɪʃən]	≒ turning from the right course, turning aside, digression 逸脱, 外れ *v.i., v.t.* deviate
168	☐ **diatribe** [dáɪətràɪb]	≒ bitter criticism, abusive denunciation 酷評, 痛烈な皮肉

Chapter 1

例文

169 The only <u>drawback</u> to the proposal for a new gymnasium is that it would be expensive to implement.

170 Lab tests were carried out to determine the <u>efficacy</u> of the chemical in removing stains from cotton material.

171 In a show of anger and protest, student activists burned a life-size <u>effigy</u> of the new military dictator.

172 The veteran police officer has been charged with 10 criminal offenses, including trafficking in stolen guns and <u>embezzlement</u> of public funds.

173 At an emergency meeting of the Security Council, it was agreed that the sudden invasion had been a clear <u>encroachment</u> on the sovereignty of a UN member state.

174 Despite the mediation of party leaders, the <u>enmity</u> between the two political camps remains strong.

169	□ **drawback** [drɔ́:bæ̀k]	≒ problem, flaw, impediment, disadvantage, fly in the ointment 欠点, 不利な点
170	□ **efficacy** [éfɪkəsi]	≒ effectiveness, usefulness, efficiency 有効性, 効き目 *adj.* efficacious
171	□ **effigy** [éfɪdʒi]	≒ model or sculpture of someone （憎い人に似せた）人形, 彫像
172	□ **embezzlement** [ɪmbézəlmənt]	≒ fraudulent use of money, misappropriation 着服, 横領
173	□ **encroachment** [ɪnkróʊtʃmənt]	≒ infringement, invasion, intrusion, trespassing 侵犯, 侵害 *v.i.* encroach
174	□ **enmity** [énməti]	≒ hostility, ill will, animus, antagonism 敵意, 憎しみ, 敵対

例文

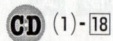

175 In his newest book, the author blames high crime rates on the steady **erosion** of family values in society.

176 The new building in the historic district is very modern inside, but when seen from the street, its **facade** preserves the district's 18th-century style.

177 The campaign to boost sales turned into a **fiasco** because sufficient funds were not made available for market research.

178 After going downstairs and finding nothing, I told myself that the strange noises I had heard were just a **figment** of my imagination.

179 It's no use saying so many nice things to me—**flattery** will get you nowhere.

175 ☐ **erosion** [ɪróuʒən]	≒ waning, weathering, deterioration, weakening 弱体化, 衰退, 蝕み *v.t.* erode
176 ☐ **facade** [fəsάːd]	≒ front view of any edifice, superficial appearance （建物の）外観, 正面, （物事のいつわりの）見かけ
177 ☐ **fiasco** [fiǽskou]	≒ utter failure, disaster 大失敗, 完敗
178 ☐ **figment** [fígmənt]	≒ something imaginary, thing existing only in *one's* imagination 想像の産物, 作りごと, 幻想
179 ☐ **flattery** [flǽṭəri]	≒ false or exaggerated praise, adulation, blandishment, sycophancy お世辞, へつらい *v.t.* flatter

例文

180 Our baseball team is terrible this year, so it was just a **fluke** that we beat the best team in the league last week.

181 The evening news program showed video **footage** of emergency workers rescuing a family from their flooded home.

182 The manufacturer recalled some of its computers after a **glitch** in the hard drive caused them to crash repeatedly.

183 In spite of a series of setbacks, the project team continued to make **headway** as the deadline approached.

184 In **hindsight**, I regret not following my father's advice to go to college.

185 After the singer's tragic death, fans gathered at the place where he had been shot and lit candles to pay **homage** to him.

186 Acting on a **hunch** that the new company's stock price would rise, I phoned my broker and bought 100 shares.

180	☐ **fluke** [fluːk]	≒ lucky accident, stroke of luck まぐれ当たり
181	☐ **footage** [fútɪdʒ]	≒ (amount of) motion-picture or video film （ある出来事の）映像
182	☐ **glitch** [glɪtʃ]	≒ fault, bug, malfunction, failing, flaw （小さな）欠陥
183	☐ **headway** [hédwèɪ]	≒ progress, improvement 進歩，前進
184	☐ **hindsight** [háɪndsàɪt]	≒ perception gained after an event あと知恵 ⇔ foresight
185	☐ **homage** [há(ː)mɪdʒ]	≒ respect, reverence, veneration （権威あるものに対する）敬意
186	☐ **hunch** [hʌntʃ]	≒ intuition about the future 予感，直感，虫の知らせ

名詞

例文

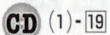

187 The peace talks had reached an **impasse**, as neither party was willing to compromise further.
188 The airline offers some special advance-booking fares as an **incentive** to customers to make early reservations.
189 Since its **inception**, this foundation has provided financial assistance to many deserving university students.
190 The teacher was struck by the **incongruity** between the student's excellent final exam results and his previous low test scores.
191 At the auction for the painting, potential buyers were asked to place bids in thousand-dollar **increments** beginning at $50,000.
192 Historically, voters tend to favor **incumbents** seeking reelection rather than candidates running for the first time.

187	☐ **impasse** [ímpæs]	≒ deadlock, dead end, standstill, cul-de-sac 行き詰まり，行き止まり
188	☐ **incentive** [ɪnséntɪv]	≒ motivation, stimulus, spur 刺激，誘因； *adj.*（行動などを）促すような，励みになる ⇔ disincentive
189	☐ **inception** [ɪnsépʃən]	≒ start, beginning, birth 開始，はじめ，発端 *adj.* inceptive
190	☐ **incongruity** [ìnkəngrúːəṭi]	≒ incompatibility, inconsistency, discrepancy 不一致，ギャップ，不調和
191	☐ **increment** [íŋkrɪmənt]	≒ amount of increase, addition 増加，増額
192	☐ **incumbent** [ɪnkʌ́mbənt]	≒ office holder, holder of an office, occupant 現職者，在職者； *adj.* 現職の，義務として当然の

Chapter 1

例文

193 There was **jubilation** and great relief among his supporters when the candidate won the closely contested election.

194 At this critical **juncture** in the negotiations, it's important that we stay unified in our demands.

195 My brother has a **knack** for repairing things. Whenever something around the house gets broken, he knows how to fix it.

196 The actress sued the newspaper for **libel** when it published an article falsely accusing her of illegal drug use.

197 When the airline company asked customers for their opinions about quality of service, the public responded with a **litany** of complaints.

198 The lawyer found a **loophole** in the tax laws that allowed the company to save a great deal of money.

193	☐ **jubilation** [dʒùːbɪléɪʃən]	≒ joy, happy celebration 歓喜、祝祭
194	☐ **juncture** [dʒʌ́ŋktʃər]	≒ point, stage, time, moment 時点、時期
195	☐ **knack** [næk]	≒ flair, gift, talent こつ、要領、才覚
196	☐ **libel** [láɪbəl]	≒ defamation, calumny, slander, vilification 名誉毀損、中傷 *adj.* libelous
197	☐ **litany** [lítəni]	≒ enumeration, list, recital, recitation 長い説明、並べたてること
198	☐ **loophole** [lúːphòul]	≒ means of escape, dodge, subterfuge （法律などの）抜け穴、逃げ道、言い逃れ

例文

199 The politician's huge victory in the election provided a clear <u>mandate</u> for his plan to eliminate corruption.

200 If you want to get ahead in the business world, it's important to have a <u>mentor</u>—an older executive who will help you with your career.

201 Most of the players had serious <u>misgivings</u> about the coach's strategy but said nothing for fear of being cut from the team.

202 As more data became available to the public, opposition to the new dam gained <u>momentum</u>.

203 The company established a <u>niche</u> at the high end of the automobile market with its technologically superior sports cars.

199	☐ **mandate** [mǽndeɪt]	≒ approval, authority, support, command 委任，民意，任期，命令 *adj.* mandatory
200	☐ **mentor** [méntɔːr]	≒ experienced and trusted adviser, faithful adviser よき助言者
201	☐ **misgiving** [mìsgívɪŋ]	≒ feeling of doubt, qualm, worry, apprehension, anxiety ＜通例複数形＞疑念，不安
202	☐ **momentum** [moʊméntəm]	≒ impetus, drive, force, energy 弾み，勢い，機動力
203	☐ **niche** [nɪtʃ]	≒ comfortable position, cubbyhole 得意分野，適所

Chapter 1

例文

204 Every year on this date, a memorial ceremony is held in **observance** of the city's destruction in the Great Earthquake.

205 At the **onset** of malaria, the patient experiences symptoms such as fever and shivering.

206 Monetary aid is not a **panacea** for the problems of Third World nations. They must learn to help themselves.

207 After receiving a warning of a possible terrorist attack, the commander increased the number of guards patrolling the **perimeter** of the base.

208 Although the suspect begged for another chance to tell his side of the story, his **pleas** fell on deaf ears.

209 Moved by the **plight** of flood victims broadcast on TV, people around the country donated food, blankets and clothing.

204	☐ **observance** [əbzɔ́:rvəns]	≒ commemoration, religious rite 遵守, 記念, 儀式 *v.t.* observe
205	☐ **onset** [á:nsèt]	≒ beginning, inception, assault, attack 始まり, 兆候, 襲来
206	☐ **panacea** [pæ̀nəsí:ə]	≒ cure-all, universal remedy 万能薬, すべての問題の解決策
207	☐ **perimeter** [pərímətər]	≒ outer boundary, periphery, border （飛行場・軍事基地などの）周辺
208	☐ **plea** [pli:]	≒ appeal, entreaty, petition, solicitation ＜〜を求める＞嘆願, 懇願＜for 〜＞
209	☐ **plight** [plaɪt]	≒ bad state, difficulty, predicament 窮状, 苦境

既出例文

名詞

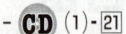

例文

210 The child's misbehavior was little more than a **ploy** to attract attention from his parents.

211 The court's decision set a **precedent** for later laws dealing with personal information available on the Internet.

212 By suggesting that living organisms have always been divided into distinct types, the professor challenged the basic **precepts** of evolution.

213 Because **precipitation** levels in the region had been well below normal all summer, residents were advised to conserve water.

214 Sean had a **premonition** that something bad was going to happen, and sure enough, he lost all his savings on the stock market the very next day.

210	☐ **ploy** [plɔɪ]	≒ stratagem, maneuver 策略, 試み
211	☐ **precedent** [présɪdənt]	≒ example, model, prior case, yardstick 先例, 判例; *adj.* 先立つ, 前の *v.t.* precede
212	☐ **precept** [príːsept]	≒ principle, aphorism, (guiding) rule, law 教え, 金言, 決まり
213	☐ **precipitation** [prɪsɪpɪtéɪʃən]	≒ amount of rain 降雨量 *v.t.* precipitate (を突然引き起こす, を真っ逆さまに落とす)
214	☐ **premonition** [prèmənɪ́ʃən]	≒ presentiment, foreboding, hunch (悪い) 予感, 徴候 *adj.* premonitory

例文

215 To promote better relations with Japan, universities in some Asian countries are considering making Japanese language skills a **prerequisite** for admission.

216 A police **probe** into the affair revealed that a number of executives in the company had attempted to bribe city officials.

217 The growing popularity of the Internet has caused a **proliferation** of affordable, low-end computers aimed at customers who use them primarily to view Web sites and send e-mail.

218 Jeffrey had a **propensity** to blame others when things went wrong, so we were surprised when he took full responsibility for the accident.

219 At a conference held last weekend, gun-control **proponents** from across the nation gathered to plan new strategies for making gun possession illegal.

215	☐ **prerequisite** [priːrékwəzɪt]	≒ requirement, condition 前提条件，必要条件
216	☐ **probe** [proʊb]	≒ investigation, enquiry, search 厳密な調査； *v.t.* を厳密に調査する
217	☐ **proliferation** [prəlìfəréɪʃən]	≒(rapid) spread, rapid increase, expansion 拡散，まん延 *v.t., v.i.* proliferate
218	☐ **propensity** [prəpénsəti]	≒(bad) tendency, proclivity, inclination, leaning （悪い）傾向
219	☐ **proponent** [prəpóʊnənt]	≒ advocate, supporter, promoter, defender 支持者，賛成者 ⇔ opponent

名詞

例文

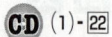

220　The festival planning committee had made **provision** for bad weather by reserving a spacious indoor arena.
221　Those living in close **proximity** to the accident site were forced to evacuate their homes until the chemical spill had been cleaned up.
222　Sam had no **qualms** about trampling over his colleagues in order to get to the top.
223　Given the unstable market conditions, managers found themselves in a **quandary** over whether to increase or decrease production.
224　The night road construction going on outside caused so much **racket** that none of us could sleep.
225　The sales manager maintains a good **rapport** with his staff, finding that open lines of communication lead to increased efficiency.

220	☐ **provision** [prəvíʒən]	≒ preparation, rearrangement, supply 用意，備え，供給
221	☐ **proximity** [prɑ(ː)ksíməti]	≒ being close in space and time, closeness, nearness, adjacency 近接 *adv.* proximate
222	☐ **qualm** [kwɑːm]	≒ compunction, pang, twinge, misgiving, apprehension 良心の呵責，不安
223	☐ **quandary** [kwá(ː)ndəri]	≒ predicament, dilemma, perplexity 困惑，ジレンマ
224	☐ **racket** [rǽkət]	≒ noise, disturbance, trick, fraud 騒音，騒ぎ，密売買 *n.* racketeer（密輸入，ゆすり，不法者）
225	☐ **rapport** [rӕpɔ́ːr]	≒ harmonious relationship 信頼関係，いい関係

Chapter 1

例文

226 The common **rationale** for regularly taking large doses of vitamin C is that it strengthens the body's immune system.

227 The singer's creative **rendition** of the popular Christmas carol was well received by the audience.

228 Even though it wasn't my fault, I was made a **scapegoat** for our department's poor performance and lost my job.

229 When the workers were laid off as a result of corporate downsizing, they received **severance** pay equal to six months' salary.

230 During rare weekends away from the movie set, the director would seek **solace** in the quiet of his mountain hideaway to recharge his creative batteries.

231 The party members maintained **solidarity** during the election campaign but broke into several factions when it was over.

226	☐ **rationale** [rǽʃənæ̀l]	≒ reason, reasoning, explanation 理由づけ，論理的根拠
227	☐ **rendition** [rendíʃən]	≒ interpretation （音楽などの）解釈，表現，演奏，翻訳 *v.t.* render
228	☐ **scapegoat** [skéɪpgòut]	≒ victim, whipping boy 他人の罪を負う者，身代わり
229	☐ **severance** [sévərəns]	≒ ending of employment, termination of a contract, separation （雇用の）契約解除，退職，分離，絶縁 *v.t.* sever
230	☐ **solace** [sá(:)ləs]	≒ consolation, reassurance, help, relief 慰め
231	☐ **solidarity** [sɑ̀(:)lədǽrəti]	≒ state of being undivided or united, unanimity 団結，結束 *adj.* solid *v.t., v.i.* solidify

名詞

例文

232 The newly elected prime minister said he was determined to widen his nation's **sphere** of influence in the strategically important Gulf region.

233 As soon as Martha got her first bonus, she went on a shopping **spree** and bought gifts for herself and everyone in her family.

234 In my opinion, the authorities should take a stricter **stance** on excessive noise pollution.

235 The organization will not be able to pay you a full-time salary for this job, but you will receive a small **stipend** to cover your daily expenses.

236 The two-year-old child threw a terrible **tantrum** when her mother refused to give her the candy.

237 Though he was justified in firing the employee for poor performance, the manager felt a **twinge** of regret for not having provided better training.

232	☐ **sphere** [sfɪər]	≒ range, area, domain, ball, globe, orb 範囲、領域、球体
233	☐ **spree** [spri:]	≒ extravagant outing, splurge, romp 浮かれ騒ぎ、金を湯水のように使うこと
234	☐ **stance** [stæns]	≒ position, stand <～に対する>立場、姿勢<on ～>
235	☐ **stipend** [stáɪpend]	≒ fixed sum of money paid periodically, pay, remuneration, fee 俸給、手当て、固定給、報酬
236	☐ **tantrum** [tǽntrəm]	≒ fit of anger, rage, fury, flare-up かんしゃく、不機嫌
237	☐ **twinge** [twɪndʒ]	≒ pang, prick, spasm 呵責、心痛、刺すような痛み

Chapter 1

例文

238 The lawyer delivered an **ultimatum** to the construction company: If they continued to use noisy equipment late at night, local citizens would take them to court.

239 Responding to increased incidents of slashed tires, broken windows, and other acts of **vandalism**, the mayor requested that additional police be assigned to patrol downtown neighborhoods.

240 We've chosen the dates for next year's convention but have not yet located a **venue** that can accommodate 1,500 participants.

241 The manufacturer was delighted to receive an unexpectedly large contract from the government, a **windfall** that assured the company's financial stability for years to come.

238	☐ **ultimatum** [ʌ̀ltɪméɪṭəm]	≒ final term(s), final condition(s), last offer 最後通告，最終提案
239	☐ **vandalism** [vǽndəlìzm]	≒ willful destruction （公共物の）破壊行為 *n.* vandal（破壊者）
240	☐ **venue** [vénjuː]	≒ place for an event, location where an event takes place 開催地，現場
241	☐ **windfall** [wíndfɔ̀ːl]	≒ unexpected acquisition, godsend, bonanza 予期せぬ幸運，もうけもの，たなぼた

既出例文

形容詞

既出例文—形容詞

日本語訳 → p.355

CD (1)-24

例文

242 The new mayor took a tour of the slum and was shocked at the **abject** poverty all around him.

243 With both sides unwilling to compromise, the increasingly **acrimonious** nature of the trade talks led to their indefinite postponement.

244 By **adroit** political maneuvering, the minority party pushed its health bill through the legislature.

245 The governor is under investigation for his **alleged** misuse of public funds.

246 Since the President was a persuasive and **articulate** speaker, he had no difficulty in gathering support for his educational reforms.

242	☐ **abject** [ǽbdʒekt]	≒ miserable, wretched, woeful, pitiful 悲惨な、絶望的な *n.* abjection
243	☐ **acrimonious** [æ̀krɪmóuniəs]	≒ harsh, bitter, caustic, rancorous 辛らつな、とげとげしい *n.* acrimony
244	☐ **adroit** [ədrɔ́ɪt]	≒ skillful, dexterous, ingenious, expert 巧みな、器用な
245	☐ **alleged** [əlédʒd]	≒ claimed, suspected, purported 申し立てられている、疑われている *n.* allegation *v.t.* allege
246	☐ **articulate** [ɑːrtíkjulət]	≒ speaking distinctly or coherently, intelligible はっきりと話す、理路整然とした；*v.t.* をはっきり表現する *n.* articulation

例文

247 Hoping to get on good terms with the board of directors, Kevin was **astute** enough to join the country club where many board members golfed.

248 The doctor discovered a tumor in the patient's stomach during a routine examination, but fortunately it turned out to be **benign**.

249 The man's careless driving habits showed **blatant** disregard for the safety of others.

250 The actress was perfectly **candid** during the TV interview, answering even the most probing questions about her personal life.

251 For this directorial position, salary is **commensurate** with experience. Managers with an excellent track record are encouraged to apply.

252 The company offered the lawyer two very **compelling** reasons for him to leave his present law firm: a higher salary and shorter working hours.

247	☐ **astute** [əstjúːt]	≒ shrewd, sagacious, clever, canny, perspicacious 抜け目ない，機敏な，ずるい
248	☐ **benign** [bənáin]	≒ harmless, nonfatal, not malignant, curable, kind 良性の，優しい
249	☐ **blatant** [bléɪtənt]	≒ flagrant, obvious, brazen, shameless, 紛れもない，露骨な，図々しい *n.* blatancy
250	☐ **candid** [kǽndɪd]	≒ frank, ingenuous, forthright 率直な，包み隠しのない
251	☐ **commensurate** [kəménsərət]	≒ proportionate to <～に>比例した，釣り合った<with ～>
252	☐ **compelling** [kəmpélɪŋ]	≒ rousing strong interest, very interesting, convincing 注目せずにはいられない，説得力のある *v.t.* compel（を強いる）

形容詞

例文

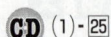

253 Even though we currently have the largest market share, let's not be **complacent**. We can't just rest on our success.

254 I always go to the library to prepare for tests because the atmosphere in my dormitory isn't **conducive** to study.

255 The computer maker recalled their latest PC model because a **defective** chip was found.

256 By projecting current **demographic** trends, we can predict that birthrates will continue to fall in industrialized countries.

257 The baseball manager was criticized for making **derisive** comments about some of his players in a radio interview.

253 □ **complacent** [kəmpléɪsənt]	≒ self-satisfied, content 自己満足の、ひとりよがりの *n.* complacence [complacency]
254 □ **conducive** [kəndjúːsɪv]	≒ leading (to), favorable, helpful ＜～の＞助けとなる＜to ～＞ *v.i.* conduce
255 □ **defective** [dɪféktɪv]	≒ faulty, flawed, imperfect 欠陥のある、不完全な *n.* defect
256 □ **demographic** [dèməgrǽfɪk]	≒ related to the statistical study of human populations 人口統計学の *n.* demography
257 □ **derisive** [dɪráɪsɪv]	≒ mocking, disdainful, scornful, contemptuous, jeering, taunting ばかにした、嘲笑するような *n.* derision *v.t.* deride

Chapter 1

例文

258 Everyone left the town when the silver mine closed down. What was once a lively community is now completely **desolate**.

259 Learning that the factory was to close next month, the workers came away from the meeting disappointed and **despondent**.

260 The injured cyclist was in **dire** need of medical attention, but there was no hospital for miles around.

261 To respect the privacy of the people involved in the scandal, the reporter asked only a few **discreet** questions.

262 The film critic apologized for her earlier **disparaging** remarks about the quality of Asian movies.

---

258 ☐ **desolate**
[désələt]
≒ deserted, dreary, ruined, abandoned
閑散とした、寂れた
n. desolation

259 ☐ **despondent**
[dɪspá(:)ndənt]
≒ dejected, depressed, sad, sorrowful, disheartened
落胆した、失望した
n. despondency

260 ☐ **dire**
[daɪər]
≒ urgent, desperate, dreadful
緊急の、ものすごい

261 ☐ **discreet**
[dɪskríːt]
≒ prudent, careful, cautious, circumspect, wary
分別のある、慎重な
n. discretion

262 ☐ **disparaging**
[dɪspǽrɪdʒɪŋ]
≒ derogatory, slanderous, defamatory, calumnious
けなす、軽蔑する
n. disparagement

形容詞

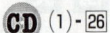

例文

263 A group of **dissident** students got together and organized anti-government protests.
264 Students at this school used to have the reputation of being **docile** and obedient, but now they're causing many discipline problems.
265 The bill for a new national tax plan failed miserably, so the issue remained **dormant** for several years until two newly elected politicians revived it.
266 Before you invest, you should realize that low risk and high return are mutually **exclusive**.

263 ☐ **dissident** [dísɪdənt]	≒ dissentient, disagreeing, nonconformist, rebellious, unorthodox 反体制の，意見を異にする；*n.* 反体制派 *n.* dissidence
264 ☐ **docile** [dá(:)səl]	≒ submissive, obedient 素直な，従順な *n.* docility
265 ☐ **dormant** [dɔ́ːrmənt]	≒ latent, unexpressed, asleep, inactive 潜伏している，眠っている，活動休止中の *n.* dormancy
266 ☐ **exclusive** [ɪksklúːsɪv]	≒ incompatible, irreconcilable, excepting, leaving out, unshared 互いに相容れない，矛盾する，＜～を＞含まない＜of ～＞，独占的な *v.t.* exclude　*n.* exclusion ⇔ inclusive

例文

267 Warning: This movie contains scenes of **explicit** violence and is therefore inappropriate for children.

268 Faced with the **exponential** growth of the world's population, we must make a greater effort to preserve natural resources for future generations.

269 There were no witnesses to the crime, but **forensic** evidence such as hair and fingerprints soon led to the suspect's arrest.

270 With new computer viruses constantly emerging, ensuring complete Internet security is a **formidable** task.

271 The proposed mountain expedition would be **fraught** with danger, so only the strongest and most experienced climbers were invited to take part.

272 Efforts to bail water out of the leaking boat proved **futile**, and we had to swim to shore.

267	☐ **explicit** [ɪksplísɪt]	≒ clearly expressed, clear, distinct, outspoken 露骨な，明確な，率直な ⇔ implicit
268	☐ **exponential** [èkspənénʃəl]	≒ rapidly increasing （増加などが）急激な，指数の *n.* exponent（説明者，主唱者）
269	☐ **forensic** [fərénsɪk]	≒ suitable for a law court or public debate 法廷の，弁論の *n.* forensics
270	☐ **formidable** [fɔ́ːrmɪdəbl]	≒ difficult, burdensome, onerous, intimidating 困難な，手ごわい，恐れを抱かせる
271	☐ **fraught** [frɔːt]	≒ replete (with), filled (with) ＜～を＞伴った，＜～で＞一杯の＜with ～＞
272	☐ **futile** [fjúːṭəl]	≒ unsuccessful, fruitless, ineffective 無駄な，成果の上がらない *n.* futility

形容詞

例文

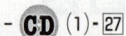

273 The refugees found themselves in a **hapless** situation. They could neither return to their own country nor stay in the country they'd fled to.

274 Even with her **hectic** schedule, the CEO regularly took time to speak to individual workers on the assembly line.

275 People who defend capital punishment argue that some crimes are **heinous** enough to warrant the death penalty.

276 The art collector was delighted to find such a fine eighteenth-century vase in **immaculate** condition for sale at the flea market.

277 Although the flood waters were rising, the town was in no **imminent** danger.

278 The rumors of **impending** layoffs had a devastating effect on company morale.

273	☐ **hapless** [hǽpləs]	≒ unlucky, unfortunate 不運な, 不幸な
274	☐ **hectic** [héktɪk]	≒ busy, frantic, confused, chaotic, frenetic てんてこまいの, 多忙な
275	☐ **heinous** [héɪnəs]	≒ wicked, flagrant, atrocious 極悪の, 憎むべき
276	☐ **immaculate** [ɪmǽkjʊlət]	≒ clean, unblemished, undefiled, spotless 汚れひとつない, 完全な *n.* immaculacy
277	☐ **imminent** [ímɪnənt]	≒ immediate, threatening, impending 差し迫った *n.* imminence
278	☐ **impending** [ɪmpéndɪŋ]	≒ forthcoming, imminent, approaching 差し迫った, まさに起ころうとしている

Chapter 1

例文

279 It is **imperative** that the government do more to enforce recycling measures to reduce the total amount of garbage.

280 We would like to assure you that the billing error was **inadvertent**. We never intended to overcharge you.

281 The candidate's **incendiary** remarks about his opponent's personal life touched off the most negative campaign in the city's political history.

282 Involvement in the bribery scandal left an **indelible** stain on the mayor's reputation and eventually forced him to resign.

283 The ferry was constantly being overloaded with passengers. Sooner or later, an accident was **inevitable**.

284 The engineers came up with an **ingenious** way to fix the problem without access to the proper equipment.

279	☐ **imperative** [ɪmpérətɪv]	≒ urgent, important, necessary, crucial, mandatory 絶対必要な，命令的な
280	☐ **inadvertent** [ìnədvə́ːrtənt]	≒ inattentive, unintended, unintentional 不注意な，うっかりした *n.* inadvertence
281	☐ **incendiary** [ɪnséndièri]	≒ tending to stir up strife, provocative, inflammable 扇動的な，火災を起こす
282	☐ **indelible** [ɪndéləbl]	≒ ineradicable, lasting, permanent 消すことができない，忘れられない *n.* indelibility
283	☐ **inevitable** [ɪnévətəbl]	≒ unavoidable, inescapable 避けられない，必然的な
284	☐ **ingenious** [ɪndʒíːniəs]	≒ clever, gifted, deft, shrewd, resourceful 巧みな，器用な，独創的な *n.* ingenuity

形容詞

例文

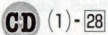

285 We are tired of the same old suggestions. What we need is some **innovative** solutions to this problem.

286 The real estate agent warned us that once we signed the purchase agreement it would be **irrevocable**. There would be no going back.

287 According to investigators, burglars were able to steal the paintings due to an extremely **lax** security system at the museum.

288 Considering the baseball player's previous bad conduct, the coach's decision to make him sit out only one game was quite **lenient**.

289 The casino business was proving so **lucrative** that the owners decided to expand into other cities.

285	☐ **innovative** [ínəvèɪtɪv]	≒ original, new, breaking new ground 斬新な，革新的な *v.i.*, *v.t.* innovate　*n.* innovation
286	☐ **irrevocable** [ɪrévəkəbl]	≒ irreversible, irreparable, irretrievable, final 取り消せない，最終的な
287	☐ **lax** [læks]	≒ slack, negligent, slipshod, loose 手ぬるい，だらしない *n.* laxation
288	☐ **lenient** [líːniənt]	≒ forgiving, merciful, tolerant 寛大な，（罰が）ゆるやかな *n.* leniency
289	☐ **lucrative** [lúːkrətɪv]	≒ profitable, moneymaking, remunerative 儲かる，利益の上がる

例文

290 Living on a **meager** salary, Frank could rarely afford to eat out with his friends.

291 The rave review of the Broadway show in the newspaper had convinced us to go, but we were rather disappointed by the **mediocre** performance.

292 The newly employed software engineer was assigned the **menial** job of sweeping the floor of the computer room.

293 This hospital relies on a team of lawyers to deal with the **myriad** legal issues surrounding organ transplants.

294 Two hours into our voyage, I began to feel **nauseous** and had to take medicine for my upset stomach.

295 Because they hadn't heard the warnings, the skiers remained **oblivious** to the danger of an avalanche until it was too late.

290	☐ **meager** [míːgər]	≒ inadequate, scanty, insufficient, paltry わずかな，乏しい，貧弱な *n.* meagerness ⇔ ample
291	☐ **mediocre** [mìːdióukər]	≒ average, run-of-the-mill, second-rate 並みの，二流の *n.* mediocrity
292	☐ **menial** [míːniəl]	≒ unskilled, humble, servile, degrading つまらない，卑しい；*n.* 使用人
293	☐ **myriad** [míriəd]	≒ a great number of 無数の；*n.* 無数
294	☐ **nauseous** [nɔ́ːʃəs]	≒ squeamish, nauseated, sick 吐き気を催させる，不快な *n.* nausea
295	☐ **oblivious** [əblíviəs]	≒ heedless, unobservant, blind 気にしていない，忘れっぽい *n.* oblivion

形容詞

例文

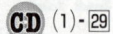

296 Ski officials were pleased to report that this morning's snowfall would provide **optimum** conditions for the race.

297 The palace's **opulent** dining room with its crystal chandeliers was too costly to reconstruct after the fire.

298 The audience were appalled. They had never heard such **outrageous** comments by a public speaker.

299 Much to the disappointment of shareholders, the company's stock value has only increased by a **paltry** 0.1% over the past year.

300 The ranger warned the trekkers that the already **perilous** climb up the mountain would be made even more dangerous by the changing weather conditions.

296	☐ **optimum** [á(:)ptɪməm]	≒ best, most favorable 最適の；*n.* 最適条件 *v.t.* optimize（を最大限に利用する）
297	☐ **opulent** [á(:)pjʊlənt]	≒ luxurious, sumptuous, deluxe, rich, plush, posh 豪華な，贅沢な *n.* opulence
298	☐ **outrageous** [aʊtréɪdʒəs]	≒ disgraceful, indecent, offensive, abusive ひどい，良識に欠けた *n.* outrage
299	☐ **paltry** [pɔ́:ltri]	≒ trifling, petty, meager, puny わずかな，無価値な
300	☐ **perilous** [pérələs]	≒ dangerous, hazardous とても危険な，冒険的な *n.* peril

Chapter 1

例文

301 What you are saying is not **pertinent** to this discussion. Please just stick to the subject.

302 If I'd known you were taking me to such a **posh** restaurant, I would've dressed more appropriately. I'm the only one here without a jacket and tie!

303 "We're running out of time, and this plan is far too unrealistic," the executive said. "We need to take a more **pragmatic** approach to the problem."

304 It was **presumptuous** of you to think you could get an A in this course just by getting a good score on the final exam. Attendance is just as important.

305 To move giant rocks over long distances without the aid of machinery must have required a **prodigious** effort from the builders of the pyramids.

301	☐ **pertinent** [pə́:rtənənt]	≒ relevant, appropriate, fitting, suitable <〜に>関連する，適切な<to 〜> *n.* pertinence
302	☐ **posh** [pɑ(:)ʃ]	≒ luxurious, deluxe, fashionable, stylish 豪華な，気取った
303	☐ **pragmatic** [præɡmǽtɪk]	≒ practical, businesslike, expedient 実利的な，実際的な *n.* pragmatism
304	☐ **presumptuous** [prɪzʌ́mptʃuəs]	≒ audacious, insolent, brazen, cheeky, uppity 図々しい，厚かましい *n.* presumption（厚かましさ，推定）
305	☐ **prodigious** [prədídʒəs]	≒ extraordinary, tremendous, enormous 並外れた，驚異的な，莫大な *n.* prodigy（天才，驚異）

形容詞

例文

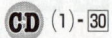

306 In light of the president's failing health, the board members decided it would be **prudent** to begin searching for someone to replace him.

307 TV reporters have been racing each other to locate the **reclusive** author ever since rumors surfaced that he had been seen in public.

308 The Victorian hotel was like a museum, **replete** with antique furniture and ornaments.

309 The author eagerly discussed her new novel with the interviewer, but was **reticent** about her recent divorce.

310 Even with my **rudimentary** knowledge of medicine, I could easily tell that my friend's leg injury was serious and needed immediate attention.

306	☐ **prudent** [prú:dənt]	≒ wise, sensible, reasonable, discreet 賢明な, 分別のある, 慎重な *n.* prudence
307	☐ **reclusive** [rɪklú:sɪv]	≒ secluded, solitary, hermitic 隠遁した, 孤独な *n.* recluse (隠遁者)
308	☐ **replete** [rɪplí:t]	≒ filled, stocked, jammed, brimming ＜〜で＞いっぱいで＜with 〜＞ *n.* repletion
309	☐ **reticent** [rétəsənt]	≒ quiet, silent, taciturn, reserved, tight-lipped 口の重い, 黙りがちの *n.* reticence
310	☐ **rudimentary** [rù:dɪméntəri]	≒ basic, fundamental, elementary 基本の, 初歩の *n.* rudiment

Chapter 1

例文

311 Mary had been confident that John would get the job, but the **rueful** expression on his face after the interview told her otherwise.

312 The Hollywood movie received one **scathing** review after another, but that didn't stop millions from turning out to see it.

313 Even though a cease-fire was in effect, there were reports of **sporadic** violence in parts of the region still held by the rebels.

314 The human rights group issued a report severely criticizing the **squalid** living conditions in the refugee camp.

315 Despite strong political opposition, the legislator remained **steadfast** in her support of public housing for the poor.

316 The movie critic's review of the new horror film was **succinct** and to the point: "The film itself is a horror. Don't see it."

311	☐ **rueful** [rúːfəl]	≒ mournful, sad, lamentable, showing sorrow 悲しそうな，痛ましい *v.t.* rue（を悔いる）
312	☐ **scathing** [skéɪðɪŋ]	≒ severe, harsh, acrimonious, incisive 痛烈な，辛らつな
313	☐ **sporadic** [spərǽdɪk]	≒ occasional, scattered, intermittent 散発的な，ときどき起こる
314	☐ **squalid** [skwá(ː)ləd]	≒ dirty, filthy, sordid, wretched, poor 汚い，卑しい，みすぼらしい
315	☐ **steadfast** [stédfæst]	≒ determined, resolute, unflinching, unswerving （決意などが）不動の，確固とした
316	☐ **succinct** [sʌksíŋkt]	≒ concise, precise, terse 簡潔な

形容詞

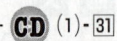

例文

317 "Treat yourself to a **tantalizing** array of cakes and handmade confections at Ye Olde Sweet Shoppe."

318 Refusing to take a lie-detector test is sometimes viewed as **tantamount** to admitting that you committed the crime.

319 Let's make **tentative** plans to meet Thursday to sign the deal, assuming the board approves the merger at its meeting on Wednesday.

320 Contrary to expectations, the public gave only **tepid** applause to the new governor's speech.

321 This may sound **trivial**, but I think we need a hyphen between these two words.

317 ☐ **tantalizing** [tǽntəlàɪzɪŋ]	≒ tempting, stimulating desire じらすような，じれったい
318 ☐ **tantamount** [tǽntəmàunt]	≒ equivalent in significance to, commensurate with <～と>同等の<to ～>
319 ☐ **tentative** [téntətɪv]	≒ provisional, experimental, not definite, hesitant 仮の，暫定的な，試験的な，おずおずした
320 ☐ **tepid** [tépɪd]	≒ unenthusiastic, uncaring, apathetic, indifferent 熱意に欠ける *n.* tepidity
321 ☐ **trivial** [trívɪəl]	≒ negligible, insignificant, petty, unimportant 些細な，取るに足らない *n.* triviality

Chapter 1

例文

322 Whereas ten years ago cellular phones were rare, now they have become **ubiquitous**.

323 The boy had **ulterior** motives for offering to wash his father's car: He was hoping to borrow it for the weekend.

324 The investment advisor had an **uncanny** ability to pick winning stocks that other investors overlooked.

325 After her pleasant first flight, the woman realized that her fear of flying had been **unfounded**.

326 The determined executive had been **unrelenting** in his pursuit of the company presidency since his very first day on the job.

327 The club's new pianist is really quite **versatile** and can play anything from jazz to classical music.

322 ☐ **ubiquitous** [jubíkwətəs]	≒ omnipresent, present everywhere （同時に）いたるところに存在する、偏在する *n.* ubiquity
323 ☐ **ulterior** [ʌltíəriər]	≒ concealed, hidden, personal, secret, covert 隠れた、秘めた
324 ☐ **uncanny** [ʌ̀nkǽni]	≒ remarkable, weird, eerie 人並み外れた、不可思議な、気味の悪い
325 ☐ **unfounded** [ʌ̀nfáʊndɪd]	≒ groundless, baseless 根拠のない *n.* foundation（根拠）
326 ☐ **unrelenting** [ʌ̀nrɪléntɪŋ]	≒ inexorable, obstinate, not yielding, determined, stern 不屈の、断固とした
327 ☐ **versatile** [vɜ́ːrsətəl]	≒ multiskilled, all-round, many-sided, resourceful 多才な、多機能の *n.* versatility

形容詞

例文

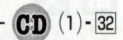

328 I'm afraid your committee's plan for investing in alternative energy sources is not <u>viable</u> at this time. We simply don't have the money to proceed.

329 It didn't take Janice long to succeed as a salesperson because customers were attracted to her <u>vibrant</u> personality.

330 Although the two warring parties have agreed to a cease-fire, the situation remains <u>volatile</u> and fighting may resume at any moment.

331 Many teenagers have <u>voracious</u> appetites. They never seem to stop eating.

328	☐ **viable** [váɪəbl]	≒ feasible, workable, practicable 実行可能な，実現性のある
329	☐ **vibrant** [váɪbrənt]	≒ lively, vivacious, resonant 明るい，活気に満ちた，響き渡る *n.* vibrancy
330	☐ **volatile** [vá(:)lətəl]	≒ unstable, changeable, erratic 不安定な，うつろいやすい *n.* volatility
331	☐ **voracious** [vəréɪʃəs]	≒ insatiable, ravenous, gluttonous がつがつしている，貪欲な *n.* voracity

Chapter 1

既出例文—副詞

日本語訳 → p.360

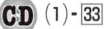

CD (1)-33

例文

332 The professor **adamantly** refused to alter his opinion, even after being shown evidence contradicting his research.

333 The intent of Lord Waldorf-Smithers was that the assets from his estate be shared **equitably** among his four children.

334 By sending troops to these uninhabited islands, your country has **flagrantly** violated your agreement with us.

335 In these harsh economic times, people are going to have to live more **frugally** if they want to make ends meet.

336 No matter how hard the teacher tried to engage her students, they sat **impassively** at their desks, unwilling to participate in the class.

332	☐ **adamantly** [ǽdəməntli]	≒ stubbornly, resolutely 頑固に，断固として *n.* adamancy
333	☐ **equitably** [ékwətəbli]	≒ fairly, squarely, judiciously 公平に，公正に *n.* equity
334	☐ **flagrantly** [fléɪgrəntli]	≒ outrageously, shamelessly, blatantly, audaciously 厚かましくも，ハレンチにも *n.* flagrancy（悪名高いこと）
335	☐ **frugally** [frúːgəli]	≒ sparingly, thriftily, abstemiously 倹約して，つつましく *n.* frugality
336	☐ **impassively** [ɪmpǽsəvli]	≒ stolidly, coolly, detachedly, callously 無感動に，冷淡に *n.* impassivity

副詞

例文

337 The other guests attending the museum opening were all **impeccably** dressed, so Chris looked out of place in just a casual sweater and jeans.

338 Despite an expensive new advertising campaign, sales for the quarter were only **marginally** higher.

339 My roommate cleans up so **meticulously** that there's never even a speck of dust on her side of the room.

340 The black clouds **ominously** building up in the distance indicated that a severe storm was developing.

341 It was **patently** obvious that the suspect was lying because of the contradictory answers he gave to the police officers' questions.

342 The movie ended so **poignantly** with the child's tragic death that the audience was in tears.

337	☐ **impeccably** [ɪmpékəbli]	≒ perfectly, faultlessly, flawlessly, very decently 申し分なく，非の打ちどころなく，きちんとして *n.* impeccability
338	☐ **marginally** [má:rdʒənəli]	≒ slightly, insignificantly, negligibly わずかに
339	☐ **meticulously** [mətíkjʊləsli]	≒ fastidiously, scrupulously, punctiliously 細心に，几帳面に
340	☐ **ominously** [á(:)mɪnəsli]	≒ portentously, inauspiciously, menacingly, with the character of ill omen 不気味にも，不吉にも *n.* omen
341	☐ **patently** [péɪtəntli]	≒ obviously, clearly, unmistakably, apparently 明らかに，はっきりと
342	☐ **poignantly** [pɔ́ɪnjəntli]	≒ excruciatingly, sadly, pathetically 痛ましく，痛烈に，感動的に *n.* poignancy

Chapter 1

例文

343 The hotel manager apologized **profusely** for the mix-up with our reservation and offered us an upgraded room.

344 Calmly and **serenely**, the great ocean liner glided out of the port on her final voyage.

345 The funeral procession for the former prime minister wound slowly and **somberly** through the streets on its way to the cemetery.

346 Undeterred by the apparent lack of concrete evidence at the scene of the crime, the investigator **tenaciously** continued to search for clues.

347 At the meeting, the motion to strike was passed **unanimously**, with every member raising his hand in agreement.

348 The teachers' union **vehemently** opposed the board's new personnel proposal because of the threat to their job security.

343	☐ **profusely** [prəfjúːsli]	≒ extravagantly, lavishly 過剰に、豊富に *n.* profusion *adj.* profuse
344	☐ **serenely** [səríːnli]	≒ quietly, peacefully, unperturbedly 静かに、穏やかに *n.* serenity
345	☐ **somberly** [sá(ː)mbərli]	≒ gravely, lugubriously, mournfully 重苦しく、悲し気に
346	☐ **tenaciously** [tɪnéɪʃəsli]	≒ persistently, stubbornly, doggedly 粘り強く、しつこく *n.* tenacity
347	☐ **unanimously** [junǽnɪməsli]	≒ all in agreement, showing complete agreement 満場一致で *n.* unanimity
348	☐ **vehemently** [víːəməntli]	≒ fervently, passionately, ardently 激しく、熱心に *n.* vehemence

既出例文—熟語

日本語訳 → p.361

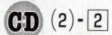

例文

349 The two main political parties, previously **at odds** over income tax reform, have finally shown signs of compromise.

350 The government has finally backed away from a controversial plan to **bail out** the ailing financial institution with public funds.

351 I'm not **banking on** his help this weekend. He's let me down so many times before.

352 After the coach's pep talk, our team **was** all **geared up** to go out and win the championship game.

353 A: You can't expect me to believe that story, Julian. I **wasn't born yesterday**.
B: But it's true! Ask anyone in my family.

349	☐ **at odds**	≒ in disagreement, quarreling <〜のことで>不和で，争って<over 〜>
350	☐ **bail out 〜**	≒ help 〜 out of difficulties （人・企業などの経済的窮地）を救う
351	☐ **bank on 〜**	≒ depend on, rely on, count on 〜を当てにする
352	☐ **be geared up**	≒ be ready in a state of excitement 準備が整って，<〜する>ばかりになって<to *do*>
353	☐ **be born yesterday**	≒ be naive <通例否定形>うぶである，世間知らずである

Chapter 1

例文

354 I've never been so busy! I**'m up to my ears** in work and I have no idea when I'll be through with it.

355 A team of specialists was organized to see how the astronauts would **bear up** under the stresses of living in a small space station for months.

356 In an effort to **beef up** security, the company installed a new high-tech alarm system and hired several more guards.

357 The President hoped that the scandal would **blow over** before the election year, but the press seemed determined not to let the matter drop.

358 The supervisor's main responsibilities **boil down to** increasing worker productivity and improving the bottom line.

359 You shouldn't keep your anger all **bottled up**, Chris. Why don't you tell me what's bothering you?

既出例文

354	☐ **be up to *one's* ears**	≒ be deeply involved ＜仕事などに＞忙殺されて，＜困難などに＞すっかり巻き込まれて＜in ～＞
355	☐ **bear up**	≒ endure, survive ＜～に＞耐える，持ちこたえる＜under, against ～＞
356	☐ **beef up ～**	≒ augment, reinforce, strengthen ～を強化する
357	☐ **blow over**	≒ fade out, pass over, be forgotten （嵐・困難などが）忘れられる，消え去る
358	☐ **boil down to ～**	≒ mean basically, amount to ～に帰着する，要約すると～になる
359	☐ **bottle up ～**	≒ control, suppress, contain, conceal, bury, hold back （感情など）を抑える

例文

360 We were all tired from working so long, so we decided to **call it a day** and go home.

361 I almost bumped into a truck when I turned the corner. It really was a **close call**!

362 How did you **come by** this information? It's supposed to be confidential.

363 The young man was always **cooking up** get-rich-quick schemes, but none of them ever amounted to anything.

364 We are stepping up our own research efforts to compete better at the **cutting edge** of communications technology.

365 Since the matter is legally complicated, we should have an agreement **drawn up** by a lawyer.

360	☐ **call it a day**	≒ stop working for the day, stop or end an activity 終わりにする，（その日の仕事を）おしまいにする
361	☐ **close call**	≒ narrow escape 危機一髪
362	☐ **come by ~**	≒ acquire, obtain, secure, get possession of ~を手に入れる，~に立ち寄る
363	☐ **cook up ~**	≒ devise, concoct, invent （話・口実など）を作る，をでっち上げる
364	☐ **cutting edge**	≒ the most advanced stage or position 最先端，刃先
365	☐ **draw up ~**	≒ draft, put into written form （報告書など）を作成する

Chapter 1

例文

366 It was hard for me not to **drift off** during the morning lecture since I hadn't slept all night.

367 The environmental group held a public meeting, hoping to **drum up** support for a ban on constructing a new factory along the river.

368 Now that your tax evasion has been discovered, you're going to have to **face the music**.

369 Despite years of planning, the project to build a new shopping complex **fell through** at the last minute because several residents refused to sell their land.

370 I know you need to ask me some unpleasant questions to complete your investigation, so **fire away**. I have nothing to hide.

371 The director was looking for an aggressive person to head the new project. She finally decided that Sandra would **fit the bill** perfectly and offered her the job.

366	☐ **drift off**	≒ drowse, doze, become drowsy うとうとする
367	☐ **drum up ～**	≒ get or obtain by canvassing or soliciting （支持・取引など）を獲得しようとする，～を募る
368	☐ **face the music**	≒ accept the consequence of *one's* deeds （失敗などの）結果を潔く受け止める，責任を取る
369	☐ **fall through**	≒ fail, come to nothing （計画などが）失敗する，実現しない
370	☐ **fire away**	≒ go ahead, begin to ask questions 始める，どんどん質問をする
371	☐ **fit the bill**	≒ be suitable, be adequate, meet the requirements, fill the bill 条件にかなう，要求を満たす

例文

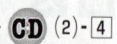

372 This is a great idea, Cathy, but we'll have to **flesh it out** with some more detailed information before we submit it to the boss.

373 When Fred failed to turn in his homework for the fourth time this week, the teacher **flew off the handle** and yelled at him in front of the whole class.

374 When our main competitor started offering products at a five-percent discount, we had no choice but to **follow suit** and reduce our prices as well.

375 My brother **frittered away** his inheritance on cars and expensive vacations, and now he's completely broke.

376 Everyone agrees this plan is unworkable. Why don't we forget it and start again **from scratch**?

377 After being down on his luck for some time, Kevin finally **got a break** when an old friend called him with a job offer.

372	☐ **flesh out ～**	≒ make ～ more substantial ～を中身のあるものとする，～を肉付けする
373	☐ **fly off the handle**	≒ become violently angry かっとなる
374	☐ **follow suit**	≒ follow the example set, do the same as another 先例に習う，追随する
375	☐ **fritter away ～**	≒ waste, squander (away), misspend ～を＜～に＞浪費する＜on ～＞
376	☐ **from scratch**	≒ from the beginning, starting with nothing 最初から，ゼロから
377	☐ **get a break**	≒ get a fair chance, get a piece of good luck 幸運をつかむ

例文

378 Dave's excuse for missing class—that he couldn't find his homework—was difficult to believe, but the teacher **gave** him **the benefit of the doubt** and didn't lower his grade.

379 Kelly **gave** her boyfriend **the cold shoulder** because she had seen him flirting with her best friend.

380 In his address, the spokesperson made a clever attempt to **gloss over** the many failures of his company.

381 Being told by the boss to accept Jonathan's proposal really **goes against the grain**. I still feel mine is much better.

382 Unfortunately, after he became famous, Ted's success **went to his head** and he began to behave very arrogantly.

383 "You've got to **hand it to** Jeremiah. He works less than anyone in the office but still manages to get all the credit."

378	☐ **give ～ the benefit of the doubt**	≒ give the concession that a person is innocent though doubt remains 疑わしきは罰せずとする，～を好意的に解釈する
379	☐ **give ～ the cold shoulder**	≒ snub, ignore, treat disdainfully, avoid, shun ～を無視する，～を冷たくあしらう
380	☐ **gloss over ～**	≒ whitewash, explain away, cover up ～を取り繕う
381	☐ **go against the grain**	≒ be something *one* does not like 意に反する，性に合わない
382	☐ **go to *one's* head**	≒ make *one* overconfident or vain （成功などが人を）うぬぼれさせる
383	☐ **hand it to ～**	≒ give credit to ～ ～の優秀さを認める

例文

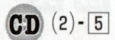

384 Jack bet everything on his favorite horse and watched the race breathlessly as his entire life's savings **hung in the balance**.

385 All you tell me to do is wait, wait, wait. I**'ve had it up to here with** these constant delays.

386 The police tried to **head off** the escaped convict before he reached the state boundary.

387 Though we looked **high and low**, we couldn't find the car keys and had to take a taxi to the movie.

388 Julie and I have been close friends since college. We met on the first day of freshman orientation and **hit it off** right away.

389 I'm so exhausted that I'm going to **hit the sack** early tonight. Let's put off washing the dishes till tomorrow.

384	☐ **hang in the balance**	≒ be in an uncertain position, be at a critical stage どうなるか分からない，重大な局面にある
385	☐ **have had it up to here with ～**	≒ have had enough of, won't tolerate any more ～にうんざりした，もうがまんできない
386	☐ **head off ～**	≒ stop, intercept ～を阻止する，～の前面に立ちはだかる
387	☐ **high and low**	≒ everywhere あらゆるところを［に，で］，くまなく
388	☐ **hit it off**	≒ have a good relationship, become good friends ＜人と＞折り合う，うまくいく＜with ～＞
389	☐ **hit the sack**	≒ go to bed, hit the hay, retire, turn in 寝る

例文

390 I can't accept the logic of the arguments you've given. They just don't **hold water**.

391 Some of my friends thought the politician's speech was convincing, but I thought it was mainly **hot air**.

392 Another title was not **in the cards** for last year's champions. They were badly beaten in the finals.

393 Arriving at the station just **in the nick of time**, we jumped onto the train as the doors closed.

394 The proposal has a few weak points, but I'm confident that we can get the problems **ironed out** before next week's deadline.

395 Good luck in your new job. Please **keep** me **posted** on how things are going.

390	☐ **hold water**	≒ be logical, sound sensible, make sense 筋が通る，妥当である
391	☐ **hot air**	≒ boastful talk, braggadocio でまかせ，大ぶろしき
392	☐ **in the cards**	≒ likely, expected, on the horizon, in the offing ありそうな，起こりそうな
393	☐ **in the nick of time**	≒ just at the right moment, just in time なんとか間に合って，ちょうどよい時に
394	☐ **iron out 〜**	≒ remove, smooth out 〜を取り除く，〜を解決する，〜を円滑にする
395	☐ **keep 〜 posted**	≒ inform, continue to give the latest information （絶えず）〜に知らせる，〜に最新の情報を伝える

例文

396 If you <u>let</u> your work <u>slide</u>, you won't be able to make that promotion.
397 The two insurance companies have nearly finalized their merger plans, but there are still some <u>loose ends</u> to tie up before an official announcement can be made.
398 The important thing to remember when an earthquake hits is to keep calm; don't <u>lose your head</u>.
399 After failing to <u>make a dent in</u> the Japanese market, the foreign carmaker was forced to close its Japanese operations.
400 Developers were very eager to buy the piece of land, so the owners <u>made a killing</u> when they sold it for three times its original value.
401 The violinist is a fine musician, but he never quite <u>measures up to</u> the high standards of the other members of the string quartet.

396	☐ **let ~ slide**	≒ be negligent of ～をおろそかにする
397	☐ **loose end**	≒ unsettled matter, final matter (to be taken care of) 未処理事項、未解決の部分
398	☐ **lose *one's* head**	≒ panic, lose control 冷静さを失う
399	☐ **make a dent in ~**	≒ make a noticeable effect on, give an appreciable effect on ～に注目すべき効果を与える、～に注目させる、～に影響を与える
400	☐ **make a killing**	≒ make a lot of money, make a sudden great profit （突然）大もうけをする
401	☐ **measure up to ~**	≒ have the necessary qualifications for （期待・標準など）に達する

Chapter 1

例文

402 As I was suddenly called upon to make the speech, I had to do it completely **off the cuff**. I wish I'd had time to prepare.

403 Since it was the minor's first offense, the judge decided to let him **off the hook**.

404 Unable to continue paying taxes on the property, the family decided to put it **on the block**.

405 The salesman says that this used car is in really good shape. But I'm not sure if he's **on the level**.

406 Not speaking a word of Spanish, Laura felt a bit **out of her element** at her Mexican friend's wedding reception.

407 At 75, my father is still very active and certainly does not think he is **over the hill**.

402	☐ **off the cuff**	≒ extemporaneously, spontaneously, offhand, impromptu, without preparation 即興で，準備なしに
403	☐ **off the hook**	≒ free of responsibility, out of trouble 義務［罰］から解放されて，困難を抜け出て
404	☐ **on the block**	≒ up for sale or auction 売りに出て，競売にかけられて
405	☐ **on the level**	≒ honest, sincere, frank, candid, unbiased 正直な，誠実な
406	☐ **out of *one's* element**	≒ out of *one's* accustomed surroundings 勝手が違って ⇔ in *one's* element
407	☐ **over the hill**	≒ declining, past the prime of life 元気な時を過ぎて，年をとって

例文

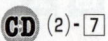

408 Monica believed she would save money by purchasing a used car, but she ended up **paying through the nose** for some very expensive repairs.

409 Some people argue that cigarette advertisements by handsome movie stars **play on** the desire of young people to look cool.

410 Though he actually supported his friend's decision to change jobs, Shawn **played the devil's advocate** by pretending to disagree.

411 The magician said he would make everything on stage disappear, but few people thought he could really **pull it off**.

412 If you have any problems finding a job, let me know. I think I can **pull** some **strings** and get you hired at my company.

413 After several months of fruitless effort, the chief engineer realized it was time to **pull the plug on** the project.

408	☐ **pay through the nose**	≒ pay much more than is reasonable, pay a great deal ＜～に＞法外な代金を払う＜for ～＞
409	☐ **play on ～**	≒ exploit, take advantage of, abuse ～につけこむ、～をうまく利用する
410	☐ **play the devil's advocate**	≒ stress the negative side of an argument あまのじゃくを演じ、わざと反論する
411	☐ **pull off ～**	≒ perform successfully, carry out despite difficulties, accomplish against odds ～をうまくやる、～をやってのける
412	☐ **pull strings**	≒ use hidden or secret influence コネを使う、陰で糸を引く
413	☐ **pull the plug on ～**	≒ stop, discontinue, put an end to ～ （計画など）を中止する

例文

414 The man's injuries were severe, but doctors were confident that, with proper treatment, he would **pull through**.

415 At the annual meeting, the shareholders **put** the directors **on the spot** by asking pointed questions about executive salaries.

416 The company **put** the electric truck **through its paces** in city traffic to see if it was practicable.

417 I've been **putting in** a lot of overtime lately. I hope it doesn't continue this way indefinitely.

418 You should go and complain to the store manager. I think you got a **raw deal** on this poor quality furniture.

419 Many investors optimistically believe they can **ride out** the lengthy downturn in the stock market.

420 When Mary was unexpectedly asked to address the conference, she **rose to the occasion** and delivered a magnificent speech.

414	☐ **pull through**	≒ recover (from an illness), survive a dangerous or difficult situation （病人が）回復する，苦境を切り抜ける
415	☐ **put ～ on the spot**	≒ put someone in an accountable position （質問などが）～を窮地に追い込む
416	☐ **put A through A's paces**	≒ test *one's* qualities or skills (in action) A（人・機械など）の能力を試す
417	☐ **put in ～**	≒ spend, pass （時間・金・労力など）を費やす
418	☐ **raw deal**	≒ unfair treatment 不当な扱い
419	☐ **ride out ～**	≒ survive, outlast, endure successfully ～を乗り切る，～を耐え抜く
420	☐ **rise to the occasion**	≒ do what suddenly becomes necessary 急場に手腕を発揮する

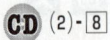

例文

421 Charlie **roped** me **into** helping him move into his new apartment.
422 Since my daughter's new boyfriend is a very studious young man, I'm hoping his influence will **rub off on** her.
423 Neither the murder victim's wallet nor his belongings had been stolen, so the police **ruled out** theft as a motive.
424 Office supervisors must maintain a certain level of discipline, but overly strict managers **run the risk of** alienating their subordinates.
425 I was very annoyed by the high-pressure **sales pitch** of the computer salesperson, so I went to another shop.
426 When I picked up my car at the repair shop, I had to **shell out** nearly twice as much as the original estimate.

421	☐ **rope ~ into ...**	≒ persuade ~ to take part in 〜を説き伏せて…させる
422	☐ **rub off on ~**	≒ be transmitted to （性質などが）に伝わる，に影響を与える
423	☐ **rule out ~**	≒ dismiss, exclude 〜を除外する，〜はあり得ないとする
424	☐ **run the risk of ~**	≒ expose *oneself* to the danger of, take the chance of 〜の危険を冒す
425	☐ **sales pitch**	≒ salesperson's way of talking, selling approach 売り込み口上，宣伝
426	☐ **shell out ~**	≒ pay (out) ＜〜のために＞（大金）をしぶしぶ支払う＜for, on 〜＞

Chapter 1

例文

427 As part of the divorce settlement, Bill was ordered by the court to <u>sign over</u> his rights to the house to his ex-wife.

428 I've told my assistant time and time again not to take such long lunch breaks, but it just doesn't seem to <u>sink in</u>.

429 The large electronics store had an outdated security system and was located on a quiet street, so it was a <u>sitting duck</u> for robbers.

430 Our boss was distressed about losing his best client, so we had to <u>skirt around</u> the subject for several days.

431 <u>Spurred on</u> by the cheering crowd, the local favorite managed to overtake the national champion in the last few meters of the marathon.

432 If there are planets orbiting other stars, it <u>stands to reason</u> that there may be other planets that can support life.

427	☐ **sign over ～**	≒ waive, relinquish, give up *one's* claim to （文書に署名して）を＜～に＞譲渡する＜to＞
428	☐ **sink in**	≒ become well understood or felt 理解される、心にしみ込む
429	☐ **sitting duck**	≒ easy or defenseless target for attack or criticism, easy mark いいカモ、だまされやすい人、楽な目標
430	☐ **skirt around ～**	≒ shun, avoid, circumvent, fight shy of, ward off, keep away from ～を回避する
431	☐ **spur on ～**	≒ incite, prod, urge, egg on, goad ～を刺激する、～に拍車をかける
432	☐ **stand to reason**	≒ be logical, be obvious, be clear to all sensible people 当然である、理にかなう

例文

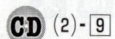

433 Thank you for **sticking up for** me at the meeting today. Without your backing, my proposal would not have been approved.

434 The old woman sitting on the bench looked lonely, so Linda sat down next to her and **struck up** a conversation.

435 You are far too naive. You shouldn't **take** everything car salespeople say **at face value**.

436 The upbeat forecasts about the future of the economy need to be **taken with a grain of salt** considering how often past predictions have been inaccurate.

437 If you don't mind my **taking a crack at** it, I think I can fix your computer.

438 I know you're frustrated with your job, but don't **take it out on** me! It's not my fault that they passed you over for promotion.

433	☐ **stick up for 〜**	≒ support, defend （人・主張など）をあくまでも支持する
434	☐ **strike up 〜**	≒ start （会話など）を始める
435	☐ **take 〜 at face value**	≒ take 〜 at the seeming value or significance, take 〜 at the value indicated or implied 〜を真に受ける，〜を額面どおりに受け取る
436	☐ **take 〜 with a grain of salt**	≒ be skeptical about, be reserved about 〜を割引いて聞く，〜について懐疑的である
437	☐ **take a crack at 〜**	≒ have an attempt at, try 〜をやってみる
438	☐ **take it out on 〜**	≒ relieve *one's* frustration by attacking 〜に当たり散らす

例文

439 I'm sorry, Sally, but I don't really want to **talk shop** over lunch. Let's discuss it when we get back to the office.

440 The newspaper editor pressured several reporters to **tone down** their criticisms of the police department.

441 We're still **toying with** the idea of moving into a larger house, but I'm not sure we can afford it.

442 Jim is afraid of flying, so I'm sure we'll have to **twist his arm** to get him to come to Hawaii with us.

443 This new software allows you to retrieve the necessary information at the click of a mouse, without having to **wade through** volumes of data.

444 Don't **waste your breath** trying to make Norman quit smoking. He won't listen to a word you say.

439	☐ **talk shop**	≒ talk about *one's* work or special interest 自分の仕事の話をする
440	☐ **tone down ～**	≒ make softer, make less harsh （表現の調子など）を和らげる
441	☐ **toy with ～**	≒ play with, fool with, flirt with 〜について漠然と考える、〜をもてあそぶ
442	☐ **twist *one's* arm**	≒ pressure or coerce someone （〜に）無理強いする
443	☐ **wade through ～**	≒ work *one's* way through, plod through （膨大な情報・人ごみなど）をかき分けていく［調べる］
444	☐ **waste *one's* breath**	≒ give advice without effect 見込みのない説得をする

例文

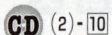

445 The best way to **wind down** after an exhausting day is to take a long, hot bath.

446 With no time to practice before the concert, the band had to just **wing it** and hope for the best.

447 The industrial robots that the company had invested in turned out to be a complete failure, so the company was forced to **write** them **off** as a loss.

448 FBI agents investigating the recent hacking incidents have **zeroed in on** three possible suspects in the Los Angeles area.

445	☐ **wind down**	≒ relax, rest, ease up （仕事・緊張の後で）くつろぐ、のんびりする
446	☐ **wing it**	≒ improvise, extemporize, get along in a makeshift manner 即興で演奏する、即興で作る［演じる］
447	☐ **write off ～**	≒ cancel the record of, dismiss as irrevocable or irreparable ～を帳簿から外す、～を帳消しにする
448	☐ **zero in on ～**	≒ focus *one's* attention on, take aim at ～に的を絞る

More to Learn

Foreign Words—外来語

ad infinitum	永遠に，無限に
à la carte	お好み料理の［で］，一品料理の［で］
bona-fide	本物の，心からの
bourgeois	中産階級者，有産者，資本家
cause célèbre	有名な裁判事件，悪名高い事件
ciao	やあ，またね
coup	大当たり，大成功，クーデター
coup d'état	クーデター，急な政変
cul-de-sac	袋小路，行き止まり
de facto	事実上の
dètente	（国際間の）緊張緩和，デタント
en masse	全体で，全部一緒に
en suite	続いて
esprit	才気，機知
esprit de corps	団結心，団体精神
fait accompli	既成事実
faux pas	過失，失礼
gratis	無料で，ただで
hors d'oeuvre	オードブル，前菜，添え物
laissez faire	（経済上の）無干渉主義，自由放任主義
modus operandi	活動方式，運用法，手口
non sequitur	不合理な推論，無関係な意見
nouveau riche	新興にわか成り金
paparazzo(-i)	（有名人を追いかける）フリーカメラマン，パパラッチ
par excellence	抜群の，とりわけ優れた
per capita	1人当たりの［で］，頭割りの［で］
per se	それ自体，本質的に
potpourri	寄せ集め，雑録
raison d'être	存在理由
status quo	＜the 〜の形で＞現状
vice versa	＜and 〜の形で＞逆もまた同じ

予想例文

日本語訳 → p.366

例文

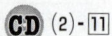

449 At the moment we seemed on the brink of defeat, the attack from the enemy **abated**, and we prevailed.

450 My mother does not **abide** anyone cursing in her house.

451 The mountain climbers seemed oblivious of the fact that they would soon reach an **abyss** too treacherous to negotiate.

452 A violent brawl broke out in a bar near the university after a drunken bully **accosted** several college students just sitting there having a beer and chatting.

453 In order to award officially recognized college credits and degrees, an institution of higher learning must undergo a process of **accreditation**.

449	☐ **abate** [əbéɪt]	≒ become less strong, subside, ease off *v.i.* 弱まる、減少する; *v.t.* を和らげる *n.* abatement
450	☐ **abide** [əbáɪd]	≒ tolerate, condone, accept *v.t.* <通例 can とともに否定文、疑問文で>を我慢する
451	☐ **abyss** [əbís]	≒ (bottomless) chasm, depth *n.* 深淵 *adj.* abysmal
452	☐ **accost** [əkɔ́(ː)st]	≒ approach and boldly speak to *v.t.* に(近寄って)話しかける
453	☐ **accreditation** [əkrèdɪtéɪʃən]	≒ the process of authorizing, authenticating, or approving, authenticating the legitimacy of an institution of higher learning *n.* 認定、承認、(学校に対する)基準合格認定

Chapter 1

例文

454 I find the <u>acrid</u> taste of vinegar quite unpleasant.
455 He often quoted a famous <u>adage</u> from folklore to enliven his lectures.
456 The presidential candidate jumped to his feet and <u>addressed</u> the assembly adamantly.
457 Even as a boy he was known for his talents and versatility, <u>adept</u> at sports, music and academics.
458 As a faithful <u>adherent</u> to Christian values, he followed the teachings of the Scripture.
459 Amazingly, the house <u>adjacent</u> to the huge fire did not burn down.

予想例文

454	☐ **acrid** [ǽkrɪd]	≒ sour, sharp, pungent, acidic, biting, astringent *adj.* （においが）つんとする，（味が）辛い
455	☐ **adage** [ǽdɪdʒ]	≒ proverb, saying, aphorism, axiom *n.* 金言，格言
456	☐ **address** [ədrés]	≒ give a talk to, speak to *v.t.* に演説をする，に話しかける
457	☐ **adept** [ədépt]	≒ talented, versed, skilled, proficient *adj.* ＜〜に＞熟練した＜at, in＞
458	☐ **adherent** [ədhíərənt]	≒ follower, supporter, advocate, believer, backer *n.* 信者，支持者；*adj.* 忠実に従う，固執する *v.t.* adhere
459	☐ **adjacent** [ədʒéɪsənt]	≒ next to, bordering, contiguous to, alongside, neighboring *adj.* ＜〜に＞隣接した，近隣の＜to 〜＞ *n.* adjacency

例文

460, 461 No matter how severely I **admonish** my son for his failure to study, he seems **impervious** to criticism.

462 A lifelong conservative, the man was **adverse** to any changes in traditional lifestyles.

463, 464 Senator Gringrich would frequently **advocate** the investigation of his opponents' personal lives but, in the end, he **unwittingly** brought about his own political demise.

465, 466 Bob was well known for his general **affability** and his strong **affinity** for good food, fine wine and fancy cars.

460 □ admonish [ədmá(:)nɪʃ]	≒ give advice to, counsel, caution *v.t.* に＜〜の件で＞注意する＜for 〜＞
461 □ impervious [ɪmpə́ːrviəs]	≒ unaffected, untouched, indifferent *adj.* ＜〜に＞影響されない＜to 〜＞
462 □ adverse [ædvə́ːrs]	≒ opposed (to), against, inimical (to), antagonistic (to) *adj.* ＜〜に＞反対の，反した，＜〜に＞不都合な＜to 〜＞ *n.* adversity
463 □ advocate [ǽdvəkət]	≒ argue for, support, champion *v.t.* を主張する，を支持する *n.* advocacy, advocate（支持者）
464 □ unwittingly [ʌ̀nwɪ́tɪŋli]	≒ unknowingly, inadvertently *adv.* それと知らずに，不注意にも
465 □ affability [æ̀fəbíləti]	≒ friendliness, approachability, kindness *n.* 愛想のよさ *adj.* affable
466 □ affinity [əfínəti]	≒ taste, fondness, liking *n.* ＜〜への＞好み＜for, to 〜＞

Chapter 1

例文

467 To discourage prowlers, the man **affixed** a beam of light to a tall pole in the middle of his lawn.

468 We used to think that the world was an **aggregate** of nation states with common interests.

469 When widespread retrenchment was necessary to save the company, the president would **agonize** over each decision to lay someone off.

470 I found that acupuncture treatments not only **alleviated** my chronic neck pain but eventually eliminated it altogether.

471, 472 Jesus Christ taught that a good Christian should behave in peaceful and **altruistic** ways toward others, and even respond to a **slap** in the face by turning the other cheek.

予想例文

467	☐ **affix** [əfíks]	≒ attach, fasten, connect *v.t.* を＜〜に＞取り付ける，を添付する＜to 〜＞
468	☐ **aggregate** [ǽgrɪgət]	≒ collection, total *n.* 集合体，集積；*adj.* 集合した，総計の
469	☐ **agonize** [ǽgənàɪz]	≒ suffer extreme anguish, worry, fret *v.i.* ＜〜で＞苦しむ，苦悶する＜over, about 〜＞ *n.* agony
470	☐ **alleviate** [əlíːvièɪt]	≒ make less severe, lessen, allay, assuage, ease *v.t.* を和らげる *n.* alleviation
471	☐ **altruistic** [æ̀ltruístɪk]	≒ concerned for other people, unselfish, humanitarian *adj.* 利他的な *n.* altruism　*n.* altruist ⇔ egoistic
472	☐ **slap** [slæp]	≒ open-handed blow *n.* 平手打ち；*v.t.* をぴしゃりと打つ

例文

473, 474 The boy was always **ambivalent** in his feelings toward his illustrious father, but he remained polite and **deferential** with him even after he himself had become a successful businessman.

475 The doctors told him that there was no permanent cure for his disease but some new medicines on the market might **ameliorate** his condition.

476, 477 Under the **amnesty** offered to **culprits** of hate crimes by the postapartheid government in South Africa, many offenders would be pardoned if they agreed to participate in a program requiring full disclosure and apology.

473	□ **ambivalent** [æmbívələnt]	≒ having a mixture of opposing feelings *adj.* ＜同一物に対して＞相反する感情がある ＜toward, about ～＞, どっちつかずの *n.* ambivalence
474	□ **deferential** [dèfərénʃəl]	≒ respectful *adj.* 敬意を持った *n.* deference
475	□ **ameliorate** [əmíːliərèɪt]	≒ improve, make better, enhance, upgrade, alleviate *v.t.* を改善する, を向上させる *n.* amelioration
476	□ **amnesty** [ǽmnəsti]	≒ general pardon *n.* 大赦, 恩赦
477	□ **culprit** [kʌ́lprɪt]	≒ criminal, offender, malefactor *n.* 犯人

Chapter 1

例文

478 To help protect the **anonymity** of the informants, the government lawyers wanted to expedite the trial as much as possible.

479 Before his speech, the President urged his **antagonists** to tone down their rhetoric and deal with the issues on a rational basis.

480 A vaccine causes people to develop **antibodies** to fight certain bacteria, which prevent them from contracting the targeted disease.

481 The woman was bitten by an unknown snake, and doctors had no **antidote** for its poison.

482 Some bacteria actually have evolved to thrive in the highly sanitary and **antiseptic** conditions found in hospitals.

予想例文

478	☐ **anonymity** [ənάnəmət̬i]	≒ state of being unidentified *n.* 匿名性、匿名者 *adj.* anonymous
479	☐ **antagonist** [æntǽgənɪst]	≒ opponent, competitor, adversary *n.* 敵対者 *v.t.* antagonize　*adj.* antagonistic
480	☐ **antibody** [ǽnt̬ibὰ(ː)di]	≒ a protein that nullifies or provides immunity to invasive bacteria *n.* ＜通例複数形＞抗体
481	☐ **antidote** [ǽnt̬idòʊt]	≒ antitoxin, antivenin, cure, remedy, countermeasure *n.* 解毒剤、解決手段
482	☐ **antiseptic** [æ̀nt̬əséptɪk]	≒ sterilized, clean, sanitary, hygienic, spotless, spic and span *adj.* 殺菌した、防腐性の、非常に清潔な *n.* 消毒剤、防腐剤

例文

483, 484 Not only did the college management seem **apathetic** toward the problems of both students and teachers, it often responded **obtusely** to the serious financial challenges ahead.

485 Despite the efforts of many Western countries to **appease** Hitler, they were eventually attacked anyway.

486 After carefully **appraising** the value of the property, I tendered an offer to purchase it.

487, 488 Although many efforts to **apprehend** the terrorists had failed, officials in the U.S. occupation force claimed they would **prevail**.

483 ☐ **apathetic** [æpəθéṭɪk]	≒ disinterested, indifferent, impassionate, lackadaisical *adj.* 無関心の，無感動な *n.* apathy
484 ☐ **obtusely** [əbtúːsli]	≒ in a thickheaded way, stupidly, foolishly, dull-wittedly *adv.* 鈍感に，鈍く，鈍角に
485 ☐ **appease** [əpíːz]	≒ placate, cater to, accommodate *v.t.* をなだめる，（欲望など）を満足させる *n.* appeasement
486 ☐ **appraise** [əpréɪz]	≒ assess, evaluate, estimate, set a price on *v.t.* を評価する，に値をつける *n.* appraisal
487 ☐ **apprehend** [æprɪhénd]	≒ arrest, seize *v.t.* を逮捕する *n.* apprehension
488 ☐ **prevail** [prɪvéɪl]	≒ achieve victory, win, triumph, be widespread *v.i.* 勝利する，まさる，広く行き渡っている *n.* prevalence *adj.* prevalent

Chapter 1

例文

489 In his <u>ardent</u> devotion to the principles of law, Mr. Thompson often rails vehemently against those who abuse those principles.

490, 491 In doing the <u>arduous</u> job of filling twelve railroad cars with coal every night, Bud says he feels more like a <u>workhorse</u> than a man.

492 Michael repeatedly urged Sally to air her grievances in a more private venue rather than the public <u>arena</u>.

493 Despite the fact that many caches of <u>armaments</u> have been uncovered in Iraq, not a single weapon of mass destruction has been found.

494 My friend's home is an <u>artful</u> mixture of elegant architecture and comfortable furnishings.

495 Just as the two archaeologists were about to give up, they spotted a rare Aztec <u>artifact</u> barely visible in the waning light.

489	☐ **ardent** [á:rdənt]	≒ enthusiastic, passionate, intense, fervent *adj.* 熱心な, 献身的な *n.* ardency
490	☐ **arduous** [á:rdʒuəs]	≒ laborious, strenuous, back-breaking *adj.* 骨の折れる
491	☐ **workhorse** [wə́rkhɔ̀:rs]	≒ horse used for labor *n.* 使役馬, 馬車馬のように働く人
492	☐ **arena** [ərí:nə]	≒ a sphere of interest or activity, a place or situation for controversy *n.* 場, 舞台, 競技場
493	☐ **armament** [á:rməmənt]	≒ military weapons or equipment *n.* ＜しばしば複数形＞軍備
494	☐ **artful** [á:rtfəl]	≒ skillful, tasteful *adj.* 巧妙な, 技巧に富んだ, ずる賢い, 人工の
495	☐ **artifact** [á:rtɪfæ̀kt]	≒ simple man-made object *n.* (簡単な) 人工 [遺] 物, 工芸品

例文

496 With the use of a few clever **artifices** for which he is well known, David Copperfield mesmerized the entire audience.

497 The judge **assailed** the convicted criminal for negligence in the care of his children.

498 The unrelenting acts of cruelty toward many minority groups in America cannot be **assuaged** by a mere apology and a few token jobs.

499 Mary Jennings was not **at loose ends**; as the coordinator of the conference, she got everything organized and going smoothly.

500 The young man tried to **augment** his inheritance by investments in stocks.

501, 502 One of the traditional customs at Chinese restaurants are fortune cookies, which suggest that **auspicious** or **foreboding** events are about to take place.

---

496 ☐ **artifice**
[ɑ́:rtɪfɪs]
≒ trickery, contrivance, strategy, maneuver
n. 策略、ごまかし、巧妙な手段

497 ☐ **assail**
[əséɪl]
≒ assault, attack violently
v.t. を非難する、を攻撃する

498 ☐ **assuage**
[əswéɪdʒ]
≒ appease, pacify, soothe
v.t. （不安・怒りなど）をなだめる、を和らげる

499 ☐ **at loose ends**
≒ without anything definite to do
特にすることもなく、定職がなくて、未解決で

500 ☐ **augment**
[ɔ:gmént]
≒ increase, enlarge, amplify, magnify, pad
v.t. を増加させる
n. augmentation

501 ☐ **auspicious**
[ɔ:spíʃəs]
≒ of good omen, favorable
adj. 縁起のよい、めでたい
n. auspice

502 ☐ **foreboding**
[fɔ:rbóʊdɪŋ]
≒ indicative of (coming evil)
adj. 不吉な；*n.* 予感、虫の知らせ

Chapter 1

例文

503 Economists predicted less **austere** conditions in the coming year, fueled, in part, by low interest rates and higher consumer confidence.

504, 505 During his first few decades in office Prime Minister Mahathir was highly regarded, but when he became more and more **autocratic** in his demonization of Vice Prime Minister Anwar Ibrahim, his place in history seemed **blemished**, an American newspaper reported.

506, 507 The young writer's outspoken **aversion** to capitalism led the pro-business press to **brand** him unfairly as a communist.

508 At the last minute, Captain Smith managed to **avert** disaster with an emergency landing.

予想例文

503	☐ **austere** [ɔːstíər]	≒ harsh, stern, severe *adj.* 厳しい，厳格な，質素な *n.* austerity
504	☐ **autocratic** [ɔ̀ːtəkrǽtɪk]	≒ dictatorial, tyrannical, despotic *adj.* 専制の，独裁的な *n.* autocracy
505	☐ **blemish** [blémɪʃ]	≒ spoil, stain *v.t.* を傷つける，を汚す；*n.* 欠点，汚点
506	☐ **aversion** [əvə́ːrʒən]	≒ antipathy, disinclination, loathing, dislike *n.* ＜〜に対する＞嫌悪，反感＜to 〜＞ *adj.* averse
507	☐ **brand** [brǽnd]	≒ stigmatize, label *v.t.* に（〜の）烙印を押す；*n.* 烙印，汚名，銘柄
508	☐ **avert** [əvə́ːrt]	≒ avoid, shun, sidestep, turn away *v.t.* （危険，事故など）を回避する，（視線など）をそむける

例文

509 Howard Hughes became the wealthiest man in the world, mostly because of his investments in **aviation**.

510 Vladimir Nabokov was both a great writer and an **avid** entomologist.

511, 512 Tom Hanks' **back-to-back** best-actor Oscars led a few rivals at the ceremony to hide a shamelessly **covetous** look in their eyes.

513 Due to a big **backlog** of orders, customers had to wait almost six months for their new Toyotas.

514 After his older brother had **badgered** him for years over anything he had tried to do, Hal finally decided to retaliate with some well-chosen words of sarcasm.

509	☐ **aviation** [èɪviéɪʃən]	≒ matters related to aircraft *n.* 航空機産業, 航空学, 飛行 *v.t.* aviate
510	☐ **avid** [ǽvɪd]	≒ ardent, fervent, enthusiastic, passionate *adj.* 熱心な, どん欲な *n.* avidity
511	☐ **back to back**	≒ happening one after the other 連続した, 続けざまの
512	☐ **covetous** [kʌ́vɪṭəs]	≒ greedy, hungry, envious *adj.* むやみに欲しがる, 欲張りな *v.t., v.i.* covet
513	☐ **backlog** [bǽklɔ̀:g]	≒ build-up, pile-up, accumulation *n.* 未処理の山, 残務
514	☐ **badger** [bǽdʒər]	≒ harass, pester, annoy *v.t.* をしつこく悩ます, をいじめる

Chapter 1

例文

515 Jim always <u>bantered</u> with the ladies, often coaxing smiles from them, which seemed to make him the most popular guy in the whole school.

516 Although China continues to bolster its military power, its weapon technology <u>is</u> still <u>a far cry from</u> the advanced military capabilities of many modern industrial nations, the Post reported.

517 Although the promising young actor's last film was virtually a debacle, he is confident he will soon <u>be back on track</u>.

518 The little girl seemed so innocent she could easily <u>beguile</u> her mother into thinking she was sick by feigning a headache or some other illness.

519, 520 His father said that it would <u>behoove</u> him to observe <u>moderation</u> in all things.

予想例文

515	☐ **banter** [bǽntər]	≒ tease, jest, speak playfully *v.i.* からかう；*n.* (悪意のない) 冷やかし
516	☐ **be a far cry from ~**	≒ be a long way from ～と大きく違って，～から遠く離れて
517	☐ **be back on track**	≒ be back on the course laid out or doing O.K. again 元に戻る，調子を取り戻す
518	☐ **beguile** [bɪɡáɪl]	≒ deceive, fool, delude *v.t.* をだます，をだまして＜～に＞導く＜into ～＞ *n.* beguilement
519	☐ **behoove** [bɪhúːv]	≒ be necessary for, be in *one's* interest, serve one, benefit, help *v.t.* ＜it を仮主語に＞にとって＜…することが＞義務（利益）である＜to *do* ＞
520	☐ **moderation** [mà(ː)dəréɪʃən]	≒ avoiding excess, balance, constraint, restraint *n.* 節度，適度，緩和，温和

例文

521, 522 Edgar had always had a **belligerent** attitude, but when he **assaulted** a police officer, he was given a jail sentence.

523, 524 Virtually every time Hiroshi was told to report to the boss he was **berated** so severely that he only spoke to him with great **trepidation**.

525, 526 The couple was so **bereaved** over the death of their child that nothing anyone did helped them **reconcile** themselves to the loss.

---

521 □ belligerent
[bəlídʒərənt]
≒ contentious, bellicose, pugnacious, quarrelsome
adj. 好戦的な、けんか腰の
n. belligerence

522 □ assault
[əsɔ́(:)lt]
≒ attack
v.t. を攻撃する、を非難する

523 □ berate
[bɪréɪt]
≒ rebuke, rail at, chastise, scold
v.t. をきつく叱る

524 □ trepidation
[trèpɪdéɪʃən]
≒ feeling of fear
n. 恐れ、おののき、不安

525 □ bereave
[bɪríːv]
≒ left in a state of sadness
v.t. ＜通例受身形＞（死によって）＜家族などを＞から奪う、＜望みを＞失わせる＜of ～＞
n. bereavement

526 □ reconcile
[rékənsàɪl]
≒ accept, resign *oneself* to
v.t. ＜通例～ *oneself* または受身形＞を＜～に＞甘んじさせる、あきらめて受け入れさせる＜to ～＞、を和解させる
n. reconciliation

Chapter 1

例文

527, 528 I had secured an upper **berth** in the first-class car on the famed Orient Express, but I was unable to sleep as the train **lurched** forward and swayed violently from side to side all through the night.

529, 530 The more the editorial staff **besieged** the president to make changes before it was too late, the more he **scoffed** at their suggestions.

531 President Mandela **bestowed** a broad clemency on all those who committed crimes under the apartheid regime in South Africa.

532, 533 Students gazed in complete **bewilderment** as the professor rambled on in his customarily **obscure** and incoherent fashion.

予想例文

527	☐ **berth** [bə:rθ]	≒ fixed bunk on a train for sleeping in *n.* （列車などの）寝台
528	☐ **lurch** [lə:rtʃ]	≒ move or sway suddenly, wobble *v.i.* 急に揺れる、よろめく
529	☐ **besiege** [bisí:dʒ]	≒ beset, assail, harass *v.t.* を攻める、を取り囲む
530	☐ **scoff** [skɑ(:)f]	≒ sneer, jeer, poke fun *v.i.* ＜〜を＞あざける、嘲笑する＜at 〜＞
531	☐ **bestow** [bistóu]	≒ give, grant, confer on *v.t.* を＜人に＞授ける＜on, upon 〜＞ *n.* bestowal
532	☐ **bewilderment** [biwíldərmənt]	≒ perplexity, confusion *n.* 当惑、困惑、混乱 *v.t.* bewilder
533	☐ **obscure** [əbskjúər]	≒ unclear, ambiguous, equivocal, vague, unknown *adj.* 曖昧な、分かりにくい、世に知られていない *n.* obscurity

例文

534, 535 The appeals court ruled that the former conviction of the defendant was based on **biased** testimony that had **infringed** on his right to a fair trial.

536, 537 In the midst of widespread criticisms and false accusations, I decided simply to **bide my time** until the day came for me to be **exonerated** by the facts.

538, 539 Many codes operate on the principle of **binary** opposition, which **denotes** two elements in fundamental contrast with each other, as in the 1 and 0 of a computer programming code.

534 biased [báɪəst]	≒ prejudiced, one-sided, unfair, distorted *adj.* 偏った，偏見のある *n.* bias
535 infringe [ɪnfrɪ́ndʒ]	≒ trespass, encroach, intrude *v.i.* ＜他人の権利などを＞侵害する，侵す＜on, upon ～＞ *n.* infringement
536 bide *one's* time	≒ await *one's* best opportunity 好機を待つ
537 exonerate [ɪgzá(:)nərèɪt]	≒ free from blame, release from a duty *v.t.* の嫌疑を晴らす，を＜責任などから＞解放する＜from ～＞ *n.* exoneration
538 binary [báɪnəri]	≒ involving two (things or parts) *adj.* 二進法の，二項の
539 denote [dɪnóʊt]	≒ mean, indicate, symbolize *v.t.* を示す，を意味する *n.* denotation

Chapter 1

例文

540 He was always considered the **black sheep** of his family until he became rich from one of his strange inventions.

541 Every time someone slows him down a little he **blares** his horn and curses.

542 I stained my favorite shirt with ink and unfortunately was unable to **bleach** it out.

543 Many American and international critics of the Bush administration's foreign policy condemn the invasion of Iraq as a permanent **blight** on the moral integrity of America.

544 The art critic stated that the works of a recently acclaimed painter consisted of little more than a few **blotches** of paint squeezed sloppily onto a canvas.

545 John Dean's confession of presidential complicity in the famous Watergate case **blew the lid off** the Nixon Administration's attempt to cover up a criminal conspiracy.

予想例文

540 ☐ **black sheep**	≒ one who is seen as a disgrace or failure by family members, a prodigal (son), a renegade, a ne'er-do-well 厄介もの，異端者，面汚し
541 ☐ **blare** [bleər]	≒ honk, blast, trumpet, blow (a horn) *v.t.* をしつこく鳴らす，を大声で宣言する
542 ☐ **bleach** [bli:tʃ]	≒ whiten, lighten *v.t.* を漂白する，から染みを抜く
543 ☐ **blight** [blaɪt]	≒ stain, taint, trouble, calamity *n.* 暗影，破滅の原因；*v.t.* を破滅させる
544 ☐ **blotch** [blɑ(:)tʃ]	≒ discolored patch, stain *n.* しみ；*v.t.* に大きなしみをつける
545 ☐ **blow the lid off ~**	≒ expose 〜を暴露する

例文

546 Motorists are warned against smoking around a gas pump for fear that it might **blow up**.

547, 548 Some people think that North Korea is trying to **bluff** the international community with claims of nuclear capabilities so it can **call the shots** in further negotiations.

549, 550 Settlers of the North American continent found many **bountiful** valleys and rivers as they headed westward, but finally they decided to make the rich farm lands of southern Illinois their chosen place of **abode**.

551, 552 Some of my colleagues thought the young girl was outspoken to the point of being **brazen**, but I admired such **pluck**.

546	☐ **blow up**	≒ explode, blast, detonate, erupt, go off 爆発する, 〜を爆破する
547	☐ **bluff** [blʌf]	≒ intimidate by making a pretense of strength *v.t.* はったりで脅す, *n.* 虚勢
548	☐ **call the shots**	≒ take the initiative, be in control 支配する, 牛耳る
549	☐ **bountiful** [báʊnṭɪfəl]	≒ abundant, plentiful, copious *adj.* 豊富な
550	☐ **abode** [əbóʊd]	≒ residence, home, domicile; address *n.* 住居, 居住地, 住所
551	☐ **brazen** [bréɪzən]	≒ audacious, brash, forward, rude, brassy *adj.* 図々しい *n.* brazenness
552	☐ **pluck** [plʌk]	≒ courage, guts, mettle, intrepidity *n.* 勇気, 胆力 ; *v.t.* を引っ張る

Chapter 1

例文

553, 554 He doesn't worry much about losing money in the stock market, saying cheerfully that he will ultimately **break even down the line**.

555 Since he was a professional pianist, his having to quit playing almost **broke his heart**.

556, 557 Having been accused of **bribing** a policeman, the man on the witness stand began to shout **abrasively** at the prosecutor.

558 Although she really deserved a raise, she didn't dare to **bring** it **up** to her boss.

553	☐ **break even**	≒ have equal loss and profit 損得なしに終わる，（収支が）とんとんになる
554	☐ **down the line**	≒ completely, fully, entirely 完全に，徹底的に，そのうち，いつか
555	☐ **break *one's* heart**	≒ make *one* very sad, crush, hurt, shatter 〜を悲嘆にくれさせる
556	☐ **bribe** [braɪb]	≒ buy off, corrupt, fix *v.t.* に賄賂を贈る；*n.* 賄賂（の金品） *n.* bribery（贈収賄）
557	☐ **abrasively** [əbréɪsɪvli]	≒ causing irritation *adv.* 耳障りな音［声］で，イライラさせるように *v.t., v.i.* abrade（（神経）を擦り減らす；擦りむく）　*n.* abrasion（擦りむくこと）
558	☐ **bring up 〜**	≒ mention, broach, call attention to （話題など）を持ち出す，を話題にする

例文

559, 560 He would sit alone in the dark and **brood** for hours over what seemed to be **trifling** matters.

561, 562 Margaret was a shy and quiet girl, and perhaps for that reason she would have to bear the **brunt** of our section chief's **caustic** way of speaking.

563 Although he was generally **brusque** and sometimes spoke disdainfully, those who knew him well also realized he had a kinder, gentler side.

564 The car had run through the guard rail, but injuries to the driver were slight since a large bush had **buffered** the severity of the crash.

559	☐ **brood** [bru:d]	≒ ponder, deliberate, ruminate *v.i.* ＜〜について＞じっくり考える，気に病む ＜over, on, about 〜＞
560	☐ **trifling** [tráɪflɪŋ]	≒ trivial, minor, unimportant, paltry, petty *adj.* たわいない，つまらない
561	☐ **brunt** [brʌnt]	≒ force of an attack, impact *n.* （非難，攻撃などの）ほこさき，矢面
562	☐ **caustic** [kɔ́:stɪk]	≒ bitter, cutting, scathing, acrimonious, harsh, virulent, corrosive *adj.* 辛らつな，腐食性の *n.* causticity
563	☐ **brusque** [brʌsk]	≒ blunt, curt, terse *adj.* ぶっきらぼうな，そっけない
564	☐ **buffer** [báfər]	≒ cushion, soften, lessen *v.t.* の衝撃を和らげる；*n.* 緩衝剤

Chapter 1

例文

565, 566 An examination of the heart patient revealed that a **bulge** in one of the major arteries carrying blood from the heart needed an emergency operation to keep it from **rupturing**.

567 When the former sumo wrestler needed an operation, doctors said it would be complicated by his enormous **bulk**.

568 An attempt to rescue the hostages had to be aborted when two helicopter pilots **bungled** the mission by colliding into each other on take off.

569 As spring came to the valley, trees everywhere were blossoming, and it seemed that flowers were **burgeoning** from every leaf and stem.

570, 571 The great Gothic cathedrals of Medieval Europe made use of the flying **buttress**, which served not only to **fortify** the support structures of the building but also as elegant elements of its overall design.

565	☐ **bulge** [bʌldʒ]	≒ lump, swelling *n.* 肥大、膨らみ、増加; *v.i.* 膨らむ
566	☐ **rupture** [rʌ́ptʃər]	≒ break, burst, tear apart *v.i.* 破裂する、決裂する; *n.* 破裂、決裂
567	☐ **bulk** [bʌlk]	≒ size, volume, mass, amplitude, substance *n.* 大きさ、かさ、巨大なもの、積荷、(〜の) 大部分
568	☐ **bungle** [bʌ́ŋgl]	≒ blunder, botch, screw up, louse up *v.t.* をしくじる; *n.* へま
569	☐ **burgeon** [bə́ːrdʒən]	≒ put forth young shoots, sprout, flourish *v.i.* 萌え出る、急成長する; *n.* 新芽
570	☐ **buttress** [bʌ́trəs]	≒ prop, reinforcement, support *n.* 控え壁、支え (となるもの)、バットレス
571	☐ **fortify** [fɔ́ːrtəfàɪ]	≒ strengthen, protect, brace, prop up, support *v.t.* を強化する、の防備を固める *n.* fortification

例文

572 Although there were some weak points in her acting debut, <u>by and large</u>, it was an impressive performance.

573, 574 Much of the material now found in the Gospels had spread <u>by word of mouth</u> for many years before it was written in the form we read it today, so many scholars find its historical accuracy very <u>dubious</u>.

575 The crash of the American stock market in 1929 was an economic <u>calamity</u> for America and the world.

576, 577 So many candidates of very high <u>caliber</u> applied for the two positions we were advertising that we could simply ignore all the <u>lackluster</u> applicants who sent us their resumes.

572	☐ **by and large**	≒ for the most part, mostly, when all is said and done 大体、全般的に
573	☐ **by word of mouth**	≒ verbally 口承で、口頭で
574	☐ **dubious** [djúːbiəs]	≒ debatable, unreliable, suspicious *adj.* 懐疑的で、疑わしい
575	☐ **calamity** [kəlǽməti]	≒ disaster, catastrophe, misfortune, cataclysm, tragedy *n.* 大惨事、大きな不幸 *adj.* calamitous
576	☐ **caliber** [kǽləbər]	≒ ability, talent, competence, quality *n.* 才幹、力量
577	☐ **lackluster** [lǽklʌstər]	≒ undistinguished, uninteresting *adj.* 冴えない、くすんだ

Chapter 1

例文

578 Abraham Lincoln had the rare ability to speak both with <u>candor</u> and grace at the same time.

579, 580 Even after she married and had children of her own, Elizabeth was <u>capricious</u> and unpredictable, and often acted more out of <u>whim</u> than from logical deliberation.

581 Witnesses said that the bus suddenly <u>careened</u> out of control, went off the road and finally came to a screeching halt, teetering on the edge of a cliff.

582, 583 As soon as the hula hoop hit the market, it <u>caught on</u>, and sales began to <u>snowball</u> until millions of people around the world had purchased one.

584 Some say that death is really defined by the permanent <u>cessation</u> of brain function, rather than by the absence of a heart beat.

578	☐ **candor** [kǽndər]	≒ honesty, frankness *n.* 率直さ, 誠実さ
579	☐ **capricious** [kəpríʃəs]	≒ unpredictable, impulsive, whimsical *adj.* 気まぐれな, 移り気な *n.* caprice
580	☐ **whim** [hwɪm]	≒ caprice, fancy, impulsiveness *n.* 気まぐれな考え, とっさの思いつき *adj.* whimsical
581	☐ **careen** [kərí:n]	≒ swerve, lurch, tilt, lean over *v.i.* （走りながら）傾く,（揺れながら）暴走する *n.* careenage
582	☐ **catch on**	≒ become popular ヒットする, 人気を得る
583	☐ **snowball** [snóʊbɔ̀:l]	≒ increase rapidly *v.i.* 雪だるま式に大きくなる
584	☐ **cessation** [seséɪʃən]	≒ stopping, ending, arrest *n.* 中止, 停止 *v.t.* cease

予想例文

例文

585 Gregorian <u>chant</u> is probably the best known example of Western monophonic music.

586, 587 When a <u>chartered</u> plane went down in a rugged mountainous area in Peru, most of the bodies of the <u>deceased</u> passengers were never recovered.

588, 589 The behavior and attitudes of so-called "male <u>chauvinists</u>" toward women's rights have <u>galvanized</u> human rights groups around the world to struggle for equality of the sexes.

585 ☐ **chant** [tʃænt]	≒ liturgical song, intonation *n.* 聖歌, 詠唱歌 ; *v.t.* を詠唱する, を調子をそろえて繰り返し唱える
586 ☐ **chartered** [tʃɑ́ːrtərd]	≒ hired *adj.* 借り切った *n.* charter (契約使用, 憲章, 設立許可)
587 ☐ **deceased** [dɪsíːst]	≒ dead, those who have died *adj.* 死去した, <the ~>死者
588 ☐ **chauvinist** [ʃóuvənɪst]	≒ person showing excessive support or loyalty to *one's* group or sex *n.* 狂信的排他主義者 *n.* chauvinism
589 ☐ **galvanize** [gǽlvənàɪz]	≒ excite, prod, rouse *v.t.* を活気づかせる, を刺激して駆り立てる *n.* galvanization

Chapter 1

例文

590, 591 At first I thought taking my son to Disneyland for his birthday would be too expensive, but when my parents **chipped in** to help cover the cost, I **jumped at** the chance to take him there.

592, 593 First we **churned** cream and ice until it thickened while adding sugar and flavoring, until finally we **ladled** our fresh, homemade ice cream into the children's bowls.

594 On many occasions Michael Jordan scored the points needed to **cinch** victory for his team.

595 The lawyer for the defense argued that the entire case against his client boiled down to merely **circumstantial** evidence.

596 Although their fists were **clenched** and their expressions grim, the two enemies reluctantly agreed to bury the hatchet.

予想例文

590	☐ **chip in**	≒ contribute (money) （金を）出し合う，提供する
591	☐ **jump at ～**	≒ accept eagerly *v.t.* （すぐに）～に飛びつく
592	☐ **churn** [tʃəːrn]	≒ agitate, stir *v.t.* をかき回す
593	☐ **ladle** [léɪdl]	≒ spoon, scoop *v.t.* を（ひしゃくなどで）すくう
594	☐ **cinch** [sɪntʃ]	≒ secure, finalize, complete *v.t.* を確実にする；*n.* 確実なこと，たやすいこと
595	☐ **circumstantial** [sə̀ːrkəmstǽnʃəl]	≒ inferred, presumed, deduced *adj.* 状況に基づく，付随的な
596	☐ **clench** [klentʃ]	≒ grasp firmly *v.t.* （こぶし）を堅く握る，（歯）を食いしばる； *n.* 握りしめること

例文

597 The last few points were enough to **clinch** the victory for the San Antonio Spurs.

598 They knew it would be hard to get a permit to build the new shopping mall, so they contacted a friend who had some **clout** with City Hall.

599 When the thief tried to grab the old lady's wallet, she **clutched** it with both hands and refused to let it go.

600 His behavior was unschooled and **coarse**, but it gave him a kind of innocent charm.

601 The Bible says that the end of the world will some day **come to pass**.

597 ☐ **clinch** [klɪntʃ]	≒ secure, settle, determine, safeguard, assure; triumph *v.t.* (勝利)を得る，に決着をつける，を取り決める
598 ☐ **clout** [klaʊt]	≒ power, influence *n.* 権力，影響力
599 ☐ **clutch** [klʌtʃ]	≒ cling to, grasp, hold onto tightly *v.t.* を握りしめる，をつかむ；*n.* しっかりとつかむこと，把握，影響力
600 ☐ **coarse** [kɔːrs]	≒ crude, vulgar, rough *adj.* 粗野な，下品な，（きめが）粗い
601 ☐ **come to pass**	≒ happen, come about, occur 起こる，実現する

Chapter 1

例文

602, 603 Throughout American history many religious and politically motivated <u>communes</u> have been formed from groups of people who shared similar values and longed for a <u>cohesive</u> lifestyle.

604, 605 Studies that claim that intellectual <u>competency</u> can be correlated with race, as the book *The Bell Curve* has done, have been shown to be blatantly <u>spurious</u>.

606 Einstein <u>conceived</u> of his theory of relativity through his imaginative use of thought problems.

607, 608 Although the speaker was asked to speak <u>concisely</u>, she had a <u>loquacious</u> nature and couldn't stop talking for almost twenty minutes.

602 ☐ **commune** [ká(:)mju:n]	≒ group of people sharing the same political ideas *n.* コミューン，共同体	
603 ☐ **cohesive** [kouhí:sɪv]	≒ sticking together *adj.* 結束力のある，粘着力のある *n.* cohesion	
604 ☐ **competency** [ká(:)mpətənsi]	≒ ability, capability *n.* 能力，力量 *n.* competent	
605 ☐ **spurious** [spjúəriəs]	≒ forged, feigned, sham, fake, phony *adj.* にせものの，擬似の	
606 ☐ **conceive** [kənsí:v]	≒ think of, invent, create *v.i.* ＜考えなどを＞思いつく，考える＜of ～＞; *v.t.* （考え，感情など）を抱く *n.* concept, conception	
607 ☐ **concisely** [kənsáɪsli]	≒ briefly, compactly *adv.* 簡潔に	
608 ☐ **loquacious** [loʊkwéɪʃəs]	≒ talkative, garrulous, verbose *adj.* おしゃべりな	

予想例文

例文

609 Gary Van Den Heuvel <u>condensed</u> the 1,200-page masterpiece of Suzanne Langer into a single-volume text, called *Mind: An Essay on Human Feeling*.

610 Many citizens would not <u>condone</u> insolent behavior from ordinary people but they don't seem to mind when it applies to movie stars or rock musicians.

611 When I trained as a laboratory technician for a tomato cannery, I learned to recognize under the microscope the <u>configurations</u> of certain species of mold.

612 The Spanish Inquisition censured and <u>confiscated</u> any materials not considered compatible with Roman Catholic beliefs.

613 It took him two days to muster the courage to face the impending <u>confrontation</u> with his boss over the raise he had been promised.

609	☐ **condense** [kəndéns]	≒ shorten, abbreviate, compress, boil down *v.t.* ＜～に＞を要約する＜into ～＞, を短縮する, を凝縮する *n.* condensation
610	☐ **condone** [kəndóun]	≒ overlook, sanction voluntarily, excuse *v.t.* (罪など)を大目に見る, 赦す
611	☐ **configuration** [kənfìgjəréɪʃən]	≒ shape, pattern, arrangement, formation *n.* 形状, 輪郭, 配置, 事情
612	☐ **confiscate** [ká(:)nfɪskèɪt]	≒ expropriate, seize by authority *v.t.* を没収する, を差し押さえる *n.* confiscation
613	☐ **confrontation** [kà(:)nfrʌntéɪʃən]	≒ conflict, argument, fight, struggle *n.* 対決, 対立 *v.t.* confront

Chapter 1

例文

614 Despite being a lazy fellow, he did well in life because he was always <u>congenial</u> and kind toward others.

615 Recently, Worldview Corporation announced a huge merger, making a <u>conglomerate</u> of several media and entertainment companies.

616 Police cordoned off one square block around the bomb scene to prevent onlookers from <u>congregating</u> there during the cleanup operation.

617 When a theory lacks <u>congruity</u> with observable facts, we need to modify it.

618 Leaks to the press of some crucial information related to a possible suspect have led the public to <u>conjecture</u> that the police will soon make an arrest.

予想例文

614	☐ **congenial** [kəndʒíːniəl]	≒ friendly, affable, collegial *adj.* 友好的な, 気性の合った *n.* congeniality
615	☐ **conglomerate** [kəngláː)mərət]	≒ large corporation formed by the merging of separate firms *n.* 巨大複合企業体, コングロマリット
616	☐ **congregate** [káː)ŋgrɪgèɪt]	≒ gather into a crowd *v.i.* 集まる, 会合する *n.* congregation
617	☐ **congruity** [kəngrúːəti]	≒ agreement, concurrence, accordance, compatibility, good fit *n.* 一致, 調和 *adj.* congruous
618	☐ **conjecture** [kəndʒéktʃər]	≒ guess, surmise, assume, infer *v.t.* <…であると>推測する<that ...>, を推測する; *n.* 推測

117

例文

619 Auto companies are cutting back on their orders for luxury cars next year, since the ones they now have on **consignment** are not selling fast enough.

620 The new company president invited all employees to air their grievances, though it was small **consolation** for the sharp pay cuts they received.

621 Once a person has been convicted of a felony, he or she cannot legally **consort** with other ex-convicts.

622 He claimed to be shy but he was always **conspicuous** in his brightly colored ties and strange hats.

623 Married couples with reasonable incomes and plenty of leisure time seem to have more **constancy** in their relationships.

619	☐ **consignment** [kənsáınmənt]	≒ <on ~> turned over to an agent for sale *n.* 委託（販売） *v.t.* consign
620	☐ **consolation** [kà(:)nsəléıʃən]	≒ comfort, solace, relief *n.* 慰め *v.t.* console
621	☐ **consort** [kənsɔ́ːrt]	≒ associate with, spend time with *v.i.* ＜望ましくない人と＞交際する＜with ~＞
622	☐ **conspicuous** [kənspíkjʊəs]	≒ showy, flamboyant, ostentatious, visible, having a high profile *adj.* 目立つ，人目を引く，著しい
623	☐ **constancy** [ká(:)nstənsi]	≒ faithfulness, fidelity *n.* （愛情などの）不変性，忠実性，貞節

Chapter 1

例文

624 No matter what **constellation** he was supposed to identify, all he could ever see was a random scattering of stars.

625, 626 Doctors discovered that not only were the elderly woman's coronary arteries seriously **constricted**, they also needed to **implant** a pacemaker to regulate her heartbeat.

627 We can **construe** a wide variety of meanings for almost any complex text.

628 Old professor Nishiyama never feels more contented than when he works in his garden, where he can **contemplate** nature's deepest secrets.

予想例文

624 ☐ **constellation** [kɑ̀(:)nstəléɪʃən]	≒ a shape recognized in a group of stars, a group of persons or things unified by some common purpose or characteristic *n.* 星座、一連のもの
625 ☐ **constrict** [kənstríkt]	≒ make narrower, tighten, compress *v.t.* を収縮させる、を圧縮する *n.* constriction
626 ☐ **implant** [ɪmplǽnt]	≒ insert (in a living body) *v.t.* を埋め込む、を移植する *n.* implantation
627 ☐ **construe** [kənstrúː]	≒ interpret, conceptualize, infer *v.t.* を＜～と＞解釈する＜as ～＞
628 ☐ **contemplate** [kɑ́(:)ntəmplèɪt]	≒ gaze at, ponder on, deliberate over, mull over, think about, intend *v.t.* を鑑賞する、をじっと見つめる、を意図する *n.* contemplation

例文

629, 630 A **contentious** debate was held over whether or not a painting attributed to Van Gogh was really **authentic** or just a hoax.

631, 632 The lawyers for the defense requested a two-day **continuance** of the trial to investigate the prosecution's charges of **perjury** against their main witness.

633 The defendant in the trial told the judge that he was **contrite** about any wrongdoing he had committed.

634 We knew that our opponents were cooking up a special strategy to stop our team's powerful offense, so we **contrived** a different attack to take them by surprise.

629	☐ **contentious** [kənténʃəs]	≒ quarrelsome, belligerent, controversial *adj.* 論争好きの、議論のある、けんか腰の *v.i., v.t.* contend
630	☐ **authentic** [ɔːθéntɪk]	≒ veritable, reliable, indubitable *adj.* 本物の、根拠のある、信頼できる *n.* authenticity
631	☐ **continuance** [kəntínjuəns]	≒ process of continuing, duration *n.* 継続、持続
632	☐ **perjury** [pə́ːrdʒəri]	≒ giving false evidence, falsification, lying *n.* 偽証（罪） *v.t.* perjure ＜*oneself*＞
633	☐ **contrite** [kəntráɪt]	≒ sorry, regretful, remorseful *adj.* 罪を深く悔いている、悔恨の *n.* contrition
634	☐ **contrive** [kəntráɪv]	≒ scheme, plan *v.t.* （手だてなど）を考え出す、（悪事など）をたくらむ *n.* contrivance

Chapter 1

例文

635, 636 The Security Council of the United Nations **convened** in an emergency meeting to try to **defuse** the volatile situation surrounding North Korea's nuclear program.

637 When German, French and Russian opposition to the Iraqi War **converged**, these three members of the Security Council of the United Nations constituted a powerful opposition to the American policy.

638 The university was looking for a guest lecturer who was **conversant** with the latest research in linguistics, so it seemed that Professor Noam Chomsky would certainly fit the bill.

635 ☐ **convene** [kənvíːn]	≒ assemble, gather, meet together *v.i.* （会議に）集まる，参集する *n.* convention	
636 ☐ **defuse** [dìːfjúːz]	≒ ease, moderate, temper, alleviate *v.t.* の危険性を弱める，（爆発物）から信管を取り除く	
637 ☐ **converge** [kənvə́ːrdʒ]	≒ join, unite, come together *v.i.* 一つにまとまる，（同じ目的に向かって）集中する *adj.* convergent	
638 ☐ **conversant** [kənvə́ːrsənt]	≒ well-acquainted, familiar with *adj.* ＜〜に＞精通している，詳しい＜with 〜＞ *adj.* conversance	

予想例文

例文

639, 640 Directly after being **convicted** of Murder One, the ruthless criminal **vowed** to get revenge on those who had brought him to justice.

641 We had to take our baby to the hospital when he developed a high fever and began to **convulse**.

642 Professor Nishiyama distributed **copious** handouts of the writings of the American transcendentalists for his students to read and comment on by the next class meeting.

643 When an opportunity came along for the workers in the office to form a softball team, they unanimously agreed to **count** us **in**.

639	☐ **convict** [kənvíkt]	≒ find guilty *v.t.* を有罪とする，に＜犯罪の＞判決を下す＜of ~＞ *n.* conviction
640	☐ **vow** [vaʊ]	≒ swear, pledge, promise *v.t.* ＜…すること＞を誓う＜to *do*＞，を誓う； *n.* 誓い
641	☐ **convulse** [kənvʌ́ls]	≒ to have a seizure, shake violently *v.i.* けいれんする，身悶えする；*v.t.* を震動させる *n.* convulsion
642	☐ **copious** [kóʊpɪəs]	≒ abundant, plentiful, providing much information *adj.* 多量の，おびただしい，豊富な
643	☐ **count in ~**	≒ include ～を仲間に入れる，～を勘定に入れる ⇔ count out ~

Chapter 1

例文

644 President Bush met his Japanese **counterpart**, Prime Minister Koizumi, in a series of meetings in Tokyo.

645 The Watergate scandal was basically an attempt by the Nixon administration to **cover up** a criminal conspiracy.

646 The **covert** operations of the CIA and FBI have increasingly come under criticism both from domestic and international commentators.

647 The comedian Robin Williams is famous for being so funny that even his co-stars sometimes **crack up** over his crazy antics during rehearsals.

648 I packed my shirts carefully but the way I had put them in the suitcase created a strange-looking **crease** in all of them.

649 She was so **credulous** that I think she believed everything anyone told her.

644	☐ **counterpart** [káʊntərpɑ̀ːrt]	≒ analogue, correspondent, complement *n.* 対応する人〔物〕、同等の人〔物〕
645	☐ **cover up ~**	≒ hide, conceal, obfuscate （事実など）を隠す
646	☐ **covert** [kóʊvəːrt]	≒ secretive, hidden, clandestine *adj.* ひそかな、隠れた ⇔ overt
647	☐ **crack up (~)**	≒ laugh, break up, amuse 急に笑い出す、大笑いする、壊れる；~を笑わせる
648	☐ **crease** [kriːs]	≒ crimp, pleat, wrinkle *n.* しわ、折り目；*v.t.* にしわをつける
649	☐ **credulous** [krédʒələs]	≒ gullible, naive, green *adj.* 信じやすい、だまされやすい、ばか正直な *n.* credulity

例文

650 The boss did not state it outright, but I still inferred from his comments that my job was on the line over my handling of the budget **crunch**.

651, 652 Greenpeace is now trying to pressure leading industrial nations to **curb** the current **deplorable** depletion of the world's tropical forests.

653 Even a **cursory** survey of the world's known oil and gas supplies will tell us that by the middle of this century, the fossil fuels available will fall far short of the demand.

654, 655 Some students requested that Professor Nishiyama reduce the volume of outside readings he required of them, but they were **curtly rebuked** for being lazy students.

650	□ **crunch** [krʌntʃ]	≒ crisis, critical moment *n.* 危機、緊張、財政ひっ迫
651	□ **curb** [kəːrb]	≒ restrain, bridle, control, repress *v.t.* を抑制する、を制御する
652	□ **deplorable** [dɪplɔ́ːrəbl]	≒ lamentable, reprehensible, shameful *adj.* 嘆かわしい *v.t.* deplore
653	□ **cursory** [kə́ːrsəri]	≒ hasty, perfunctory, rapid, superficial *adj.* 急いだ、ぞんざいな
654	□ **curtly** [kə́ːrtli]	≒ snappishly, bluntly *adv.* ぶっきらぼうに
655	□ **rebuke** [rɪbjúːk]	≒ scold, reprimand, reprove, dress down *v.t.* を＜〜のことで＞厳しくしかる＜for 〜＞ *adv.* rebukingly

Chapter 1

例文

656 In the past young ladies of good character were expected to be **dainty** and discreet in their public behavior.

657 Many politicians assume that the key to political success depends mostly on **dangling** a carrot in front of the people, who will be easily duped into believing their entire platform.

658, 659 School officials were concerned about the large number of junior high school boys **dawdling** on their way to school and annoying people with behavior and speech that many witnesses considered **gauche**.

660, 661 Despite the **dearth** of evidence, Inspector Hearns could **ascertain** where and how the murder occurred.

662 After the hostages had been released by the terrorists, they were detained for a few days to be thoroughly **debriefed**.

656	☐ **dainty** [déɪnti]	≒ delicate, graceful, pleasing *adj.* 上品な, 優美な
657	☐ **dangle** [dǽŋgl]	≒ hold out, flaunt, brandish *v.t.* をぶら下げる, をちらつかせる ; *v.i.* ぶら下がる
658	☐ **dawdle** [dɔ́:dl]	≒ linger, loiter, walk slowly and idly *v.i.* だらだらする, ぶらぶらと進む
659	☐ **gauche** [gouʃ]	≒ awkward, lacking grace, crude *adj.* 無作法な, ぎこちない, がさつな
660	☐ **dearth** [də:rθ]	≒ scarcity, deficiency *n.* <～の>不足, 欠乏<of ～>
661	☐ **ascertain** [æsərtéɪn]	≒ find out accurately, make certain *v.t.* を正確に知る, を確かめる *n.* ascertainment
662	☐ **debrief** [dì:brí:f]	≒ interrogate about a completed mission *v.t.* （任務を終えた人）に報告を求める

例文

663 The police were utterly baffled with the brilliant heist, contrived by some of the world's most devious criminal minds, all involved in a masterful **deception**.

664 His formal upbringing taught him to behave in a **decorous** and dignified manner, even when angry or under stress.

665 The company always **deducted** about 25% of the employees' gross monthly salary for health insurance, taxes and the pension fund.

666, 667 In matters involving proper etiquette, I always **defer** to Professor Nishiyama's **flawless** judgment.

---

663 □ deception
[dɪsépʃən]
≒ duplicity, deceit
n. 欺くこと、詐欺
v.t. deceive *n.* deceit

664 □ decorous
[dékərəs]
≒ proper, acceptable, seemly, appropriate
adj. 上品な、礼儀正しい
n. decorum

665 □ deduct
[dɪdʌ́kt]
≒ subtract, take out, take away from
v.t. を控除する
n. deduction

666 □ defer
[dɪfə́ːr]
≒ accede, submit
v.i. ＜～に＞従う＜to ～＞
n. deference

667 □ flawless
[flɔ́ːləs]
≒ perfect, uncorrupted, impeccable
adj. 完璧な、欠点のない

Chapter 1

例文

668, 669 Some commentators have remarked that the more extreme measures of Greenpeace would **deflect** public attention from the main goal of saving the earth and therefore **detract** from the effectiveness of their efforts.

670 André Agassi, one of the oldest players to win Wimbledon, is still successful partly due to his clever, **deft** maneuvers on the baseline.

671 Studies discovered that a common drawback of some popular cold medicines is that they may cause or contribute to **dehydration**.

672 During the Christmas season in the United States the postal service is **deluged** with holiday cards and packages.

668	☐ **deflect** [dɪflékt]	≒ turn aside, divert, sidetrack *v.t.*（注意・非難など）を＜〜から＞そらす ＜from 〜＞，の方向を変えさせる *n.* deflection
669	☐ **detract** [dɪtrǽkt]	≒ diminish, reduce *v.i.* ＜価値などを＞損なう＜from 〜＞ *n.* detraction
670	☐ **deft** [deft]	≒ skillful, dexterous, graceful *adj.* 器用な，巧みな，手際のよい
671	☐ **dehydration** [dìːhaɪdréɪʃən]	≒ deficiency of water or bodily fluids *n.* 脱水症状，脱水 *v.t.* dehydrate
672	☐ **deluge** [déljuːdʒ]	≒ engulf, overrun, inundate, flood, drown, swamp *v.t.* ＜通例受身形＞を氾濫させる，に殺到する ＜with, by 〜＞；*n.* 大洪水，殺到

予想例文

例文

673 The young woman is suffering from the **delusion** that she was abducted by aliens.

674, 675 Congress again is asking for a special prosecutor to **delve** into the latest Washington scandal, but the White House is keeping everything **under wraps**.

676, 677 In less than an hour the **demolition** team was able to **topple over** a huge building that occupied a pretty large portion of the center of the city.

678 My brother admitted that when he was in the Army, he was once **demoted** for insubordination.

673 ☐ **delusion** [dɪlúːʒən]	≒ false idea or belief, hallucination, illusion, deceit, deception *n.* 妄想, 思い違い, だます [だまされる] こと *v.t.* delude
674 ☐ **delve** [delv]	≒ search, investigate *v.i.* ＜〜を＞徹底的に調査する, 探求する＜into 〜＞
675 ☐ **under wraps**	≒ in secrecy 秘密にされて, 隠されて
676 ☐ **demolition** [dèməlíʃən]	≒ tearing down, pulling down *n.* 取り壊し, 破壊 *v.t.* demolish
677 ☐ **topple over 〜**	≒ cause to fall down, knock down 〜を倒す
678 ☐ **demote** [diːmóut]	≒ reduce in rank, bust, relegate, kick downstairs *v.t.* を降格する, の級を落とす *n.* demotion ⇔ promote

Chapter 1

例文

679 When old Professor Nishiyama once again misplaced his key, we had to break into his **den** by picking the lock to the door.

680 Japan agreed to **deploy** oil tankers to help fight the war against the Taliban in Afghanistan but ruled out direct military involvement.

681, 682 Although he had to cover the expenses of 10% annual **depreciation** in the value of his equipment, it was **gratifying** to know that these expenditures would reduce his level of taxation.

683 A respected British scientist recently committed suicide after becoming despondent over allegedly **despicable** treatment from the government.

684 The most advanced forensic laboratories can **detect** even tiny traces of human blood.

679	☐ **den** [den]	≒ (small) private room for pursuing *one's* hobby or work *n.* 研究室, 仕事部屋, 隠れ家
680	☐ **deploy** [dɪplɔ́ɪ]	≒ place in position, station *v.t.* (軍隊, 兵器など) を配置する, を展開させる *n.* deployment
681	☐ **depreciation** [dɪpriːʃiéɪʃən]	≒ decrease in value *n.* 減価償却費, 価値の低下 *v.t., v.i.* depreciate
682	☐ **gratifying** [grǽtɪfàɪɪŋ]	≒ satisfying, pleasurable *adj.* 満足できる, 心地よい *n.* gratification
683	☐ **despicable** [dɪspíkəbl]	≒ shameful, contemptible, reprehensible *adj.* 卑劣な, 卑しむべき *v.t.* despise
684	☐ **detect** [dɪtékt]	≒ discover, uncover, find *v.t.* を見つける, を検出する *n.* detection

予想例文

例文

685 Police say they have in <u>detention</u> a suspect in a recent capital murder case.

686 One of the greatest fears of those now dealing with the threats posed by terrorists is the ominous possibility that they will acquire the ability to <u>detonate</u> a nuclear device in a major urban center.

687 Even as a child she was <u>dexterous</u> and athletic.

688 Everyone in the room froze when the speaker glared at them with a <u>diabolic</u> look in his eyes.

689 The philosopher Suzanne Langer has challenged the traditional <u>dichotomy</u> between reason and emotion.

685 ☐ **detention** [dɪténʃən]	≒ being held in custody, confinement, imprisonment, detainment, internment, retention *n.* 拘留、引き留め、（放課後の）居残り
686 ☐ **detonate** [détənèɪt]	≒ explode (with a loud noise) *v.t.* （爆弾など）を爆発させる *n.* detonation
687 ☐ **dexterous** [dékstərəs]	≒ skillful, deft, coordinated *adj.* 機敏な、頭の切れる、器用な *n.* dexterity
688 ☐ **diabolic** [dàɪəbá(:)lɪk]	≒ devilish, satanic, evil *adj.* 悪魔のような、残忍な *n.* diabolism
689 ☐ **dichotomy** [daɪká(:)ṭəmi]	≒ opposing concepts, contrast *n.* 二分法、二分すること

Chapter 1

例文

690 The student was bright but so **diffident** and docile that she could not make the best use of her abilities.

691 The department chairperson told me that she spent much of her time **diffusing** the interpersonal conflicts of faculty members.

692, 693 One of the biggest scientific hoaxes of all time was when the complete skeleton of a human "missing link" that had been **dug up** in Turkey turned out to be **fraudulent**.

694, 695 A vaccine is a **diluted** sample of an infectious bacteria that is **injected** into a person's bloodstream to bring about the production of antibodies.

690	☐ **diffident** [dífɪdənt]	≒ shy, bashful, withdrawn *adj.* 内気な，自信のない *n.* diffidence
691	☐ **diffuse** [dɪfjúːz]	≒ mitigate, weaken, spread out *v.t.* を和らげる，を拡散させる，を広める *n.* diffusion
692	☐ **dig up ～**	≒ unearth, find, disinter ～を掘り起こす，～を発見する
693	☐ **fraudulent** [frɔ́ːdʒələnt]	≒ counterfeit, falsified, forged *adj.* 詐欺的な，人をだます，ねつ造された *n.* fraud
694	☐ **dilute** [daɪlúːt]	≒ water down, thin out *v.t.* を希釈する，を薄める *n.* dilution
695	☐ **inject** [ɪndʒékt]	≒ shoot in, introduce *v.t.* を＜～に＞注入する，を注射する＜into ～＞ *n.* injection

例文

696 He appeared to be innocent and <u>disarming</u>, but he was actually very adroit at manipulating the political process for personal gain.

697 A well-known mutual-fund company recently <u>discharged</u> several of its top executives for shady practices.

698, 699 I discovered a large <u>discrepancy</u> in my bank account this week: my account had been <u>debited</u> three hundred dollars for a mistaken credit card charge.

700 As I was passing through Japanese customs, the immigration official looked at me with <u>disdain</u>.

696 ☐ **disarming** [dɪsá:rmɪŋ]	≒ harmless, allaying hostility *adj.* 敵意［疑惑］を解くような、心を和ませる（ような）
697 ☐ **discharge** [dɪstʃá:rdʒ]	≒ fire, terminate, let go, give a pink slip to *v.t.* を解雇する、を放出する
698 ☐ **discrepancy** [dɪskrépənsi]	≒ disparity, inequality, gap, difference *n.* 矛盾、食い違い
699 ☐ **debit** [débət]	≒ enter on the debit side of an account, charge, bill *v.t.* を借り方に記入する、（金額）を引き落とす； *n.* 借方（記入）、引き落とし ⇔ credit
700 ☐ **disdain** [dɪsdéɪn]	≒ contempt, disregard, condescension *n.* 軽蔑；*v.t.* を軽蔑する *adj.* disdainful

Chapter 1

例文

701 Some commentators believe that we are witnessing the gradual **disintegration** of the traditional world order, once dominated by independent nation states.

702 Cheap labor may be a great boon to a country's Gross National Product, but it ensures huge economic **disparity** between workers and management.

703, 704 Not only has Iran **disputed** charges that it is developing nuclear weapons, it promises to **debunk** all the evidence upon which these charges have been based.

705 In the Middle Ages, pioneer students of medicine **dissected** bodies of executed criminals, which they had to steal from graveyards due to the taboo against cutting open a human body.

701	☐ **disintegration** [dɪsìntəgréɪʃən]	≒ collapse, falling apart, decomposition *n.* 崩壊, 分解 *v.t.* disintegrate ⇔ integration
702	☐ **disparity** [dɪspǽrəti]	≒ discrepancy, unevenness, difference *n.* 不釣り合い, 相違 *adj.* disparate
703	☐ **dispute** [dɪspjúːt]	≒ challenge, argue against, impugn *v.t.* に反論する, に意義を唱える ; *n.* 論争, 紛争
704	☐ **debunk** [dìːbʌ́ŋk]	≒ expose as a sham of falsehood *v.t.* を暴露する, の正体を暴く
705	☐ **dissect** [dɪsékt]	≒ cut up to examine its parts *v.t.* を解剖する *n.* dissection

例文

706, 707 Scholars know that the **dissemination** of the first humans began in Africa, and then they **dispersed** toward the Asian and European continents.

708, 709 Moralists often claim that the **dissipated** lifestyles portrayed in popular films as heroic have **debased** the values of the younger generation.

710, 711 In the California recall election, women's groups tried to **dissuade** various factions from **endorsing** Arnold Schwarzenegger, due to recent allegations of sexual misconduct.

---

706 □ **dissemination** [dɪsèmɪnéɪʃən]	≒ propagation, dispersal, spread *n.* 広まり,普及 *v.t.* disseminate
707 □ **disperse** [dɪspə́ːrs]	≒ spread, dissipate *v.i.* 分散する,広まる; *v.t.* を普及させる,を分散させる
708 □ **dissipated** [dísɪpèɪtəd]	≒ self-indulgent, dissolute, depraved, profligate *adj.* ふしだらな,放蕩の *n.* dissipation *v.t.* dissipate
709 □ **debase** [dɪbéɪs]	≒ degrade, lower *v.t.* を堕落させる,の品質［価値］を落とす *n.* debasement
710 □ **dissuade** [dɪswéɪd]	≒ discourage *v.t.* （人）に＜…することを＞思いとどまらせる ＜from *doing*＞ *n.* dissuasion ⇔ persuade
711 □ **endorse** [ɪndɔ́ːrs]	≒ support, back up *v.t.* を支持する,（小切手など）に裏書きをする

Chapter 1

例文

712 Astigmatism refers to a **distortion** of visual perception caused by defects in the lens of the eyeball.

713 We found a poor old man lying drunk in a drainage **ditch**.

714 When I told her that I decided to order the Salisbury steak, she said "**Ditto** for me."

715 To his detriment as a scientist, he was too **dogmatic** in his beliefs to look at problems and solutions with an open mind.

716 When he lost his job a few years back, he had no choice but to go on the government **dole**.

717 Whenever he looks into a mirror, his aging face seems to him the face of **doom**.

予想例文

712	☐ **distortion** [dɪstɔ́:rʃən]	≒ blurring, skewing, misrepresentation, confusion *n.* ゆがみ, ねじれ, わい曲 *v.t.* distort　*adj.* distorted
713	☐ **ditch** [dɪtʃ]	≒ furrow, trench, drain *n.* 溝, 排水溝
714	☐ **ditto** [dítou]	≒ the same *n.* 同上, 写し ; *adv.* 同様に
715	☐ **dogmatic** [dɔ:gmǽtɪk]	≒ assertive, imperious *adj.* 独善的な, 独断的な *n.* dogma
716	☐ **dole** [doʊl]	≒ money paid by a government to the unemployed, social welfare, handout, charity, allowance *n.* 失業手当, 施し物
717	☐ **doom** [du:m]	≒ ultimate disaster, destruction *n.* 悲運, 破滅, 死

例文

718 Sigfried had always **doted** on his youngest son, but now he realized that he had made the big mistake of spoiling him as a child.

719 He put his savings into the stock market, but in less than a year most of it went **down the drain**.

720, 721 During this period of gradual economic **downtrend**, many investors are **divesting** themselves of their more volatile stocks and investing in bonds.

722 For days they had experienced a steady downfall of icy rain, and the house felt cold, **drafty**, and a little depressing.

723, 724 We had **drilled** for oil in the area for weeks without success, when suddenly black gold began to **gush** out of the ground in several spots at the same time.

718	☐ **dote** [doʊt]	≒ be excessively fond of, idolize *v.i.* <〜を>溺愛する<on, upon 〜>
719	☐ **down the drain**	≒ wasted, squandered, frittered away 無駄になって、だめになって
720	☐ **downtrend** [dáʊntrend]	≒ downward trend *n.* 下降、(景気などの) 下押し気配
721	☐ **divest** [daɪvést]	≒ dispossess, rid, free *v.t.* <〜を>放棄する、脱ぐ<*oneself* of 〜>
722	☐ **drafty** [dræfti]	≒ letting in currents of air *adj.* すきま風の入る *n.* draft (すきま風、下書き、為替手形)
723	☐ **drill** [drɪl]	≒ bore, make a hole with a drill, train *v.i.* 穴をあける、反復練習する
724	☐ **gush** [gʌʃ]	≒ spurt, spout *v.i.* (液体・言葉などが) どっと流れ出る

Chapter 1

例文

725, 726 When my classmates laughed at me for my shabby clothing, I predicted that one day they would have to **eat their words** when they themselves were **destitute**.

727, 728 This tiny stream **ebbing** at its banks began as a powerful mountain river but **diverges** at several places as it grows weaker and weaker on its way to the sea.

729 The Bush Administration's Secretary of State, Colin Powell, reached the highest **echelon** in the U.S. military.

730, 731 Last month we visited a new type of museum, which reflected the **eclectic** tastes of its curator and displayed **miscellaneous** artifacts from around the world.

予想例文

725	☐ **eat *one's* words**	≒ admit that *one* was wrong 前言を取り消す、過ちを認める
726	☐ **destitute** [déstɪtjùːt]	≒ poor, poverty-stricken, indigent, penurious *adj.* 困窮した、貧しい *n.* destitution
727	☐ **ebb** [eb]	≒ subside, slacken *v.i.* (力などが) 弱くなる、減る、潮が引く
728	☐ **diverge** [dəvə́ːrdʒ]	≒ fork, branch off, divide *v.i.* 分岐する、それる、離れる *adj.* divergent
729	☐ **echelon** [éʃəlà(ː)n]	≒ position, level, rank, degree, grade *n.* (組織などの) 地位、階層、段階
730	☐ **eclectic** [ɪkléktɪk]	≒ deriving ideas from various sources *adj.* 折衷的な、折衷主義の *n.* eclecticism
731	☐ **miscellaneous** [mìsəléɪniəs]	≒ varied, diverse, motley *adj.* 種々雑多な、多才な *n.* miscellany

例文

732 Despite his enormous achievements, he is still embarrassed by **effusive** praise.

733, 734 Investigators of a series of mysterious murders hoped that a new witness could **elucidate** the motive for the killings, but their questions only **drew a blank**.

735, 736 Abraham Lincoln vowed to **emancipate** the American slaves and to end the **suppression** of their personal liberty.

737 In the early part of the sixteenth century, Ferdinand Magellan **embarked** on a journey to circumnavigate the globe.

732	□ **effusive** [ɪfjúːsɪv]	≒ extravagant, gushing, excessive *adj.* 仰々しい，感情をあらわにした *v.t.* effuse *n.* effusion
733	□ **elucidate** [ɪlúːsɪdèɪt]	≒ explain *v.t.* を解明する，を明瞭にする *n.* elucidation
734	□ **draw a blank**	≒ elicit no response 空くじを引く，失敗する
735	□ **emancipate** [ɪmǽnsɪpèɪt]	≒ liberate, set free, deliver *v.t.* (束縛などから) を解放する，を自由にする *n.* emancipation
736	□ **suppression** [səpréʃən]	≒ repression, restraint *n.* 抑圧，鎮圧 *v.t.* suppress
737	□ **embark** [ɪmbáːrk]	≒ go aboard, start, enter *v.i.* <～に>搭乗する，<事業などに>乗り出す <on ～> *n.* embarkation

Chapter 1

例文

738 One of the main differences between English and Japanese is the position of **embedded** adjectival clauses and prepositional phrases.

739 The feminist movement has gradually succeeded in **empowering** many women in their struggle for equal rights.

740 I have always sought to **emulate**, rather than envy, Professor Nishiyama's air of detachment.

741 The new prime minister **enacted** a stringent fiscal policy to combat a long recession.

742 The great philosopher, Professor Suzanne Langer, was a meticulous scholar, whose writings **encompass** an astonishing range of academic disciplines and vast knowledge.

743 Although the hikers were **encumbered** by heavy packs and a terrible ice storm, they showed great tenacity in making their way out of the forest.

738	☐ **embed** [ɪmbéd]	≒ place (firmly), fix *v.t.* ＜通例受身形＞をはめ込む、（心などに）を深く留める
739	☐ **empower** [ɪmpáuər]	≒ energize, strengthen, bolster *v.t.* に権限を与える、に力を与える
740	☐ **emulate** [émjulèɪt]	≒ try to equal or excel *v.t.* と競う、を見習う、に匹敵する *adj.* emulation
741	☐ **enact** [ɪnǽkt]	≒ legislate, initiate, implement, act upon *v.t.* を制定する、を法律化する、を実行に移す *n.* enactment
742	☐ **encompass** [ɪnkʌ́mpəs]	≒ include, contain *v.t.* を包括する、を包み込む
743	☐ **encumber** [ɪnkʌ́mbər]	≒ hamper, impede, inconvenience *v.t.* を妨げる、を煩わす *n.* encumbrance

例文

744 Harvard University has annual **endowments** of many millions of dollars.

745 Not only were the children enthralled with the circus performance, the adults also seemed equally **engrossed** by the events.

746 Doctors studying a strange new disease could not explain the **enigma** of a dormant gene suddenly coming to life and triggering an attack on the patient's nervous system.

747, 748 When it became clear that people in the highest levels of government were **enmeshed** in the huge corporate trading scandals, the public suspected **foul play**.

749 Some people believe that **entities** from outer space have visited our planet.

744	**endowment** [ɪndáʊmənt]	≒ gift, contribution, donation, benefit, benefaction, charity, bestowal, legacy *n.* 寄付, 寄贈
745	**engross** [ɪŋgróʊs]	≒ absorb the attention of *v.t.* ＜通例受身形＞を没頭させる *adj.* engrossing
746	**enigma** [ɪnígmə]	≒ puzzle, mystery *n.* 謎 *adj.* enigmatic
747	**enmesh** [ɪnméʃ]	≒ entangle (in a net) *v.t.* ＜通例受身形＞＜困難などに＞を巻き込む＜in ～＞, を網にからませる
748	**foul play**	≒ unfair play 不正行為, 反則プレー
749	**entity** [éntəti]	≒ being, thing, individual *n.* 実在のもの, 人物, 存在

Chapter 1

例文

750 When a famous actress was arrested for forgery, her lawyers argued that she was merely a victim of police **entrapment**.

751 When Mr. Matsumoto was preparing his students for a speech contest, he implored them to **enunciate** their words slowly and clearly.

752 It is often very effective in concluding an essay to quote a succinct **epigram** from a great author to highlight one's main point.

753, 754 We finally had to hire experts to **eradicate** the moles that **burrowed** holes all over our yard and were destroying the garden.

755, 756 My grades had been **erratic** throughout high school but in my senior year I finally decided to **hit the books**.

757 Old Professor Nishiyama's forgetfulness is exceeded only by his **erudition**.

750	☐ **entrapment** [ɪntrǽpmənt]	≒ inducement to commit a crime *n.* わな
751	☐ **enunciate** [ɪnʌ́nsièɪt]	≒ pronounce, state *v.t.* (言葉など)をはっきり発音する, を宣言する
752	☐ **epigram** [épɪgræ̀m]	≒ adage, aphorism, old saying *n.* 警句, エピグラム, 風刺詩
753	☐ **eradicate** [ɪrǽdɪkèɪt]	≒ root out, get rid of, destroy completely *v.t.* を根絶する, を一掃する
754	☐ **burrow** [bə́:roʊ]	≒ dig, tunnel, bore *v.t.* (動物が穴)を掘る; *v.i.* もぐりこむ; *n.* 穴, 隠れ場
755	☐ **erratic** [ɪrǽṭɪk]	≒ inconsistent, irregular *adj.* 一貫性のない, とっぴな
756	☐ **hit the books**	≒ study hard, bone up, burn the midnight oil 猛勉強する
757	☐ **erudition** [èrjudíʃən]	≒ great learning, scholarship, knowledge *n.* 学識, 博識 *adj.* erudite

例文

758 My father told me that his most difficult hour was having to deliver a **eulogy** for his closest friend.

759 Rather than using the clothes dryer I often hang my laundry outside so it can dry from **evaporation**.

760, 761 When a humble peasant was **exalted** to the highest post in the land by a grateful nation, many citizens participated in the **buoyant** celebration that took place across the land.

762 Although our **exasperation** over our failure to score increased during the match, we kept our composure and finally got a goal.

---

758 ☐ **eulogy** [júːlədʒi]
≒ funeral tribute, commendation, high praise
n. 追悼演説, 賛辞, ほめ言葉

759 ☐ **evaporation** [ɪvæpəréɪʃən]
≒ the process of drying out
n. 蒸発, 発散
v.i. evaporate

760 ☐ **exalt** [ɪgzɔ́ːlt]
≒ raise in rank or power, promote, extol
v.t. を昇進させる, を称揚する
n. exaltation

761 ☐ **buoyant** [bɔ́ɪənt]
≒ lively, cheerful, jaunty, bouncy, floating
adj. 浮かれた, 楽しい, 浮力のある
n. buoy（浮標）, buoyancy（浮力, 回復力）

762 ☐ **exasperation** [ɪgzæspəréɪʃən]
≒ irritation, vexation, pique
n. いらだち, 憤激
v.t. exasperate

例文

763 In order to apply political pressure to certain countries, the United States can threaten to revoke the status of "favored nation," which **exempts** that nation from certain tariffs.

764 The United Nations tried to **exert** pressure on what they called a "rogue nation" by issuing it an ultimatum to cease hostilities against its neighbors.

765 Disgusted with so many complacent students having little interest in a world outside themselves, Mr. Suzuki **exhorted** them to think more deeply about their future.

766 Ayatollah Khomeini had been a political dissident against the regime of the Palahvi Shah and returned from **exile** to lead the Islamic revolution in 1979.

763 ☐ **exempt** [ɪgzémpt]	≒ free, absolve, excuse *v.t.* に＜課税・義務などを＞免除する＜from ～＞； *adj.* ＜～を＞免除された＜from ～＞； *n.* 免除されている人 *n.* exemption
764 ☐ **exert** [ɪgzə́ːrt]	≒ bring to bear, exercise *v.t.* （圧力など）を＜～に＞加える＜on ～＞，を行使する *n.* exertion
765 ☐ **exhort** [ɪgzɔ́ːrt]	≒ advise earnestly *v.t.* に熱心に勧める，に勧告する *n.* exhortation
766 ☐ **exile** [éksaɪl]	≒ banishment, expulsion *n.* 追放，亡命； *v.t.* ＜通例受身形＞を国外追放にする

例文

767, 768 Scholars do not know when early humans' first great **exodus** out of Africa began, but they do know that it was the **impetus** for the differentiation of human genes and the evolution of modern man.

769 In a pattern that has been repeated throughout history, despots have selected certain minority groups as scapegoats, who then become victims of liquidation, or **expulsion** from their homelands.

770 During the dark period of American history known as "McCarthyism," ordinary citizens were coerced into admitting that they were communists, money was **extorted** from possible suspects, and many lives were ruined.

767	☐ **exodus** [éksədəs]	≒ departure, flight *n.* （大勢の）脱出，出国 the Exodus（イスラエル人のエジプトからの脱出）
768	☐ **impetus** [ímpətəs]	≒ incentive, motivation, goad *n.* はずみ，刺激，推進力
769	☐ **expulsion** [ɪkspʌ́lʃən]	≒ banishment, exile *n.* 追放，排除，駆逐
770	☐ **extort** [ɪkstɔ́ːrt]	≒ wrest (away), obtain by force *v.t.* （金銭など）を＜～から＞強奪する＜from ～＞ *n.* extortion

Chapter 1

例文

771, 772 The Nobel Committee was **exuberant** in their praise for the two men, whom they **lauded** for their creation of magnetic resonance imaging (MRI), which allowed doctors to observe the inside of the body without using harmful X-rays or intrusive surgery.

773 Doctors told the man that his ulcer was caused by gastric acids being **exuded** by the stomach.

774 The boxer **exulted** after being awarded a unanimous vote for victory over his opponent in a match for an Olympic gold medal.

775, 776 President Clinton's combination of social liberalism and fiscal conservatism allowed him to draw on diverse **factions** of the electorate, which **defied** some of the traditional alliances of Democrats but won the election.

771	☐ **exuberant** [ɪgzjúːbərənt]	≒ effusive, lively high-spirited, lavish *adj.* 熱狂的な、生気あふれる、豊かな、華麗な *n.* exuberance
772	☐ **laud** [lɔːd]	≒ praise, extol, applaud *v.t.* をほめたたえる；*n.* 賞賛 *adj.* laudable
773	☐ **exude** [ɪgzjúːd]	≒ cause to escape gradually, ooze, emit *v.t.* をにじみ出させる
774	☐ **exult** [ɪgzʌ́lt]	≒ rejoice, triumph *v.i.* 大喜びする、勝ち誇る
775	☐ **faction** [fǽkʃən]	≒ group, camp, clique *n.* 派閥、党派
776	☐ **defy** [dɪfáɪ]	≒ flout, go against, resist *v.t.* を無視する、に（公然と）反抗する *n.* defiance

例文

777 Even a man with such impeccable judgment as Professor Nishiyama is occasionally and unavoidably **fallible**.

778 Over time, Timothy's stories became more and more **far-fetched**, and much of what he told us turned out to be completely bogus.

779 He had always had a somewhat servile nature, but it was humiliating to see him **fawning** so blatantly on the boss.

780 Although experts agreed that the new medical procedure was theoretically **feasible**, many doubted the efficacy of its use.

781 The poet was a nature-lover, able to make himself almost selfless in the woods — a life of **felicity** and divinity.

782 It has proven much more difficult than originally thought to **ferret out** Osama Bin Laden from his hiding places.

777 ☐ **fallible** [fǽləbl]	≒ liable to be erroneous *adj.* 間違いを犯すことのある，誤りやすい *n.* fallibility
778 ☐ **far-fetched** [fàːrfétʃt]	≒ unconvincing, unnatural *adj.* こじつけの，不自然な
779 ☐ **fawn** [fɔːn]	≒ behave servilely, court favor, cringe *v.i.* ＜人に＞へつらう，（犬が）じゃれる＜on, over ～＞
780 ☐ **feasible** [fíːzəbl]	≒ workable, practicable, viable *adj.* 実行可能な，可能性のある *n.* feasibility
781 ☐ **felicity** [fəlísəti]	≒ great happiness *n.* 至福，非常な幸福 *adj.* felicitous
782 ☐ **ferret out ～**	≒ force out of hiding, flush, extract ～を捜し出す

Chapter 1

例文

783, 784 The Russian ambassador said that he **fervently** hoped that the other nations on the U.N. Security Council would be **amenable** to his country's proposal.

785 She was an inexperienced young teacher but no one could doubt her **fervor**.

786 The principal of the school chastised several boys for attempting to **filch** the school mascot.

787 I had spent so many hours in the chemistry lab **filtering out** the impurities of my experimental solution, then I spilled it all over my clothes!

788 It was bad enough to hear that he had **fixed** the poker game by bribing a crooked dealer, but it was simply incredible that he was loudly boasting about it to his friends.

783	☐ **fervently** [fə́:rvəntli]	≒ eagerly, ardently, zealously *adv.* 熱心に, 熱烈に *n.* fervency
784	☐ **amenable** [əmí:nəbl]	≒ ready to comply, obedient, responsible, accountable *adj.* <〜に>快く従う, 従順な<to 〜>
785	☐ **fervor** [fə́:rvər]	≒ passion, devotion, commitment *n.* 熱意, 熱心, 熱烈 *adj.* fervid
786	☐ **filch** [fɪltʃ]	≒ pilfer, steal *v.t.* （ささいなもの）を盗む, をくすねる
787	☐ **filter out 〜**	≒ remove by means of a filter 〜をろ過して取り除く
788	☐ **fix** [fɪks]	≒ influence a result to *one's* advantage by trickery *v.t.* の八百長をはかる, の結果を操作する

例文

789 Even as a young child, jazz artist Charles Mingus showed a remarkable <u>flare</u> for music.

790 They decided to hold the party under tents but they proved to be too <u>flimsy</u> to withstand the strong winds.

791 British poet Mina Loy is as well known for <u>flouting</u> traditional values as she is for her poetry.

792, 793 As stock prices have <u>fluctuated</u> due to economic uncertainty, many retired people depending on <u>dividends</u> and interest payments from their investments are experiencing hard times.

794 The slightest attention from a male <u>flustered</u> the young lady so much that she could barely speak.

789	☐ **flare** [fleər]	≒ talent, knack, gift *n.* 才能, 傾向, 激発
790	☐ **flimsy** [flímzi]	≒ fragile, weak, wobbly, unsubstantial *adj.* もろい, 壊れやすい, 薄弱な, 説得力のない
791	☐ **flout** [flaʊt]	≒ defy, disregard, spurn, thumb *one's* nose at *v.t.* を軽視する, をばかにする
792	☐ **fluctuate** [flʌ́ktʃuèɪt]	≒ be unstable, undulate, vacillate *v.i.* （不規則に）変動する, 上下する *n.* fluctuation
793	☐ **dividend** [dívɪdènd]	≒ sum of money paid to shareholders *n.* （株式・保険などの）配当（金）, 分け前
794	☐ **fluster** [flʌ́stər]	≒ embarrass, confuse, confound, befuddle, discombobulate *v.t.* を当惑させる, を混乱させる

Chapter 1

例文

795 The grand homestead of what was once a Southern plantation outside New Orleans was closed to the public so that the **foyer** and parlor could be refurbished.

796 In a serious car accident, the driver of the vehicle suffered a compound **fracture** of the right leg, but a passenger in the back seat amazingly escaped without a scratch.

797 We were worried that our friend had been worn to a **frazzle** by the relentless pressure she'd been under.

798 We kept telling Mom that there was no reason for her to **fret** over such trivial matters, but she just couldn't help it.

799 He not only earns a lucrative salary but gets excellent **fringe** benefits.

800 The adage "Hell knows no **fury** like a woman scorned" is viewed as sexist by many modern women.

予想例文

795	☐ **foyer** [fɔ́iər]	≒ entrance hall *n.* 入口の間，ロビー，ホワイエ
796	☐ **fracture** [fræktʃər]	≒ breaking of a bone *n.* 骨折，割れ目
797	☐ **frazzle** [fræzl]	≒ exhausted state *n.* くたくたの状態，擦り減った状態
798	☐ **fret** [fret]	≒ be upset, be irritated *v.i.* <～のことで>いらいらする，くよくよ思い悩む<about, over, at ～>
799	☐ **fringe** [frindʒ]	≒ additional, extra *adj.* 付加の，二次的な
800	☐ **fury** [fjúəri]	≒ rage, wrath, fierceness *n.* 憤激，憤怒の状態，猛威 *adj.* furious

例文

801　In physics, "**fusion**" is the union of two atomic nuclei, producing enormous energy.

802　My mother always made a big **fuss** when her grandchildren would come to visit.

803　He was delightfully old fashioned, both **gallant** and magnanimous, but not too stuffy to pull a few pranks now and then.

804　When the two most **garrulous** members of our office were absent from work, it seemed as silent as a tomb.

805　Nothing could be more disparate from traditional Japanese taste than pachinko parlors, full of ostentation with their **gaudy** colors and raucous noise.

801	☐ **fusion** [fjúːʒən]	≒ union, combining, joining *n.* 融合、融解、連合 ⇔ fission
802	☐ **fuss** [fʌs]	≒ excitement, commotion, ado *n.* 無用な騒ぎ、空騒ぎ ; *v.i.* つまらないことで騒ぎ立てる *adj.* fussy
803	☐ **gallant** [gǽlənt]	≒ markedly attentive to women, chivalrous, dauntless, courageous, bold, valiant *adj.* 女性にいんぎんな、勇敢な
804	☐ **garrulous** [gǽrələs]	≒ talkative, loquacious, blabber-mouthed, motor-mouthed *adj.* おしゃべりな、多弁な
805	☐ **gaudy** [gɔ́ːdi]	≒ showy, flashy, tawdry, vulgar, ostentatious *adj.* (服装・装飾・色などが) けばけばしい、派手な

Chapter 1

例文

806, 807 By the time the United Nations relief team reached the famine-torn African country, millions of refugees could be seen, their faces **gaunt** and their bellies **distended** from hunger.

808 The interviewers regarded the candidate intensely, as if to **gauge** his character.

809, 810 Old Professor Nishiyama is known as a **genial** fellow who likes to take **catnaps** in his office from time to time, while students wait patiently outside his door.

811 He made a very small salary, but it was enough to **get by** due to his modest lifestyle.

812 Engineers tried to save the tower from collapsing by **girding** it with steel belts.

806	☐ **gaunt** [gɔːnt]	≒ scraggy, haggard, bony *adj.* げっそりやせた，やつれた，荒涼とした
807	☐ **distend** [dɪsténd]	≒ swell, dilate, expand *v.t.* （内部の圧力によって）を膨張させる *n.* distension
808	☐ **gauge** [geɪdʒ]	≒ judge, assess, evaluate, take stock of, size up *v.t.* を判断する，を評価する，を測定する
809	☐ **genial** [dʒíːnjəl]	≒ friendly, affable, kindly, hospitable, good-natured *adj.* 温厚な，親切な *n.* geniality
810	☐ **catnap** [kǽtnæp]	≒ doze, snooze, forty winks, siesta *n.* うたた寝
811	☐ **get by**	≒ survive, make ends meet, make it 何とかやっていく，通り抜ける
812	☐ **gird** [gəːrd]	≒ bind, encircle, strengthen *v.t.* ＜ベルトなどを＞に巻きつける＜with ～＞

例文

813 At our faculty meeting I was asked to reiterate the **gist** of the keynote speech at the international conference on language that I attended last month.

814 In sumo competition it is not considered good form for a wrestler to **gloat** after a victory.

815 Economic conditions were not at all conducive to new business ventures, so many new companies **went broke**.

816 When the girl was seriously injured in an automobile accident, all her dreams **went up in smoke**.

817 She admitted she would **gorge** at night and then regurgitate, an illness called "bulimia."

813	☐ **gist** [dʒɪst]	≒ essence, point *n.* 要点, 主旨
814	☐ **gloat** [gloʊt]	≒ exult with a malicious delight *v.i.* 得意そうに眺める, ほくそ笑む
815	☐ **go broke**	≒ go bankrupt, become financially ruined 破産する
816	☐ **go up in smoke**	≒ be lost, wasted, be drained off 煙のように消える, はかなく消える, むなしい結果に帰する
817	☐ **gorge** [gɔːrdʒ]	≒ overeat, gluttonize, gormandize, pig out *v.i.* たらふく食べる, むさぼり食う

Chapter 1

例文

818, 819 A political outsider, Jimmy Carter became President of the United States through a **grass roots** campaign, gaining popularity from deeply felt Christian values **cherished** by ordinary people.

820 Far from holding a **grudge** against his prodigal son, his father embraced him and had a feast prepared in his honor.

821 What we took to be a satanic apparition at the university festival was really Professor Nishiyama in the **guise** of a demon.

822 Aquatic mammals like dolphins and dugongs spend most of their lives underwater but must come up to the surface occasionally to **gulp** some air.

823 Simon's behavior was usually impeccable, but whenever he had **guzzled** a few beers, he would wobble down to the beach to bask in the sun.

818	☐ **grass roots**	≒ ordinary people 草の根，民衆
819	☐ **cherish** [tʃérɪʃ]	≒ treasure, hold dear, prize, value highly, cling to *v.t.* を大切にする，（希望，信念など）を心に抱く
820	☐ **grudge** [grʌdʒ]	≒ rancor, ill will, bitterness, resentment *n.* ＜人に対する＞恨み，遺恨＜against ～＞
821	☐ **guise** [gaɪz]	≒ pretence, look, appearance *n.* 見せかけ，ふり，外見，様子
822	☐ **gulp** [gʌlp]	≒ breathe hastily, swallow, gobble *v.t.* （息）を大きく吸い込む，（液体）をごくごく飲む，（食物）を急いで食べる，（涙など）をこらえる
823	☐ **guzzle** [gʌ́zl]	≒ drink or eat greedily *v.t.* をがぶがぶ飲む，をがつがつ食う

例文

824, 825 Although the parties **haggled** for weeks over minute details, in the end they were able to **hammer out** an agreement.

826 Instead of waiting to deposit the employees' bonuses in their bank accounts, the president decided to call a meeting and **hand out** their bonuses on the spot.

827 A few years ago our company had trouble drumming up any business at all, but lately we have been making money **hand over fist**.

828 The children appear so hapless, as if they have nothing to do all day but **hang out** on the street asking total strangers for pocket money.

829 When he moved to the next state, he had to hire a large trailer to **haul** his belongings.

824	☐ **haggle** [hǽgl]	≒ dicker, squabble *v.i.* <～について>言い争う<over, about ～>
825	☐ **hammer out ～**	≒ work out the details of ～を苦心して考え出す，知恵を絞って～を解決する
826	☐ **hand out ～**	≒ distribute, award ～を配る，～を与える
827	☐ **hand over fist**	≒ very quickly どんどん
828	☐ **hang out**	≒ loiter, hang around, dally ぶらぶらして時を過ごす
829	☐ **haul** [hɔːl]	≒ transport, carry, lug *v.t.* ～を運ぶ，～を運搬する，～を強く引っ張る

例文

830 An earthquake struck in the middle of rush-hour traffic, creating total **havoc** for the rescue team.

831 When Jack met Jill, not only did they hit it off but in no time they were **head over heels** in love.

832, 833 The president promised to prosecute all law-breakers equally and without exception, but when his own son was arrested for bribery, he began to **hedge**, arguing that there were **extenuating** circumstances in his son's case.

834 The film was number one at the box office because everyone agreed that it was **hilarious** and sure to become a classic someday.

835 Around five o'clock, Professor Nishiyama usually leaves the office and **hits the road** for home.

830	☐ **havoc** [hǽvək]	≒ chaos, disorder; damage, destruction n.（天災・戦争などによる）混乱，破壊，大損害
831	☐ **head over heels**	≒ utterly, completely 深くはまりこんで，激しく（恋して），まっさかさまに
832	☐ **hedge** [hedʒ]	≒ equivocate, evade commitment v.i. 言葉を濁す，確答を避ける；v.t. を囲い込む
833	☐ **extenuating** [ɪksténjuèɪtɪŋ]	≒ mitigating the seriousness of guilt adj.（罪などを）酌量できる n. extenuation
834	☐ **hilarious** [hɪléəriəs]	≒ very funny, uproarious, side-splitting adj. とても楽しい，陽気な
835	☐ **hit the road**	≒ depart, leave, set out 出発する，立ち去る

例文

836 If you're waiting for a gorgeous woman to marry you, please don't **hold your breath**.
837 The terrorists were trapped in a cave without food or water, so we didn't think they could **hold out** much longer.
838 **Holographic** imaging is a method of creating the illusion of a three-dimensional object.
839 She really acted as if she were **hot stuff**, draped with expensive jewelry and dangling a Gucci bag from her arm.
840 Amazingly, a few people have been discovered who seem to have a natural **immunity** to AIDS.

836	☐ hold *one's* breath	≒ wait in eager anticipation 期待して待つ
837	☐ hold out	≒ endure, survive, wait 持ちこたえる，耐える
838	☐ holographic [hòʊləgræfɪk]	≒ made by light beams *adj.* ホログラフィー（レーザー光線を利用する立体写真術）の *n.* holography
839	☐ hot stuff	≒ narcissist, egomaniac, conceited person, someone, usually female, who is sexually attractive to others 並外れた人，セクシーな人，流行のもの，特ダネ
840	☐ immunity [ɪmjúːnəti]	≒ protection against disease or legal action *n.* ＜〜に対する＞免疫（性）＜to, against 〜＞，（債務，兵役などの）免除 *adj.* immune

Chapter 1

例文

841 Though he claims he has lost his grip, old Professor Nishiyama is still **imparting** knowledge to his students.

842 The American legal system guarantees any person charged with a crime the right to be tried by an **impartial** jury of his or her peers.

843 Although the **impeachment** of President Clinton failed, it seriously impaired his effectiveness in his last few years in office.

844 Even the world's most powerful army cannot **impel** an entire nation to accept a hostile, occupying force.

845 The great illusionist moved **imperceptibly**, and before the audience knew it, he was standing suddenly at the other end of the stage.

846 Mr. Simpson urged his daughter not to be **impetuous** about her future but to choose a college only after careful deliberation.

予想例文

841	☐ **impart** [ɪmpáːrt]	≒ communicate, convey knowledge *v.t.* ＜～に＞を伝える，を知らせる＜to ～＞
842	☐ **impartial** [ɪmpáːrʃəl]	≒ unbiased, unprejudiced, fair *adj.* 偏見のない，公平な *n.* impartiality
843	☐ **impeachment** [ɪmpíːtʃmənt]	≒ charging the holder of a public office with misconduct, indictment *n.* 弾劾，告訴
844	☐ **impel** [ɪmpél]	≒ force, compel, coerce *v.t.* を強いて…させる＜to *do*＞
845	☐ **imperceptibly** [ìmpərséptɪbli]	≒ invisibly, without anyone knowing *adv.* 気づかれないうちに，それとわからないほどに
846	☐ **impetuous** [ɪmpétʃuəs]	≒ impulsive, rash, precipitate, unplanned *adj.* 性急な，衝動的な *n.* impetus

例文

847 The O. J. Simpson defense team argued that racial prejudice had **impinged** on its client's right to a fair trial.

848 Somewhat **implausibly**, the news media is touting a new miracle drug as a kind of panacea for everything that ails us.

849, 850 The government is investigating a secret society **implicated** in a **collusion** to steal nuclear technology.

851 He is an **impulsive** young man who often talks back impudently, even to the dean.

852 **In a nutshell**, Einstein's theory of relativity was a major breakthrough in modern physics because it called into question the universality of Newton's law of gravity.

847	☐ **impinge** [ɪmpíndʒ]	≒ interfere with, affect *v.i.* <～を>侵害する,犯す<on ～>
848	☐ **implausibly** [ɪmplɔ́:zəbli]	≒ unlikely, improbably *adv.* 信じがたく,もっともらしくなく
849	☐ **implicate** [ímplɪkèɪt]	≒ involve, embroil, entangle *v.t.* を<犯罪などに>関係させる,を連座させる <in ～> *n.* implication
850	☐ **collusion** [kəlú:ʒən]	≒ artifice, intrigue, collective fraud, plot *n.* 共謀,結託 *v.i.* collude <with ～>
851	☐ **impulsive** [ɪmpʌ́lsɪv]	≒ impetuous, unthinking, instinctive *adj.* 直情的な,衝動的な *n.* impulse
852	☐ **in a nutshell**	≒ in a few words, in a brief statement 簡潔に言えば,要するに

Chapter 1

例文

853, 854 When the Senator heard that his re-election was **in the bag**, he was **elated**.

855 Many educators regret that the modern media has begun to supplant works of classical literature with **inane** material that targets the lowest possible intellectual level.

856 A virus exhibits traits both of animate and **inanimate** entities.

857 Leaders gathered from around the world to attend the august occasion of President Kennedy's **inauguration**.

858 Burning **incense** became a very popular fad among hippies in the 1960s.

853	☐ **in the bag**	≒ certain 成功確実で
854	☐ **elated** [ɪléɪṭəd]	≒ exhilarated, jubilant, ecstatic *adj.* 大得意の、意気盛んな *n.* elation
855	☐ **inane** [ɪnéɪn]	≒ absurd, silly, nonsensical, fatuous, dumb *adj.* 意味のない、つまらぬ、空虚な *n.* inanity
856	☐ **inanimate** [ɪnǽnɪmət]	≒ of a non living thing, lifeless, inorganic, inert, related to anything in the mineral kingdom *adj.* 無生物の、死んだ、生気のない ⇔ animate
857	☐ **inauguration** [ɪnɔ̀ːgjəréɪʃən]	≒ investiture, installation *n.* 就任式、就任、起業 *v.t.* inaugurate
858	☐ **incense** [ínsens]	≒ a substance that when burned produces a fragrant aroma *n.* 香、香料

例文

859 We were kept awake all night by the <u>incessant</u> beating of the rain on the window pane.

860 Scientists refer to the <u>incipient</u> development of life on earth as starting with a kind of "primeval soup," in which life gradually evolved.

861 The invention of laser surgical technology permitted many operations to be done with minimal invasiveness, often without requiring a major <u>incision</u>.

862, 863 When his son was charged with trying to <u>incite</u> a crowd to riot, the mayor hired the best <u>attorney</u> in the country to defend him.

859	☐ **incessant** [ɪnsésənt]	≒ constant, continuous, without stopping *adj.* 絶え間ない，ひっきりなしの
860	☐ **incipient** [ɪnsípiənt]	≒ initial, first, nascent, original *adj.* 初期の，始まりの *n.* incipience
861	☐ **incision** [ɪnsíʒən]	≒ cut, slit *n.* 切開，切り込み，切れ目 *v.t.* incise
862	☐ **incite** [ɪnsáɪt]	≒ urge, prompt, instigate, egg on *v.t.* を＜…へ＞駆り立てる，をそそのかす＜to do＞ *n.* incitation
863	☐ **attorney** [ətə́ːrni]	≒ lawyer, person appointed to act for another *n.* 弁護士，代理人

例文

864 Even Albert Einstein was skeptical about the major breakthroughs of quantum mechanics since he said that the idea that atomic structure was characterized by mere chance was **inconceivable**.

865 What began as a small trading post grew into a large city, **incorporating** one small town after another.

866 Under American law a person cannot be forced to **incriminate** his or her spouse in a court of law.

867, 868 The instructions for the experiment were to **incubate** in separate Petri dishes two species of bacteria for six hours and then put them together for several hours until they intermingle and **coalesce**.

869 My uncle told me that he often made brief **incursions** into enemy territory when he fought in Germany in World War II.

864	□ **inconceivable** [ìnkənsíːvəbl]	≒ unthinkable, impossible, improbable *adj.* 想像もつかない、信じがたい、驚くべき
865	□ **incorporate** [ɪnkɔ́ːrpərèɪt]	≒ assimilate, join, add, amalgamate *v.t.* を組み入れる、を合同させる、を法人化する *n.* incorporation
866	□ **incriminate** [ɪnkrímɪnèɪt]	≒ accuse, blame, implicate, finger *v.t.* を告発する、を有罪にする、を密告する *n.* incrimination
867	□ **incubate** [íŋkjubèɪt]	≒ breed, grow, raise *v.t.* （細菌など）を培養する、（卵）を孵化させる *n.* incubation
868	□ **coalesce** [kòʊəlés]	≒ come together, form one whole *v.i.* 合体する、（政党などが）合併する *n.* coalescence
869	□ **incursion** [ɪnkɔ́ːrʒən]	≒ foray, infiltration, encroachment *n.* ＜〜への＞侵入、襲撃＜into 〜＞ *adj.* incursive

例文

870 Years of war and economic mismanagement have impoverished a number of African nations, leading to thousands of <u>indigent</u> and homeless refugees.

871 The famous movie star became loudly <u>indignant</u> when airline security officers informed her that she had to be frisked for a possible concealed weapon.

872 Totalitarian governments often use their nation's educational system to <u>indoctrinate</u> their country's children.

873 He was jocular and well-liked by his teachers, despite his <u>indolent</u> nature.

874, 875 We were sure we could <u>induce</u> Mr. Hopkins to accept the position of department chair, but when he declined we realized that we had presented our argument rather <u>ineptly</u>.

870	☐ **indigent** [índɪdʒənt]	≒ poor, poverty-stricken, down and out, hard up *adj.* 貧しい，貧窮した； *n.* 貧困者
871	☐ **indignant** [ɪndígnənt]	≒ irritated, peeved, resentful, irked *adj.* 憤慨した，憤った
872	☐ **indoctrinate** [ɪndá(:)ktrɪnèɪt]	≒ instruct, brainwash, program *v.t.* を洗脳する，（教義・信条などを人）に教え込む *n.* indoctrination
873	☐ **indolent** [índələnt]	≒ lazy, sluggish, slothful *adj.* 怠惰な，不精な *n.* indolence
874	☐ **induce** [ɪndjú:s]	≒ lead, prevail upon, bring about *v.t.* を説得して…する気にさせる，を引き起こす *n.* inducement
875	☐ **ineptly** [ɪnéptli]	≒ inappropriately, bunglingly, clumsily *adv.* 的外れに，不適当に，不器用に *n.* ineptitude

Chapter 1

例文

876, 877 He had been a confirmed bachelor until he became completely **infatuated** with Karen, whose gentle and **demure** nature took him by surprise.

878, 879 After the fall of Saddam Hussein's government in Iraq, the country experienced a degree of **infiltration** by Islamic **insurgents**.

880 Even though the enemy had **inflicted** massive losses on the Allied troops, there was no question that they would continue to persevere until they achieved victory.

881 The boy's behavior was often so audacious and reckless that he could **infuriate** his father just by walking into a room.

876	☐ **infatuated** [ɪnfǽtʃuèɪṭəd]	≒ fascinated, enamored, possessed, obsessed *adj.* <～に>夢中になった<with ～> *n.* infatuation
877	☐ **demure** [dɪmjúər]	≒ modest, shy, decorous *adj.* 控えめな、内気な
878	☐ **infiltration** [ìnfɪltréɪʃən]	≒ gradual entrance, permeation *n.* 浸透、潜入
879	☐ **insurgent** [ɪnsə́ːrdʒənt]	≒ insurrectionist, resister *n.* <通例複数形>反対分子、暴徒 *n.* insurgency
880	☐ **inflict** [ɪnflíkt]	≒ administer, deal, impose *v.t.* (打撃・傷など)を<～に>与える、(罰など)を<～に>課する<on ～> *n.* infliction
881	☐ **infuriate** [ɪnfjúərièɪt]	≒ cause to be furious, enrage *v.t.* を激怒させる *n.* infuriation

例文

882 Unlike his more sophisticated colleagues, Jim was too **ingenuous** to get along well in the world of corporate competition and ruthless ambition.
883 He admitted he smoked marijuana but claimed he did not **inhale** it.
884 Rousseau espoused the view that human beings are not **inherently** evil but that they are conditioned by society to be that way.
885 King Henry the Eighth displayed an **insatiable** appetite for food, drink and women.
886 Our teacher would sometimes look at us with an **inscrutable** expression on her face.
887 The famous writer was outraged to read that a critic had insinuated in a review that his works were fundamentally **insipid**.

882	☐ **ingenuous** [ɪndʒénjuəs]	≒ innocent, unsophisticated, credulous, artless *adj.* 純真な、正直な、うぶな
883	☐ **inhale** [ɪnhéɪl]	≒ breathe in, respire *v.t.* (空気など)を吸い込む、を肺まで吸い込む ⇔ exhale
884	☐ **inherently** [ɪnhíərəntli]	≒ innately, naturally, intrinsically *adv.* 本質的に、先天的に *n.* inherence
885	☐ **insatiable** [ɪnséɪʃəbl]	≒ limitless, unsatisfiable, unquenchable, unappeasable *adj.* 飽くことを知らない、貪欲な ⇔ satiable
886	☐ **inscrutable** [ɪnskrúːṭəbl]	≒ mysterious, enigmatic, unfathomable, unreadable, deadpan, poker face *adj.* 不可解な、なぞの、計り知れない
887	☐ **insipid** [ɪnsípɪd]	≒ dull, vapid, uninteresting, unexciting *adj.* 退屈な、無味乾燥な、風味のない

Chapter 1

例文

888, 889 A new head master was appointed to reform the girls' boarding school when it was learned that not only were the girls rude and **insolent**, but that violations of the 10 P.M. curfew were **rampant**.

890 After many years police managed to solve a case they had once declared **insoluble**.

891 The good old days of widespread affluence were gone when it was learned that many companies were virtually **insolvent**.

892 The nation's leader claimed that rebel groups were simply trying to **instigate** chaos in rural areas of the country.

893 His parents **instilled** in him a deep appreciation for the suffering of less fortunate people in the world.

888	☐ **insolent** [ínsələnt]	≒ rude, disrespectful, pert, saucy, cheeky *adj.* 横柄な, 無礼な *n.* insolence
889	☐ **rampant** [rǽmpənt]	≒ unchecked, uncontrolled, rife *adj.* 流行する, 激しい, 自由奔放な
890	☐ **insoluble** [ɪnsá(:)ljəbl]	≒ unsolvable, hopeless *adj.* (問題が) 解決できない, (物質が) 溶解しない ⇔ soluble
891	☐ **insolvent** [ɪnsá(:)lvənt]	≒ bankrupt, broke, on the rocks *adj.* 支払い不能の, 破産した; *n.* 支払不能者 *n.* insolvency
892	☐ **instigate** [ínstɪgèɪt]	≒ provoke, stir, rouse *v.t.* (反乱など) を扇動する, (人) をけしかけて行動させる
893	☐ **instill** [ɪnstíl]	≒ ingrain, inculcate, infuse *v.t.* (思想・感情など) を＜人の心に＞しみ込ませる＜in, into ～＞

予想例文

例文

894, 895 The professor complained that his students' theses were wholly **insubstantial**, not only lacking in profundity but essentially consisting of **extraneous** material that could have better served as a few footnotes.

896 Marcel Marceau, who is considered the greatest mime in the world, is able to express **intangible** human emotions without the use of words.

897 Defense systems aimed at **intercepting** enemy missiles are still far from perfect.

898 When my brother and sister would argue, no one else could **interject** a single word.

894	□ **insubstantial** [ìnsəbstǽnʃəl]	≒ insignificant, flimsy, unconvincing *adj.* 実体のない、内容のない ⇔ substantial
895	□ **extraneous** [ıkstréıniəs]	≒ unrelated, irrelevant, external *adj.* 筋違いの、無関係の、外来の、異質の
896	□ **intangible** [ıntǽndʒəbl]	≒ abstract, subtle, impalpable, untouchable *adj.* 実体のない、無形の、ぼんやりした ⇔ tangible
897	□ **intercept** [ìntərsépt]	≒ cut off, block, intervene *v.t.* を迎撃する、を途中で止める、（通信など）を傍受する *n.* interceptor（途中で阻止する物［人］）
898	□ **interject** [ìntərdʒékt]	≒ cut in with, break in with, interpose *v.t.* （言葉）を差しはさむ *n.* interjection

例文

899 The police **interrogated** the suspect for twelve hours before he confessed to the crime.

900 Critics remain divided over whether a powerful nation has the right to **intervene** in the subjugation of less powerful countries.

901 As a cardiac specialist, Doctor Grumfeld was often called upon to perform operations of great **intricacy**.

902 When I watched the fight between a mongoose and a snake, I wondered if the mongoose had been trained to attack the snake, or if it was just **intrinsically** hostile.

903 Wanting to get out of the house, we went for a walk in the cool evening air and felt somewhat **invigorated**.

904 Some believe that the safe at Fort Knox, which holds America's gold reserves, is impregnable, but experts know that no security system is **invincible**.

899	☐ **interrogate** [ɪntérəgèɪt]	≒ question, grill, query, cross-examine *v.t.* に尋問［質問］する、を取り調べる *n.* interrogation　*adj.* interrogative
900	☐ **intervene** [ìnṯərvíːn]	≒ interfere, meddle, butt in *v.i.* ＜～の＞間に入る、口を出す＜in ～＞、＜2つのものの間に＞介在する＜between ～＞ *n.* intervention
901	☐ **intricacy** [íntrɪkəsi]	≒ complexity, complicatedness *n.* 複雑さ、錯綜 *adj.* intricate
902	☐ **intrinsically** [ɪntrínsɪkəli]	≒ innately, naturally, essentially *adv.* 本質的に、本来、固有に
903	☐ **invigorate** [ɪnvígərèɪt]	≒ energize, refresh, pep up *v.t.* に元気を出させる、に活力を与える
904	☐ **invincible** [ɪnvínsəbl]	≒ unconquerable, unbeatable, impregnable *adj.* 征服できない、無敵の、頑強な

例文

905 Richard Nixon's presidential legacy was **irreparably** damaged by the Watergate scandal.

906, 907 Even ancient cultures learned to build **irrigation** systems in order to bring **arid** and semi-arid land under cultivation.

908 An electric fence around fields on a cattle ranch gives cows that touch it a painful **jolt**, preventing them from escaping.

909 My grandfather was always fair and **judicious** in dealing with family conflicts.

910 The human being with the longest officially documented lifespan **kicked the bucket** at the age of 122.

905	☐ **irreparably** [ɪrépərəbli]	≒ beyond repair or correction, irrevocably, irreversibly *adv.* 取り返しのつかないほどに，修復できないほどに
906	☐ **irrigation** [ìrɪgéɪʃən]	≒ watering *n.* 灌漑，注水 *v.t.* irrigate ⇔ drainage
907	☐ **arid** [ǽrɪd]	≒ dry, parched, barren *adj.* （気候・土地が）乾燥した，不毛の
908	☐ **jolt** [dʒoʊlt]	≒ shock, impact, force *n.* 衝撃，ショック，驚き；*v.t.* を揺する，に衝撃を与える
909	☐ **judicious** [dʒudíʃəs]	≒ thoughtful, wise, prudent *adj.* 思慮分別のある，賢明な，注意深い
910	☐ **kick the bucket**	≒ die, pass away, expire, decease, croak 死ぬ，往生する，くたばる

Chapter 1

例文

911 Countries now developing nuclear weapons justify them as deterrents, just as the established nuclear powers **lambasting** them used to claim in their own defense during the Cold War.

912 The keynote speaker was a disaster: not only was his delivery **languid** and monotonous, his content seemed to be a desultory, disconnected monologue.

913 Surrounded by verdant vegetation and a variety of wild flowers in bloom, the lake's silvery waters **lapped** against its shores under a gentle breeze.

914 No one doubts the governor's brilliance, but his performance has frankly been erratic with occasional **lapses** in sound judgment.

915 Some scientists today believe that no one can truly fathom the full extent of the **latent** powers of the human mind.

916 As the daughter of a wealthy businessman, she lived **lavishly**, in a style that reflected her upbringing.

911	☐ **lambaste** [læmbéɪst]	≒ censure, rebuke, upbraid *v.t.* を酷評する, を厳しくとがめる
912	☐ **languid** [lǽŋgwɪd]	≒ weak, lethargic, apathetic, enervated *adj.* 元気のない, 物憂げな
913	☐ **lap** [læp]	≒ move gently (back and) forth *v.i.* （波などが）＜〜に＞ひたひたと打ち寄せる ＜against, at, up, on 〜＞
914	☐ **lapse** [læps]	≒ slip, error, momentary mistake, blunder *n.* ちょっとした過失, 思わぬ失敗
915	☐ **latent** [léɪtənt]	≒ beneath the surface, hidden *adj.* 潜在的な, 隠れている, 潜伏性の
916	☐ **lavishly** [lǽvɪʃli]	≒ wantonly, immoderately, extravagantly *adv.* ぜいたくに

例文

917 When the famous coach was offered the head coaching position at a major college, he insisted on total **leeway** to coach as he saw fit.

918 After working for weeks on the oil rig, the men would go to town and raise hell just to **let off steam**, but they never really did any harm to anyone.

919 Sometimes I shout at **lethargic** students, not to humiliate them but only to fire them up about the pleasures of learning.

920 Stalin was the kind of leader who thought it best simply to **liquidate** all of his adversaries before they could threaten his authority.

921 Sartre explained that many thinkers in the modern world are suffering from *ennui*, which is a kind of profound **listlessness** or weariness with a world that lacks meaning.

917	☐ **leeway** [líːwèɪ]	≒ freedom, flexibility, room *n.* 行動の自由, 余地, 余裕
918	☐ **let off steam**	≒ release tension, vent うっぷんを晴らす
919	☐ **lethargic** [ləθáːrdʒɪk]	≒ sluggish, languid, listless, phlegmatic *adj.* 無気力な, 不活発な, 昏睡状態の *n.* lethargy
920	☐ **liquidate** [líkwɪdèɪt]	≒ kill, eliminate, destroy, turn to liquid form *v.t.* を粛清する, を一掃する, を精算する, を整理する *n.* liquidation
921	☐ **listlessness** [lístləsnəs]	≒ state of weakness and inactivity, ennui, tiredness, passivity *n.* 無関心, 気力のなさ, 物憂さ *n.* listlessness

例文

922 A few years ago my sister had to find homes for a **litter** of five kittens which she had found abandoned in her backyard.

923 Bill thought he got shafted when he was passed over for a promotion, and he was **livid** about it.

924 Some senior citizens called the police to complain about the burly guys who spent their time **loitering** on street corners and making rude comments to strangers.

925 He always had a knack for positive thinking; even when things seemed hopeless, he somehow felt they were **looking up**.

926 The landscape around Denver, Colorado, is simply stunning, especially in winter, with the snow-capped mountains always **looming** above you.

927 When the governor felt he was **losing ground** in his battle to save his job, he tried to derail the opposing candidate's campaign with slanderous accusations of personal misconduct.

922	☐ **litter** [lítər]	≒ a group of new-born animals *n.* （動物の）一緒に生まれた子, 一腹の子
923	☐ **livid** [lívɪd]	≒ angry, furious, enraged, grayish blue *adj.* ひどく怒った, 土色の, 青黒い
924	☐ **loiter** [lɔ́ɪtər]	≒ linger idly, hang around, dawdle *v.i.* ぶらぶら歩く, のらくら過ごす
925	☐ **look up**	≒ improve, search for 〜, call on ＜通例進行形＞（景気などが）良くなる, 好転する；（単語など）を調べる, （人）を訪ねる
926	☐ **loom** [lu:m]	≒ be seen dimly, appear indistinctly *v.i.* （大きな姿が）ぼんやりと現れる, （危険などが）不気味に迫る
927	☐ **lose ground**	≒ fall behind, be defeated, fail to succeed, lose popularity, deteriorate 人気を失う, 負ける, （議論などで）譲歩する

例文

928 Although the recall of the governor threw the political scene in turmoil, the message from the people that things had to change was **loud and clear**.

929 Although Professor Mills was often eloquent, his students felt that his lectures would be more **lucid** if he were less verbose.

930 Abraham Lincoln grew up in poverty doing menial farm work, but he **made** quite **a splash** in the history of the world as possibly America's greatest president.

931 The discovery of the cannibalistic serial murderer, Jeffrey Dahmer, revealed a man capable of **malevolent** acts and abominations.

928	☐ **loud and clear**	≒ forceful and unambiguous, powerful and unmistakable はっきりと，明確に
929	☐ **lucid** [lúːsɪd]	≒ easy to understand, clear, unambiguous, transparent *adj.* 分かりやすい，澄んだ *n.* lucidity
930	☐ **make a splash**	≒ become famous and influential, be triumphant, succeed 注目を集める，大評判をとる，世間をあっと言わせる
931	☐ **malevolent** [məlévələnt]	≒ evil, diabolical, vicious, pernicious, satanic *adj.* 悪意のある *n.* malevolence ⇔ benevolent

Chapter 1

例文

932 When the old man was found to have a **malignant** tumor, he did not know how he could pay for treatment with no health insurance and only meager savings.

933 I informed my students that I would assess each senior thesis for its clarity, profundity and originality, and **mark down** papers that only paraphrased information from other sources.

934, 935 Race officials **marked off** a certain distance from the track, where they set up a fence to keep **bystanders** at least ten yards from the cars as they sped by.

936 The President was not only a politician but also an erudite man who could quote an appropriate **maxim** for any occasion.

937 Former U.S. President Jimmy Carter has been very helpful in the **mediation** of a number of international disputes.

予想例文

932	☐ **malignant** [məlígnənt]	≒ cancerous, spreading bad feelings, evil *adj.* 悪性の、悪意［敵意］のある *n.* malignancy
933	☐ **mark down ~**	≒ downgrade, take points away, reduce the grade of; make at a lower price 〜の点数を下げる、〜を値下げする、〜を書き留める
934	☐ **mark off ~**	≒ designate, rope off （線・境界などで）＜…から＞〜を区別する、〜を区画する＜from ...＞
935	☐ **bystander** [báɪstændər]	≒ observer, witness, spectator, passer-by *n.* 見物人、傍観者
936	☐ **maxim** [mǽksɪm]	≒ aphorism, adage, saying, proverb *n.* 格言、金言
937	☐ **mediation** [mìːdiéɪʃən]	≒ arbitration, settlement, reconciliation *n.* 仲裁、調停

例文

938 Despite the romantic portrayal of the French foreign legion, it was really a troop of **mercenaries** willing to fight anyone, anywhere, if the price was right.

939 We thought from the beginning that his strategy to reform the economy was not merely foolhardy but would completely **miss the boat**.

940 South Korea is trying its best to **mitigate** the tension created by the North Korean nuclear program, which has aroused the antagonism of the United States, Japan and others.

941 A few years ago, Malaysian Prime Minister Mohammed Mahathir issued a temporary **moratorium** on the floating of the ringgit in the world currency market, pegging it to a fixed rate of 3.8 ringgit per dollar.

942 When the girl came back home in such an outfit her mother was **mortified**, shouting at her daughter that she was dressed inappropriately.

938	☐ **mercenary** [mə́:rsənèri]	≒ soldier who fights only for payment, not for principle or loyalty *n.* （外国軍隊の）傭兵，傭人
939	☐ **miss the boat**	≒ fail to take advantage of an opportunity しくじる，チャンスを逃す
940	☐ **mitigate** [mítəgèɪt]	≒ lessen, ease, alleviate, lighten *v.t.* を和らげる，を軽くする *n.* mitigation
941	☐ **moratorium** [mɔ̀(:)rətɔ́:riəm]	≒ temporary delay, temporary law or policy, postponement, clemency *n.* モラトリアム，（支払い）猶予期間
942	☐ **mortify** [mɔ́:rtʃəfàɪ]	≒ humiliate, embarrass, shame, abash *v.t.* ＜通例受身形＞に屈辱を与える，を悔しがらせる *n.* mortification

例文

943 The meeting ended up in a **muddle**, as if we had thrown the agenda out of the window.

944 He was a bit of a snob, thinking he was urbane; he felt nothing but disdain for the **mundane** world of the average man.

945 Susie's **mute** protest indicated that she would see no more of me.

946 An alkali solution can sometimes be used to **negate** the effects of an acid.

947 We needed to certify some documents from overseas but were told that a **notary** was absolutely requisite.

948 For a **novice** in the firm, he seemed brash and overconfident, but he was prepared to back up anything he said with his performance.

943	☐ **muddle** [mʌ́dl]	≒ confusion, disorder, chaos, mess, jumble, hodgepodge *n.* 混乱状態, 当惑
944	☐ **mundane** [mʌ̀ndéɪn]	≒ ordinary, commonplace, pedestrian, of this world *adj.* 平凡な, ありふれた, 世俗的な
945	☐ **mute** [mju:t]	≒ speechless, dumb, silent, unable to speak *adj.* 無言の, 言葉に表されない, 口がきけない
946	☐ **negate** [nɪɡéɪt]	≒ invalidate, veto, overrule, reject *v.t.* を無効にする, を否定する *adj.* negative
947	☐ **notary** [nóʊṭəri]	≒ person authorized to draw up or certify contracts, deeds, etc. *n.* 公証人
948	☐ **novice** [ná(:)vəs]	≒ inexperienced person, newcomer, beginner, amateur, fledgling, greenhorn *n.* 初心者, 未熟者

例文

949, 950 Tim's selfish play in the big game was a real **nuisance** but its effect on the final outcome was not **negligible**.

951 The young presidential hopeful was advised to avoid the **oblique** manner of talking for which his opponents were often criticized.

952 Even after the sun had gone down, the light of dusk lingered on the canyon wall for nearly an hour until darkness completely **obliterated** it.

953 It seems that not long after a computer comes on the market it is considered **obsolete**.

949	☐ **nuisance** [njúːsəns]	≒ annoyance, inconvenience, bother, bothersome person or thing, pain in the neck *n.* <通例単数形>迷惑なもの［人］，厄介もの，うるさいもの
950	☐ **negligible** [néglɪdʒəbl]	≒ slight, minimal, insignificant *adj.* 取るに足らない，つまらない *n.* negligence
951	☐ **oblique** [əblíːk]	≒ roundabout, indirect, evasive, circumlocutory, slanting *adj.* 遠回しの，斜めの *n.* obliquity
952	☐ **obliterate** [əblítərèɪt]	≒ erase, efface, blot out, expunge *v.t.* を消す，を抹消する *n.* obliteration
953	☐ **obsolete** [à(ː)bsəlíːt]	≒ out-of-date, antiquated, out-moded *adj.* 時代遅れの，旧式の，古くなった

Chapter 1

例文

954 At first we thought our neighbors were just being nice, but in time they became **obtrusive** to the point of seeming overbearing.

955, 956 Although I also felt as if I were **on my last legs**, I had to maintain the morale of the men in my **brigade**, so I urged them to keep fighting.

957 The new office girl is certainly **on the ball**, having already mastered the office procedures.

958 After I had been at my new company for only a month, my boss called me **on the carpet** to remind me exactly what duties my job entailed.

959, 960 The former dictator had been **on the run** since April of 2003, and he was able to **elude** capture for eight months.

954	☐ **obtrusive** [əbtrúːsɪv]	≒ forward, impertinent *adj.* でしゃばりの，おしつけがましい *v.t.* obtrude　*n.* obtrusion
955	☐ **on *one's* last legs**	≒ at the end of *one's* resources, near the end of *one's* usefulness 万策ほぼ尽きて，疲れきって，終わりが近づいて
956	☐ **brigade** [brɪɡéɪd]	≒ large body of troops *n.* （軍隊の）旅団
957	☐ **on the ball**	≒ sharp, astute, competent, alert, with it 有能で，機敏で
958	☐ **on the carpet**	≒ be reprimanded （叱責のため）呼びつけられて
959	☐ **on the run**	≒ fleeing, in flight, escaping 逃走中で
960	☐ **elude** [ɪlúːd]	≒ escape adroitly from, dodge *v.t.* を（巧みに）逃れる，を回避する *n.* elusion

予想例文

例文

961 How frustrating it is when you can't remember a word that is just **on the tip of your tongue**!

962 The windows of many luxury cars look **opaque** from the outside but transparent from the inside.

963 As a salesman of optical equipment, I felt that being seated next to an optometrist on my flight from New York to Los Angeles was **opportune**.

964 The wealthiest man in our town had **opted** not to go to college after high school but instead to start his own business.

965 Ever since Father Carlos was **ordained** twenty years ago as a Roman Catholic priest, he has held his vows of obedience, charity and chastity to be sacrosanct in the eyes of God.

961	☐ **on the tip of *one's* tongue**	≒ something *one* is about to say, just eluding recall 口から出かかっている，思い出せそうで思い出せない
962	☐ **opaque** [oupéɪk]	≒ impervious to light, non-transparent *adj.* 光を通さない，不透明な，不明瞭な
963	☐ **opportune** [à(:)pərtjúːn]	≒ felicitous, timely, offering a good chance, lucky, fortunate *adj.* 好都合の，適切な，タイミングのよい
964	☐ **opt** [ɑ(:)pt]	≒ choose, decide, prefer, select, go for *v.i.* <…する方を>選ぶ<to *do*>
965	☐ **ordain** [ɔːrdéɪn]	≒ initiate and confirm as a priest, order, determine *v.t.* （人）を聖職に任命する，（神，運命などが）を定める，（法などが）を規定する

例文

966 Doctors said that he survived his **ordeal** of ten days in the desert because he was so robust and possessed a tremendous will to live.

967 A metronome **oscillates** at a regular frequency, so it can be used to establish a musical rhythm.

968 When I was invited to a banquet honoring famous show business celebrities, I felt very much **out of place**.

969 Yoyo Ma was given a standing **ovation** for his sublime performance of a Bach cello concerto.

970 The young man's prestige as a serious actor may be questioned since his recent performances all seem to be more and more **over the top**.

971 All week long the skies have been nebulous with a threat of rain, and today when I woke up the sky was still **overcast**.

966	☐ **ordeal** [ɔːrdíːl]	≒ painful and difficult experience, travail, distress, trial, tribulation, hardship, misfortune *n.* 厳しい試練, 苦難
967	☐ **oscillate** [á(ː)sɪlèɪt]	≒ pendulate, seesaw, vibrate *v.i.* (振り子のように2点間を) 往復する, 振動する
968	☐ **out of place**	≒ not belonging, in the wrong position, unsuited, unfit, uncomfortable 場違いな, 不適当な
969	☐ **ovation** [ouvéɪʃən]	≒ loud clapping in praise of, applause, acclamation, big hand *n.* 大喝采, 熱烈な歓迎
970	☐ **over the top**	≒ overdone, melodramatic, histrionic, excessive 度を越した, 芝居がかった, 目標を超えた
971	☐ **overcast** [òuvərkǽst]	≒ cloudy, clouded over, murky, hazy *adj.* (空が) 曇った, 憂うつな

例文

972 We decided we really had to pinch pennies for a while after we learned we had **overdrawn** our account at the bank.

973 When Mr. Higgins was **overdue** on his house payments to the bank, he was cautioned not to be delinquent again.

974 I took my colleagues to a restaurant where the food is usually excellent, but for some reason on that night the food was barely **palatable**.

975 After Mrs. Stanton's close call with a heart attack, she looked **pallid** and weak for several months.

976 Whatever you do in life, happiness is **paramount**.

977 When the Senator was found guilty of bribery, the press vilified him in the newspapers, and he was treated like a **pariah** even by some of his so-called friends.

972	☐ **overdraw** [òuvərdrɔ́ː]	≒ place *one's* bank account in deficit, draw a sum of money in excess of the amount credited to *one's* account *v.t.* （預金）を借り越す
973	☐ **overdue** [òuvərdjúː]	≒ delinquent, in arrears, behind, late, past the deadline *adj.* 支払期限を過ぎた，予定の日時より遅れた
974	☐ **palatable** [pǽləṭəbl]	≒ tasty, pleasant to the taste, fit to be eaten *adj.* 口に合う，味のよい
975	☐ **pallid** [pǽlɪd]	≒ pale, white, ashen *adj.* （病気で）青白い，青ざめた
976	☐ **paramount** [pǽrəmàunt]	≒ most important, foremost, primary, dominant *adj.* 最高の，最も重要な，主要な
977	☐ **pariah** [pəráɪə]	≒ outcast, persona non grata *n.* （社会の）のけ者

Chapter 1

例文

978 A common feature among administrators is their tendency to **pass the buck** to someone lower in the company or university hierarchy.

979, 980 No matter how **pathetic** his condition really gets, on the surface he remains **jovial** and optimistic.

981 The vitality of the society is threatened by the great **paucity** of imaginative people with new ideas for solving old problems.

982 A technique that has recently become popular in writing classes is that of **peer** review.

983 Aldous Huxley wrote a famous book on the effects of hallucinogenic drugs on **perception**.

978 ☐ **pass the buck**	≒ shift responsibility <〜に>責任を押し付ける<to 〜>
979 ☐ **pathetic** [pəθétɪk]	≒ pitiable, wretched, doleful *adj.* 痛ましい、悲しい
980 ☐ **jovial** [dʒóuviəl]	≒ merry, jolly, lighthearted *adj.* 陽気な、楽しい *n.* joviality
981 ☐ **paucity** [pɔ́ːsəti]	≒ dearth, shortage, insufficiency *n.* <通例単数形>不足、少量、少数
982 ☐ **peer** [pɪər]	≒ colleague, social equal, associate, coequal, mate *n.* 仲間、同僚、同輩
983 ☐ **perception** [pərsépʃən]	≒ consciousness of sensory stimuli, awareness, cognizance *n.* 知覚、認識、洞察、概念 *adj.* perceptive

予想例文

例文

984 All around the king's splendid domicile **perennial** flowers and blossoming trees were planted.

985 If he continues to treat his studies in such a **perfunctory** way, he will probably flunk out before his sophomore year begins.

986, 987 The police arrested a man for acts so **pernicious** that even the most experienced officers were shocked at his confession and his **callow** attitude toward his own behavior.

988, 989 Inspector Davidson was certain he had caught the **perpetrators** of the bank heist, but the evidence at the trial completely **exculpated** them.

984	☐ **perennial** [pəréniəl]	≒ lasting several years, enduring, imperishable *adj.* （植物が）多年生の，四季を通じて続く，永続的な
985	☐ **perfunctory** [pərfʌ́ŋktəri]	≒ without effort or sincerity, cursory, unthinking, superficial, mechanical, automatic *adj.* おざなりの，いい加減な，やる気のない
986	☐ **pernicious** [pərníʃəs]	≒ destructive, ruinous, fatal, harmful *adj.* 破壊的な，非常に有害な
987	☐ **callow** [kǽlou]	≒ inexperienced, immature, green, unsophisticated *adj.* 未熟な，青二才の
988	☐ **perpetrator** [pə́:rpətrèitər]	≒ one who does something evil or commits a crime *n.* 犯人，加害者 *n.* perpetration
989	☐ **exculpate** [ékskʌlpèit]	≒ clear of a charge, free from blame *v.t.* を無罪とする，の潔白を立証する *n.* exculpation

例文

990 The philosophical and scientific legacies of the ancient Greeks **pervade** all of Western intellectual history.

991 The boy's mother corrected him for **pestering** his little sister.

992 The **petition** received over ten thousand signatures of people hoping to compel the mayor to shut down a dangerous nuclear reactor operating at the edge of the city.

993 Fossils result when organic life-forms are covered with clay, and are turned into stone, or **petrified**.

994 He resented being **pigeonholed** as a classical, jazz or popular composer; to him it was all just music.

995 My grandfather always locked his room when he went out so that no one could **pilfer** his things.

990	☐ **pervade** [pərvéɪd]	≒ spread everywhere through, penetrate, permeate *v.t.* に浸透する，に普及する *n.* pervasion
991	☐ **pester** [péstər]	≒ bother, trouble, agitate, hassle, bug *v.t.* を悩ます，を困らせる
992	☐ **petition** [pətíʃən]	≒ formal written request, entreaty, plea, supplication *n.* 嘆願書
993	☐ **petrify** [pétrɪfàɪ]	≒ fossilize, turn to stone, solidify *v.t.* を石化する，を硬直させる *n.* petrifaction
994	☐ **pigeonhole** [pídʒənhòul]	≒ assign to a preconceived category, classify, categorize, put in a narrow niche *v.t.* ＜～として＞を分類する＜as ～＞，(書類など)を整理棚に入れる；*n.* 分類棚
995	☐ **pilfer** [pílfər]	≒ commit petty thievery, steal, purloin, pinch *v.t.* を盗む，をくすねる

例文

996 He is such a clever politician that it is almost impossible to **pin him down** to a definite statement about his resources.

997 After struggling for years as a poverty-stricken actor, he finally reached the **pinnacle** of success when he won an Academy Award.

998 Early explorers gave the Pacific Ocean its name because, somewhat erroneously, they thought it was peaceful or **placid**.

999, 1000 As an elementary student I was asked daily to **pledge allegiance** to the United States flag and "to the republic for which it stands."

1001 We all hoped to attend the **plenary** session at the annual TESOL convention, but all the seats were filled before we could get there.

996	☐ **pin down ~**	≒ determine or establish clearly, nail down, clarify, confine 〜をはっきりさせる，〜を見分ける，〜にはっきり言わせる
997	☐ **pinnacle** [pínəkl]	≒ peak, acme, height, summit *n.* 頂点，絶頂
998	☐ **placid** [plǽsɪd]	≒ calm, tranquil, serene *adj.* 穏やかな，落ち着いた *n.* placidity
999	☐ **pledge** [pledʒ]	≒ swear, vow, promise *v.t.* を誓う；*n.* 誓約，担保
1000	☐ **allegiance** [əlíːdʒəns]	≒ loyalty, faithfulness, patriotism *n.* 忠節
1001	☐ **plenary** [plíːnəri]	≒ to be attended by all members, general, unconditional, complete *adj.* （有資格者）全員出席の，無条件の

Chapter 1

例文

1002 At first there seemed to be a shortage of oil on the market, but after several countries tried to capitalize on the situation quickly, in no time there was a **plethora**, and prices plummeted.

1003 Modern sculptors, hoping to find more **pliable** materials than marble or even bronze, have turned to plastics, clays and other surprising substances to create three-dimensional forms.

1004 Many of the Egyptian pyramids were excavated only centuries after they had already been **plundered** by thieves.

1005 If illegal profiteers continue to **poach** gorillas merely to be used as trophies, it is possible this magnificent species will become extinct.

1006 Everyone was impressed that so young a girl, merely 13, performed in her first ballet with such **poise** and elegance.

1002 ☐ plethora [pléθərə]	≒ oversupply, excess, abundance, surfeit *n.* 過多, 過剰 *adj.* plethoric
1003 ☐ pliable [pláɪəbl]	≒ flexible, plastic, malleable, pliant, adaptable *adj.* しなやかな, 従順な, 順応性に富む *n.* pliability
1004 ☐ plunder [plʌ́ndər]	≒ loot, pillage, ravage *v.t.* を荒らす, を略奪する
1005 ☐ poach [poutʃ]	≒ capture or kill illegally *v.t.* を密猟する, を侵害する
1006 ☐ poise [pɔɪz]	≒ composure, self-possession, aplomb, assurance *n.* (心の)落ち着き, 平静, 態度, 釣り合い; *v.t.* を安定させる

例文

1007 The president of the college was probably one of the most **pompous** men I had ever met, always acting as if he were among the most important men the world had ever seen.

1008 In his effort to support the existence of God with a logical argument, Thomas Aquinas **postulated** the principle of first causes.

1009 The poison of the cobra is so **potent** that it can kill a person in a matter of minutes.

1010 Through the heavy foliage we could see a wild cat, poised and ready to **pounce**.

1011 Those boys are very mischievous, so nothing makes them happier than a successful **prank**.

1007 ☐ **pompous** [pá(:)mpəs]	≒ arrogant, haughty, pretentious, putting on airs, vain, self-important, snooty *adj.* 尊大な，もったいぶった，気取った *n.* pomposity
1008 ☐ **postulate** [pá(:)stʃəlèɪt]	≒ create a principle or solution, assume, propose, articulate *v.t.* を前提とする，を仮定する *n.* postulation
1009 ☐ **potent** [póʊtənt]	≒ effective, powerful, strong, lethal *adj.* 効能のある，有力な，強大な ⇔ impotent
1010 ☐ **pounce** [paʊns]	≒ leap, jump, spring *v.i.* 急に飛びかかる，（機会などに）飛びつく
1011 ☐ **prank** [præŋk]	≒ practical joke, trick, caper, tomfoolery, shenanigan(s) *n.* いたずら，悪ふざけ

Chapter 1

例文

1012, 1013 On the slippery, **precarious** mountain road, our car suddenly started to **fishtail** and nearly careened out of control.

1014 Computer-guided laser surgery can perform operations with much greater **precision** than surgeons using traditional scalpels.

1015 There were a few drawbacks in Jennifer's signing of a long-term recording contract with RCA, one of them being the **preclusion** of future deals with other companies.

1016 Recent American policy has defended the concept of a **preemptive** strike as a justifiable principle of self-defense.

1017 His argument was based on a **premise** as faulty as 2 + 2 = 5.

予想例文

1012 ☐ precarious [prɪkéəriəs]	≒ insecure, uncertain, unsteady, unstable *adj.* 不確かな、あてにならない
1013 ☐ fishtail [fíʃtèɪl]	≒ move the rear side to side uncontrollably *v.i.* （自動車がスリップして）尻を振る
1014 ☐ precision [prɪsíʒən]	≒ great accuracy and clarity, correctness, exactitude, meticulousness *n.* 正確、精密 *adj.* precise
1015 ☐ preclusion [prɪklúːʒən]	≒ prevention, removal, exclusion, obstruction, blockage *n.* 除外、防止、阻止 *v.t.* preclude
1016 ☐ preemptive [priémptɪv]	≒ anticipatory for the purpose of preventing a future problem *adj.* 先制の、優先的な *v.t.* preempt
1017 ☐ premise [prémɪs]	≒ assumption, given, a first principle, a basis *n.* 前提、根拠、＜複数形で＞土地、屋敷； *v.t.* を前提とする＜that ...＞

例文

1018 When Janice agreed to marry Leonard, she made it clear that it would be her **prerogative** to decide where and how the ceremony would take place.

1019, 1020 Although he lived in large urban centers for most of his life, he never lost his image of the **pristine** nature of an **idyllic**, rural lifestyle.

1021 She has struggled with a lifelong **proclivity** to overeat.

1022 He worked hard all of his life to **procure** a comfortable home and a few luxuries for himself and his family.

1023 The teacher tried his best to **prod** every student to realize his or her potential.

1018 ☐	**prerogative** [prɪrá(:)gətɪv]	≒ right to make a certain decision, privilege, choice, liberty *n.* 特権, 特典, 大権
1019 ☐	**pristine** [prísti:n]	≒ unspoiled, pure *adj.* 素朴な, 初期の, 清純な
1020 ☐	**idyllic** [aɪdílɪk]	≒ pastoral, rustic, bucolic *adj.* 牧歌的な, のどかで美しい
1021 ☐	**proclivity** [proʊklívəti]	≒ tendency, inclination, preference, habit *n.* <…する, 〜の>性癖, 傾向<to *do*, for, toward 〜>
1022 ☐	**procure** [prəkjúər]	≒ get, obtain, secure *v.t.* (苦労して)を手に入れる, を確保する *n.* procurement
1023 ☐	**prod** [prɑ(:)d]	≒ push, motivate, instigate, pressure, move someone to action *v.t.* <…するように>を刺激する<to *do*>, を駆り立てる

Chapter 1

例文

1024 When Mr. Tweedy visited the doctor, he was told he had cancer but that the **prognosis** was good for his type of tumor.

1025 Isaac Asimov is regarded as one of the most **prolific** science fiction and popular science writers of all time.

1026, 1027 Though working as a mere copyright clerk, Albert Einstein rose to **prominence** in 1905 with his special theory of relativity, but after his publication of the general theory of relativity in 1916, his **eminence** throughout the world was unrivaled.

1028 When one of the steaks he was grilling fell into the burning charcoal, he used a **prong** to extract it.

1024 ☐ prognosis [prɑ(:)gnóʊsəs]	≒ prediction (for chances of recovering from illness), likely outcome, diagnosis *n.* （病気の）予後，予測 *v.t.* prognosticate（を予言する）
1025 ☐ prolific [prəlífɪk]	≒ productive, abundant, voluminous, fecund *adj.* 多作の，多産の，豊富な
1026 ☐ prominence [prɑ́(:)mɪnəns]	≒ fame, celebrity, reputation, eminence *n.* 目立つこと，著名 *adj.* prominent
1027 ☐ eminence [émɪnəns]	≒ distinction *n.* （地位・名声などが）高いこと，高位，高名 *adj.* eminent
1028 ☐ prong [prɔ(:)ŋ]	≒ a instrument with a sharp point on its end, used mostly in cooking *n.* 大きなフォーク，フォークのとがった先

例文

1029 The ancient Romans often resorted to oracles, who they believed could **prophesy** the future.

1030 Statements of truth or falsehood are often expressed in the form of **propositions**.

1031 My grandmother was often more concerned about the social **propriety** of an action than with purely logical "correctness."

1032 Mr. Edwards is a capable fellow, a hard working technocrat, but his writing is so **prosaic** it puts anyone with an ounce of imagination fast asleep.

1033 The former heavyweight boxing champion Mike Tyson has been arrested numerous times for assault, with or without **provocation**.

1029 ☐ prophesy [prá(:)fəsi]	≒ predict, foretell, divine, foresee, soothsay, prognosticate *v.t.* を予言する *n.* prophet, prophecy
1030 ☐ proposition [prà(:)pəzíʃən]	≒ assertion, principle, axiom *n.* 陳述, 主張, 提案, 定理, 命題 *v.t.* propose *n.* proposal
1031 ☐ propriety [prəpráıəti]	≒ decorum, good manners, correct etiquette *n.* 礼節, 作法, 適切(性) *adj.* proper
1032 ☐ prosaic [prouzéıık]	≒ boring, methodical, unimaginative, unpoetic *adj.* 単調な, 平凡な
1033 ☐ provocation [prà(:)vəkéıʃən]	≒ cause of something bad, incitement, instigation *n.* 挑発, 立腹 *v.t.* provoke

Chapter 1

例文

1034 Recent studies of domesticated cats have shown that they are still highly lethal killers that will **prowl** the streets and backyards of their neighborhoods looking for prey.

1035 Nearly everyone knows about the big bad wolf in the story of the "Three Little Pigs," who threatened the pigs, "I'll huff and I'll **puff**, and I'll blow your house down."

1036 The school principle was so gullible that students thought it was fun to **pull his leg** once in a while.

1037 One of the unpleasant aspects of printing black-and-white photographs in one's own darkroom is the **pungent** smell of the chemicals.

1038 The Holocaust in Nazi Germany was an attempt by Hitler to **purge** the country of its Jewish population.

1039 As the coordinator for a conference on modern language teaching, I received over two hundred **queries**.

1034 ☐ **prowl** [praʊl]	≒ walk stealthily in search of victims, stalk, patrol *v.t.* （獲物・機会などを求めて）をうろつく，を徘徊する
1035 ☐ **puff** [pʌf]	≒ blow out, breathe out *v.i.* ふっと吹く，息を切らす
1036 ☐ **pull** *one's* **leg**	≒ joke, tease, put on, trick をからかう，をばかにする
1037 ☐ **pungent** [pʌ́ndʒənt]	≒ sharp, acid, penetrating, sour, caustic *adj.* 鼻を刺激するような，辛らつな
1038 ☐ **purge** (*oneself of* ～) [pəːrdʒ]	≒ get rid of, remove, expel, purify *v.t.* （反対分子などを）から粛正する，から取り除く
1039 ☐ **query** [kwíəri]	≒ request for information, inquiry, question *n.* 質問，問い合わせ

例文

1040 A <u>quip</u> attributed to Mark Twain asserted that quitting smoking was easy, because in fact, he had done it many times.

1041 Madame and Pierre Curie won a Nobel Prize for their work on <u>radiation</u>.

1042 The <u>radius</u> of a circle is a significant value in a wide number of mathematical calculations.

1043 The <u>ramifications</u> of quantum theories have not yet been fully explored.

1044 The Chinese representative said that China would agree to <u>ratify</u> the treaty if the other nations would consent to amend the clause concerning intellectual property rights.

1045 The man's analyst urged him to <u>reach out</u> for help in controlling his pent-up animosity toward his father.

1040	**quip** [kwɪp]	≒ epigram, wisecrack *n.* 警句, 辛辣な言葉, 気の利いた言葉
1041	**radiation** [rèɪdiéɪʃən]	≒ the emission of radioactive or other kinds of waves *n.* 放射線, 放射能 *v.i.* radiate
1042	**radius** [réɪdiəs]	≒ half the length of the diameter of a circle *n.* 半径
1043	**ramification** [ræmɪfɪkéɪʃən]	≒ result, implication, consequence *n.* 派生問題, 結果, 分枝, 支脈, 分派 *v.t.* ramify
1044	**ratify** [rǽṭəfàɪ]	≒ approve, sanction, confirm *v.t.* (条約など) を批准する *n.* ratification
1045	**reach out**	≒ stretch out the hand ＜～に向かって＞手を伸ばす, 努力する＜for ～＞

例文

1046 The Ford Motor Company announced last week that it was offering a five-hundred dollar **rebate** for every new car purchased before December of 2003.

1047 In his summation to the jury, the lawyer for the defense thoroughly **rebutted** the argument of the prosecution.

1048 Galileo was forced to **recant** his statements supporting a heliocentric solar system.

1049 The teacher asked one of the students to **recapitulate** the basic meaning of the text he had assigned the class to read.

1050 After the terrible flood, it took more than a month before the waters of the Mississippi River had **receded** enough for everyone to return to their homes.

予想例文

1046 ☐ **rebate** [ríːbeɪt]	≒ payback, refund, bonus *n.* 払い戻し，割戻し，リベート
1047 ☐ **rebut** [rɪbʌ́t]	≒ refute, negate, nullify, invalidate *v.t.* に反論する，の反証を挙げる *n.* rebuttal
1048 ☐ **recant** [rɪkǽnt]	≒ retract, take back *v.t.* （主張など）を（公式に）撤回する
1049 ☐ **recapitulate** [rìːkəpítʃulèɪt]	≒ summarize, repeat, recount, paraphrase, go over the same ground *v.t.* を要約する，を総括する *n.* recapitulation
1050 ☐ **recede** [rɪsíːd]	≒ ebb, retreat, subside, move away, decrease *v.i.* 後退する，遠ざかる，（価値などが）薄れる，低下する *n.* recession

例文

1051 According to the **reckoning** of some analysts, the eventual costs of the war and reconstruction of Iraq will exceed 350 billion dollars.

1052 The Japanese Government spent trillions of yen to **reclaim** land from the ocean.

1053 One of my uncles flew **reconnaissance** flights over Germany for the U.S. Army during World War II.

1054 Professor Yasuda often **recounted** stories from his student days at the University of Tokyo just after the war.

1055 Instead of arresting the boy for theft, the victimized store owner offered him a chance to **rectify** what he had done by working to replace the value of the stolen goods.

1051 ☐ reckoning [rékəniŋ]	≒ calculation, estimation *n.* 計算, 決算, 見積もり
1052 ☐ reclaim [rikléim]	≒ retrieve, recover, get back, restore *v.t.* <海・沼地など>を干拓する, を再利用する, を矯正する *n.* reclamation
1053 ☐ reconnaissance [riká(:)nəzəns]	≒ information gathering, intelligence gathering, spy *n.* 偵察, 偵察隊 *v.t., n.* reconnoiter
1054 ☐ recount [rikáunt]	≒ tell, narrate, describe, relate *v.t.* を詳しく話す
1055 ☐ rectify [réktifài]	≒ redress, amend, compensate for, make good on *v.t.* (誤り)を正す, を調整する *n.* rectification

Chapter 1

例文

1056 It took my brother almost six months to **recuperate** from his operation.

1057 It took many decades for the United States Government to try to **redress** its shameful treatment of Japanese Americans in World War II.

1058 When a book I had ordered arrived with twenty pages missing, I wrote the company and demanded a **refund**.

1059 Mary recovered well from leukemia, until she apparently began to **regress** after a remission of two years.

1060 Once he became disliked by the company management, he was **relegated** to a basement office without even a window to look out of.

予想例文

1056 ☐ **recuperate** [rɪkjúːpərèɪt]	≒ recover, heal, get well *v.i.* （病気などから）回復する，元気になる *n.* recuperation
1057 ☐ **redress** [rɪdrés]	≒ make amends for, compensate for, make up for, square, recompense, correct *v.t.* （損害など）を賠償する，（不正など）を直す，を正す
1058 ☐ **refund** [ríːfʌnd]	≒ money returned for something one has bought, repayment *n.* 返金，払い戻し（金）
1059 ☐ **regress** [rɪgrés]	≒ come or go back, backslide, relapse, return *v.i.* 逆戻りする，後退する
1060 ☐ **relegate** [rélɪgèɪt]	≒ assign to a lower position, demote *v.t.* を（低い地位や状態に）追いやる，を左遷する *n.* relegation

例文

1061 The old man ran the company until he died of a stroke, refusing to <u>relinquish</u> power even after he was incapable of thinking or speaking clearly.

1062 In June I was notified that I had not yet <u>remitted</u> the proper amount of city tax to the tax office.

1063 Psychopaths are often unable to feel <u>remorse</u> for anything they have done.

1064 In addition to generous <u>remuneration</u>, the job provided many attractive benefits as special incentives for its employees.

1065 <u>Renegades</u> from both the South and North in the American Civil War were often hanged or shot.

1061 ☐ **relinquish** [rɪlíŋkwɪʃ]	≒ give up, yield, cede, waive, surrender, abdicate *v.t.*（地位・権力など）を放棄する，を譲渡する，を手放す *n.* relinquishment
1062 ☐ **remit** [rɪmít]	≒ pay, send (money) in payment *v.t.*（金銭）を送る，送金する *n.* remittance
1063 ☐ **remorse** [rɪmɔ́:rs]	≒ sorrow for *one's* own mistakes or bad behavior, regret *n.* 良心の呵責，自責の念，悔恨 *adj.* remorseful
1064 ☐ **remuneration** [rɪmjù:nəréɪʃən]	≒ payment, salary, reward *n.* 報酬
1065 ☐ **renegade** [rénɪgèɪd]	≒ traitor, deserter, escapee, rebel *n.* 裏切り者，背教者；*v.i.* 裏切る

例文

1066, 1067 When we first moved into the 19th century farmhouse, we decided to **renovate** it by **elongating** the family room and remodeling the kitchen.

1068 Japanese authorities hope to **repatriate** the Japanese nationals kidnapped and abducted to North Korea.

1069 After eight hours of bloody fighting, the enemy troops were finally **repelled**.

1070 Cloning is a process of **replicating** the DNA of an organism and creating a viable duplicate.

1071 Many sincere Muslims find the actions of Islamic terrorists **reprehensible**.

1066 □ renovate
[rénəvèit]
≒ restore, modernize, refurbish
v.t. を改築する、を刷新する
n. renovation

1067 □ elongate
[ilɔ́:ŋgeit]
≒ lengthen, extend, expand
v.t. を引き伸ばす
n. elongation

1068 □ repatriate
[ri:péitrièit]
≒ return to *one's* country of origin
v.t. を帰国させる、を本国へ送還する
n. repatriation

1069 □ repel
[ripél]
≒ drive back, push back, rebuff, put to flight
v.t. （攻撃・侵入など）を撃退する、をはねつける、（人）を不快にする
n., adj. repellent（防虫剤、不快な、寄せつけない）

1070 □ replicate
[réplikèit]
≒ copy, duplicate
v.t. を複製［模写］する、のレプリカを作る
n. replication, replica（複製品）

1071 □ reprehensible
[rèprihénsəbl]
≒ despicable, odious, hateful
adj. 非難されるべき、とがめられて当然の
v.t. reprehend

例文

1072 Freud believed that mental illness is the result of social **repressions** that inhibit human beings' natural instincts.

1073 The students were all severely **reprimanded** for smoking on the school premises.

1074 The dean **repudiated** several teachers for failing to find an equitable solution for handling the problem students in their courses.

1075 As a nurse in World War II, his mother told us she was often **repulsed** by the horrible things she had to witness.

1076 His **repute** varied widely, depending on whom you happened to talk to.

1072 ☐ **repression** [rɪpréʃən]	≒ control, suppression, inhibition *n.* 抑圧 *adj.* repressive
1073 ☐ **reprimand** [réprɪmænd]	≒ scold, correct, upbraid *v.t.* を懲戒する、を叱責する *n.* reprimand
1074 ☐ **repudiate** [rɪpjúːdièɪt]	≒ reject, renounce *v.t.* を退ける、を否認する、を破棄する
1075 ☐ **repulse** [rɪpʌ́ls]	≒ disgust, revolt, nauseate, appall *v.t.* ＜通例受身形＞気分を悪くさせる、不快にさせる、を拒絶する
1076 ☐ **repute** [rɪpjúːt]	≒ reputation, state of being esteemed *n.* 評判、好評；*v.t.* ＜通例受身形＞（人・物）を（～と）考える

Chapter 1

例文

1077 A mental patient tried to escape from the institution and had to be physically <u>restrained</u>.

1078 A turning point in the trial came when one of the key witnesses for the prosecution <u>retracted</u> his former accusations against the defendant.

1079 Mike Tyson is the kind of fighter who is continuously aggressive in the ring, never <u>retreating</u> even when he is getting hit.

1080 A sestina is an intricate and ancient 12th-century French poetic form, whose end-line words follow the pattern of <u>retrogradation</u>.

1081 As time has passed since the assassination of Abraham Lincoln, the world has come to <u>revere</u> him even more than it did during his lifetime.

1082 The psychiatric diagnosis had assured the authorities that the man was safe to return to society, but within a week he had <u>reverted</u> to his former sociopathic behavior.

予想例文

1077	**restrain** [rɪstréɪn]	≒ shackle, fetter, subdue, control *v.t.* を拘束する、（感情など）を抑える、（行動など）を制止する *n.* restraint
1078	**retract** [rɪtrǽkt]	≒ recant, deny, take back, renege *v.t.* （約束など）を取り消す
1079	**retreat** [rɪtríːt]	≒ give up, turn back, submit, backpedal *v.i.* 後退する、退く、（約束などを）撤回する
1080	**retrogradation** [rètrəgreɪdéɪʃən]	≒ recapitulation, repetition, reiteration *n.* 反復、逆行、後戻り、後退 *adj.* retrograde
1081	**revere** [rɪvíər]	≒ honor, respect, adulate *v.t.* を崇敬する
1082	**revert** [rɪvə́ːrt]	≒ return, regress, go back *v.i.* （もとの悪い状態に）逆戻りする、戻る

例文

1083 On television programs like *Survival* people do dangerous stunts or eat **revolting** things like cheese covered with maggots.

1084 After the earthquake, chaos broke out everywhere and looting was **rife**.

1085 I hoped I could help heal the **rift** that had developed between my parents, but I was not optimistic.

1086 When Eric was hired by the company, he was told that under no circumstances should he try to **rock the boat** regarding the company's traditions.

1087 The old man was able to **roll up** a fortune by investing in various kinds of technology.

1083 ☐ **revolting** [rɪvóultɪŋ]	≒ disgusting, vile, nauseating, repugnant, repulsive, putrid *adj.* ひどく不快な、ぞっとするような *v.t., n.* revolt (に嫌悪の念を抱かせる、反抗)	
1084 ☐ **rife** [raɪf]	≒ widespread, rampant, uncontrolled *adj.* (好ましくないことが) 流行して、おびただしく広まって	
1085 ☐ **rift** [rɪft]	≒ fight, discord, split *n.* 不和、断絶	
1086 ☐ **rock the boat**	≒ rebel, defy, flout, challenge, upset the applecart 波風を立てる、波乱を起こす	
1087 ☐ **roll up ~**	≒ amass, accumulate, build up, acquire gradually 〜を蓄える、〜を徐々に増やす、〜を包む	

Chapter 1

例文

1088 The time span of one full day and night represents the time it takes for one complete <u>rotation</u> of the Earth on its axis.

1089 It has been a <u>rough ride</u> during the recession, but business is finally starting to pick up.

1090 Once enemy forces broke through the front line, our troops lost their confidence and were soon <u>routed</u>.

1091 After he spent the night at the airport waiting for a late flight, his suit and shirt looked completely <u>rumpled</u>.

1092 He seemed to be doing very well, but he started to <u>run afoul of</u> the law by evading taxes and getting involved in other illegal practices such as fraudulent accounting.

1093 I awoke in the middle of the night because a light autumn breeze was <u>rustling</u> the leaves outside my window.

予想例文

1088 ☐ **rotation** [roʊtéɪʃən]	≒ turning, completion of one cycle of a repeated circular or oval motion *n.* 回転（運動），自転，循環
1089 ☐ **rough ride**	≒ ordeal, trial, tough time 試練，逆境
1090 ☐ **rout** [raʊt]	≒ repel, drive off, defeat, disperse *v.t.* を敗走させる； *n.* 敗走，大敗北
1091 ☐ **rumple** [rʌ́mpl]	≒ wrinkle, crumple *v.t.* をしわくちゃにする
1092 ☐ **run afoul of ～**	≒ conflict, clash, disagree (with) ～と衝突する，～ともめごとを起こす
1093 ☐ **rustle** [rʌ́sl]	≒ make a sound like that of leaves rubbing together in a breeze or papers being shuffled *v.t.* にかさかさと音を立てさせる； *n.* かさかさという音

例文

1094 Genghis Khan had a reputation for being totally **ruthless**, but in many ways he brought stability and order to the lands he conquered.

1095 An excellent public speaker often saves his most **salient** points for last.

1096 Keith and Amy asked Father Brooks to **sanctify** their marriage with a special ceremony in the same chapel that Amy's parents were married in.

1097 Even millions of executions still failed to **satiate** Joseph Stalin's lust for blood.

1098 After working on his cars in his front yard for almost a year, Jim found the ground so **saturated** with oil that he had to bring in topsoil to grow grass there again.

1099 The young puppies **scampered** around on the lawn as their mother watched them anxiously.

1094	☐ **ruthless** [rúːθləs]	≒ heartless, cruel, merciless, brutal *adj.* 冷酷な、無慈悲な、断固とした
1095	☐ **salient** [séɪliənt]	≒ major, most important, primary *adj.* 大事な、顕著な、目立つ *n.* salience
1096	☐ **sanctify** [sǽŋktɪfàɪ]	≒ make sacred, bless *v.t.* を神聖にする
1097	☐ **satiate** [séɪʃièɪt]	≒ satisfy, fulfill, complete *v.t.* （欲望など）を満足させる、をうんざりさせる *n.* satiety
1098	☐ **saturate** [sǽtʃərèɪt]	≒ soak, fill up with, permeate, sate *v.t.* に＜〜を＞すっかり染み込ませる、を＜〜で＞満ちあふれさせる＜with 〜＞ *n.* saturation
1099	☐ **scamper** [skǽmpər]	≒ cavort, skip, bound *v.i.* （子どもなどが）はね回る、ふざけ回る

Chapter 1

例文

1100 When the power in the office short-circuited, we had to find a **schematic** of the electrical system to locate the problem.

1101 In the Middle Ages the black plague was a **scourge** transmitted by rats that killed millions of Europeans.

1102 As the deadline for our report drew near, the committee members were **scrambling** to complete the project.

1103 My friend joined the Navy, he said, to see the world, but all he did for half a year was to **scrape** the deck of the ship, then paint and repaint it.

1104 My boss's favorite line was "You **scratch my back**, and I'll scratch yours."

1105 Igor spent most of his youth in a community home, **scribbling** the word "revenge" all over brown paper bags.

予想例文

1100 ☐ schematic [skiːmǽtɪk]	≒ blueprint, diagram *n.* 図表，配線図 ; *adj.* 図式的な，概略的な
1101 ☐ scourge [skəːrdʒ]	≒ devastating disease or catastrophe, illness, plague, epidemic *n.* 災難，難儀，天罰
1102 ☐ scramble [skrǽmbl]	≒ hasten, hurry, rush around in confusion *v.i.* 争って〜しようとする\<to *do*\>
1103 ☐ scrape [skreɪp]	≒ remove something from a surface by a vigorous scrubbing motion, scour, grate *v.t.* をこすり落とす，をこする
1104 ☐ scratch *one's* back	≒ do *one* a favor, help *one* （見返りを期待して〜に）好意を示す，親切にする
1105 ☐ scribble [skrɪ́bl]	≒ scrawl, scratch *v.t.* を書きなぐる ; *n.* 走り書きしたもの

例文

1106 We stood on the beach and watched crabs <u>scuttle</u> into the water.
1107 American writer Henry David Thoreau lived in a <u>secluded</u> cabin in the woods next to Walden Pond.
1108 By the time we got to the president's office, he was <u>seething</u> in anger.
1109, 1110 America is called a "melting pot" because so many groups of immigrants, even those once <u>segregated</u>, are gradually being <u>assimilated</u> into the mainstream population.
1111 After his accident, the man could no longer form a <u>semantically</u> acceptable sentence.

1106 □ **scuttle** [skʌ́tl]	≒ move quickly, scurry, scoot, dart *v.i.* 急いで行く、あわてて走る
1107 □ **secluded** [sɪklúːdɪd]	≒ isolated, remote, reclusive, out of the way *adj.* 人里離れた、隠遁した
1108 □ **seethe** [siːð]	≒ vent some powerful emotion, smolder *v.i.* （怒りなどで）煮えくり返る、煮えたぎる、動揺する
1109 □ **segregate** [ségrɪgèɪt]	≒ set apart, separate, partition *v.t.* を分離する、を隔離する *n.* segregation ⇔ integrate
1110 □ **assimilate** [əsíməlèɪt]	≒ absorb (into the main cultural body) *v.t.* を同化させる、（知識など）を吸収する *n.* assimilation
1111 □ **semantically** [səmǽntɪkəli]	≒ referring to the formal rules of acceptable usage of a language, referring to the meaning of something *adv.* 意味の上で *n.* semantics（意味論）

Chapter 1

例文

1112, 1113 Although he was expected to be **servile** as a servant in the Royal Palace, he seemed to **lay it on** too thick at times.

1114 One of the reasons for the American Civil War was to free African-American slaves from their **servitude**.

1115 The child seemed to be getting better, when a severe infection **set in**, putting him in critical condition.

1116 The troop of boy scouts strapped on their back packs and **set out** through the woods.

1117, 1118 Although the action received widespread criticism from the international community, Washington argued that **shelling** the suspected terrorist camp was simply a matter of **expediency**.

予想例文

1112 □ servile [sə́:rvəl]	≒ slavish, obsequious, menial, ingratiating *adj.* 盲従的な、奴隷の、卑屈な
1113 □ lay it on	≒ flatter, butter up へつらう、むやみにお世辞を言う
1114 □ servitude [sə́:rvətjùːd]	≒ slavery, bondage, subjugation, serfdom, under the yoke *n.* 奴隷の境遇、隷属
1115 □ set in	≒ begin, take hold, take root （よくないことが）始まる、起こる
1116 □ set out	≒ set forth, take off, embark 出発する、始める
1117 □ shell [ʃel]	≒ bombard, fire *v.t.* を砲撃する、の殻をとる
1118 □ expediency [ɪkspíːdiənsi]	≒ usefulness, suitability, propitiousness *n.* 便宜、好都合、方便 *adj.* expedient

例文

1119, 1120 Although he was hunted by law enforcement officers and military personnel all over the world, he had been **shrewd** enough to **evade** capture for over thirty years.

1121, 1122 We walked through a landscape **shrouded** in fog, knowing that danger lay just **around the corner**.

1123 Although Jodie Foster has been a movie star since childhood, she **shuns** publicity.

1124 In the 1970s a temporary gas shortage caused prices to rise rapidly, and many people put locked gas caps on their cars so hoodlums couldn't steal their gas at night by **siphoning** it out with a hose.

1119 ☐ **shrewd** [ʃruːd]	≒ clever, astute, calculating, crafty *adj.* 抜け目ない，洞察力の鋭い
1120 ☐ **evade** [ɪvéɪd]	≒ escape (from), avoid, dodge *v.t.* （義務・問題など）を避ける *n.* evasion *adj.* evasive
1121 ☐ **shroud** [ʃraʊd]	≒ veil, wrap, cover *v.t.* ＜通例受身形＞＜～で＞を覆い隠す ＜in, by ～＞
1122 ☐ **around the corner**	≒ very near, imminent すぐ近くに
1123 ☐ **shun** [ʃʌn]	≒ avoid, shy away from, eschew, evade *v.t.* （反感・嫌悪などから日常的に）を避ける
1124 ☐ **siphon** [sáɪfən]	≒ extract or draw off through suction, suck out *v.t.* を（サイフォンで）吸い上げる，（利益など）を横取りする

Chapter 1

例文

1125 The man's wife was enraged when her husband just **sat on his hands** and did nothing while she was being insulted.
1126 Whenever the Governor wasn't sure about the policy the people liked most, he would **sit on the fence** until he saw which direction the wind was blowing.
1127 A survey of too few subjects may **skew** the results.
1128, 1129 She walked into the vast boutique and **skimmed** a wide **array** of evening gowns before her.
1130 The colt was **sleek** and beautiful under the bright October sun.

予想例文

1125 ☐ **sit on *one's* hands**	≒ remain idle, do nothing, refuse to meet one's responsibility 手をこまねいている、傍観する
1126 ☐ **sit on the fence**	≒ be equivocal, be ambivalent, be indecisive, be evasive, be ambiguous, equivocate, talk out both sides of the mouth どっちつかずの態度をとる、決定を避ける
1127 ☐ **skew** [skjuː]	≒ distort, twist, misrepresent, warp *v.t.* を歪める、をわい曲する
1128 ☐ **skim** [skɪm]	≒ glance through, look over hastily, scan *v.t.* にざっと目を通す
1129 ☐ **array** [əréɪ]	≒ grouping, arrangement, collection *n.* ずらりと並んだもの、陳列
1130 ☐ **sleek** [sliːk]	≒ glossy, lustrous, gleaming, shiny, glistening *adj.* (皮膚・毛などが)つやのある、なめらかな、栄養のよい、人当たりのよい

例文

1131 The boy scout troop went on a canoe trip every summer, but they spent much of the time carrying their canoes in shallow water as they <u>slogged</u> for miles through mud and sand.

1132 It was only a rumor, but a good man's reputation can be ruined by such <u>slurs</u>.

1133 The coach sometimes got so frustrated with his players that he would <u>smack</u> the back of their heads to get their attention.

1134 Political candidates usually claim that their opponents' criticisms are really efforts to <u>smear</u> them.

1135 Witnesses said that the policeman suddenly seemed to <u>snap</u>, as he opened fire on innocent bystanders.

1131 ☐ **slog** [slɑ(:)g]	≒ move forward slowly against resistance, trudge, plod, schlep, drudge *v.i.* ＜～を＞重い足取りで歩く、辛抱強く進む ＜on, through ～＞、辛抱強く精を出す
1132 ☐ **slur** [slə:r]	≒ slander, epithet, aspersion *n.* 中傷、誹謗
1133 ☐ **smack** [smæk]	≒ slap, hit, cuff *v.t.* をぴしゃりと打つ
1134 ☐ **smear** [smɪər]	≒ slander, besmirch, malign, spread rumors of *v.t.* の名声を汚す、を中傷する、を汚す
1135 ☐ **snap** [snæp]	≒ lose control, go crazy, lose it, flip out *v.i.* 自制心を失う、かっとなる、ぱちんと音を立てる

Chapter 1

例文

1136 The monkeys around the park became so tame that they would sneak up to tourists and <u>snatch</u> whatever they could and run away.

1137 His words were formally polite but his tone was arrogant and <u>snide</u>.

1138 He is the kind of person who can be very nice to you one day but the next day openly <u>snubs</u> you.

1139 The golden eagle <u>soared</u> into the clouds and disappeared.

1140 The <u>solvency</u> of many large banks in Japan has been in question since the bursting of the economic bubble in the 1990s.

1141 Mrs. Hilliard was so upset over the accident that no one could say or do anything to <u>soothe</u> her.

1142 The press soon got hold of the <u>sordid</u> details surrounding the political scandal which threatened to implicate the highest levels of the government.

1136 ☐ **snatch** [snætʃ]	≒ grab, seize, snag	*v.t.* をひったくる, を強奪する, のチャンス[時間]をすばやくつかむ; *n.* ひったくり, 短時間
1137 ☐ **snide** [snaɪd]	≒ disparaging, contemptuous, insulting	*adj.* 意地悪な, 嫌味な, あてこすりの
1138 ☐ **snub** [snʌb]	≒ ignore, disregard, look past, brush off	*v.t.* にそっけない態度をとる, を無視する
1139 ☐ **soar** [sɔːr]	≒ ascend into the sky, fly high, rise up	*v.i.* 高く舞い上がる, 急上昇する, 急騰する
1140 ☐ **solvency** [sá(ː)lvənsi]	≒ economic stability, economic viability	*n.* 支払い能力 *adj.* solvent
1141 ☐ **soothe** [suːð]	≒ comfort, calm down, relieve	*v.t.* を和らげる, を落ち着かせる
1142 ☐ **sordid** [sɔ́ːrdəd]	≒ immoral, disgusting, reprehensible, dirty	*adj.* 汚い, 浅ましい

予想例文

例文

1143 The state of Montana is so **sparsely** populated that one can travel for miles without seeing a single human soul, let alone a human dwelling place.

1144 She promised to follow her mother's orders, but her voice was full of **spite**.

1145 When the child accidentally cut an artery on a rusty can, blood **spurted** from his wrist.

1146 Microsoft's opponents argued that the software company was trying to **squeeze** them **out** of competition with its Internet browser.

1147 When I received the bills for our last vacation, the sum total truly **staggered** me.

1148 Even as a young boy, my nephew **stood out** from the crowd as a talented singer.

1143 □ **sparsely** [spá:*r*sli]	≒ thinly, characterized by few in number, insufficiently *adv.* まばらに, 散在して, 薄く *adj.* sparse
1144 □ **spite** [spaɪt]	≒ malice, contempt, loathing, vengeance *n.* 悪意, 意地悪, 恨み *adj.* spiteful
1145 □ **spurt** [spə:rt]	≒ spout, spray, gush, jet, squirt, shoot out or up *v.i.* 噴出する, 全力で走る；*n.* 噴出, 奮闘
1146 □ **squeeze out ～**	≒ eliminate, oust, expel *v.t.* を＜～から＞締め出す＜of ～＞
1147 □ **stagger** [stǽgər]	≒ shock, stun, astound *v.t.* を呆然とさせる；*v.i.* よろめく *adj.* staggering
1148 □ **stand out**	≒ excel, distinguish *oneself* （～より）傑出している, 目立つ, 際立つ

Chapter 1

例文

1149 Many educators are concerned that putting weak students in special classes marks them with a **stigma**.

1150 In the 1960s and early '70s the Beetles really caused a **stir**, drawing huge crowds until "Beetle mania" virtually engulfed the entire teenage population.

1151 A **stowaway** was discovered on a boat going from India to England.

1152 The military academy was known around America for its **stringent** rules and high standards of education.

1153 A now-famous rebellion in 1971 at Attica prison was brutally **subdued** by prison guards and the New York State Police and National Guard, killing 33 prisoners and ten of their hostages.

1154 After two months of almost constant rain, the monsoon finally **subsided** but left the village devastated by flood damage.

予想例文

1149 ☐ **stigma** [stígmə]	≒ mark of, shame, blemish *n.* 汚名, 恥辱 *adj.* stigmatic
1150 ☐ **stir** [stəːr]	≒ commotion, excitement *n.* 旋風, 騒ぎ, 興奮
1151 ☐ **stowaway** [stóuəwèɪ]	≒ hideaway, someone who hides on a ship to get free passage *n.* 密航者, もぐりこんだ無賃乗客
1152 ☐ **stringent** [stríndʒənt]	≒ strict, rigorous, severe *adj.* 厳格な, 厳重な, 徹底した
1153 ☐ **subdue** [səbdjúː]	≒ put down, control, restrain *v.t.* （反乱・敵など）を鎮圧する, を制圧する, （勢いなど）を弱める
1154 ☐ **subside** [səbsáɪd]	≒ slow down, stop, cease *v.i.* 静まる, 落ち着く

例文

1155 Many wealthy countries **subsidize** certain favored domestic agricultural products, but it is a practice that often angers undeveloped countries.

1156 During the McCarthy era of the 1950s, many gifted artists and film makers were blacklisted for alleged **subversive** activities.

1157 Elderly patients often don't die from the injuries or illnesses they are suffering from but **succumb** instead to pneumonia.

1158 When a five-star general was abruptly **summoned** to the White House, no one knew if he would be promoted or fired.

1155 ☐ subsidize
[sʌ́bsɪdàɪz]
≒ support financially in part or totally, sponsor, bankroll, fund
v.t. に助成金を支給する
n. subsidy

1156 ☐ subversive
[səbvə́ːrsɪv]
≒ seditious, treasonous, traitorous, unpatriotic, destabilizing
adj. （秩序などを）破壊する，（体制を）転覆させる，反逆の
n. subversion

1157 ☐ succumb
[səkʌ́m]
≒ die from, perish, fall victim to, yield, expire, be overcome by, give in
v.i. ＜〜がもとで＞死ぬ，倒れる＜to 〜＞，屈服する

1158 ☐ summon
[sʌ́mən]
≒ call, call in, beckon, order to report
v.t. を召喚する，を召集する，（力など）を奮い起こす

Chapter 1

例文

1159 One thing that angered the Iranian people so much about the former Shah was his **sumptuous** palace.

1160 The stock market **surged** after most of the usual economic indicators were positive for the third straight quarter.

1161 He worked hard to **surmount** a childhood of abject poverty.

1162, 1163 We took a boat ride through the **swamps**, not knowing what creatures might **lurk** in the branches just above our heads or under the surface of the water.

1164 Just last week, John was told that his head was on the block over his sales record for the past few months and he would just have to **sweat it out**.

予想例文

1159 ☐ **sumptuous** [sʌ́mptʃuəs]	≒ luxurious, posh, extravagantly opulent *adj.* 壮麗な、ぜいたくな
1160 ☐ **surge** [səːrdʒ]	≒ accelerate, increase, boost *v.i.* 沸き立つ、急騰する、押し寄せる、込み上げる
1161 ☐ **surmount** [sərmáunt]	≒ overcome, prevail, win an uphill battle over *v.t.* を乗り越える、を克服する
1162 ☐ **swamp** [swɑ(ː)mp]	≒ marsh, bog *n.* 湿地、沼地
1163 ☐ **lurk** [ləːrk]	≒ hide, wait stealthily, go furtively *v.i.* 潜む、待ち伏せする、（危険、疑念などが）潜在する
1164 ☐ **sweat it out**	≒ wait nervously for a problem to be resolved, worry about, agonize over, be on pins and needles about はらはらして待つ、不愉快なことを最後まで我慢して待つ

例文

1165 Scholars have noted that the **symmetry** of art imitates that of nature.

1166 The dance group rehearsed six hours a day for two weeks prior to the concert to be sure their movements were **synchronized** perfectly.

1167 Professor Takahashi was a brilliant lecturer and scholar, but he was often **tactless** and insensitive in his contact with colleagues and students.

1168 He had worked on his novel for five years, and it was finally beginning to **take shape**.

1169 When old Professor Nishiyama entered the room, everyone present insisted he **take the floor**.

1165 □ symmetry [símətri]	≒ aesthetic balance, having perfect proportionality, harmony *n.* 均整（美）、釣り合い、左右対称 *adj.* symmetrical ⇔ asymmetry
1166 □ synchronize [síŋkrənàız]	≒ cause to occur at the same time *v.t.* を同時に起こるようにする；*v.i.* 同時に起こる、一致する
1167 □ tactless [tǽktləs]	≒ rude, insensitive, brusque, impolite *adj.* 機転がきかない
1168 □ take shape	≒ come together, make progress 形ができる、具体化する
1169 □ take the floor	≒ take the stage or podium, command the attention of an audience or group as a speaker 発言のために立つ、発言する

Chapter 1

例文

1170 The election doors closed some hours ago, but it will take almost a full day for the votes to be **tallied**.

1171 A storm shook the windows and doors of the house, until it finally **tapered off** to a light drizzle.

1172 His superiors would **taunt** him for his strange deviations from normal practice, but he often found creative and effective ways for dealing with problems.

1173 I was so appalled at the poor quality of my essay that I **tore** it **up** and started over.

1174 The work is **tedious** and demanding, but he hoped in the end to produce a useful and unique text for young learners.

1175 It is generally true that the world's most fertile farmland can be found in the **temperate** weather zones.

1170 ☐ tally [tǽli]	≒ count up, calculate, total (up), sum *v.t.* を勘定する、の総計を出す、(得点) を記録する
1171 ☐ taper off	≒ slow by small increments, wind down, come to a close *v.i.* 先細になる、次第に減少する
1172 ☐ taunt [tɔːnt]	≒ tease, mock, poke fun at *v.t.* をあざける、を嘲笑する；*n.* あざけり
1173 ☐ tear up ～	≒ destroy by tearing completely を破り捨てる
1174 ☐ tedious [tíːdiəs]	≒ drudging, boring, tiresome, humdrum *adj.* つまらない、退屈な、冗長な
1175 ☐ temperate [témpərət]	≒ mild, moderate, without excess *adj.* 温暖な、穏やかな、穏健な、緩やかな

例文

1176, 1177 We thought the colt was securely <u>tethered</u> to the railing, when he suddenly <u>bolted</u> toward the gate and escaped at a gallop.

1178 When some suspects were given a serious <u>thrashing</u> by the police, they would confess to crimes they didn't commit.

1179 "What fine <u>threads</u>!" my father muttered sarcastically as soon as he noticed my slovenly choice of clothing for the party.

1180 My mother was <u>thrifty</u> and resourceful and always seemed to have money when she really needed it.

1181 A great public outcry <u>thwarted</u> the government's plan to send troops into a dangerous war zone.

1182 When we had so many expenditures that we couldn't pay all our bills this month, we had to get a temporary loan to <u>tide</u> us <u>over</u>.

1176 ☐ tether [téðər]	≒ tie, rope *v.t.* を（鎖などで）＜〜に＞つなぐ，を束縛する＜to 〜＞；*n.* （家畜などをつなぐ）鎖
1177 ☐ bolt [boʊlt]	≒ run off, dart off, flee *v.i.* 急に飛び出す，逃亡する
1178 ☐ thrashing [θrǽʃɪŋ]	≒ severe beating, pummeling, pounding *n.* むち打ち，激しく打つこと
1179 ☐ threads [θredz]	≒ clothes *n.* 衣服
1180 ☐ thrifty [θrífti]	≒ restrained in spending money, frugal *adj.* 倹約的な，つましい
1181 ☐ thwart [θwɔːrt]	≒ stop, curtail, foil, prevent *v.t.* （計画など）をくじく，を妨害する
1182 ☐ tide over 〜	≒ help get by, sustain, maintain （金銭的な援助で人）に困難を切り抜けさせる

Chapter 1

例文

1183 During the recession, many Japanese families felt the need to **tighten their belts**.

1184 When we traveled to Greece, we thought the food was **tolerable** but not great.

1185 In order to complete the geological survey of the area, we need to refer to a **topographical** map.

1186 It is clear that the old professor Nishiyama has **transcended** the normal boundaries of time and space.

1187 It took me hours to **transcribe** the president's speech due to his many grammatical and lexical errors.

予想例文

1183 ☐ **tighten *one's* belt**	≒ economize, cut expenses, budget *oneself*, be thrifty, scrimp, pinch pennies 倹約して暮らす
1184 ☐ **tolerable** [tá(:)lərəbl]	≒ fairly good, acceptable, mediocre, so-so, bearable, endurable *adj.* まあまあよい、まずまずの、我慢できる *v.t.* tolerate ⇔ intolerable
1185 ☐ **topographical** [tà(:)pəgrǽfɪkəl]	≒ referring to precise physical features of a geographical area *adj.* 地形学の、地勢上の *n.* topography
1186 ☐ **transcend** [trænsénd]	≒ to go beyond, surpass, overcome, surmount *v.t.* を超越する、にまさる *adj.* transcendent(al)
1187 ☐ **transcribe** [trænskráɪb]	≒ write out an oral text, express the meaning or sound of a text in a writing system different from the original *v.t.* を書き取る、を文章に起こす、を書き写す

例文

1188, 1189 The boy often came late for work and left early, but when these <u>transgressions</u> became a direct <u>affront</u> to the boss, he was fired.

1190 Fame is <u>transient</u> and life is short.

1191 It took him hours to realize that his mathematical mistake was caused when he <u>transposed</u> two of the digits of one of the numbers he was working with.

1192 His remarks at the conference were accurate enough but full of <u>trite</u> phrases and bad jokes.

1193 During the general commotion of the festival, a great <u>tumult</u> suddenly rose from the crowd as the parade came into sight.

1188 ☐ **transgression** [trænsgréʃən]	≒ violation, misbehavior, offense, fault *n.* 違反，逸脱，罪 *v.t., v.i.* transgress	
1189 ☐ **affront** [əfrʌ́nt]	≒ rudeness, discourtesy, insult *n.* 侮辱；*v.t.* ＜通例受身形で＞侮辱される	
1190 ☐ **transient** [trǽnziənt]	≒ brief, evanescent, fleeting, ephemeral, momentary *adj.* 一時的な，つかの間の *n.* transience	
1191 ☐ **transpose** [trænspóuz]	≒ invert, switch, reverse, flip-flop *v.t.* （複数のもの）を入れ替える，を置き換える *n.* transposition	
1192 ☐ **trite** [traɪt]	≒ hackneyed, worn out, commonplace, shallow *adj.* ありふれた，使い古された，陳腐な	
1193 ☐ **tumult** [tjúːmʌlt]	≒ commotion, disquiet, disturbance, ado *n.* 騒ぎ，騒動，喧騒 *adj.* tumultuous	

Chapter 1

例文

1194 In these **turbulent** times in the Middle East, the Bush Administration's "road map" for peace seems all but lost in the accelerating violence.

1195 After years of derisive treatment from his peers in the entertainment business, he was pleased to **turn the tables** when he became a film and television critic.

1196 My cat often runs away for days at a time, but sooner or later she will **turn up** again.

1197 His defiant speech was an **unabashed** rejection of the government policy.

1198 In my home my mother considered it **uncouth** for her sons to come to the dinner table without wearing a shirt.

1199 After a few moves, the grand master chess player asked his opponent whether he wanted to concede the game, but the challenger was **undaunted** and insisted on continuing.

1194 □ turbulent [tə́ːrbjulənt]	≒ volatile, dangerous, violent, changeable, stormy *adj.* （世情などが）不穏な，激しい，（波，風などが）荒れ狂う
1195 □ turn the tables	≒ reverse the situation or relationship 形勢を逆転させる
1196 □ turn up	≒ appear, arrive, show up, return 姿を現す，ひょっこりやってくる，生じる
1197 □ unabashed [ʌ̀nəbǽʃt]	≒ bold, unapologetic, cheeky, impudent *adj.* 臆することのない，平然とした，厚かましい
1198 □ uncouth [ʌ̀nkúːθ]	≒ crude, coarse, impolite, ill-mannered, gauche *adj.* 無作法な，野暮な，無骨な
1199 □ undaunted [ʌ̀ndɔ́ːntɪd]	≒ unswerving, unyielding *adj.* ＜通例叙述用法＞不屈の，くじけない

例文

1200 Mr. Stanton's wife always had him **under her thumb**.
1201 Every evening I would sit at the edge of the lake adjacent to the campus, watching the waves **undulate** in the setting sun.
1202 The Army, Navy, Marines, Air Force and National Guard form the **unitary** branches of the American armed forces.
1203 We let the boys play outside as often as possible, but when they become so **unruly** that they disturb the neighbors, we make them come inside and play games quietly.
1204 It was incredible that the race-car drivers in that terrible crash came through the accident completely **unscathed**.

1200 ☐ **under *one's* thumb**	≒ under control, subservient, submissive, dominated あごで使われて、人の言うなりになって
1201 ☐ **undulate** [ʌ́ndʒəlèɪt]	≒ move up and down in wave-like motions, oscillate, vibrate *v.i.* うねる、波打つ、大きくなったり小さくなったりする
1202 ☐ **unitary** [júːnətèri]	≒ unified, whole, connected in belief, character or action, closely affiliated *adj.* 単一の、単位の、中央集権の
1203 ☐ **unruly** [ʌ̀nrúːli]	≒ out of control, wild, uncontrollable *adj.* 手に負えない、言うことを聞かない
1204 ☐ **unscathed** [ʌ̀nskéɪðd]	≒ unharmed, untouched, without a scratch, safe and sound, in one piece *adj.* 無傷の、無事な

Chapter 1

例文

1205 We all thought that the professor's <u>unseemly</u> attire was an embarrassment to his wife.

1206 Even when his position seemed <u>untenable</u> in the light of obvious facts, he would refuse to alter his opinions one iota.

1207 David finally dumped his girlfriend because she would <u>vacillate</u> from week to week regarding her feelings about him.

1208 Over the past decade one could see more and more <u>vagrants</u> living in large train stations in Tokyo.

1209 Despite fighting <u>valiantly</u> for years, the native American general Geronimo was finally defeated.

1210 Cosmetic companies and beauty salons want to exploit the inherent <u>vanity</u> of their potential customers.

予想例文

1205 □ unseemly [ʌnsíːmli]	≒ unattractive, inappropriate, vulgar *adj.* 見苦しい、みっともない、不適当な
1206 □ untenable [ʌnténəbl]	≒ indefensible, unconvincing, insupportable *adj.* （議論・立場などが）支持できない
1207 □ vacillate [væsɪleɪt]	≒ waver, oscillate, be fickle, be wishy-washy *v.i.* 揺らぐ、迷う、ためらう
1208 □ vagrant [véɪgrənt]	≒ bum, tramp, the homeless, the unemployed *n.* 浮浪者、放浪者 *n.* vagrancy
1209 □ valiantly [væljəntli]	≒ bravely, courageously, intrepidly, heroically *adv.* 勇敢に
1210 □ vanity [vænəti]	≒ narcissism, conceit over looks or accomplishments, self-pride, arrogance *n.* 虚栄心、うぬぼれ、空しさ

例文

1211 Terrorists threatened to **vaporize** a large population center if authorities refused to meet their demands.
1212 American English offers numerous **variants** in spelling from British English.
1213 The world will soon see if the young boxer can live up to his much-**vaunted** prowess.
1214 At his memorial service not long ago, thousands of people gathered to pay homage to one of the most **venerable** actors of his generation, Gregory Peck.
1215 He would often **vent** his anger on innocent bystanders.

1211 □ **vaporize** [véɪpəràɪz]	≒ kill, annihilate, eliminate, convert from a liquid to a gaseous state *v.t.* を絶滅させる，を気化する *n.* vapor
1212 □ **variant** [véəriənt]	≒ form derived from something else, alternative, option *n.* 変形，異形；*adj.* (標準から) 異なる，変化しやすい *n.* variance (変化，相違)
1213 □ **vaunted** [vɔ́ːntɪd]	≒ highly praised, bragged about *adj.* 自慢の，誇示されている *v.t.* vaunt
1214 □ **venerable** [vénərəbl]	≒ respectable, revered, venerated *adj.* 尊敬に値する，(古びて) 神々しい *v.t.* venerate
1215 □ **vent** [vent]	≒ unleash, release, express, let loose, ventilate *v.t.* (感情など) を発散する；*n.* 排出，はけ口

例文

1216 That lady is so **verbose** that the simple word "hello" isn't in her vocabulary.

1217 Just as it seemed that Al Gore was on the **verge** of finally winning the U.S. presidency, he was defeated once again in a last-minute election reversal in Florida.

1218 Old Professor Nishiyama is well-**versed** in American intellectual history.

1219 Republican presidents regularly threaten to **veto** any bill calling for controls on the sale of hand guns.

1220 Since she had been an invalid from childhood, who had seldom left the home where she was born, she lived an exciting life **vicariously** through books and films.

1216 ☐ **verbose** [vəːrbóus]	≒ lacking conciseness, wordy *adj.* おしゃべりな、言葉数が多い、回りくどい *n.* verbosity
1217 ☐ **verge** [vəːrdʒ]	≒ brink, edge *n.* 縁、へり、境界、瀬戸際、 <on the verge of ~>~寸前で
1218 ☐ **versed** [vəːrst]	≒ knowledgeable, schooled, acquainted with *adj.* <~に>精通した、熟達した<in ~>
1219 ☐ **veto** [víːtou]	≒ cancel, reject, deny, negate, stymie, nix *n.* を拒否する、を禁じる；*n.* 拒否権（の行使）、禁止
1220 ☐ **vicariously** [vɪkéəriəsli]	≒ through an alternative medium, in contrast to real life, imaginatively, by proxy, virtually *adv.* （他人やものを通して）自分のことのように感じて、代理で

例文

1221 The twelve finalists in the speech contest will **vie** for first prize, which is a five-hundred dollar certificate and a nice trophy.
1222 Military boot camp usually involves **vigorous** exercise.
1223 The psychopathic killer wrote **vile** letters, which he sent to people whose names he selected randomly from the phone directory.
1224 She was always **vivacious** and cheerful, even as a girl, so it's not surprising that she has so many friends.
1225 In contrast to the Vietnam War era, when many men refused to fight, in World War I and World War II many young men joined one of the military services of their own **volition**.

1221 □ **vie** [vaɪ]	≒ compete, struggle, fight, contend *v.i.* 競う，張り合う
1222 □ **vigorous** [vígərəs]	≒ strenuous, active, dynamic, strong *adj.* 強健な，活発な，激しい *n.* vigor
1223 □ **vile** [vaɪl]	≒ disgusting, repugnant, repulsive, despicable, evil, immoral *adj.* ひどい，下劣な，不愉快な *v.t.* vilify
1224 □ **vivacious** [vɪvéɪʃəs]	≒ lively, full of life, cheerful, bubbly, dynamic, gregarious *adj.* （特に女性が）活発な
1225 □ **volition** [voulíʃən]	≒ choice, free will, willingness *n.* 意志，決意，選択

Chapter 1

例文

1226 In the 1950s, the **voluptuous** look of starlets like Marilyn Monroe was generally preferred over the pencil-thin appearance of the models who became popular a decade later, like Twiggy.

1227 The girl's mother told her that her outfit was too **vulgar** for her to wear out in public.

1228 The man was so obese that he **waddled** like a duck.

1229 My younger sister was known in the family as a **wet blanket**.

1230 A new helicopter being developed is so silent that one can barely hear the **whirring** of its blades.

1231 A cult of Islamic mystics, who base their worship on dancing, are called "**whirling** dervishes."

1226 ☐ **voluptuous** [vəlÁptʃuəs]	≒ sensuous and sexually attractive, sybaritic, full-figured (females), curvy *adj.* 官能的な、肉感的な
1227 ☐ **vulgar** [vÁlgər]	≒ coarse, crude, unrefined, gauche, base, boorish, tasteless, obscene, off-color *adj.* 下品な、粗野な、俗悪な
1228 ☐ **waddle** [wá(:)dl]	≒ walk like a duck, toddle, totter *v.i.* よたよた歩く、よちよち歩く
1229 ☐ **wet blanket**	≒ a negative person, grouch, misanthrope, malcontent, scrooge, curmudgeon, grouser, sourpuss, meanie けちをつける人、座をしらけさせる人
1230 ☐ **whir** [hwə:r]	≒ produce the sound of the rapid flutter of wings *v.i.* ブンブン音を立てて回る［動く］; *n.* ブンブンいう音
1231 ☐ **whirl** [hwə:rl]	≒ circle, swirl, rotate, spin *v.t.* 踊り回る、くるくる回転する

予想例文

例文

1232 Many people predicted that the new high-rise office building would become a <u>white elephant</u>, considering the weak economy.

1233 He was ready to fight the strange man if he had to, but when the guy ran toward his house <u>wielding</u> a hatchet, he changed his mind.

1234 The debate became so acrimonious that one could actually see George <u>wince</u> every time his opponent began to respond.

1235 He sometimes would get out his old photo albums and look <u>wistfully</u> through the photos of his younger days when his wife was still living.

1236 By the time their joint project was nearing its end, the participants were so much at odds with each other that they couldn't <u>wrap</u> everything <u>up</u> smoothly.

1237 The young man incurred the <u>wrath</u> of his boss by challenging the wisdom of his policies.

1232 ☐ **white elephant**	≒ a public project, usually a building, that turns out to be useless, folly, fiasco 金のかかる厄介もの、無用の長物、持て余しもの
1233 ☐ **wield** [wi:ld]	≒ brandish, wave (threateningly), manipulate *v.t.* （剣など）を振り回す、（権力）を振るう
1234 ☐ **wince** [wɪns]	≒ recoil, shrink back, flinch *v.i.* ＜～に＞たじろぐ、顔をゆがめる＜at, under ～＞
1235 ☐ **wistfully** [wístfəli]	≒ regretfully, nostalgically, sadly *adv.* 物思いに沈んで、物欲しげに
1236 ☐ **wrap up ～**	≒ finish, end, terminate ～を（滞りなく）終える
1237 ☐ **wrath** [ræθ]	≒ anger, ire, rage, fury, acrimony *n.* 激怒、天罰

Chapter 1

例文

1238 In Europe and America it is customary to hang a **wreath** over the front door at Christmas time.

1239 Just before the biggest game of the season, their star player **wrenched** his knee in practice and was unable to play for two weeks.

1240 Jesus infused his disciples with the **zeal** to follow his example and spread his teachings as far as they could.

1241 While his **zest** for life is commendable, he is often irresponsible and self-centered in his pursuit of happiness.

1238 ☐ **wreath** [riːθ]	≒ circular or oval-shaped decoration made of flowers, leaves and vines, garland, bouquet *n.* リース，花輪，輪
1239 ☐ **wrench** [rentʃ]	≒ twist, sprain, pull a muscle *v.t.* をひねる，を捻挫する，をもぎ取る
1240 ☐ **zeal** [ziːl]	≒ earnestness, fervor *n.* （目的，使命への）熱意，熱心さ *adj.* zealous
1241 ☐ **zest** [zest]	≒ eagerness, enthusiasm, zeal *n.* 情熱，強い興味 *adj.* zestful

予想例文

Roots of Words—語源から意味をつかむ

ab	(away from)	abduct
acr	(bitter, sharp)	acrimony
ambi	(both)	ambivalent
anthrop	(man)	anthropology
belli	(war)	bellicosity
ben	(good)	benevolence
bio	(life)	biotechnology
cent	(one hundred)	centennial
chron	(time)	chronology
cide	(kill)	pesticide
com	(together)	community
cy	(state of being)	democracy
demo	(people)	demography
dia	(across)	diameter
err	(wander)	erratic
fin	(limit)	infinite
gen	(birth)	generate
greg	(flock)	gregarious
hydro	(water)	dehydrate
log	(word, reason)	prologue
mor	(die)	mortal
oper	(work)	cooperation
pac	(peace)	pacifist
port	(carry)	transport
scrip	(write)	description
spec	(look, watch)	aspect
urb	(city)	urbane
vinct	(conquer)	invincible

Chapter 2

長文問題に出題される単熟語

医学	230
コンピュータ	250
科学・テクノロジー	259

経済・ビジネス	283
自然・環境	299
文化・社会	311

1 Timing Is Everything

医学

日本語訳 → p.405

例文

1 Our bodies seem wonderfully deft at maintaining balance. We sweat to cool down, and our hearts ¹²⁴²**pound** when blood pressure falls. ¹²⁴³**As it turns out**, though, our natural state is not a steady one. Researchers are finding that everything from blood pressure to brain function varies rhythmically with the cycles of sun, moon, and seasons. And their ¹²⁴⁴**insights** are yielding new strategies for ¹²⁴⁵**warding off** such common killers as heart disease and cancer.

2 In medical school, most doctors learn that people with ¹²⁴⁶**chronic conditions** should take their medicine at regular rates. "Everyone does it, but it's a terrible way to treat disease," says Dr. Richard Martin. For example, ¹²⁴⁷**asthmatics** are most likely to suffer during the night, when ¹²⁴⁸**mucus** production increases, airways narrow, and ¹²⁴⁹**inflammatory** cells work overtime. Yet most patients ¹²⁵⁰**strive** to keep a constant level of medicine in their blood day and night. In recent studies, researchers have found that a large midafternoon dose of a ¹²⁵¹**steroid** or ¹²⁵²**bronchodilator** can be as safe as several small doses, and better for warding off nighttime attacks.

3 Dr. William Hrushesky has shown that many cancer drugs are less toxic if they're used only at certain times of day. In his clinic and others, patients getting rhythmic chemotherapy through portable injection pumps have suffered less heart, stomach, and ¹²⁵³**bone-marrow** damage than those getting continuous infusions.

4 Daily rhythms aren't the only ones that could affect cancer treatment. Hrushesky analyzed the records of 41 women who'd undergone ¹²⁵⁴**surgery** for breast cancer and found that those operated on midway through the ¹²⁵⁵**menstrual cycle** enjoyed better 10-year survival rates than those treated at other times of the month.

5 Unlike most new treatments, this one would cost no more than what it replaced. Time, after all, is free.

1242 □ **pound** [paʊnd]	≒ beat, pulse, hammer, strike, batter, pulverize *v.i.*（心臓が）激しく鼓動する，続けざまに打つ； *v.t.* を打ち砕く
1243 □ **as it turns out**	≒ in the end, when all is said and done, in fact, as a matter of fact 結局のところ，結果的には
1244 □ **insight** [ínsàɪt]	≒ deep understanding, perceptiveness, perspicacity, discernment, acumen *n.* 洞察力，見識 *adj.* insightful（洞察に満ちた）
1245 □ **ward off ~**	≒ fend off, repel, repulse, fight off *v.t.*（危険・攻撃など）を防ぐ，をかわす ⇔ welcome
1246 □ **chronic condition**	≒ a frequently occurring or reoccurring medical problem, a continuous or permanent medical condition 慢性症状 ⇔ acute condition（急性症状）
1247 □ **asthmatic** [æzmǽtɪk]	≒ patients of a disease of the lungs, causing difficulty in breathing and triggered by pollutants or emotional stress *n.* 喘息患者； *adj.* 喘息の *n.* asthma（喘息）
1248 □ **mucus** [mjú:kəs]	≒ a slimy, viscous fluid secreted by the body, specifically the mucous membranes *n.* 粘液

1249 ☐	**inflammatory** [ɪnflǽmətɔ̀ːri]	≒ causing swelling and redness in the body, usually due to infection *adj.* 炎症性の，扇動的な *n.* inflammation *adj.* inflammable（引火性の，怒りっぽい）
1250 ☐	**strive** [straɪv]	≒ try, struggle for, seek, attempt *v.i.* <…しようと，〜を求めて>努力する<to do, for 〜>
1251 ☐	**steroid** [stíərɔɪd]	≒ organic compounds characterized by four rings of carbon molecules including many hormones, alkaloids and vitamins *n.* ステロイド
1252 ☐	**bronchodilator** [brɑ̀ːŋkoʊdaɪléɪtər]	≒ a medicine that widens or expands the bronchial tubes in the lungs *n.* 気管支拡張剤 *n.* bronchus（気管支），bronchitis（気管支炎）
1253 ☐	**bone marrow**	≒ soft, fatty substances in the cavities of the bones that produce blood cells 骨髄
1254 ☐	**surgery** [sə́ːrdʒəri]	≒ invasive form of medical treatment requiring the cutting of bodily tissue *n.* 外科手術，外科 *adj.* surgical
1255 ☐	**menstrual cycle**	≒ menses or menstruation, the monthly process of ovulation in women and female primates, characterized by monthly blood flow 月経周期

Chapter 2

2 Scientists Searching for Fountain of Youth

日本語訳 → p.406

例文

1 **1256 Gerontologists**, those scientists who study aging, have been trying to unravel the mysteries of aging. Aside from normal **1257 wear and tear**, they have identified three primary mechanisms, one **1258 genetic** and two chemical, that lead to the body's breakdown.

2 Genetically, the cells that compose us seem programmed to have a **1259 finite** **1260 life span**. All cells, whether from humans or worms, are able to reproduce themselves only a certain number of times. After that, their **1261 metabolic** functions begin to **1262 deteriorate**, their **1263 membranes** weaken and they (and, eventually, we) die. Researchers still don't know what drives this cellular timetable. Until they can find a way to overcome it, the lives of humans seem to be limited to about 120 years.

3 Unfortunately, two types of chemical reactions conspire to reduce our actual life span well below that theoretical limit. The first is called **1264 free-radical oxidation**. Like an electric power plant, the body produces waste products as it burns its fuel (food) for energy. These wastes are called oxygen free radicals: highly reactive oxygen **1265 molecules** that bond with virtually any biological substances they come into contact with. When free radicals bind to **1266 proteins** and membranes, they weaken **1267 tissues** and internal organs. When they bind to DNA, they can produce cancer-causing **1268 mutations**. The second destructive mechanism is called glycosylation, a process whereby sugars in the **1269 blood stream** coat proteins, causing them to stick together and bind to places they normally wouldn't. This, in turn, stiffens joints, blocks **1270 arteries**, and causes numerous other problems. Originally associated with **1271 diabetes**, it is now thought to play a major role in the aging process and researchers are hoping to develop drugs that block it.

4 Despite years of research, scientists have identified only two treatments that extend life without being aimed at specific diseases:

¹²⁷²**caloric** restriction and ¹²⁷³**hormone** replacement therapy. Gerontologists have demonstrated in animals that reducing food consumption by about 30 percent below normal levels, while maintaining adequate levels of vitamins and minerals, can lead to a 40 to 50 percent increase in life span. However, maintaining such a diet ¹²⁷⁴**regimen** requires a massive exercise of willpower that is probably beyond the reach of most people. What the researchers are seeking is a drug that would allow people to eat any of the foods they want, but enable them to still get the beneficial effects of caloric restriction. But that's probably 20 years away at least.

5 Hormone replacement therapy, in contrast, is much easier and, in terms of quality of life, more beneficial. Recent studies have shown that hormone replacement therapy, which replaces naturally decreasing amounts of such female hormones as ¹²⁷⁵**estrogen**, can help prevent a variety of ills as well as reduce wrinkling and keep teeth sound. On average, hormone replacement therapy increases ¹²⁷⁶**life expectancy** by about eight years, with the greatest benefits among women who have high risk factors for heart disease. Studies in males taking estrogen also show a sharply reduced risk of heart disease. For most men, however, the ¹²⁷⁷**feminizing effects** ¹²⁷⁸**outweigh** the potential benefits.

1256 ☐ **gerontologist** [dʒèrəntá:lədʒɪst]	≑ doctor or scientist who studies and treats the problems of aging *n.* 老人学者 *n.* gerontology
1257 ☐ **wear and tear**	≑ decay, deterioration, erosion, corrosion, depreciation *n.* 消耗,磨耗,劣化

1258 ☐ **genetic** [dʒənéṭɪk]	≒ hereditary, related to genes, ancestral *adj.* 遺伝学の，遺伝子の *n.* gene, genetics
1259 ☐ **finite** [fáɪnaɪt]	≒ limited, terminable, restricted *adj.* 有限の，限定されている *n.* finiteness, finitude ⇔ infinite
1260 ☐ **life span**	≒ longevity, length of a person's life *n.* 寿命
1261 ☐ **metabolic** [mètəbá(:)lɪk]	≒ of chemical processes in the body that sustain life functions *adj.* （新陳）代謝の *n.* metabolism
1262 ☐ **deteriorate** [dɪtíəriərèɪt]	≒ decline, degenerate, decay, erode, worsen *v.i.* 悪化する；*v.t.* を悪化させる *n.* deterioration
1263 ☐ **membrane** [mémbreɪn]	≒ a pliable, sheetlike structure acting as a lining, boundary or partition in living organism *n.* （細胞）膜，膜組織
1264 ☐ **free-radical oxidation**	≒ a chemical reaction in the body whereby oxygen molecules are formed by a waste product, which binds with other compounds to weaken tissue or cause cancerous tumors フリーラジカル酸化作用，遊離基による酸化
1265 ☐ **molecule** [má(:)lɪkjùːl]	≒ atoms bound together to form the smallest unit of a chemical compound that is capable of taking part in a chemical reaction *n.* 分子，微粒子 *adj.* molecular

1266 ☐ **protein** [próuti:n]	≒ organic compounds that consist of one or more long chains of amino acids essential for living structures, especially muscle and hair *n.* タンパク質	
1267 ☐ **tissue** [tíʃu:]	≒ the fabric of cells and their products forming the organic matter of a living thing *n.* 組織	
1268 ☐ **mutation** [mjutéɪʃən]	≒ alteration in a gene, usually negative, a change, a transformation *n.* 突然変異, 変質 *v.t., v.i.* mutate	
1269 ☐ **bloodstream** [bládstrì:m]	≒ the blood circulating through the body of an organism *n.* 血流	
1270 ☐ **artery** [á:rtəri]	≒ a blood vessel that carries oxidized blood away from the heart *n.* 動脈 *adj.* arterial ⇔ vein（静脈）	
1271 ☐ **diabetes** [dàɪəbí:təs]	≒ a disease caused by a malfunction of the pancreas, which can no longer produce the correct amount of insulin necessary for the processing of blood sugar *n.* 糖尿病 *adj., n.* diabetic	
1272 ☐ **caloric** [kəlɔ́(:)rɪk]	≒ related to the amount of energy in food or fuel *adj.* カロリーの, 熱の *n.* calorie	

1273 ☐	**hormone** [hɔ́ːrmoun]	≒ a substance in the body that regulates certain bodily processes, such as sexuality or other metabolic functions *n.* ホルモン，ホルモン物質 *adj.* hormonal
1274 ☐	**regimen** [rédʒɪmən]	≒ a prescribed diet or course of medical treatment *n.* 療法，養生，食餌療法
1275 ☐	**estrogen** [éstrədʒən]	≒ a type of steroid hormone responsible for the development and maintenance of female characteristics in the body *n.* エストロゲン（女性ホルモン）
1276 ☐	**life expectancy**	≒ life span, the statistical estimate of a person's probable life span 平均余命，寿命
1277 ☐	**feminizing effect**	≒ a process that increases or accentuates the female attributes of a person or situation 女性化の影響
1278 ☐	**outweigh** [àutwéɪ]	≒ be of greater importance or significance, overcome, win out over, outdo, predominate *v.t.* より重要である，より重い

3 Bugs Fighting Back

例文

1 Sixty years ago, the landmark discovery of penicillin as a weapon against bacterial illnesses ushered in a golden era during which [1279]**scores of** [1280]**infectious diseases** could be controlled—if not entirely wiped out. With the increasingly large [1281]**arsenal** of powerful [1282]**antibiotics** developed in [1283]**subsequent** years, [1284]**pneumonia**, [1285]**typhoid fever**, and other illnesses became curable in much of the world where drugs were readily available. Now, as a result of the overuse and misuse of these same antibiotics, drug-resistant forms of these and other diseases are staging a comeback, presenting a global threat to public health.

2 Despite medical advances, infectious diseases remain the world's leading cause of death, according to the World Health Organization, which notes that in the past two decades alone, more than 30 new [1286]**strains** of infectious diseases have appeared. Ironically, hospitals themselves are the most common incubators of many of these drug-resistant [1287]**germs**. When harmful bacteria are not completely killed, they undergo genetic mutations, multiply, and come back even stronger. Recently, even vancomycin—considered the most powerful antibiotic available—could not stop the spread of a strong strain of bacteria found in New York City.

3 Although resistance varies greatly from region to region, studies have shown that some bacterial strains are now up to 55% resistant to penicillin and up to 30% resistant to the more powerful methicillin. Drug-resistant varieties of [1288]**tuberculosis**, an infectious coughing disease, have appeared, with up to 40% of cases showing an ability to survive the initial antibiotic attack.

4 How has this come about? The causes are several: unnecessary [1289]**prescription** of antibiotics by doctors for [1290]**viral illnesses** or other [1291]**maladies** not caused by bacteria, patients failing to follow [1292]**dosage**

instructions or stopping an antibiotics course too soon, and use of antibiotics in feed supplements for livestock whose meat and milk enter the human food chain. Four common bacteria have now developed resistant forms after having been transmitted from animals to humans.

5 With the rise of international travel, many of these drug-resistant strains of bacteria are spreading quickly on a global scale. As a result, developed countries are almost as [1293]**vulnerable** as developing countries to the danger of diseases that cannot be stopped. Despite the common threat, however, there has so far been little coordinated effort to monitor the full extent of the problem across borders or to design a systematic campaign to educate doctors, patients, [1294]**livestock breeders**, and others about ways they can help prevent the spread of these [1295]**superbugs**.

6 National and international health organizations should help to focus global resources to educate the medical community about the proper use of antibiotics. Some have already begun to lead the way by sharing data and information about the resistance of specific bacterial strains while promoting the development of new antibiotics.

1279 ☐ **scores of ~**	≒ a lot of, a great deal of 多数の〜, 何十（種）の〜
1280 ☐ **infectious disease**	≒ a bacterial or viral disease that can be contracted by other organisms after contact with the diseased organism 伝染病, 感染症
1281 ☐ **arsenal** [ɑ́ːrsənəl]	≒ a store or supply, weaponry, means of defense, arms, firepower *n.* 蓄積, 在庫, 武器庫, 防衛手段

1282 ☐ antibiotic [æntibaiá(:)tɪk]	≒ drugs used to combat bacterial diseases *n.* <通常複数形>抗生物質；*adj.* 抗生作用のある、抗生物質の
1283 ☐ subsequent [sʌ́bsɪkwənt]	≒ following, next, successive, ensuing *adj.* それに続く、その次の
1284 ☐ pneumonia [njumóʊniə]	≒ a bacterial disease that attacks the lungs *n.* 肺炎
1285 ☐ typhoid fever	≒ a bacterial disease that is characterized by red spots, high fever, and severe intestinal disorders 腸チフス
1286 ☐ strain [streɪn]	≒ the breed, stock or variety of an animal or plant organism, a type of a particular disease *n.* 品種、種族、（遺伝的）素質；*v.t.*（体など）を痛める ⇒ Keep in mind the fact that too much exercise might strain your heart. （運動もあまりしすぎると心臓を悪くするかもしれない、ということを忘れないで）
1287 ☐ germ [dʒəːrm]	≒ a harmful bacteria that causes disease or infection in its host organism *n.* 細菌、微生物
1288 ☐ tuberculosis [tjubəːrkjulóʊsəs]	≒ a disease of the lungs *n.* 結核
1289 ☐ prescription [prɪskrɪ́pʃən]	≒ a dosage of some medicinal drug issued by a licensed doctor or other medical practitioner *n.* 処方、処方箋 *v.t.* prescribe *adj.* prescriptive（規定する、規範的な）
1290 ☐ viral illness	≒ a disease caused by a virus rather than a bacterium ウィルス感染症

1291 ☐ **malady** [mǽlədi]	≒ illness, disease, sickness, pathology *n.* 病気，弊害
1292 ☐ **dosage** [dóusɪdʒ]	≒ the amount of a medicinal drug a person is instructed to consume at one sitting, the overall amount of a medicinal drug one is authorized to administer or consume *n.* （1回分の）服用量 *n.* dose（一服）
1293 ☐ **vulnerable** [vʌ́lnərəbl]	≒ open, weak, exposed, defenseless, unguarded *adj.* 弱い，攻撃されやすい，傷つきやすい
1294 ☐ **livestock breeder**	≒ a person who raises cattle or other farm animals for profit 畜産業者
1295 ☐ **superbug** [súːpərbʌ̀g]	≒ a strain of unusually powerful bacteria that is resistant to antibiotic treatment *n.* 強力微生物

4 To Cure Snoring

例文

1 "Laugh and the world laughs with you. Snore and you sleep alone." So wrote British author Anthony Burgess. But for the 25 percent of adults who have a chronic snoring problem, sleeping solo is only a small drawback compared with the more serious health problems that may arise from this often [1296]**satirized** malady.

2 The condition is caused by breathing obstructions in the airways of sufferers. As air reaches the passages at the back of the throat, it is obstructed by the collapsible structures where the tongue meets the soft [1297]**palate**, from which dangles the loose piece of flesh known as the uvula. When these body parts strike each other and vibrate, the characteristic grunts and [1298]**wheezes** of snoring are produced.

3 This obstruction may arise from a number of factors: poor muscle tone in the tongue and throat which can result from drinking alcohol, taking [1299]**sleep-inducing drugs**, or just a very deep sleep. This leads to the tongue falling backwards into the airway or the throat muscles [1300]**contracting** inwards. Another cause is excessive bulkiness of throat tissue—large [1301]**tonsils** or [1302]**adenoids**, for example—or simply an overly fleshy neck as a result of [1303]**obesity**. Sometimes the structure of the palate or uvula may be unusually long and both may dangle too far into the airway, or there may be a [1304]**blockage** in the [1305]**nasal airways** from causes such as a cold, [1306]**hay fever**, or allergies.

4 In extreme cases, the condition of sleep apnea may occur. This happens when loud snoring is interrupted by frequent periods of totally obstructed breathing. Sufferers may stop breathing for 10 seconds at a time, up to seven times in an hour. Sleep apnea patients are never able to fully relax and gain the benefits of deep sleep. In the short term, this leads to daytime sleepiness and impaired job performance—and in the long term, to high blood pressure and an enlarged heart.

Chapter 2

5 The United States Patents Office has over 300 anti-snoring aids registered, but none have proven totally effective. Surgery has also been developed for extreme cases, but this is [1307]**invasive** and costly. Recently, however, Dr. Scott E. Brietzke has developed a new technique which he believes may eradicate snoring for most sufferers. Brietzke's injection snoreplasty involves an injection of [1308]**sodium** tetradecyl sulfate into the soft palate. This chemical promotes the formation of scar tissue which stiffens the structures at the back of the throat, thus preventing the [1309]**fluttering** of the palate that creates snoring.

6 Of the 27 patients treated so far with Brietzke's technique, only two responded that snoring is still a problem. As for [1310]**side effects**, the patients reported that they experienced mild discomfort similar to a sore throat that lasted between two and three days, but that it did not interfere with their work. Although an injection into the palate sounds painful, even the most sensitive patient rated the discomfort as merely a 3 on a scale of 1 to 10. Besides, who wouldn't be prepared to suffer a little short-term pain for the chance of a quiet and restful sleep?

1296 ☐ **satirize** [sǽṭəràɪz]	≒ subject a person or thing to ridicule through the use of sarcasm or abusive irony, make fun of *v.t.* をからかう、を風刺する *n.* satire *adj.* satirical
1297 ☐ **palate** [pǽlət]	≒ the tissue of the mouth that contains the taste buds *n.* 口蓋、味覚 *adj.* palatal
1298 ☐ **wheeze** [*h*wiːz]	≒ heavy breath producing a high pitched sound *n.* ゼイゼイいう息 [音] ; *v.i.* ゼイゼイ息を切らす

1299 ☐	**sleep-inducing drugs**	≒ chemical substances that induce sleep in anyone who consumes them, soporific drugs 睡眠薬
1300 ☐	**contract** [kəntrǽkt]	≒ collapse or shrink from within, diminish, draw together, constrict, compress *v.i.* 収縮する；契約を結ぶ；*v.t.*（重い病気）にかかる ⇒ Much later that night it was found that my son had contracted whooping cough. （その晩ずっと遅くなって，私の息子が百日ぜきにかかっていたことが分かった） *n.* contraction
1301 ☐	**tonsils** [tá(:)nsəlz]	≒ two masses of lymphoid tissue found in the throat at the base of the tongue, one on each side *n.* 扁桃腺
1302 ☐	**adenoids** [ǽdənɔ̀ɪdz]	≒ a mass of lymphatic tissue found at the back of the nose and throat, sometimes impeding clear speech or breathing in young children *n.* アデノイド，咽頭扁桃腺
1303 ☐	**obesity** [oʊbíːsəti]	≒ excessive fatness, corpulence, grossness, fleshiness *n.* 肥満 *adj.* obese
1304 ☐	**blockage** [blá(:)kɪdʒ]	≒ obstruction, obstacle, impediment, barrier *n.* 障害（物），封鎖 *v.t.* block
1305 ☐	**nasal airways**	≒ the cavities that carry air from the nostrils to the throat, nasal passages *n.* 鼻の空気の通り道

Chapter 2

1306 ☐ **hay fever**	≒ an allergic condition caused by pollen, causing a running nose, sneezing, burning eyes, coughing, difficulty in breathing and other cold-like symptoms 花粉症
1307 ☐ **invasive** [ɪnvéɪsɪv]	≒ intrusive; in medicine, related to the introduction of instruments or other objects into bodily cavities or to the cutting of body tissue for medical purposes *adj.*（メスなどの器具が体に）押し入る、侵略的な *v.t.* invade
1308 ☐ **sodium** [sóʊdiəm]	≒ a silver-white metallic element *n.* ナトリウム
1309 ☐ **flutter** [flʌ́tər]	≒ flap, flop, wave, waver, oscillate *v.i.* 速く不規則に動く、震える
1310 ☐ **side effect**	≒ a secondary consequence of medication, usually unintended and negative *n.* ＜通例複数形＞副作用、副産物

5 Blood Substitutes

例文

1 There is no commodity more precious than blood, since having enough is the difference between life and death. Too often, hospitals have not had enough. Since the seventeenth century, doctors have experimented with blood substitutes, giving ¹³¹¹**transfusions** of everything from animal blood to oil and even milk to hapless patients, but a safe and effective substitute has remained ¹³¹²**elusive** until just recently.

2 In May of 1999, doctors at an American hospital attempted a radical new procedure on a patient whose ¹³¹³**immune system** had mysteriously begun to attack her ¹³¹⁴**red blood cells**. With no known way to counter the patient's loss of red blood cells, doctors had little hope for the dangerously ¹³¹⁵**anemic** young woman. In one last desperate attempt, Dr. George Giacoppe, head of the ¹³¹⁶**intensive-care unit**, contacted one of the companies attempting to develop an effective blood substitute. With the patient near death, Giacoppe obtained permission from authorities and began giving his patient transfusions of Hemopure, an experimental blood substitute derived from highly purified cow's blood. Chances for success were low—the blood substitute was still in ¹³¹⁷**clinical trial**, and no substitute had ever passed this stage. Amazingly, it worked. Hemopure carried badly needed oxygen to the patient's anemic cells without provoking an attack from her immune system. A few hours later, she was sitting up and chatting with doctors.

3 If health regulators give the go-ahead for blood-substitute usage, it will be none too soon. Due to the fear of contamination from such diseases as ¹³¹⁸**AIDS** and ¹³¹⁹**mad cow disease**, restrictions on who can donate blood have been expanding steadily. As a result, blood is in short supply. Moreover, the substitutes also promise several benefits over normal blood transfusions. They do not ¹³²⁰**spoil** as quickly as human blood and do not require refrigeration. Doctors would no longer have to worry about the deadly mistake of mismatching the blood types of donors and patients. And, importantly, substitutes are less likely to be infected by human viruses.

4 It was once believed that the need for new blood sources would spur faster approval of substitutes by the FDA, America's main health regulatory agency. But the head of that agency, Abdu Alayash, says that speedy approval is not necessarily desirable. The substitutes now being considered still do not perfectly replicate the role of blood. While they do carry oxygen even more efficiently than red blood cells, they do not offer the protective role of white blood cells, which fight disease. The oxygen-carrying particles in the substitutes are much smaller than red blood cells, which enables them to slip through [1321]clogged arteries—a real benefit. But researchers wonder if these same properties may also cause negative side effects. Researchers are also concerned about the apparent tendency of substitutes to increase blood pressure in [1322]recipients. "These products could do harm, and we have nothing to compare them with," said Alayash. He believes that cases like those of Dr. Giacoppe's patient are no substitute for long-term, [1323]in-depth clinical trials that test hundreds of patients.

1311 ☐ **transfusion** [trænsfjúːʒən]	≒ the transference of blood from the veins of one person to those of another *n.* 注入, 輸血
1312 ☐ **elusive** [ɪlúːsɪv]	≒ slippery, evasive, tricky *adj.* 捉えにくい, 理解しにくい, 巧みに逃げる

1313 ☐	**immune system**	≒ the self-defense system of the body, largely involving the creation of antibodies to fight invasive organisms 免疫システム
1314 ☐	**red blood cells**	≒ the cells in the blood that carry oxygen throughout the body to sustain life 赤血球 ⇔ white blood cells（白血球）
1315 ☐	**anemic** [əníːmɪk]	≒ having a deficiency of oxygen in the blood stream due to too few red blood cells or reduced hemoglobin in the blood *adj.* 貧血の *n.* anemia
1316 ☐	**intensive-care unit**	≒ a special facility in a hospital to care for critically ill patients 集中治療室，ICU
1317 ☐	**clinical trial**	≒ an experimental process whereby new medical treatments and new drugs are tested under careful scientific controls 臨床実［試］験
1318 ☐	**AIDS** [eɪdz]	≒ Acquired Immune Deficiency Syndrome, a viral disease that destroys the body's immune system *n.* エイズ（後天性免疫不全症候群）
1319 ☐	**mad cow disease**	≒ Bovine Spongiform Encephalopathy, a disease that destroys the brain in cattle 狂牛病，BSE
1320 ☐	**spoil** [spɔɪl]	≒ go bad, go off, perish *v.i.* だめになる，台なしになる，腐る
1321 ☐	**clogged artery**	≒ the blockage of a blood vessel carrying blood to or from the heart 動脈がつまること，動脈硬化

1322 ☐ recipient
[rɪsípiənt]

≒ the receiver of something, such as a transplanted organ or a particular treatment
n. 受容者，レシピエント（ドナーから臓器提供を受ける人）

1323 ☐ in-depth
[ìndépθ]

≒ deeper level, extensive, thorough, leaving no stone unturned
adj. 詳細な，徹底的な

1 Virus Writers

コンピュータ

日本語訳 → p.411

例文

1 Virus writers create the ¹³²⁴**digital pests** that ¹³²⁵**cripple** computer systems and cause millions of dollars in damage. While much has been written about viruses, little has been known about the writers themselves until recently. Sarah Gordon, a computer security expert, has done extensive research into the psychology of virus writers, and what she has found may surprise you. Because the skills required for virus writing are not nearly as demanding as those required for ¹³²⁶**hacking**, the perpetrators are often very young—some only 10 or 11 years old. That's why virus writers find themselves on a lower ¹³²⁷**rung** of the underground technical ¹³²⁸**hierarchy**. As these ¹³²⁹**sinister** ¹³³⁰**whiz kids** get older, they usually move beyond virus writing, working their way through the ranks to take up other technical pursuits.

2 Gordon also discovered that for some people, entry into the world of virus writing is unintentional. By playing around with ¹³³¹**self-replicating** programming codes, perhaps in the process of investigating viruses and their effects on computer systems, ¹³³²**well-meaning** programmers can ¹³³³**unleash** new viruses. Nevertheless, most virus writers carefully plan the chaos they create, whether in pursuit of ¹³³⁴**notoriety** or to make a political or personal statement. Writers bent on destruction frequently make use of the latest technology, often building on existing viruses. That's why we can predict that future outbreaks will be increasingly complex and ¹³³⁵**devastating**.

3 How should society respond? According to Gordon, this depends on the age of the offender. In her studies, she found that adult virus writers are most effectively deterred by fear of punishment. "For adults," says Gordon, "it's not the laws that are important, but their perception of the likelihood of being prosecuted under those laws." Minors, on the other hand, are unlikely to be intimidated by the threat of legal intervention.

Chapter 2

Education is a more effective ¹³³⁶**countermeasure**, and Gordon argues that society has a moral obligation to teach children how to behave on the computer and on the Internet.

1324 ☐ **digital pest**	≒ a computer disease, a kind of plague that attacks computer hardware or software programs and damages data デジタルペスト，（ウィルスによる）コンピュータ伝染病
1325 ☐ **cripple** [krípl]	≒ destroy or damage the ability of something to carry out its functions *v.t.* を無力化する，の機能を麻痺させる
1326 ☐ **hacking** [hǽkɪŋ]	≒ illegal breaking into a computer to read, steal or damage its data or ability to function *n.* ハッキング（コンピュータに不正に侵入すること）
1327 ☐ **rung** [rʌŋ]	≒ a certain level in a hierarchy, a step or phase in a process that moves from beginning to advanced phases （社会的な）段階，（はしごの）段
1328 ☐ **hierarchy** [háɪərɑ̀ːrki]	≒ chain of commands, order from top to bottom, ranking system *n.* ヒエラルキー，階層制度 *adj.* hierarchical
1329 ☐ **sinister** [sínɪstər]	≒ evil, malevolent, perverse, pernicious *adj.* 邪悪な，不吉な

コンピュータ

1330 ☐ **whiz kid**	≒ very young experts at computer operations, including hacking 神童，達人の子ども（特にコンピュータ操作に）長けた子ども
1331 ☐ **self-replicating**	≒ something that can generate copies of itself or generate a repetition of a particular process *adj.* 自己増殖できる
1332 ☐ **well-meaning** [wèlmíːniŋ]	≒ benevolent, of positive intention, desirous of doing good *adj.* 善意で行なった，善意の
1333 ☐ **unleash** [ʌ̀nlíːʃ]	≒ release, stimulate into action, put in motion (usually considered negative) *v.t.* （抑えていたもの）を解放する，を発散させる
1334 ☐ **notoriety** [nòutəráɪəṭi]	≒ infamous reputation, infamy, disrepute *n.* 悪評，悪名 *adj.* notorious
1335 ☐ **devastating** [dévəstèɪtɪŋ]	≒ with terrible effects, horrible, damaging *adj.* 破壊的な，痛烈な，ひどい *v.t.* devastate *n.* devastation
1336 ☐ **countermeasure** [káʊntərmèʒər]	≒ an action taken to nullify or overcome a previous action *n.* 対抗策，防御策

Chapter 2

2 Cheaters on the Internet

日本語訳 → p.412

例文

1 ¹³³⁷**Plagiarism** on college campuses is nothing new. But in a ¹³³⁸**new twist** to the age-old problem, some companies are using the Internet to market ready-made ¹³³⁹**term papers**.

2 Incensed over the wide availability of this cyberscholarship, educators are ¹³⁴⁰**waging war against** the high-tech term paper mills. Under a new Texas law backed by colleges, companies can be fined $500 for selling papers over the Internet. In another example, Boston University is ¹³⁴¹**suing** eight on-line companies **for** fraud and ¹³⁴²**racketeering**.

3 Educators defend these efforts in the name of ¹³⁴³**academic integrity**. But focusing their fury on the source of the scholarship—instead of its fraudulent use by students—misses the point. They let college kids escape responsibility for plagiarism, a serious offense, while trying to police the ¹³⁴⁴**amorphous** world of ¹³⁴⁵**on-line scholarship**.

4 The Web sites offer term papers on a wide range of subjects, and posting and selling research on the Internet doesn't constitute fraud. Canned term papers are easy to obtain ¹³⁴⁶**off line**, too, through campus-based entrepreneurs and mail-order companies that place classified ads in student publications. Even if educators could shutter every electronic term paper factory in the USA, they couldn't stop them from joining the 40% of Internet sites that are based outside the United States.

5 Prosecuting Internet-based term paper mills raises serious constitutional questions. Last year, the Supreme Court struck down a federal law designed to protect kids from ¹³⁴⁷**cyberporn**. There's no reason to think courts will ¹³⁴⁸**be** more **tolerant of** attempts to censure free speech to ¹³⁴⁹**fend off** cyberplagiarists.

6 The most sensible way to stop plagiarism is to target students looking for a shortcut. Whether a student ¹³⁵⁰**cribs** material from cyberspace or mail-order catalogue, professors say ready-made term papers are easy to spot. They stand out as off-point and superficial, particularly to professors who give original assignments and do their own grading.

7 With or without the Internet, there will always be students looking for ways to beat the education system. By targeting the source of the faked research instead of the person ¹³⁵¹**passing it off**, students are denied a lesson in the value of high standards—in ethics as much as in scholarship.

1337 ☐ **plagiarism** [pléɪdʒərìzm]	≒ the theft of ideas, information or intellectual property without permission or without acknowledging the source *n.* 盗用，剽窃（ひょうせつ） *v.t.,v.i.* plagiarize
1338 ☐ **new twist**	≒ a new way of doing or looking at something 新案，新方式
1339 ☐ **term paper**	≒ academic reports due at the end of an academic term 学期末レポート
1340 ☐ **wage war against ~**	≒ fight against, struggle against, compete with agressively ~に対し戦争をする，~と戦う
1341 ☐ **sue *A* for *B***	≒ take legal action to seek compensation for some financial or other damage done to someone *A* を *B* のかどで訴える

1342	**racketeering** [rǽkətíəriŋ]	≒ blackmailing or illegal activities (by a criminal or a swindler) *n.* 恐喝行為 *v.i., n.* racketeer
1343	**academic integrity**	≒ maintaining high ethical standards in matters related to the profession of teaching and scholarship 学問上の高潔さ
1344	**amorphous** [əmɔ́ːrfəs]	≒ lacking organization, shapeless, ruleless *adj.* はっきりしない, 形のない, 無秩序な
1345	**on-line scholarship**	≒ any academic activity pursued through the Internet, taking a course of study via the Internet オンライン上の学問の世界
1346	**off line**	≒ disconnected from the Internet or World Wide Web オフラインで［の］
1347	**cyberporn** [sáɪbərpɔ̀ːrn]	≒ obscene material [pornography] that is available on the Internet サイバー［インターネット上の］ポルノ
1348	**be tolerant of ~**	≒ accepting, open-minded to, permissive of ~に寛容である *v.t.* tolerate *n.* tolerance
1349	**fend off ~**	≒ fight against, struggle against （打撃・質問など）をかわす, を払いのける
1350	**crib** [krɪb]	≒ steal or plagiarize information (for an academic report or examination) *v.t.* を盗作する, を剽窃（ひょうせつ）する
1351	**pass off ~**	≒ forge, fabricate, sell ~ as authentic だまして~を通用させる, ~を＜~だと＞偽る ＜as ~＞

コンピュータ

3 The New Auction Arena

例文

1 Only a few short years ago, stock-market analysts wondered how anyone could make money from the Internet. Sure, millions of people were ¹³⁵²**logging on**, but relatively little cash was ¹³⁵³**changing hands** on all those free sites with winking ¹³⁵⁴**banner ads**. Since then, however, the Net has transformed itself into the ultimate global bazaar, and the stock prices of the leading companies are soaring into the ¹³⁵⁵**stratosphere**. Among the fastest growing are online auctioneers, who offer free access to buyers while ¹³⁵⁶**charging** small **commissions** to sellers. The pioneer and leader, eBay, lists more than two million items daily—in more than fifteen hundred categories—that nearly four million registered users bid for over the Internet.

2 ¹³⁵⁷**Bidding for** an item at eBay is similar to placing a bid at a traditional auction, with a few variations. First, a bidder clicks on a category or runs a search for an item—say an autographed picture of Elvis Presley. If such an item is being auctioned, she can make a secret maximum bid for it—say $50. If someone bids $20, the site automatically places a ¹³⁵⁸**counterbid** on her behalf for the stated minimum increment—say $20.50. If she is still the highest bidder when the auction closes, she contacts the seller by e-mail to arrange for shipment and then sends her payment. Not long after, if all goes well, a signed Elvis photo hangs on her wall. And selling is just as simple. Set up shop at an online auction house and you can offer anything from fishing lures to Ferraris.

3 Aren't there dangers, one might wonder? The online-auction equivalent of snake-oil salesmen? Undoubtedly there are, but satisfied customers seem to far ¹³⁵⁹**outnumber** ¹³⁶⁰**rip-off victims**. And before you bid on the Brooklyn Bridge, note that eBay offers a feedback system whereby potential buyers can judge a seller's reputation by reading comments about past transactions. Other safeguards include an escrow system that allows successful bidders to place their payments in a secure account until purchased items are delivered. Also, though eBay does not try to police every transaction—an impossibility given the thousands of deals done daily—the company has tried to [1361]**crack down on** the more flagrant abuses, including ingenious software programs called "bid bots" that jump into an auction at the last possible moment to make a higher bid at the lowest possible increment.

4 Potential rip-offs aside, many bidders find themselves victims of their own obsessions. Instead of spending days, weeks, or even years poking around flea markets and thrift shops for that antique glass vase that graced your grandmother's cupboard, you can find one—or even dozens—instantly on an auction site. Soon your own cupboards are bulging with antique glassware and your bank account is running low. But don't despair. There is a way to [1362]**replenish** it—become an auction-site seller!

1352 ☐ **log on**	≒ connect to the Internet, log in ログオンする，インターネットに接続する
1353 ☐ **change hands**	≒ exchange information or money from one person or group to another （金が）やりとりされる，所有主が変わる
1354 ☐ **banner ad**	≒ advertisement that highlights some product with a flashy visual display that blinks on and off バナー広告

1355 ☐	**stratosphere** [strǽtəsfìər]	≒ figuratively, reaching great heights or accomplishing a great achievement, a level of the earth's atmosphere far above the surface of the earth between the troposphere and the mesosphere *n.* 最高位，成層圏 *adj.* stratospheric
1356 ☐	**charge a commission**	≒ charge a fee usually based on a percentage of some sale 手数料を課す
1357 ☐	**bid for ~**	≒ offer to pay a certain sum for a product in a competitive auction, attempt to do something or get something ～に入札する，～を得ようと努める
1358 ☐	**counterbid** [káuntərbìd]	≒ a bid in response to a previous bid, a competitive offer to perform a task or pay a sum, in response to a previous offer *n.* 対抗買い注文
1359 ☐	**outnumber** [àutnʌ́mbər]	≒ to have greater numbers of people or other entities than an already established number *v.t.* より数でまさる，より多い
1360 ☐	**rip-off victim**	≒ a person who has been cheated or defrauded 詐欺の被害者
1361 ☐	**crack down on ~**	≒ enforce the law more strictly upon, become less flexible and more severe in enforcing a rule or regulation on ～を厳しく取り締まる，～に厳しく法を適用する
1362 ☐	**replenish** [rɪplénɪʃ]	≒ replace something that has been lost *v.t.* を補充する，を補給する *n.* replenishment

1 Don't Monkey with Female Peacekeepers

1 If you're looking for a criminal class in the animal kingdom, look no further than the higher male **primate**. Gorilla males coolly murder infants fathered by other males to free up nursing mothers for breeding; rival gangs of chimpanzees wage bloody border wars to protect their **turf** or enlarge their harems; and the human male has a criminal record too long to contemplate. The latest research, however, shows that in one species of great ape, the bonobo, males engage in none of this **barbarism**. Bonobo society is one in which behavioral limits are set, the peace generally kept, and transgressors quickly punished. The reason for such order is simple: Among bonobos it is the females that enforce the laws.

2 While female chimpanzees (relatives to the bonobos) form only casual bonds, female bonobos establish lifelong relationships, spending much of their time socializing with one another. For males with an **aggressive bent**, such a powerful sisterhood **spells trouble**. If a mature bonobo male shows a female unwanted attention, she has merely to sound a distress call to bring an avenging group of females quickly to the scene. Males that misbehave at a feeding site, where they may try to hoard a **cache** of fruit, are similarly intimidated and chased off. Even males that reserve their aggression solely for one another find their behavior unrewarded. The whole purpose of such **macho combat** is to secure breeding rights to females, but since bonobo females are powerful enough to resist even the strongest male, the results of the contest mean nothing.

3 How such female-policed **pacifism** evolved is unclear, but the answer appears to lie in the food supply. Chimpanzees eat a rich man's diet of meat and ripe fruit, while gorillas can get by on an austere menu of leaves and stems. Bonobos are adapted to both types of food, and this **confers an advantage**: They can stay in one place and survive on whatever's available, allowing them to form more or less permanent groups. Such ¹³⁷²<u>lifelong homesteading</u> doesn't do much for naturally competitive males, but for females it provides the chance to form the kinds of alliances that free them from ¹³⁷³<u>overbearing</u> males.

4 For human beings the cultural lesson from this is obvious. Feminist groups have long argued that many of humanity's most persistent problems, from war to domestic abuse, stem directly from the male tendency to settle questions first by ¹³⁷⁴<u>coming to blows</u> and only later ¹³⁷⁵<u>coming to terms</u>. The success of this primate suggests that power sharing between the sexes may make political sense.

1363 ☐	**primate** [práɪmeɪt]	≒ an animal of the same mammalian order as homo sapiens, including monkeys and apes *n.* 霊長類，霊長目の動物
1364 ☐	**turf** [təːrf]	≒ area or region occupied and controlled by an animal, soil, earth *n.* 縄張り，芝生
1365 ☐	**barbarism** [báːrbərìzm]	≒ absence of civilized behavior, vicious, cruel and violent behavior *n.* 野蛮行為，野蛮，未開状態 *adj.* barbaric, barbarian
1366 ☐	**aggressive bent**	≒ a tendency toward violent or pushy behavior 攻撃的な性向
1367 ☐	**spell trouble**	≒ be likely to create problems 面倒なことになる

Chapter 2

1368 ☐ **cache** [kæʃ]	≒ a hiding place for keeping provisions or valuables, repository, storage place *n.* （隠してある）貯蔵品，隠し場所
1369 ☐ **macho combat**	≒ aggressive male fighting 雄の闘争
1370 ☐ **pacifism** [pǽsɪfìzm]	≒ opposition to the use of force under any circumstances, behavior that is peaceful and lacks aggression *n.* 平和主義，不戦論 *v.t.* pacify *n.* pacifist
1371 ☐ **confer an advantage**	≒ provide the means to make someone or something stronger, provide something that gives an edge to or helps a competitor 利点を生む，優位を与える
1372 ☐ **lifelong homesteading**	≒ living in the same place or with the same social group permanently 生涯同じ場所に定住すること
1373 ☐ **overbearing** [òʊvərbéərɪŋ]	≒ aggressive, pushy *adj.* 横柄な，威圧的な
1374 ☐ **come to blows**	≒ result in a violent conflict 暴力沙汰になる，殴り合いを始める
1375 ☐ **come to terms**	≒ reach an agreement or settlement 和解する，折り合う

科学・テクノロジー

2 Astronomy and Reality

例文

1 Sometimes astronomy is unreal. Really.

2 Those spectacular pictures from the Hubble Space Telescope of exploding stars and ¹³⁷⁶**nebulous** gas clouds and stars emerging from ¹³⁷⁷**dusty cocoons** are all—to one extent or another—computer-enhanced. The images are processed, ¹³⁷⁸**spruced up**, airbrushed, and painted like so many Hollywood stars.

3 People sometimes look through ordinary backyard telescopes and feel betrayed. They don't see enormous green and purple glowing clouds of gas. Saturn looks mostly black and white. But is it deception, really?

4 Curiously, when Galileo first looked through his ¹³⁷⁹**crude** telescope and saw mountains on the moon and moons around Jupiter, people thought he was seeing an optical illusion. His telescope, they said, was creating distortions. Anything you couldn't see with your naked eye, in other words, wasn't really real.

5 Today, we don't worry about the reality of the things we see through lenses. In fact, many of us walk around with lenses floating on our eyeballs or ¹³⁸⁰**perched** on our noses, the better to see the world. Moreover, we know that the images we see in our mind's eye are exhaustively processed by our brains. The brain rights the upside-down images on our ¹³⁸¹**retinas**, fills in blind spots, erases unnecessary "noise" such as ¹³⁸²**blood vessels** and floating bits of fluff from our field of vision. The brain adjusts for motion, "corrects" colors, and puts things in their proper perspective.

6 In their own way, that's just what the Hubble scientists do. The astronomers have to clean up "noise" in the images, such as cosmic ray tracks, and clear up distortions. What's more, the Hubble images come down in black and white. They're processed through different filters sensitive to different colors. The astronomers put them back together.

That's also more or less the way the human eye works—color-sensitive cells process images, which the brain reassembles.

7 So it would be difficult to argue that the Hubble images are somehow dishonest. After all, there's no such thing as an unprocessed, unfiltered image. For that matter, there's no such thing as an [1383]**unprocessed** [1384]**sense perception**, be it sight, sound, touch, taste, or smell. The truth of the matter is hard to explain: Yes, the Hubble images are processed, filtered, reassembled, artificially colored, and generally [1385]**jazzed up**. But they are no more jazzed up than the images we see with our own two eyes.

1376 ☐ **nebulous** [nébjʊləs]	≒ like or having the appearance of interstellar dust, cloudlike, belonging to some luminous material that glows when observed *adj.* 星雲状の，不透明な，あいまいな
1377 ☐ **dusty cocoon**	≒ forms in outer space made of stellar debris that appear to be cocoons full of dust ちり状の繭（のようなもの）
1378 ☐ **spruce up (〜)**	≒ improve and clarify the appearance of something, clean up and embellish 〜をこぎれいにする，身なりを整える，めかす
1379 ☐ **crude** [kru:d]	≒ unrefined, rough, primitive *adj.* 粗末な，粗製の，天然のままの
1380 ☐ **perch** [pəːrtʃ]	≒ set or place (as a bird does itself on a tree limb) *v.t.* （人・物）を＜〜に＞据える，止まらせる ＜on 〜＞；*v.i.* （鳥が枝などに）止まる

1381 ☐ **retina** [rétənə]	≒ the light-sensitive membrane that reflects light and allows the eye to transmit images of the external world to the brain *n.* 網膜	
1382 ☐ **blood vessel**	≒ the channel or conduit for blood to circulate around the body 血管	
1383 ☐ **unprocessed** [ʌ̀nprá(:)sest]	≒ pure and unadulterated, unchanged, directly perceived without alteration or change of any kind *adj.* 未処理の，加工されていない ⇔ processed ⇒ The processed cheese I had there was absolutely first-rate. (私がそこで食べたプロセスチーズは間違いなく一級品だった)	
1384 ☐ **sense perception**	≒ the ability of special organs in the body to recognize stimuli from the physical world: seeing, hearing, smelling, tasting, touching 感覚，五感	
1385 ☐ **jazz up ～**	≒ make something more interesting and attractive ～を多彩にする，～をおもしろくする	

3 Life on Other Planets

1 The search for life on other planets is a quest of vast intrinsic interest, but of extreme difficulty in practice. Its root logic, though, is simple enough: If life was brewed on the planet Earth in a ¹³⁸⁶**primordial** soup of chemicals 4 billion to 4.5 billion years ago, why shouldn't it have happened on at least one other planet in the universe, too? Astronomers calculate that hundreds of millions of Earth-like planets must exist throughout the universe.

2 Space exploration has not yet turned up life elsewhere: Mars is dry and ¹³⁸⁷**sterile**, Venus is a raging ¹³⁸⁸**inferno**, and Jupiter is a ball of gas. Scientists who are skeptical about life's ever having arisen elsewhere have ¹³⁸⁹**had a strong case**, given the precise conditions that used to seem essential for life to develop and survive. Planets that are too small cannot retain an atmosphere at all. Those that are too hot or cold have no liquid water. And without water, the chemical process of ¹³⁹⁰**photosynthesis**, which converts sunlight into chemical energy, is impossible. Without an atmosphere of oxygen, the chemical reactions that allow a cell to extract energy from other chemicals cannot normally run, either.

3 But recent findings from our own planet have led scientists to wonder if they have taken too ¹³⁹¹**parochial** a view of life. ¹³⁹²**Microbes** have been discovered ¹³⁹³**thriving** under circumstances once thought impossible: in ¹³⁹⁴**volcanic vents**, in hot springs, in ¹³⁹⁵**geysers**. The rocks and the cold waters deep beneath the surface of Antarctica and the ¹³⁹⁶**subterranean ground** water in the Columbia River Basin may harbor ¹³⁹⁷**terrestrial** models for the rise of life on Mars and other planets. And some tantalizing, if still highly controversial, evidence from Mars at least hints that some similar forms of life may indeed have arisen there, even if they subsequently died out.

4 Evidence of life in ¹³⁹⁸**inhospitable** environments began to pile up in recent years as highly sensitive ¹³⁹⁹**gene-sequencing techniques** made it possible to identify ¹⁴⁰⁰**microorganisms** that could not grow in laboratory conditions. Deep-diving submarines have found organisms whose metabolism is powered by heat from ¹⁴⁰¹**geothermal** sources. Geologists boring two miles below the Columbia River Basin have found organisms that ¹⁴⁰²**propagate** using ¹⁴⁰³**hydrogen**—created from a ¹⁴⁰⁴**chemical reaction** between ¹⁴⁰⁵**basalt** and ground water—as their energy source.

5 Some researchers argue that many of these microbes belong to a distinct and previously unrecognized branch of life called "archaea," perhaps the oldest life forms on Earth. If they are correct, then life did not absolutely need the warm, hospitable primordial soup to form, but could have formed in extreme, hostile environments, too. This would make it possible for archaea-like microbes to exist in extreme circumstances below the surface where water would remain in a liquid state—and that would mean that there could be life on Mars.

1386 ☐ **primordial** [praɪmɔ́ːrdiəl]	≒ basic, fundamental, primitive, at the beginning *adj.* 原始の，最初から存在する，原初期の，根源的な
1387 ☐ **sterile** [stérəl]	≒ void of life, incapable of sustaining life, incapable of biological reproduction *adj.* 不毛の，不妊の，無菌の *v.t.* sterilize (を殺菌する) *n.* sterilization (不毛にすること，殺菌) ⇔ fertile
1388 ☐ **inferno** [ɪnfɔ́ːrnoʊ]	≒ a very hot, burning place, a raging fire *n.* 地獄さながらの場所，灼熱地獄，大火 *adj.* infernal

1389 ☐	**have a strong case**	≒ have a valid argument for something, be persuasive 言い分が十分ある、申し立てをする ⇔ have a weak case
1390 ☐	**photosynthesis** [fòʊṭoʊsínθəsɪs]	≒ the process by which chlorophyll cells of green plants produce energy from light and make organic compounds out of inorganic compounds *n.* 光合成
1391 ☐	**parochial** [pəróʊkiəl]	≒ restricted, limited, narrow-minded *adj.*（考えなどが）狭い、偏狭な
1392 ☐	**microbe** [máɪkroʊb]	≒ a microorganism that can only be seen through a microscope *n.* 微生物、細菌
1393 ☐	**thrive** [θraɪv]	≒ flourish, prosper, able to reproduce in great numbers *v.i.* 繁茂する、成長する、栄える *adj.* thriving
1394 ☐	**volcanic vent**	≒ a passage or opening in a volcano that emits volcanic gas and other material 火山の噴火口
1395 ☐	**geyser** [gáɪzər]	≒ a natural spring under pressure that periodically ejects water and steam into the air *n.* 間欠泉
1396 ☐	**subterranean** [sʌ̀btəréɪniən]	≒ under the surface of the earth, beneath ground level *adj.* 地下の、地中の
1397 ☐	**terrestrial** [təréstriəl]	≒ related to earth, related to the soil or ground-level (in contrast to trees or objects above the ground) *adj.* 地球（上）の、陸上の、陸生の ⇔ celestial（空の、天上の）

1398 □ **inhospitable** [ìnhá(:)spɪṭəbl]	≒ unfriendly (to life forms, referring to a domain or atmospheric condition in which life cannot survive or can survive only with difficulty) *adj.* 過酷な，荒れ果てた，宿るところのない，無愛想な
1399 □ **gene-sequencing technique**	≒ a method that can determine the order of genes in an organism 遺伝子配列技術
1400 □ **microorganism** [màɪkrouɔ́:rɡənɪzəm]	≒ a tiny, microscopic animal that cannot be seen by the naked eye *n.* 微生物
1401 □ **geothermal** [dʒì:ouθə́:rməl]	≒ source of heat produced by volcanic activity *adj.* 地熱の
1402 □ **propagate** [prá(:)pəɡèɪt]	≒ reproduce, increase their own numbers, replicate *v.i.* 増殖する；*v.t.* を繁殖させる
1403 □ **hydrogen** [háɪdrədʒən]	≒ the lightest and most abundant gaseous element known to exist *n.* 水素
1404 □ **chemical reaction**	≒ the process in which two or more chemical substances come in contact with each other and combine to form another substance, produce a by-product of some kind, or are changed in some other way 化学反応
1405 □ **basalt** [bəsɔ́:lt]	≒ a hard, dense, dark volcanic rock *n.* 玄武岩

Chapter 2

4 Small Wonders

日本語訳 → p.418

例文

1 Al Globus, a project manager at Ames Research Center (a division of NASA), explains his vision to make "excellent computers in really small spacecraft." He means really small—maybe a couple of thousand [1406]**nanometers** (billionths of a meter). Globus is talking about designing a microscopic spaceship that will fly to other planets and do productive work. "But you wouldn't send just one," he says, "you would send millions."

2 This is the basic idea of nanotechnology. Simply put, nanotech is the science of building things out of individual atoms and molecules, and it promises the ultimate in [1407]**miniaturization**. For decades, technology has pursued "top-down" miniaturization: devising smaller and smaller machines run by smaller and smaller microchips crammed with smaller and smaller transistors. Nanotechnologists, by contrast, believe in a "bottom-up" approach. Take atoms and molecules, they say, and [1408]**custom build** them into larger objects—ultra-strong materials, designer foods, even tiny robots. If the nanotechnologists accomplish even a fraction of what they [1409]**envision**, the implications for humanity's future are so dramatic they make the Internet look as insignificant as an extra channel on your TV.

3 The famous American physicist, Richard Feynman, outlined nanotech's basic concepts in an [1410]**offhand talk** in 1959. The major prophet of nanotech, however, is a less exalted engineer-turned-dreamer named Eric Drexler. Drexler had his first vision of nanotech while still an undergraduate at the Massachusetts Institute of Technology in the mid-1970s as he read about the new field of [1411]**genetic engineering**. At a time when biologists were just learning to manipulate molecules that make up DNA, Drexler was wondering why [1412]**inorganic machines** couldn't be built out of atoms.

科学・テクノロジー

4 For Drexler, the vision became an ¹⁴¹³<u>obsession</u>. Why not, he later decided, build machines with the ability to replicate themselves? One machine becomes two, two become four, then eight…indefinitely. Add this to the capacity to produce specific, nonbiological objects from simple raw materials, and the only possible result, he thought, would be wealth beyond imagination. Tiny robots, which Drexler called assemblers, could ¹⁴¹⁴<u>churn out</u> limitless quantities of food for the hungry and innumerable houses for the homeless, and they could cruise through the human bloodstream and repair cells, thus putting an end to disease and aging. In fact, someday human beings could just kick back and relax while nanobots, as science fiction writers have ¹⁴¹⁵<u>dubbed</u> them, did all the work in the world.

5 There was, of course, the possible ¹⁴¹⁶<u>downside</u>. Self-replicating machines could theoretically spin out of control, consuming the matter around them, replicating, then consuming twice as much matter, then replicating again, and so on, until they'd eaten up the entire ¹⁴¹⁷<u>physical world</u>.

6 While skeptics still ¹⁴¹⁸<u>predominate</u>, Drexler is ¹⁴¹⁹<u>winning</u> more and more <u>converts</u>. Harnessing the atom, nature's primal building block, would be one of those moments in history after which nothing is the same. And Drexler insists that wide-scale nanotech applications are possible within 15 years—given sufficient research and funding.

1406 ☐ **nanometer** [nǽnəmìːṭər]	≒ one-billionth (1/1,000,000,000) of a meter *n.* ナノメートル（10億分の1メートル）
1407 ☐ **miniaturization** [mìniətʃərəzéɪʃən]	≒ the process of making something small, the tendency to make things small *n.* 小型化

1408 ☐	**custom build**	≒ build or make to order 注文生産する，客の希望に合わせて作る
1409 ☐	**envision** [ɪnvíʒən]	≒ picture in the mind, imagine or plan for the future *n.* （未来のこと）を心に描く
1410 ☐	**offhand talk**	≒ extemporaneous talk, casual chatting, informal conversation 非公式の談話，即席の話，何気ない会話
1411 ☐	**genetic engineering**	≒ changing or controlling the growth or function of certain genes for a specific end 遺伝子工学，遺伝子組み換え
1412 ☐	**inorganic machine**	≒ a nonliving mechanism 無機質のメカニズム
1413 ☐	**obsession** [əbséʃən]	≒ extreme preoccupation, fixation, mania *n.* 強迫観念，妄想 *v.t.* obsess *adj.* obsessive
1414 ☐	**churn out ～**	≒ turn out, produce in large numbers quickly ～を（機械的に）つぎつぎと大量生産する
1415 ☐	**dub** [dʌb]	≒ name, call, coin or create a new term for *v.t.* に名をつける，を＜～と＞呼ぶ＜as ～＞
1416 ☐	**downside** [dáʊnsàɪd]	≒ the negative aspects of a situation *n.* マイナス面，否定的側面，下側
1417 ☐	**physical world**	≒ the world of concrete reality, the world of objects that can be perceived through the senses and are governed by scientific laws 物質界，自然界
1418 ☐	**predominate** [prɪdá(:)mɪnèɪt]	≒ possess greater force, importance, or influence, rule, control *v.i.* 優位を占める，優勢である
1419 ☐	**win converts**	≒ succeed in convincing or persuading people 人を同調させる，人を転向させる

科学・テクノロジー

5 Machine Translation

日本語訳
→ p.419

例文

1 In the 1950s, the surging Cold War demand for English versions of Russian technical documents ¹⁴²⁰**figured into** an exciting belief, held by many computer scientists, that machines could be designed to produce accurate automatic translations. Today, several software programs claim to have accomplished this ¹⁴²¹**feat**. But just how realistic is their claim?

2 Three decades ago, under contract from the U.S. government, a company called Systran pioneered the field of machine translation. ¹⁴²²**Prototype models** were "direct systems," producing literal translations by looking up each word or phrase in a ¹⁴²³**lexicon** and substituting an equivalent in the target language. This technology owed much to a simplistic analogy advanced by American mathematician Norbert Wiener. Computers were used during the war to help break enemy codes; ¹⁴²⁴**decoding** is a matter of transforming a set of symbols; language translation could be the same. But when scientists actually ¹⁴²⁵**fired up** their machines, the results were less than encouraging.

3 One huge ¹⁴²⁶**snag** for machine translation, or MT, is word order. The latest products seek to overcome this by incorporating grammatical rules for figuring out what words are performing what functions in a sentence. The programs construct a "parse tree," a ¹⁴²⁷**diagram** showing the grammatical function of each word in a sentence. The result is transferred to the target language with the aid of a second set of rules governing grammatical combinations in that language.

4 The latest results? That depends on whom you ask. When faced with criticism of their products' translations, MT vendors tend to ¹⁴²⁸**invoke** the "talking dog"—as in, "Don't be ¹⁴²⁹**picky**; it's amazing that a dog can talk at all." And in all fairness, outright mistranslations are far fewer than one might expect.

5 The real limitations of MT have less to do with grammatical complexity than with the fact that computers don't have any common sense. Language is full of ambiguity that correct [1430]**syntax** goes only a short way toward sorting out. Is a "bank" a place to put money, or is it the edge of a river? A five-year-old child can grasp the difference, but getting a computer to do so is another matter.

6 In other words, semantics is the key to MT, and semantics is a matter of a lot more than linguistics—it requires real-world knowledge. Indeed, one can produce near-perfect translations with just about any system by limiting its vocabulary to a narrow, specialized area. Canadian radio stations, for example, use software to translate weather [1431]**bulletins** from English to French. With a lexicon of just a few hundred words, the program achieves an accuracy rate of more than 90 percent.

7 A major effort now under way in MT circles is to develop [1432]**elaborate** classifications of meaning that will [1433]**duplicate** the knowledge that allows human beings to know which of various meanings a speaker intends. This, of course, is virtually equivalent to the challenge of [1434]**artificial intelligence**—creating a computer that thinks, or at least comes so close to human thinking that we can't tell the difference.

1420 ☐ **figure into ～**	≒ contribute to a result of, (partly) lead to ～につながる，～に導く
1421 ☐ **feat** [fiːt]	≒ achievement, exploit, attainment *n.* 偉業，手柄，離れ業
1422 ☐ **prototype model**	≒ original model for some machine or procedure, the first attempt at creating a machine or procedure, usually technical or scientific in nature 原型

1423 ☐	**lexicon** [léksəkà(:)n]	≒ a corpus of vocabulary words for a dictionary or some other resource, a stock of terms *n.* 語彙集, 辞書, 語彙目録
1424 ☐	**decode** [di:kóʊd]	≒ translate a set of symbols into a meaningful code, break down the discrete symbols of one meaning system into another meaning system *v.t.* （暗号・符号）を解く, を解読する ⇔ encode
1425 ☐	**fire up**	≒ start, warm up （機械など）を始動させる
1426 ☐	**snag** [snæg]	≒ problem, hindrance, blockage, hang-up *n.* 思わぬ障害, 故障
1427 ☐	**diagram** [dáɪəgræ̀m]	≒ a plan, sketch, drawing or scheme that represents and explains something else *n.* 図式, 図解, 図表
1428 ☐	**invoke** [ɪnvóʊk]	≒ mention, refer to, cite *v.t.* を引き合いに出す,（法）に訴える, 権威に頼る,（霊など）を呼び出す ⇒ The old woman sits on this chair and invokes spirits of children. （この女性はこの椅子に座って子どもたちの霊を呼び出す） *n.* invocation
1429 ☐	**picky** [píki]	≒ overly critical, fault-finding, particular, fastidious *adj.* 細かいことを言う, 気難しい
1430 ☐	**syntax** [síntæks]	≒ the rules of grammar for forming correct sentences in a language, systematic order for some language or code *n.* 構文（法）, 統語論, シンタックス

1431 ☐ **bulletin** [búlətɪn]	≒ a written or spoken notice, a short announcement of news or information *n.* ニュース速報，公報，紀要	
1432 ☐ **elaborate** [ɪlǽbərət]	≒ intricate, complex, complicated *adj.* 精巧な，入念な；*v.t.* 詳しく述べる ⇒ The old professor elaborated on the need of gun control. (その老教授は銃規制の必要性について詳しく述べた) *n.* elaboration ⇔ simple	
1433 ☐ **duplicate** [djúːplɪkèɪt]	≒ copy, reproduce *v.t.* を複製［写］する；*adj.* 複製［写］の，二重の	科学・テクノロジー
1434 ☐ **artificial intelligence**	≒ computer or other machine models that attempt to duplicate or simulate human thinking abilities 人工知能	

6 The Mother of All Genes

例文

1 The ¹⁴³⁵**Biblical** story of Adam and Eve, long dismissed as fiction by many, is gaining the attention of some ¹⁴³⁶**geneticists** and researchers of humanity's origins. According to recent research into the ¹⁴³⁷**human genome**, all people now living can trace their ancestry back to 10 Adams and 18 Eves, all of whom emerged from a small population of individuals in prehistoric Africa. Furthermore, all 28 can be traced back to one woman, the original Eve, who lived nearly 200,000 years ago.

2 Dr. Douglas C. Wallace of the Emory University School of Medicine in Atlanta, Georgia, has developed a human family tree based on ¹⁴³⁸**mitochondrial DNA**, which is passed from mother to daughter, starting with the ¹⁴³⁹**aforementioned** 18 Eves. Meanwhile, Dr. Peter A. Underhill and Dr. Peter J. Oefner of Stanford University have constructed a similar tree based on the ¹⁴⁴⁰**Y chromosome**, whose characteristics are handed down from father to son, beginning with the 10 Adams.

3 Geneticists believe that the ancestral human population from which the first Eve was born had about 2,000 members. Approximately 144,000 years ago, well after the first Eve, this population began to split, with some subgroups remaining in Africa and others spreading to Europe, Asia, and the rest of the world. Wallace found that nearly all Native Americans belong to the mitochondrial ¹⁴⁴¹**lineages** he labeled A, B, C, and D, while Europeans belong to two different lineage groups he called H through K and T through X. Not surprisingly, the A through D lineages are also found in Asia, confirming the widely held theory that the Americas were populated by Asians traveling across a land bridge from Siberia during the last Ice Age.

4 In 1998, however, Wallace and his colleagues discovered the rare X lineage, which is found in Europe but not in Asia, among northern Native American tribes, suggesting that prehistoric migration to the Americas was more complex and followed more routes than was originally thought.

5 The out-of-Africa theory has not gone unchallenged. Some researchers, pointing to flaws in the assumptions and findings of geneticists, support an alternative theory of [1442]**multiregional** evolution, one that holds that modern humans arose in Africa nearly 2 million years ago and evolved as a single species. They then spread from Africa over a long period and [1443]**interbred** with local populations, including Neanderthals and other [1444]**archaic** humans. Recent fossil evidence, they say, points to the interbreeding of older populations and newer groups of modern humans in places as widespread as Portugal and Australia.

6 Both sides of the debate, however, tend to agree that the old rigid divisions of race, once considered scientific [1445]**gospel**, have crumbled. Research has shown no evidence for "race" at the genetic level. As a result, the Biblical account of mankind's origin from a common ancestor has shed some of its mythical status. Commented Dr. Underhill: "We are all Africans at the Y chromosome level, and we are really all brothers."

科学・テクノロジー

1435 ☐ **Biblical** [bíblɪkəl]	≒ related to the Old or New Testament of the Bible *adj.* 聖書の(ような)，聖書に関する
1436 ☐ **geneticist** [dʒənétɪsɪst]	≒ a scientist who studies genes and how they function *n.* 遺伝学者 *n.* genetics
1437 ☐ **human genome**	≒ the pattern or map of the human genetic system, the complete haploid of human chromosomes ヒトゲノム

1438 ☐ **mitochondrial DNA**	≒ DNA, or basic hereditary elements of an organism, derived from the female parent ミトコンドリア DNA	
1439 ☐ **aforementioned** [əfɔ̀ːrménʃənd]	≒ previously stated or mentioned *adj.* 前述の	
1440 ☐ **Y chromosome**	≒ the chromosome, or linear body of the cell nuclei that determines inherited traits responsible for maleness *n.* Y 染色体	
1441 ☐ **lineage** [líniɪdʒ]	≒ ancestral line of inheritance *n.* 系統, 血統, 家系	
1442 ☐ **multiregional** [mʌ̀ltiríːdʒənəl]	≒ referring to more than one area or region *adj.* 多地域の, 複数の場所の	
1443 ☐ **interbreed** [ìntərbríːd]	≒ breed with a different race, hybridize, crossbreed, produce hybrids *v.i.* 他の種［民族］と血が混ざる, 異種交配する	
1444 ☐ **archaic** [ɑːrkéɪɪk]	≒ ancient, prehistoric, very old *adj.* 古代の, 古風な, 旧式な	
1445 ☐ **gospel** [gá(ː)spəl]	≒ unquestionable, certain or doubtless truth (coming from the Biblical stories of Jesus, which Christians consider unquestionable) *n.* 絶対の真理, 福音, 信条	

7 The Evolution of the Feather

例文

1 Feathers may not have always separated the world of birds from other animals. In fact, the first feathers did not necessarily [1446]**herald** the age of animal flight—and here is where the feathers fly between two opposing camps of [1447]**paleontologists**. One side argues that feathers initially evolved in a small group of two-legged, [1448]**carnivorous** dinosaurs. Luis Chiappe of the Natural History Museum of Los Angeles County believes that early [1449]**forerunners** of feathers initially served purposes other than flight, such as attracting potential mates and maintaining body heat. Computer simulations utilized to analyze [1450]**aerodynamics** show that flightless dinosaurs with feathered, winglike [1451]**appendages** would have been able to run faster and make quicker turns if they [1452]**flapped** their wings, enabling them to [1453]**catch prey** or escape [1454]**predators**. This theory presupposes, of course, that feathered dinosaurs were the early ancestors of modern birds.

2 Other paleontologists argue against this "ground up" theory, saying that feathers more likely evolved "from the trees down." Advocates of the latter theory hold that the evolution of modern feathers and the ability to fly happened simultaneously. Some believe that small reptiles living in trees evolved [1455]**stubby** projections, which smoothed airflow on their skin and enabled them to jump quickly away from predators. Reptiles that developed longer [1456]**filaments** from these projections could jump faster and farther. Dominique Homberger, an evolutionary biologist at Louisiana State University, maintains that these [1457]**precursors** to feathers probably did not serve all the purposes that modern feathers do, but that they did provide some clear survival advantages.

3 There are other contentious feather issues among paleontologists. Some rely exclusively on analyses of fossil records to determine how feathers may have evolved. Others focus their attention on modern birds.

The members of the first camp search for evolutionary relationships between various organisms by analyzing shared characteristics in [1458]**fossilized remains**, a science called cladistics. They construct evolutionary family trees based on the analysis of such shared traits as general body structure, the number and shape of bones, and the type of skin covering. The other scientists consider it foolish to restrict investigation to fossils. This group studies the characteristics of modern birds for clues as to how feathers may have evolved in ancient [1459]**predecessors**.

4 The debate between the fossil-focused and less restricted groups is heated. Chiappe, a proponent of the cladistics camp, calls his opponents "the arm-waving school of speculating and looking for what's [1460]**intuitively** pleasing." "Nothing's intuitively pleasing," he says, "until I see it in the fossil record." The opposing camp argues that fossil records are simply too spotty to provide a clear picture of what really happened. The situation is complicated by the fact that the earliest known bird fossil, the famous [1461]**Archaeopteryx**, appears to already have feathers.

5 If feathers did indeed evolve from something else, the fossil record has yet to produce conclusive evidence as to how or why. Paleontologists of both camps eagerly await the discovery of bird fossils that predate Archaeopteryx, in hopes that the findings will prove their respective views and close the debate [1462]**once and for all**.

| 1446 □ **herald** [hérəld] | ≒ predict, foretell, announce (a future event)
 v.t. の到来を告げる、を先触れする；*n.* 先触れ、前兆、伝達者 |

Chapter 2

1447 □ **paleontologist** [pèɪliə(ː)ntá(ː)lədʒəst]	≒ a scientist that studies the fossilized remains of past organic life *n.* 古生物学者	
1448 □ **carnivorous** [kɑːrnívərəs]	≒ meat-eating *adj.* 肉食性の，肉食動物の *n.* carnivore ⇔ herbivorous	
1449 □ **forerunner** [fɔ́ːrrʌ̀nər]	≒ a preliminary case or example, a predecessor, progenitor, precursor *n.* 先駆け，前身，先駆者，先人	
1450 □ **aerodynamics** [èəroʊdaɪnǽmɪks]	≒ science of characteristics suitable for flight *n.* 空気［航空］力学	
1451 □ **appendage** [əpéndɪdʒ]	≒ something attached, as arms, legs or wings of an animal; something added on *n.* 付属器官（手・足など），付加物	
1452 □ **flap** [flæp]	≒ move up and down in a repetitive motion, wave up and down *v.t.* をはためかす，をパタパタと動かす；*v.i.* はためく；*n.* パタパタするもの，フラップ	
1453 □ **catch prey**	≒ grasp and subdue animals for food, hunt animals to kill and eat, to prey 捕食する，獲物を捕らえる	
1454 □ **predator** [prédətər]	≒ an animal that kills and eats other animals *n.* 捕食動物，略奪者 *adj.* predatory	
1455 □ **stubby** [stʌ́bi]	≒ short *adj.* （太くて）短い *n.* stub	
1456 □ **filament** [fíləmənt]	≒ a slender, threadlike appendage *n.* 繊維，糸状の突起物	

科学・テクノロジー

1457 ☐	**precursor** [prɪkə́:rsər]	≒ a forerunner, something that precedes another related thing *n.* 先駆者，前身，前兆
1458 ☐	**fossilized remains**	≒ traces of organic material or whole species that have been turned into rock 化石化した遺物
1459 ☐	**predecessor** [prédəsèsər]	≒ precursor, forerunner *n.* 前のもの，前身，前任者
1460 ☐	**intuitively** [ɪntjú:əṭɪvli]	≒ without conscious awareness or intention, innately, instinctively *ad.* 直観的に *n.* intuition *adj.* intuitive
1461 ☐	**Archaeopteryx** [à:rkiá(:)ptərɪks]	≒ the oldest bird species known to science that has been long extinct *n.* 始祖鳥
1462 ☐	**once and for all**	≒ finally, completely, definitively これを最後に，きっぱりと

Chapter 2

経済・ビジネス

1. China's Challenge to the U.S. and to the Earth

日本語訳 → p.424

例文

1 In recent decades, many observers noted that the United States, with less than 5 percent of the world's population, was consuming a third or more of its resources. But this is no longer true. In several areas, China has overtaken the United States. For example, China now consumes more grain and red meat, uses more ¹⁴⁶³**fertilizer**, and produces more steel than the United States. Since China has 4.6 times as many people as the United States, its ¹⁴⁶⁴**per capita demands** on the earth's resources are still far less. To cite an extreme example, the average American consumes 25 times as much oil as the average Chinese citizen does.

2 Even with its still modest ¹⁴⁶⁵**per capita consumption**, China is already paying a high environmental price for its booming economy. Its heavy reliance on coal, for example, has led to air pollution nearly as bad as that once found in eastern Europe.

3 As China, with its much larger population, attempts to replicate the consumer economy developed in the United States, it becomes clear that the U.S. model is not environmentally sustainable. Ironically, it may be China that finally forces the United States to come to terms with the environmental unsustainability of its own economic system.

4 The ¹⁴⁶⁶**bottom line** is that China, with its vast population, simply will not be able to follow for long any of the development paths blazed ¹⁴⁶⁷**to date**. It will be forced to ¹⁴⁶⁸**chart a** new **course**. The country that invented paper and ¹⁴⁶⁹**gunpowder** now has the opportunity to ¹⁴⁷⁰**leapfrog** the West and show how to build an environmentally sustainable economy. If it does, China could become a shining example for the rest of the world to admire and emulate. If it fails, we will all pay the price.

1463 ☐	**fertilizer** [fə́:rṭəlàizər]	≒ a substance to make soil more productive 肥料, 化学肥料 *adj.* fertile
1464 ☐	**per capita demand**	≒ demand by each person 1人当たりの需要
1465 ☐	**per capita consumption**	≒ consumption by each person 1人当たりの消費
1466 ☐	**bottom line**	≒ the underlying truth 要点, 肝心なこと, 結論, ギリギリの線
1467 ☐	**to date**	≒ until now, so far これまで（のところ）
1468 ☐	**chart a course**	≒ map out, plot, draft 進路を策定する
1469 ☐	**gunpowder** [gʌ́npàʊdər]	≒ an explosive made of sulphur, charcoal, etc. 火薬
1470 ☐	**leapfrog** [líːpfrɑ(ː)g]	≒ move ahead of, jump past *v.t.* を跳び越す, を回避する； *n.* 馬跳び

Chapter 2

2 What's in a Name?

日本語訳
→ p.424

例文

1 The San Francisco ¹⁴⁷¹**Municipal** Transportation Agency (SFMTA) recently announced it was considering selling the rights to name certain subway stations. If the SFMTA has its way, new companies will ¹⁴⁷²**line up** to pay millions to get their names affixed to public transit stations throughout San Francisco. After all, putting a company's name in a highly trafficked area where thousands of people are likely to see it seems like great advertising.

2 However, what these companies may not know is the effect these corporate names have on the stock market. The stock market is full of superstitions and myths. Day-to-day swings in the market often have more to do with fear than economic ¹⁴⁷³**determinants**. The market reacts to signals and signs—and when a company spends millions of dollars to put its name in lights, it has historically been a sign to sell.

3 The worst-case scenario is the National Hockey League's St. Louis Blues. In 2000, the team sold naming rights to its arena to Savvis Communications, an Internet company, for cash and shares of Savvis stock. The company's stock has dropped 80 percent since then, and the team has lost millions. Unless their stock ¹⁴⁷⁴**rebounds** in the near future, the Blues may not be able to pay players or coaches, let alone continue to pay for the stadium.

4 The Blues' experience is not unique. In fact, this chain of events has become something of a familiar pattern. So why do companies continue to sponsor such ¹⁴⁷⁵**corporate titling**? Perhaps the motivation is a marketing plan ¹⁴⁷⁶**gone awry**. Or perhaps these corporate names just mirror the vain desires of CEOs to see their corporation's name large in lights. In either case, it is the portfolio of the investor that suffers in the end. Publicizing the corporate name does not always raise the corporation's value. In fact, ¹⁴⁷⁷**the opposite is** often **the case**. If marketing departments were to study the history of such corporate sponsorships, perhaps they would ¹⁴⁷⁸**think twice** about such ventures in the future.

1471 ☐ **municipal** [mjunísipəl]	≒ belonging to a town or city that has its own local government *adj.* 市の，地方自治体の	
1472 ☐ **line up**	≒ queue (up), get in line （順番待ちのために）行列する，整列する	
1473 ☐ **determinant** [dɪtə́ːrmɪnənt]	≒ determining factor *n.* 決定因子，決定要素 *adj.* determinate（明確な，決定的な）	
1474 ☐ **rebound** [rɪbáund]	≒ make a recovery, pick up, spring back *v.i.* 持ち直す，立ち直る，跳ね返る	
1475 ☐ **corporate titling**	≒ naming of a company 会社名を冠すること	
1476 ☐ **go awry**	≒ go wrong, turn bad, go off the expected course うまく行かない，見込みがはずれる，それる，間違える	
1477 ☐ **the opposite is the case**	≒ The reverse is true. 逆が真である	
1478 ☐ **think twice**	≒ be in two minds, reconsider, hesitate 二の足を踏む，考え直す，ためらう	

3 Offshore Private Banking

例文

1 Among the general public, the term "banking" most often refers to the everyday management of money in ¹⁴⁷⁹**checking** and ¹⁴⁸⁰**savings accounts** with so-called ¹⁴⁸¹**retail banks**. However, there is also a niche category of banking known as private banking, which caters exclusively to High Net Worth Individuals (HNWI)—people with the equivalent of over $1 million in ¹⁴⁸²**investable assets**.

2 Within the private-banking market, there is further ¹⁴⁸³**segmentation** into two sectors—the ¹⁴⁸⁴**offshore** sector, wherein individuals keep their money in a country not their own, and the ¹⁴⁸⁵**onshore** sector, wherein a country's citizens place their money domestically. Individuals are drawn to accounts located in so-called offshore centers such as Switzerland and Bermuda by the banking secrecy and tax-savings opportunities available in these loosely regulated foreign jurisdictions.

3 While most analysts agree that private banking overall will continue to grow at a rapid rate, they also express doubts that the offshore sector can sustain the growth it has enjoyed in the recent past. Over the past few years, the quality of onshore private banking services has improved considerably, due in part to increased political stability and lessened ¹⁴⁸⁶**currency volatility**. Moreover, offshore ¹⁴⁸⁷**tax havens** have been the target of criticism by regulatory agencies around the world, which is leading to tighter regulation of some prominent offshore centers.

4 What is the offshore sector to do? Many offshore centers have begun to take steps to strengthen reporting requirements in an attempt to alleviate fears that these tax havens are also ¹⁴⁸⁸**hotbeds** for ¹⁴⁸⁹**money laundering**. Yet, in the process, offshore private banks' primary competitive advantage over their onshore counterparts will surely be weakened. The degree to which offshore banks are able to satisfy the needs of their existing ¹⁴⁹⁰**clientele** and simultaneously attract new wealth will determine not only their own fate, but also the future financial livelihood of the foreign countries in which they are located.

1479 ☐ **checking account**	≒ a bank account which earns no interest and from which money can be drawn at any time by check 当座預金口座
1480 ☐ **savings account**	≒ a bank account that earns interest 普通預金口座
1481 ☐ **retail bank**	≒ a bank that has branches in many towns and provides services to public or small companies 小口取引銀行 ⇔ wholesale
1482 ☐ **investable asset**	≒ asset that can be invested in 投資対象になる財［資］産
1483 ☐ **segmentation** [sègmentéɪʃən]	≒ dividing 分割，分裂 *n., v.t.* segment（区切り，区分；を分割する）
1484 ☐ **offshore** [ɔ(:)fʃɔ́:r]	≒ operating abroad, based in foreign countries where the tax system is more favorable than in the home country *adj.* 海外の
1485 ☐ **onshore** [ɑ(:)nʃɔ́:r]	≒ operating in the home country, domestic, operating on land *adj.* 国内の，陸上の
1486 ☐ **currency volatility**	≒ currency instability 通貨の不安定［乱高下］

1487 ☐ **tax haven**	≒ a place or a country that people choose because the tax system is more favorable there 税金回避地
1488 ☐ **hotbed** [há(:)tbèd]	≒ breeding ground, a place where an undesirable thing can develop *n.* 温床
1489 ☐ **money laundering**	≒ (repeated) transfer of money to conceal a dubious origin マネーロンダリング，資金洗浄
1490 ☐ **clientele** [klàɪəntél]	≒ clients, customers, patrons *n.* 顧客，常連，依頼人たち

4 Firms That Never Sleep

日本語訳
→ p.426

例文

1 Call British Airways from London after 11 o'clock at night to book a flight, and you will be answered in an American accent. "You sound as if you are in New York," you say. "That's because I am in New York," comes the reply. British Airways is one of a growing number of companies that use technology to turn ¹⁴⁹¹**time zones** to advantage. No need to keep operators up half the night in Britain when the rotation of the earth provides a wide-awake American alternative.

2 The benefits are familiar. The financial markets, which pioneered the three-time-zone world, have grown used to operating 24 hours around the globe. Other businesses are heading in the same direction. One pressure for them to do so is productivity. Put together a business deal or a research project with three teams ¹⁴⁹²**working in shifts**, and you save days. Another is technology. As more and more services can be assembled far from the customer and sold down a telephone line, it becomes easier to produce them where skilled staff come cheap. Lots of the paperwork for things like insurance claims and credit-card records can be done in developing countries, where there are more educated workers than jobs for them.

3 The problems are familiar, too: Any ¹⁴⁹³**old-fangled** manufacturer with a continuous process knows that shift work needs careful management. The evening shift may leave a mess behind for the night shift to sort out, and the night shift may ¹⁴⁹⁴**bequeath** a worse mess for the day shift.

4 Worse, while the night shift in the average coal mine or paper plant lives ¹⁴⁹⁵**just down the road** from the day shift, the Tokyo ¹⁴⁹⁶**bond**-dealing team may never meet the ¹⁴⁹⁷**chaps** in New York, and analysts in Singapore may know their counterparts in London only through telephone conversations squeezed between the end of one day and the start of another. At the least, companies need to ensure that international

Chapter 2

teams know what is expected of them, and find substitutes for the congeniality of teams of the old-fashioned, unvirtual variety.

5 Customers, too, can be an obstacle to global shiftworking. People who live in different time zones are likely to laugh at different jokes and [1498]**take offense** at different phrases. Some large banks have found that customers prefer to push buttons and hear a recorded voice rather than talk to a human being in a faraway country.

1491 ☐ **time zone**	≒ any of the 24 parts of the earth divided by standard time 標準時間帯
1492 ☐ **work in shifts**	≒ work in relay with others 交替で働く
1493 ☐ **old-fangled** [òuldfǽŋgld]	≒ old-fashioned, out-moded, obsolete *adj.* 旧式の ⇔ new-fangled
1494 ☐ **bequeath** [bɪkwíːð]	≒ leave, hand down *v.t.* を残す，を（後世に）伝える *n.* bequeathal（遺産）
1495 ☐ **just down the road**	≒ near, around the corner 近くに
1496 ☐ **bond** [bɑ(ː)nd]	≒ a paper or a certificate issued by a government or an industrial firm to pay back with interest money that has been lent *n.* 債券

経済・ビジネス

1497 ☐ **chap** [tʃæp]	≒ fellow *n.* 連中，仲間，やつ，男	
1498 ☐ **take offense**	≒ take umbrage, feel indignant, feel resentful <～に＞腹を立てる，怒る<at ～>	

5 The Brand Barons of Asia

1 Stroll along Orchard Road, Singapore's main shopping street, and you'll be besieged by luxury brands shouting out from the shops. The same is true in Hong Kong and even outside of Asia's traditional shopping paradises, due primarily to the determination of the region's middle class to wear the right thing. ¹⁴⁹⁹**Invariably**, the label Asians want is Western, making Asia the fastest-growing market for the West's top brands. Today, a third of all luxury-goods sales are to Asia, and some predict that Asia will make up half of the world's market within a decade.

2 By then, however, Asians may own many of the brands they covet. Many of the region's retailers and wholesalers are turning into powerful international groups who are no longer content to merely ¹⁵⁰⁰**franchise** Western goods in their home market. Some Asian groups want to make their own products for the brands they are pushing, while others want to buy brands ¹⁵⁰¹**outright**. Consider Ong Beng Seng, for instance, who is assembling a formidable ¹⁵⁰²**portfolio** of clothing and food brands. He represents more than 40 top American brands—not just in Asia, but also in Australia and Britain. Ong recently formed a joint venture with DKNY, a fashion brand founded by Donna Karan, which will build a string of boutiques in Japan and other parts of Asia.

3 Other brand ¹⁵⁰³**barons** fear overextending ¹⁵⁰⁴**up-market** brands too much—and turning off the market in the process. They are, therefore, adding mid-market lines and trying to build regional brands of their own. In Hong Kong, retailers are trying to build local fashion brands, often mid-market, with Western-sounding names. Hong Kong-based Giordano, for example, has established a successful chain of stores selling its own brand of low-priced casual clothes throughout Asia.

4 Can Asia build global brands of its own? The Japanese have, but mostly for such technological products as cars, cameras and televisions.

Some Japanese "lifestyle" brands have made the world stage, like Kenzo, but in general, they are much less well-known than Honda, Canon or Sony. So how can Asian companies add the magic ¹⁵⁰⁵**elixir** that turns lifestyle brands into global products? Brands involve a certain geographical ¹⁵⁰⁶**caricature**—¹⁵⁰⁷**swanky** clothes are supposed to be French, the best leather Italian, and top watches Swiss. The Western fashion brands coveted in Asia rely for their appeal on a host of nebulous qualities, including the lifestyle they represent. Finding the right combination of factors for success isn't easy.

1499 ☐ **invariably** [ɪnvéəriəbli]	≒ always, on every occasion, without exception *adv.* 常に、変わることなく *v.i.* vary（異なる） *adj.* invariable（変わりやすい、不安定の） ⇔ variably	
1500 ☐ **franchise** [fræntʃaɪz]	≒ authorize the sale of, grant a franchise to *v.t.* の専売権を与える；*n.* 専売権、専売権を持つ企業	
1501 ☐ **outright** [àʊtráɪt]	≒ entirely, altogether *adv.* すっかり、その場で、率直に； *adj.* [áʊtràɪt] まったくの、率直な	
1502 ☐ **portfolio** [pɔːrtfóʊlioʊ]	≒ a wide array of merchandise, a range of investments *n.* 品揃え、一連の投資	
1503 ☐ **baron** [bærən]	≒ magnate, important businessman, tycoon *n.* 大物、（財界の）実力者、男爵	

1504 ☐ **up-market** [ʌ̀pmáːrkət]	≒ of very good quality and expensive, intended for a high social class *adj.* 高級な，高級品市場向けの ⇔ down-market（大衆向けの）	
1505 ☐ **elixir** [ɪlíksər]	≒ magic drug, panacea, something with a magical power to solve any problems 妙薬，万能薬	
1506 ☐ **caricature** [kǽrɪkətʃùər]	≒ exaggeration, satire, parody, lampoon *n.*（人物や出来事の特徴の）誇張，風刺，風刺画	
1507 ☐ **swanky** [swǽŋki]	≒ very fashionable, stylish, chic, posh *adj.* 気取った，派手な，粋な	

経済・ビジネス

6 Putting Globalization in Perspective

例文

1 The media loves to both ¹⁵⁰⁸**tout** and decry globalization. Tom Friedman of The New York Times calls it "a flowering of both wealth and technological innovation the likes of which the world has never before seen," while David Korten, a well-known detractor, speaks of "market ¹⁵⁰⁹**tyranny**... extending its reach across the planet like a cancer." But whether ¹⁵¹⁰**pro or con**, the hype about globalization is just that: hype. True, there has been a trend toward mergers, acquisitions, and increasing international trade. But international trade accounts for only 10% of America's national income. That percentage is unlikely to grow much higher.

2 Global companies must contend with an economic principle known as ¹⁵¹¹**the law of diminishing returns**, which states that there is an upper limit to company size beyond which complexities, inefficiencies, and breakdowns begin to hamper profitability. In banking, for instance, while mergers and acquisitions often ¹⁵¹²**steal the headlines**, Federal Reserve researchers found that after banks reach a fairly modest size (of about $100 million in assets), there is no cost advantage to further expansion. Some evidence even suggests diseconomies of scale for very large banks. Another study, sponsored by the Financial Markets Center, found that banks lending within a limited regional area were typically twice as profitable as those with nationwide portfolios. Despite the coverage of national and global mergers, the more active trend has been toward community banks, credit unions, and ¹⁵¹³**microloan** funds.

3 Similar forces are at work in the rapid worldwide growth of community-supported agriculture. Farmers once received 50 cents on the dollar for agricultural products sold to consumers; in today's corporate farming, only 9 cents of every consumer dollar goes to the farmer. Marketers, who have little to do with the product itself, get 67 cents. But when farmers are in closer contact with consumers, both benefit, for consumers are able to purchase fresher, higher-quality products at reasonable prices, and farmers get a higher return on their products. If nothing else, the world is a big place, and a factor that [1514]**chips away at** the bottom line is that global companies have to distribute goods over larger areas. With the price of oil having [1515]**quadrupled** in the last four years, shipping costs are no small consideration.

4 Global producers often make efforts to produce specialized products to meet local tastes, but global companies compete at a disadvantage. Local operations, by being better equipped to communicate with retailers and consumers and provide timely delivery, are better suited to design and produce goods for local markets. Small companies are also able to take advantage of information technology to carry out such business functions as management, accounting, communications, and publishing, while the Internet enables small and even home-based businesses to compete against the major players.

5 These trends do not necessarily [1516]**spell doom** for globalization, for it is simply not feasible to produce all goods locally. Global trade will likely remain, as it is today, a minor part of most economies.

1508 □ **tout** [taʊt]	≒ praise very highly; highly recommend *v.t.* を賞賛する、を褒めちぎる、をしつこく勧める
1509 □ **tyranny** [tírəni]	≒ autocracy, despotism, dictatorship, cruelty, brutality *n.* 暴虐、横暴 *n.* tyrant（暴君）

1510	**pro or con**	≒ an argument for or against 賛否のいずれか
1511	**the law of diminishing returns**	≒ the fact that after a certain point in the increase of capital, taxation, expenditure, etc., productivity ceases to increase proportionately 収益逓減の法則
1512	**steal the headlines**	≒ attract prominent attention as news 新聞紙上をにぎわす
1513	**microloan** [mάɪkroʊlòʊn]	≒ mini-loan 小規模融資
1514	**chip away at ～**	≒ cut pieces off ～を徐々に減らす，～から少しずつ削り取る
1515	**quadruple** [kwɑ(ː)drúːpl]	≒ increase fourfold *v.i.* 4倍になる；*v.t.* を4倍にする；*adj.* 4倍の，4からなる
1516	**spell doom**	≒ add up to ruin 凶運［破滅］をもたらす

自然・環境

Chapter 2

1 Ozone Fungus

日本語訳
→ p.430

例文

1 Gases such as ¹⁵¹⁷**CFCs**—originally developed for use in refrigeration units and air conditioners—are most often blamed for the ¹⁵¹⁸**depletion** of the ¹⁵¹⁹**ozone layer**, but many of the gases ¹⁵²⁰**eating away** at the ozone are actually not man-made. Until recently, the origin of these substances had eluded scientists. ¹⁵²¹**Preliminary tests**, however, suggest that a common type of forest ¹⁵²²**fungus** may be responsible for at least some of the ozone-depleting gases in the earth's atmosphere. The fungus grows around the roots of trees, where it gathers ¹⁵²³**nitrogen** and ¹⁵²⁴**phosphorus** from the soil and shares these ¹⁵²⁵**vital nutrients** with the trees. In return, the fungus receives ¹⁵²⁶**carbohydrates** from its tree hosts.

2 This helps to maintain the health of temperate rain forests, where the fungus is found. The same may not be true for the ozone layer. While each gram of the fungus gives out only a few millionths of a gram of gas per day, it makes up as much as 15% of organic matter in the soil in which it grows in forests throughout the world. Among the gases the fungus gives out are methyl bromide, which is believed to cause about 10% of ozone destruction, and methyl ¹⁵²⁷**chloride**, which is blamed for another 15% of the destruction. Scientists have long known that some of the methyl bromide in the atmosphere comes from farming and other human activities, but they have not been able to identify the source of at least a quarter of the atmosphere's methyl bromide. The search may soon be over.

3 Further tests are being conducted to see whether the fungus really is responsible for a significant amount of ozone-depleting gases. In addition, scientists want to know how the world's changing climate may cause changes in fungus activity. In any case, the seemingly benign forest fungus is being ¹⁵²⁸**looked at in a** completely **new light**.

1517 ☐	**CFC** [sìːefsíː]	≒ gas used in refrigerator units and for other purposes that contribute to the depletion of the ozone layer, chlorofluorocarbon *n.* フロンガス，クロロフルオロカーボン
1518 ☐	**depletion** [dɪplíːʃən]	≒ gradual destruction, diminishing, damaging *n.* 減少，消耗，破壊
1519 ☐	**ozone layer**	≒ the layer of the atmosphere that protects earth from the ultraviolet rays of the sun オゾン層
1520 ☐	**eat away 〜**	≒ deplete, destroy in large increments （徐々に）〜を侵食する
1521 ☐	**preliminary test**	≒ an initial or early phase of an investigation 予備調査
1522 ☐	**fungus** [fʌ́ŋɡəs]	≒ a type of plant of the subkingdom Thallophytic that lacks chlorophyll, including yeast, molds, smuts, and mushrooms *n.* 真菌類，菌類，キノコ
1523 ☐	**nitrogen** [náɪtrədʒən]	≒ an nonmetallic element making up 80% of the air by volume *n.* 窒素
1524 ☐	**phosphorus** [fá(ː)sfərəs]	≒ a (poisonous) highly reactive, nonmetallic element (P) *n.* リン
1525 ☐	**vital nutrient**	≒ a substance that is essential for the survival of living organisms 生命維持に必要な栄養［素］

1526 ☐ **carbohydrate** [kɑ̀ːrbouháɪdreɪt]	≒ a group of chemical compounds made up of carbon, hydrogen and oxygen, which include sugars, starches, and cellulose *n.* 炭水化物, 含水炭素
1527 ☐ **chloride** [klɔ́ːraɪd]	≒ a binary compound of chlorine, a substance partly responsible for destruction of the ozone *n.* 塩化物 *n.* chlorine（塩素）
1528 ☐ **look at ∼ in a new light**	≒ find another way of understanding or thinking about something 〜に対して新しい見方をする, 〜について見直す

自然・環境

2 Private Conservation

例 文

1 Reflecting the growing public awareness about environmental destruction, concerned citizens are ¹⁵²⁹**digging into their** own **pockets** to protect their countries' natural heritage. Many people are buying parcels of land ¹⁵³⁰**earmarked** for ¹⁵³¹**logging** or development, either on their own or by pooling resources with friends.

2 Similarly, citizens are helping to purchase ¹⁵³²**at-risk land** by donating to the many ¹⁵³³**land-conservation trusts** that have sprung up. The U.S.-based Nature Conservancy is America's largest and richest conservation group, with an annual ¹⁵³⁴**turnover** of $450 million, as much as its six nearest rivals combined. The vast majority of land trusts employ the "revolving fund" strategy—buying land, placing a legal ¹⁵³⁵**covenant** on it, and then reselling it. A legal covenant forbids development of a property, and is permanent, remaining valid even if the land changes hands. Because covenants are considered the most effective means of ¹⁵³⁶**safeguarding** land, they are fast becoming the most popular nature-preservation tool.

3 In Australia, the Australian Bush Heritage Fund recently generated publicity with the purchase of a 59,000-hectare cattle property in one of the country's land-clearing ¹⁵³⁷**hotspots** in Queensland. CEO Doug Humann believes that conservation trusts still have great growth potential, a thought supported by the recent flood of contributions. "I'm convinced we haven't even scratched ¹⁵³⁸**the tip of the iceberg** of community understanding and interest in this area," he says.

4 The genesis of Bush Heritage has become almost legendary in environmental circles. An activist from Tasmania created the trust in 1990, using a $50,000 environment prize he had won to make a ¹⁵³⁹**down payment** on a piece of privately owned Tasmanian wilderness that was earmarked for the chainsaw. Since then the fund has bought an additional

13 properties and helped hundreds of individuals and groups with similar aims. Humann asserts private trusts are [1540]**swelling** because of a growing public conviction that governments lack the will and resources to properly protect Australia's natural heritage.

1529 **dig into** *one's* **pocket**	≒ procure money from *one*, get money from *one*, take out *one's* money 自分の金を使う，自腹を切る
1530 **earmark** [íərmàːrk]	≒ mark, designate, target, select, set aside *v.t.* を＜〜の目的で＞指定する，＜特別な目的のために＞を取っておく＜for 〜＞
1531 **log** [lɔ(ː)g]	≒ to cut down trees for lumber *v.i.* （木材を）切って丸太にする
1532 **at-risk land**	≒ land that is in danger of being used up and destroyed for business profits 危険な状態の土地
1533 **land-conservation trust**	≒ a group which protects land by an agreement that no matter who owns it, it cannot be sold for purposes of development 土地保護トラスト
1534 **turnover** [tə́ːrnòuvər]	≒ gross revenue, income, sales *n.* 取引高，総売上高，（商品などの）回転率 ⇒ The turnover of merchandise is rising at a moderate rate. （商品の回転率はゆっくり上昇している）

1535 ☐	**covenant** [kʌ́vənənt]	≒ agreement, contract *n.* 約款, 契約, ＜the C-で＞（神とイスラエル人との）契約 ⇒ God told Moses that it was his Covenant. （神はそれが神の契約だとモーゼに言った）
1536 ☐	**safeguard** [séɪfgɑ̀ːrd]	≒ protect, save, preserve *v.t.* を保護する, を守る ; *n.* 保護手段
1537 ☐	**hotspot** [hɑ́(ː)tspɑ̀(ː)t]	≒ a place or area where some activity is occuring frequently *n.* 議論を呼んでいる土地
1538 ☐	**the tip of the iceberg**	≒ a small part of the whole, that which is visible from a much larger sphere of activity 氷山の一角, 大きな問題のほんの一部
1539 ☐	**down payment**	≒ the initial sum of money that is paid to purchase something, usually a small portion of the total cost （分割払いの）頭金
1540 ☐	**swell** [swel]	≒ increase, augment, get larger *v.i.* 増大する, 膨張する, 大きくなる ; *n.* 増加, 膨張 ; *adj.* すてきな, 素晴らしい ⇒ The people at the party were swell; they didn't have a lot of petty little theories about what's wrong in the world. （パーティに来た人たちは素晴らしかった。世界の諸問題に小賢しい理論をいろいろ言わなかった）

3 The Blue Revolution

1 The first agricultural revolution brought domestication of crops and animals. Now, another revolution is ¹⁵⁴¹**unfolding**. Already, one of every five fish on the world's dinner tables comes from ¹⁵⁴²**fish farms**, and that share is expected to increase. This "blue revolution," like the ¹⁵⁴³**green revolution** on land, promises greater efficiency and steadier supplies.

2 With stocks of many popular fish species plummeting, clearly ¹⁵⁴⁴**aquaculture** is ¹⁵⁴⁵**here to stay**. But just as the green revolution had its dark side, so too has the blue revolution. We may see more pollution, disease, loss of genetic diversity, and shortages of fresh water and other scarce resources. Still, something must be done.

3 One solution to the crisis is to limit the species farmed: Instead of enjoying a variety of wild fish, we should prepare to eat a lot of tilapia. Tilapia, the chicken of the fisheries world, are moderate-sized African fish that will eat almost anything, grow quickly, and tolerate incredible crowding. Scientists are now breeding better tilapia through the selective breeding skills that have worked so well with crops and animals.

4 But the low-tech fish farms of developing countries still often have to raise high-value species such as shrimp and salmon, to ¹⁵⁴⁶**raise the hard cash** to repay Western loans. Cheaper fish that could be sold in local markets often cannot ¹⁵⁴⁷**make it into** large-scale culture, even though the fish ¹⁵⁴⁸**beloved** of Western palates will never feed a hungry world, no matter how many we manage to farm. These expensive species are near the top of the food chain, and even in fish farms demand a high-protein diet, which usually means ¹⁵⁴⁹**ground-up** fish from the sea. This myth of aquaculture, that farming cod or salmon will "take the pressure off the oceans," is simply false.

5 Intensive aquaculture has its own drawbacks, too. Artificial ponds can cause severe fresh water shortages. Serious water pollution can occur, since a densely stocked fish cage can pour waste directly into a waterway. And when large numbers of one species crowd together, the risk of disease increases—another problem shared with agriculture.

6 Then even if disease and pollution can be overcome, where will we put all the fish farms? About half the area used for shrimp ponds in Thailand was once [1550]**rice paddy**, and China actually already prohibits conversion of [1551]**arable land** to aquaculture.

7 Turning over the North American prairies to agriculture left a great ecosystem [1552]**in tatters**. Yet the cornfields that replaced them became one of the world's most productive [1553]**breadbaskets**. Can we justify a similar [1554]**trade-off** in our coastal waters? Can we learn from experience and attempt a more balanced development? We must decide soon, before unplanned exploitation races ahead.

1541 ☐ **unfold** [ʌnfóuld]	≒ take place, be revealed or uncovered *v.i.* 展開する、（真相などが）明らかになる； *v.t.* を開く、を明らかにする
1542 ☐ **fish farm**	≒ man-made ponds where fish are bred for profit 養魚場
1543 ☐ **green revolution**	≒ the dramatic increase in crop production created by improved seeds and other innovations in agriculture 緑色革命、農作物革命
1544 ☐ **aquaculture** [á:kwəkʌ̀ltʃər]	≒ the raising of fish and other fresh-water and sea-water animals for profit *n.* 水産養殖
1545 ☐ **here to stay**	≒ not transitory, permanent, long-lasting 定着して、普及して

1546	**raise the hard cash**	≒ find ways to procure capital or funds for investment 現金を稼ぐ，資金を募る
1547	**make it into ～**	≒ become generally accepted or used, be introduced successfully ～に受け入れられる make it（成功する，間に合う）⇒ Suzie got dressed faster than usual. She had to make it for the meeting. （スージーはいつもより早く着替えた。会議に間に合う必要があったのだ）
1548	**beloved** [bɪlʌ́vɪd]	≒ favored, preferred; dear *adj.* ＜～に＞愛される，好かれる＜of ～＞，最愛の ⇒ People were abandoning their beloved ones, who were dying of the new epidemic. （人々は最愛の人たちを見捨てていたが，それは彼らが新しい流行病で死につつあったためだった）
1549	**ground-up** [ɡráʊndʌ̀p]	≒ chopped or cut into extremely fine pieces 細かく切り刻まれた，すりつぶされた *v.t.* grind（を粉にひく，を粉々にする）
1550	**rice paddy**	≒ field where rice is grown 水田，稲田
1551	**arable land**	≒ land that can grow crops 耕地
1552	**in tatters**	≒ in a state of decay, falling apart, disintegrating ぼろぼろになって，打ち砕かれて
1553	**breadbasket** [brédbæ̀skət]	≒ a major source of some food supply *n.* 穀倉地帯
1554	**trade-off** [tréɪdɔ̀(ː)f]	≒ an exchange or balance between two entities *n.*（より好ましいものとの）転換，交換，一方をたてるための他方の犠牲，妥協

4 Weighing the Consequences

例文

1 Decisions do not always come easy for public policymakers. Faced with financial constraints, competing political interests, and limited if not often inadequate evaluation and assessment data, they frequently find themselves trapped in a ¹⁵⁵⁵**no-win situation**.

2 ¹⁵⁵⁶**A case in point** is the Tellico Dam project. In 1967, the U.S. Congress unanimously approved construction of a dam along the Little Tennessee River. The public would benefit twofold: Construction would create much-needed local employment, and completion would provide the public with inexpensive electricity and water in times of drought. Six years later, with the dam 75% complete, a snail darter—a variety of fish listed in the Endangered Species Act—was discovered in the ¹⁵⁵⁷**vicinity**. Ecologists petitioned to have construction terminated, arguing that the dam threatened the fish's survival as a species. Policymakers were at odds. Do you continue construction on a dam that is nearly finished and will provide economical electricity for the people you serve, or do you stop construction to save an already endangered fish? For five years debate ¹⁵⁵⁸**ensued**. In 1979, on a split vote, Congress decided to complete the dam.

3 Policymakers outside American borders find themselves in similar ¹⁵⁵⁹**predicaments**. An estimated 800,000 small dams, 40,000 large dams, and 300 major dams contribute one-fifth of the world's electricity. Unfortunately, this power hasn't come as cheaply as the ¹⁵⁶⁰**ledgers** first claimed it would. According to International Rivers Network, a network of academics monitoring the status of rivers, about 400,000 square kilometers of fertile land—the size of the state of California—have been inundated behind dams; 20% of the globe's freshwater fish are now endangered or extinct; and 30 to 60 million people have been evicted from their homes in order to make way for dams. These figures are only the tip of the iceberg when considering the ^{1561}**hydrological effects** of inland and coastal erosion, and the fact that deforestation along natural flood plains, now dry as a result of large dam construction, will lead to severe land degradation in the future.

4 The United States, once the leader in dam construction, declared a moratorium in 1994, and in an ironic twist, the agency once in charge of dam building in that country now has a mandate as an environmental regulatory agency. But dam construction continues elsewhere, to the tune of approximately 260 new locations every year, and until a ^{1562}**commercially viable** eco-friendly alternative is developed, policymakers in these countries will face tough dilemmas.

5 Ecologist-activist Barry Commoner, author of *The Closing Circle*, in advocating the Principle of Minimal Interference warned that if humans tampered with nature's own screening process that decides the fate of a species, the global ecosystem would fall into unbalance. So put yourself ^{1563}**in the shoes of** a public policymaker. Knowing that dam construction threatens more than just the survival of the snail darter, what would your decision be? How would you weigh the consequences?

1555 ☐ **no-win situation**	≒ a choice one must make that cannot have a successful outcome 絶望的状況, うまく行きそうもない状態
1556 ☐ **a case in point**	≒ an example that is related to the present reference, concerned with the topic or issue being mentioned at that moment 適切な例
1557 ☐ **vicinity** [vəsínəṭi]	≒ neighborhood, surrounding area, region *n.* 近所, 付近

1558 ☐ **ensue** [ɪnsjúː]	≒ follow, emerge from something, be the result or consequence *v.i.* 続いて起こる，結果として起こる	
1559 ☐ **predicament** [prɪdíkəmənt]	≒ dilemma, problem, serious situation *n.* 苦境，窮地	
1560 ☐ **ledger** [lédʒər]	≒ a sheet of paper on which calculations are made concerning the positive or negative effects, a book in which data are recorded *n.* 台帳，元帳	
1561 ☐ **hydrological effect**	≒ effects created or caused by water 陸水学［水文（すいもん）学］上の影響	
1562 ☐ **commercially viable**	≒ profitable as a business venture 商業的に利益の上がる	
1563 ☐ **in the shoes of ~**	≒ in someone's point of view or situation 〜の立場に立って	

文化・社会

Chapter 2

1 A New Approach to Traffic

日本語訳 → p.434

例文

1 Look at a road map of almost any major metropolitan area and you are apt to see a pattern of ¹⁵⁶⁴**concentric circles**. These lines, indicating bypasses, resemble the ¹⁵⁶⁵**contours** of tree rings and are evidence of a similar type of growth: the growth of an urban area as it has swelled outward. Municipal authorities around the world seek to accommodate higher volumes of vehicular traffic by building what are ¹⁵⁶⁶**aptly** called ring roads. Because traffic engineers regard them as the obvious solution to clogged roads, such bypasses have become as ubiquitous as the trucks and automobiles they carry.

2 While many governments promote bypasses as an effective means of easing traffic jams, citizens' drives to halt them are sometimes creating policy jams. City planners in Melbourne have hit ¹⁵⁶⁷**roadblocks** as people object to additional asphalt. Australia's Anti Ring Road Organization (ARRO) believes a new bypass would ¹⁵⁶⁸**amplify** road ¹⁵⁶⁹**congestion** in Melbourne, exacerbate pollution, and produce a ¹⁵⁷⁰**sprawling** car-dependent city with a ¹⁵⁷¹**dead center**.

3 ARRO would like local municipal leaders to mirror the vision of the mayor of Hasselt, a Belgian town that has just under 70,000 residents, plus another 200,000 people commuting in and out on a daily basis. Faced with escalating debt and ¹⁵⁷²**sluggish** traffic, Hasselt's mayor abandoned plans to construct a third ring road around the town. In a related move, he also closed one of Hasselt's two existing ring roads and converted it to a greenbelt with pedestrian and cycling paths. He also improved the quality and frequency of the bus service while at the same time making all rides free. According to one source, within a year the use of public transport had soared a stratospheric 800%, merchants had begun to enjoy ¹⁵⁷³**brisker** business, and accidents and road casualties had declined.

4 Granted, Hasselt's award-winning approach to congestion and pollution will not work universally. However, as some traffic engineers now realize, bypasses can be bypassed.

1564 ☐	**concentric circle**	≒ a series of circles, one inside the other, having the same center 同心円 ⇔ eccentric circle（中心を異にする円）
1565 ☐	**contour** [ká(:)ntuər]	≒ the outline of a figure or other form, delineation, shape, curvature, lineament *n.* 輪郭，輪郭線，外形
1566 ☐	**aptly** [ǽptli]	≒ accurately, correctly, appropriately *adv.* 適切に，ふさわしく
1567 ☐	**roadblock** [róudblà(:)k]	≒ obstacle, hindrance, blockage, problem *n.* 障害，バリケード，道路封鎖
1568 ☐	**amplify** [ǽmplɪfàɪ]	≒ expand, magnify, augment *v.t.* を増強する，を拡充する *n.* amplification, amplifier（アンプ）
1569 ☐	**congestion** [kəndʒéstʃən]	≒ crowded road condition, clogging, jam, blockage *n.* 渋滞，混雑，密集
1570 ☐	**sprawl** [sprɔːl]	≒ spread out, disorderly expand, stretch in all directions *v.i.*（都市・建物などが）無計画に広がる，だらしなく手足を伸ばす
1571 ☐	**dead center**	≒ a lifeless middle point (in the city), a city center with little or no economic activity 空洞化した中心，ど真ん中

Chapter 2

1572 □ **sluggish**
[slʌ́gɪʃ]

≒ slow moving
adj. 動きののろい, 不活発な, 怠惰な
n. slug（ナメクジ, 怠け者）, sluggard（怠け者）

1573 □ **brisk**
[brɪsk]

≒ active, energetic, fast-moving
adj. 活発な, きびきびした, 活況の

2 Sleeping on the Job?

1 The nap has never ranked high on the list of grown-up pursuits. Somewhere along the way to adulthood, napping is usually overtaken by coffee breaks and trips to the water cooler. But now, the nap is ¹⁵⁷⁴**working its way into** the corporate culture. Recent studies suggest that employees are spending more time than ever at the office and that half of them are chronically ¹⁵⁷⁵**deprived** of sleep. Companies are discovering that coffee breaks are mere ¹⁵⁷⁶**band-aids**. What employees truly need, they are concluding, is a nap room.

2 Martin Moore-Ede, professor of psychology at Harvard Medical School, often recommends to companies that they establish napping policies. "The initial reaction is almost invariably a negative one," he says. But Moore-Ede goes on to cite research about the productivity-diminishing effects of sleep deprivation: short-term memory loss, ¹⁵⁷⁷**debilitated** immune systems, and loss of alertness. And two-thirds of his clients end up encouraging their workers to take nap breaks.

3 The need to nap is particularly strong roughly eight hours after you wake, says James Maas, a Cornell University psychologist who offers "Power Sleep" seminars to large companies. "That's when you have a huge ¹⁵⁷⁸**dip** in alertness," he explains. "By napping for 15 to 20 minutes, you can regain creativity and problem-solving skills."

4 Companies have started to notice some ¹⁵⁷⁹**tangible**, bottom-line benefits to napping. Since one company created a nap room, its expenditures on soda and coffee for employees have dropped 30 percent. Still, some companies are wary of exposing their nap rooms to the public. Some call it the "relaxation room," and most are reluctant to discuss naps. They are afraid that it gives people the wrong impression.

5 That hesitance doesn't surprise William Anthony, who wrote a comical guide, *The Art of Napping*. Anthony is trying to get folks to go public with their stories. In the meantime, he says, napping remains a quiet revolution.

1574 □ **work** *one's* **way into ~**	≒ slowly become accepted and popular ~に徐々に受け入れられる
1575 □ **deprive** [dɪpráɪv]	≒ prevent one from (getting) *v.t.* （人）から＜~を＞奪う，（人）に＜~を＞与えない＜of ~＞ *n.* deprivation *adj.* deprived（恵まれない）⇒ You often say you want to help people deprived of means of living, but remember, charity begins at home. （困っている人を助けたいと君は言うが，よく言われているとおり，慈善は家からだ）
1576 □ **band-aid**	≒ temporary and insufficient method for solving a problem or treating an illness *n.* 応急措置，一時しのぎの処置，＜Band-Aidで＞バンドエイド
1577 □ **debilitate** [dɪbílɪtèɪt]	≒ damage, weaken, hamper *v.t.* を衰弱させる *n.* debilitation, debility
1578 □ **dip** [dɪp]	≒ drop, decline, decrease *n.* 低下，下落；*v.t.* を（水などに）つける
1579 □ **tangible** [tǽndʒəbl]	≒ clear and demonstrable, based on physical evidence *adj.* 感知できる，有形の，明白な，実際の ⇔ intangible

3 A Worthwhile Vacation

例文

1 If the word "volunteering" ¹⁵⁸⁰**evokes** images of picking up garbage from the streets or collecting cans for ¹⁵⁸¹**fundraising**, think again. With a little planning and an open mind, volunteering can be a ¹⁵⁸²**philanthropic recess** from the office and a valuable cultural experience. Although it's hard work, spending vacation time in the field is a great way to learn about a country. The ¹⁵⁸³**spectrum** of opportunities in Asia for willing—and paying—volunteers is vast and varied. Among the options: work camps in Bangladesh, construction projects in South Korea, and ¹⁵⁸⁴**archaeological** digs in Thailand.

2 If a volunteer vacation sounds like a worthwhile alternative to an easygoing holiday, be warned: Travelers lacking serious commitment or realistic expectations could ¹⁵⁸⁵**be in for** a hard time. "I would caution people against a casual approach to these vacations," says David Minich of Habitat for Humanity, a U.S. Christian organization that arranges construction projects worldwide. "Management of expectation is critical. A 10-day contribution on a building site will allow you to see only a portion of a lengthy process. Don't expect to save the world in a week."

3 That said, ¹⁵⁸⁶**immersion** in a job provides an excellent opportunity to learn about the customs of local coworkers. And leave the guidebook behind. "For people who want to play the part of a carefree tourist," says Blue Magruder of Earthwatch, which offers a wide spectrum of volunteer opportunities, "this is the wrong thing."

4 Many international work camps are run by local organizations that focus on social welfare and community development. Volunteers generally are placed in ¹⁵⁸⁷**harsh** conditions with no access to modern conveniences such as ¹⁵⁸⁸**running water**, and are asked to bring their own sleeping bags.

1580	**evoke** [ɪvóʊk]	≒ remind *one* of, call up (the image of), bring to mind, suggest *v.t.* （感情など）を呼び起こす，を喚起する *n.* evocation *adj.* evocative
1581	**fundraising** [fʌ́ndrèɪzɪŋ]	≒ gathering funds from different sources, raising money *n.* 資金集め，募金
1582	**philanthropic recess**	≒ a break in the routine that will benefit others more than oneself, a rest from daily work for the purpose of helping others ボランティア活動などのために仕事を一時離れること *n.* philanthropy（博愛）
1583	**spectrum** [spéktrəm]	≒ range, wide number of options *n.* 範囲，広がり，スペクトル
1584	**archaeological** [àːrkiəlá(ː)dʒɪkəl]	≒ referring to the study of prehistoric culture, usually through artifacts from ancient times *adj.* 考古学の
1585	**be in for ～**	≒ will experience ～に直面しそうである，～を味わうことになる
1586	**immersion** [ɪmɚ́ːrʒən]	≒ complete involvement, being surrounded by an experience totally *n.* ＜～に＞没頭すること，熱中＜in ～＞ *v.t.* immerse
1587	**harsh** [hɑːrʃ]	≒ hard, difficult, trying, severe, rough, crude *adj.* 過酷な，厳しい，粗い，ひどい
1588	**running water**	≒ water that comes out of a pipe and does not have to be carried from its source 水道［水］

文化・社会

4 Guiding the Crystal Ball

例文

1 Sally's Psychic Gallery is not an obvious place to seek the future. Located in a small brick building behind a gas station, the shop offers no outward sign of the ¹⁵⁸⁹**supernatural**. Prospective customers, be reassured: Sally possesses a fortune-telling license from the government of Cecil County, Maryland.

2 In an age when consumers are otherwise expected to look out for themselves, Cecil County is one of a handful of places that want to protect the ¹⁵⁹⁰**gullible**. Anyone who wants to tell fortunes in the county needs a "License for ¹⁵⁹¹**Palm Readers**, ¹⁵⁹²**Fortune-Tellers**, and ¹⁵⁹³**Soothsayers**." The county clerk checks a prospective fortune-teller's background for any "crimes of moral ¹⁵⁹⁴**turpitude**" and then, if satisfied, collects a license fee of $250.

3 But attempts to license fortune-tellers do not seem to have changed the nature of the industry. Because fortune-telling services are inexpensive to provide and the ¹⁵⁹⁵**credentials** of ¹⁵⁹⁶**would-be seers** difficult to check, the profession attracts more than its share of shady characters. When a California court ruling overturned a local ban on fortune-telling businesses, the town of Huntington Beach responded with a four-page licensing law designed to, in the words of a local policeman, "make people ¹⁵⁹⁷**jump through a few hoops**." Predictably, this did not prevent one fortune-teller from ¹⁵⁹⁸**conning** more than $150,000 from her clients a few years later. The moral of the story? Let the buyer beware.

4 If only so much can be done to safeguard the unwary, why not abandon these policies altogether? Such a move may actually be to the customer's advantage—an unscientific survey by this correspondent suggested that fees for fortune-telling services were higher in regulated Cecil County than elsewhere. Whether the county's ¹⁵⁹⁹**sages** would benefit from future deregulation is ¹⁶⁰⁰**anybody's guess**. Well, maybe not: Presumably, Sally and company have already seen the future.

1589 ☐ **supernatural** [sùːpərnǽtʃərəl]	≒ beyond ordinary natural laws, unexplainable by known laws of cause and effect, magical or spiritual or "other worldly" *adj.* 超自然の
1590 ☐ **gullible** [gʌ́ləbl]	≒ naive, easily fooled or tricked, unsophisticated *adj.* だまされやすい *n.* gullibility
1591 ☐ **palm reader**	≒ someone who claims to tell future events from the lines on a person's palm *n.* 手相占い師
1592 ☐ **fortune-teller** [fɔ́ːrtʃəntèlər]	≒ *one* who claims to see the future and professes to foretell or predict future events *n.* 占い師，易者
1593 ☐ **soothsayer** [súːθsèiər]	≒ a fortune-teller *n.* 占い師，予言者
1594 ☐ **turpitude** [tɔ́ːrpətjùːd]	≒ degeneracy, evil, wickedness, depravity *n.* 卑劣，堕落，卑劣な行為
1595 ☐ **credential** [krədénʃəl]	≒ qualification, evidence of authenticity *n.* 資格証明書，信任状，資格
1596 ☐ **would-be seer**	≒ someone who wants to be a fortune-teller or soothsayer 占い師志望者

文化・社会

1597 ☐	**jump through the [a few] hoops**	≒ follow rules, regulations and orders, follow useless regulations to demonstrate signs of submissiveness and obedience 規則に従う，（人の）言いなりになる，（多くの）試練をくぐり抜ける
1598 ☐	**con** [kɑ(:)n]	≒ cheat one of, swindle one out of *v.t.* （金など）をだまし取る，（人）をだます *n.* con man [confidence man]（詐欺師）⇒ Soon the old man was persuaded to trust the con man.（間もなく，その老人は口説かれて詐欺師を信じてしまった）
1599 ☐	**sage** [seɪdʒ]	≒ wise person, expert, authority *n.* 賢人，哲人；*adj.* 賢い，分別のある
1600 ☐	**anybody's guess**	≒ something no one could know for sure だれにも予測がつかないこと

Chapter 2

5 A New Bronze Age

日本語訳 → p.438

例文

1 ¹⁶⁰¹**When it comes to** challenging the ¹⁶⁰²**conventional wisdom**, few businesses can match the ¹⁶⁰³**chutzpah** of the $4 billion-a-year indoor tanning industry. Faced with condemnation from health organizations and government agencies, trade groups representing the nation's 50,000 tanning salons are fighting back with a media campaign. "New research shows that moderate tanning prevents cancer," one ¹⁶⁰⁴**press release** announces.

2 The industry faces a slight PR obstacle, however: No leading expert accepts such claims. They all warn consumers to stay away from tanning booths, saying that the ultraviolet rays from the sun—and tanning lamps—can cause skin cancer. Scientists generally accept the view ¹⁶⁰⁵**espoused** by the American Academy of ¹⁶⁰⁶**Dermatology**: "There's no such thing as a safe tan."

3 It's exactly that sort of ¹⁶⁰⁷**downbeat message** that prompted Joseph Levy, the executive director of the leading trade group, to start running monthly ads this year. "We're trying to undo years of totally negative conditioning by the medical community," Levy says. But critics insist that the industry is trying to make its case by drawing on unproven theories and exaggerating current research. For instance, the group's ads and press releases highlight a study that "suggests that 30,000 cancer deaths could be avoided every year if more people tanned regularly." The study was actually a review paper ¹⁶⁰⁸**positing** that sunlight exposure can prevent such deadly cancers as ¹⁶⁰⁹**colon** and breast cancer, because people who live in sunnier climates have lower rates of those cancers. But ¹⁶¹⁰**epidemiologists** say that other key factors, such as diet and exercise, also differ in warmer and colder climates, so sunlight can hardly be proclaimed as a cure for cancer.

4 The incessant attacks by health organizations may be having an impact. A decade ago, indoor tanning was among the fastest-growing industries, but growth has slipped to less than 4 percent this year, compared with 54 percent between 1986 and 1988. Still, Levy is confident that the 21st century will be a "[1611]**Bronze Age**" for the tanning industry.

1601 ☐	**when it comes to ～**	≒ if one does ～, under specific circumstances or conditions (stating a condition in which something else happens) （話が）～ということになると
1602 ☐	**conventional wisdom**	≒ the usual way of thinking, what most people consider the best policy or strategy 従来培われてきた知恵，社会通念
1603 ☐	**chutzpah** [hútspə]	≒ brazenness, gall, boldness, audacity *n.* 図々しさ，厚かましいこと
1604 ☐	**press release**	≒ news bulletin, information given to the public via the media 新聞発表，報道用文書
1605 ☐	**espouse** [ɪspáuz]	≒ support, adopt, state a belief in *v.t.* （思想・主義など）を支持する，を擁護する
1606 ☐	**dermatology** [də̀ːrmətá(ː)lədʒi]	≒ the study and treatment of skin and skin diseases *n.* 皮膚病学 *n.* dermatologist
1607 ☐	**downbeat message**	≒ negative news, gloomy news 悲観的な発言 ⇔ upbeat message

Chapter 2

1608 posit
[pá(:)zət]

≒ propose, hypothesize, suggest, present a view about
v.t. ＜…＞と仮定する＜that …＞
n. position

1609 colon
[kóʊlən]

≒ a section of the large intestine that extends to the rectum
n. 結腸

1610 epidemiologist
[èpɪdì:miá(:)lədʒɪst]

≒ a scientist who specializes in widespread, contagious diseases
n. 伝染病研究者, 疫学者

1611 Bronze Age

≒ a period of progress and growth, referring to the time frame in human culture between the Stone Age and the Iron Age
青銅器時代

文化・社会

6 Plastic Bankruptcy

1 The road to bankruptcy is paved with plastic. This year Americans filed a record number of personal bankruptcies, peaking just ¹⁶¹²**shy of** 1 million. Although some bankruptcies were due to high medical expenses and downsizing, a great many had to do with credit-card debt. There was something like 2.7 billion ¹⁶¹³**credit offers** that went out last year. Card issuers encourage their consumers to go into debt with incentives like ¹⁶¹⁴**frequent-flier miles**, cash back and low introductory interest rates. "We're finding a lot of people are ¹⁶¹⁵**living off** their credit cards, and they're even making their credit-card payments with a credit card," says Bernie Kaiser, executive director of Cincinnati's Consumer Credit Counseling Service (CCCS), a national ¹⁶¹⁶**nonprofit organization** that offers free financial counseling. "They're using a credit card to supplement their income." Credit cards give holders a feeling of ¹⁶¹⁷**largesse**, but the reality is far different.

2 Originally, bankruptcy was intended to give people relief for debts due to circumstances beyond their control, says Matt Gerald, education director of CCCS. But bankruptcy has now become so common that it has lost much of its stigma. "In fact, there are a lot of people who have filed a second time," says Kaiser.

3 The root of overspending for many people lies in childhood, says psychotherapist Olivia Mellan. Some people try to fulfill emotional needs—either by mirroring ¹⁶¹⁸**overindulgent** parents or filling the ¹⁶¹⁹**voids** of negligent ones. Contemporary American culture, with its fragmented families and emphasis on consumption, leaves people feeling disconnected and lonely. But shopping doesn't make over-spenders feel loved, valued or wanted, says Mellan. It leaves them wanting more.

4 Bad credit can have long-term consequences. Prospective employers, landlords and insurance companies can review credit records, where bankruptcies remain on file for 10 years. "If a person applies for a loan, there's a question on the loan application that asks if you have ever ¹⁶²⁰**filed for** bankruptcy," says Gerald. If the question is not answered truthfully, applicants commit fraud. Banks are looking into fraud loss more and more every day.

1612 □ **shy of ~**	≒ insufficient of, short of, lacking 〜に達しない，〜が不足で
1613 □ **credit offer**	≒ an offer to buy things on credit クレジットカードでの買い物のオファー［提案］
1614 □ **frequent-flier miles**	≒ special programs that offer benefits to travelers who fly many miles in a certain time period （飛行機を頻繁に利用する人のための）マイレージサービス
1615 □ **live off ~**	≒ support oneself through, get money from 〜によって生きる，〜で暮らしをたてる
1616 □ **nonprofit organization**	≒ an organization that does not make money after expenditures are covered 非営利組織
1617 □ **largesse** [lɑːrdʒés]	≒ a sense of generosity, money and gifts bestowed *n.* 気前よく与えること，気前のよい施し，援助
1618 □ **overindulgent** [òuvərɪndʌ́ldʒənt]	≒ being too lax or lenient with others, permissive, bestowing gifts and favors excessively and unwisely *adj.* 甘やかしすぎの，わがままにさせる *n.* overindulgence

1619 □ **void** [vɔid]	≒ emptiness, condition of something missing or lacking *n.* むなしさ，空虚，何もない空間；*adj.* 欠落した，空の，無効の ⇒ The contract signed by your former wife is void. （あなたの先妻がサインした契約は無効だ）
1620 □ **file for 〜**	≒ register for some legal process, make an official request in writing for a legal process 〜の申請をする，〜を申し込む

7 Teacher-Cops

例文

1 ¹⁶²¹**In a bid to** extend the disciplining arm of the law into schools, Singapore police have begun selecting teachers to be made honorary Volunteer Special ¹⁶²²**Constabulary** (VSC) officers: teacher-cops with jurisdiction in schools. Details of the scheme, which was introduced as a ¹⁶²³**pilot program** in several schools in 1997, were given recently at a seminar on reducing ¹⁶²⁴**juvenile delinquency**.

2 The appointees will work to ¹⁶²⁵**counter** delinquent behavior by managing ¹⁶²⁶**school discipline**. They will be trained in police procedures, wear police uniforms, and work to maintain order in the classroom by dealing with problem students. Though not expected to participate in police work outside of school, these new VSC officers will have the right to exercise certain police powers on campus.

3 The Volunteer Special Constabulary was formed in 1946 to supplement the regular Singapore police force, and now has a membership of 1,600 officers. VSC ¹⁶²⁷**recruits** undergo basic training at a police academy, which includes training in firearms, techniques for ¹⁶²⁸**unarmed combat**, and a course in basic legal knowledge.

4 ¹⁶²⁹**Home Affairs Minister** Wong Kan Seng said the scheme was another way to give authority to schoolteachers. "With their additional powers," he said, "they will be seen not just as teachers but as police officers."

5 The news caused a stir in the audience of 500, many of whom were teachers. Some were worried about what powers and how much power the teacher-cops should wield. Senior Assistant Commissioner Benedict Cheong, a police director, responded by saying that there is still a need to "discuss ¹⁶³⁰**the likely scenarios** schools will face."

6 Mr. Wong said police-school ties would be strengthened. Unlike before, when principals called the police only when they could not deal with a student, the police will be more aggressive in the future and ensure that students, particularly those who have [1631]**committed minor offenses**, are [1632]**kept in check**. He said: "Police will adopt the student, visit him, and ensure that it is not just his school principal and teachers, but also the police who are interested in [1633]**keeping him on the straight and narrow**."

1621 □ **in a bid to** *do*	≒ in an effort to *do*, trying to *do* …しようとして
1622 □ **constabulary** [kənstǽbjəlèri]	≒ police, police force *n.* 警察，警察隊 *n.* constable（巡査）
1623 □ **pilot program**	≒ trial program, experimental attempt to see if a certain approach will be successful 試行プログラム，実験プログラム
1624 □ **juvenile delinquency**	≒ criminal behavior by children 未成年非行，青少年による犯罪 juvenile delinquent（非行少年［少女］）
1625 □ **counter** [káʊntər]	≒ fight against, nullify, balance out or mitigate *v.t.* に立ち向かう，に反対する
1626 □ **school discipline**	≒ good behavior of children in schools 学校の規律やしつけ
1627 □ **recruit** [rɪkrúːt]	≒ a new worker *n.* 新参者，新署員；*v.t.*（新社員・新兵など）を募る
1628 □ **unarmed combat**	≒ fighting without weapons 武器を持たないでの闘い

1629 ☐	**Home Affairs Minister**	≒ a government official who handles domestic issues and problems 内務大臣
1630 ☐	**likely scenario**	≒ what is likely to happen 起こりそうなこと
1631 ☐	**commit a minor offense**	≒ break a rule or law that is not so serious 軽犯罪を犯す
1632 ☐	**keep ~ in check**	≒ control, restrict the behavior of 〜を監視する，〜を抑える
1633 ☐	**keep *one* on the straight and narrow**	≒ cause *one* to continue to behave properly （人）にきちんとした生活をさせる

8 In the News

例文

1 Until about a decade ago, American newspapers had a clear idea what the "news" was. It was what the prime ministers and presidents of leading countries announced at press conferences. It was politics and diplomacy and [1634]**cabinet shuffles**. It was economic statistics and [1635]**business mergers** and Wall Street. But over the last dozen years, there has been a growing movement in American newspapers away from that conception of news and toward something looser, more [1636]**feature-oriented**, and more [1637]**trend-driven**.

2 Max Frankel, who ruled as executive editor of *the New York Times* from 1986 through 1994 and thus helped [1638]**set the** journalistic **agenda**, pioneered the concept of soft features on the front page. Frankel wanted newspapers to be read, and he argued that articles about country music and miniskirts were not only engaging but also reflected important trends: Many readers probably cared more about [1639]**hemlines** than about [1640]**arms-control talks**.

3 Under Frankel, *the Times* also began to search for new and compelling ways to cover [1641]**foreign affairs** in the post-Cold War world. Editors felt that politics mattered less than before, and that correspondents should write increasingly about the people of foreign countries rather than just the governments. Correspondents were pushed to spend less time in the national capitals talking to cabinet ministers and more time in rural areas talking to farmers and homemakers. There was more attention to trends; indeed, Frankel emphasized that "sometimes the most important news doesn't happen on any one day."

4 Other newspapers, particularly *the Washington Post* and *Los Angeles Times*, pursued a similar approach. They all beefed up their science and medical reporting, and soon nobody blinked when stories about health or fitness—Does vitamin C prevent colds? Does weightlifting help [1642]**shed**

pounds as well as running does?—were promoted to the front page. *The Wall Street Journal* led the way in pioneering skeptical reporting about corporations, and soon all major newspapers ware assigning ¹⁶⁴³**investigative reporters** to look at ¹⁶⁴⁴**corporate executives** as well as politicians.

5 Yet critics complained that while newspapers were becoming perhaps more ¹⁶⁴⁵**readable**, they were also becoming somewhat ¹⁶⁴⁶**dispensable**. An article about vitamin C might be engaging, but it did not matter if you missed it. Front pages were becoming ¹⁶⁴⁷**clogged with** so many articles about fascinating people that it was difficult to tell what, if anything, had happened that was truly of any consequence. Moreover, as the Internet joined television in providing the public with an alternative source of information, many young people simply ¹⁶⁴⁸**spurned** newspapers altogether.

6 The debate remains unresolved. Newspaper executives do worry that their relevancy may decrease as they reduce their ¹⁶⁴⁹**coverage** of ¹⁶⁵⁰**hard news**, but they say that in a world if 24-hour news on the Internet and cable television, they simply cannot compete effectively at being the first to inform the public of the latest events. They must take a different approach.

1634 ☐ **cabinet shuffle**	≒ when all or many of the leading officials or ministers of a particular government are changed 内閣改造
1635 ☐ **business merger**	≒ the joining of two or more businesses or corporations into one large corporation 企業合併

1636 ☐	**feature-oriented** [fíːtʃərɔ̀ːrientɪd]	≒ emphasizing general, human-interest stories instead of news items 特集記事志向の
1637 ☐	**trend-driven** [tréndrìvən]	≒ guided by fads and what is popular with the public 流行を追った
1638 ☐	**set the agenda**	≒ determine the topics dealt with or discussed （会議の）話題を決める，方針を決める
1639 ☐	**hemline** [hémlàɪn]	≒ the bottom edge of a skirt or dress n.（スカートなどの）裾の線
1640 ☐	**arms-control talks**	≒ discussions among the leaders of nations regarding the issue of reducing and restricting weaponry 軍縮会議
1641 ☐	**foreign affairs**	≒ international issues, dealings among nations 外交問題，外務，海外事情
1642 ☐	**shed pounds**	≒ lose weight 減量する
1643 ☐	**investigative reporter**	≒ journalist whose job is to uncover hidden information, such as public or private scandals 調査報道記者，事件記者
1644 ☐	**corporate executive**	≒ the leader of a company, the boss or one of the bosses in a company 法人幹部，会社役員
1645 ☐	**readable** [ríːdəbl]	≒ appealing to general public interest, more interesting or entertaining to read adj.（本・記事などが）読んでおもしろい，読みやすい

1646	**dispensable** [dɪspénsəbl]	≒ not essential, not needed *adj.* なくても済む，たいして重要でない *v.t.* dispense（を分配する，を販売する） ⇔ indispensable
1647	**clogged with ～**	≒ crowded with, filled up with ～でいっぱいになって，～が詰まって
1648	**spurn** [spəːrn]	≒ reject, disregard, ignore *v.t.* をはねつける，を鼻であしらう
1649	**coverage** [kʌ́vərɪdʒ]	≒ news that gets reported by the media *n.* 報道，取材，取材範囲
1650	**hard news**	≒ news of serious events in the world, information that affects public welfare 堅いニュース報道，重大なニュース報道

文化・社会

9 A Golden Opportunity?

日本語訳
→ p.443

1 In the spring of 1999, a Swiss scientist named Ingo Potrykus announced that his team had successfully created "golden rice," a powerful weapon in the fight against world hunger and disease. Potrykus and his chief [1651]**collaborator**, Peter Beyer, took the genes responsible for making [1652]**beta carotene** in daffodils and inserted them into the DNA structures of a [1653]**bacterium** known as Agrobacterium tumefaciens. Altered bacteria were allowed to infect rice [1654]**embryos**, and in so doing they carried the genes that produce beta carotene into the endosperm of the rice. Beta carotene, which gives the new rice its golden color, does not normally occur in polished rice and is a vital ingredient in the body's production of vitamin A. Potrykus's dream is to use golden rice as a [1655]**staple crop** in those countries where 1 million children die and another 350,000 go blind each year because of [1656]**vitamin A deficiency**.

2 Predictably, not everyone is applauding golden rice. According to Dr. Richard Horton, editor of the British medical journal *The Lancet*, "Seeking a technological food fix for world hunger may be not only the biggest scientific controversy of our time but also the most commercially malevolent [1657]**wild goose chase** of the new century." The debate over [1658]**genetically modified food** is now familiar to most people. On one side are scientists and agribusinesses pushing the Green Revolution. They encourage intensive farming of a range of genetically modified crops with various attributes—from pest resistance to larger crop yields—built into their DNA. On the opposite side are other scientists and environmental groups who urge extreme caution, warning that the long-term results of genetic manipulation are not yet known, and that the consequences of widespread interference in our [1659]**foodstuffs**' genetic makeup may prove harmful further down the line.

3 Another key issue for golden-rice opponents is that even if Potrykus's creation turns out to be a safe and controllable form of genetic modification, it still may not be the answer to the issue of vitamin A deficiency. There is a host of other issues that need to be addressed. Simply making a new crop available, argue the critics, does not guarantee that it will reach the people who need it. In fact, nearly three-fourths of ¹⁶⁶⁰**malnourished** children live in countries that boast food surpluses. As a spokesperson for the environmental group Greenpeace commented, "The real causes of hunger and malnutrition are poverty, poor food distribution, and a failure of political will."

4 It remains to be seen whether golden rice and other products of genetic engineering can provide the most effective solution to world hunger. But how ¹⁶⁶¹**choosy** can we afford to be? As this debate grows more complex, the scourge of malnutrition spreads unabated. Those opposed to genetically modified foods will continue to raise important issues, but for a starving child in a developing nation these issues are largely irrelevant. As the old saying goes: "With food there are many problems. Without food there is only one problem."

1651 ☐ **collaborator** [kəlǽbərèɪṭər]	≒ associate, colleague, fellow worker, co-researcher *n.* 協力者, 合作者 *n.* collaboration
1652 ☐ **beta carotene**	≒ a plant pigment that acts as a source of vitamin A, a nutritional supplement ベータカロチン
1653 ☐ **bacterium** [bæktíəriəm]	≒ a one-celled microscopic animal that exists either as a free-living organism or as a parasite *n.* ＜複数形：bacteria＞バクテリア, 細菌

文化・社会

1654 ☐	**embryo** [émbriòu]	≒ an organism in its earliest phase of development *n.* 胚，胎児，未発達のもの
1655 ☐	**staple crop**	≒ the major, most essential food crop of a nation or community within a single nation 主要作物
1656 ☐	**vitamin A deficiency**	≒ lacking enough vitamin A to be healthy ビタミンA欠乏症
1657 ☐	**wild goose chase**	≒ a useless effort or pursuit, a major effort that has no chance of success 無駄なこと，見込みのないこと，骨折り損
1658 ☐	**genetically modified food**	≒ food that has been altered at the genetic or most basic biological level 遺伝子組み換え食品
1659 ☐	**foodstuff** [fúːdstÀf]	≒ food supplies *n.* ＜しばしば複数形＞食糧，食料品
1660 ☐	**malnourished** [mælnə́ːrɪʃt]	≒ lacking adequate calories or other nutrients *adj.* 栄養不良の
1661 ☐	**choosy** [tʃúːzi]	≒ selective, particular, picky *adj.* 選り好みする，気難しい

Chapter 2

10 The Genetic Divide

日本語訳 → p.444

例文

1 In recent years, tremendous advances have been made in the field of genetics. With the ability to view increasingly complex interrelationships between genes and devise exceptionally accurate tests for [1662]**predisposition** to disease, we can now alert certain individuals to future health problems years in advance of the recognition of symptoms. But while such knowledge holds great promise, genetic testing has potentially adverse effects that could [1663]**overshadow** and even impede future progress.

2 The science of genetics is widely believed to have originated with Austrian [1664]**botanist** Gregor Mendel, who discovered the principle of the inheritance of physical [1665]**traits** through the combination of genes from parent cells. As genetics evolved, researchers found that the information transmitted from parent to offspring controls more than mere physical resemblance. In fact, it plays a part in governing immunity and [1666]**pinpointing** [1667]**susceptibility** to certain diseases and disorders. This is a great step forward in medical science for those who can be treated. Problems arise, however, when we can predict illnesses in individuals for which there is no known cure.

3 In October 2000, a British government committee made an announcement that raised precisely such issues. After conducting research into genetic tests for a fatal brain condition known as Huntington's disease, the committee announced that it is now possible to accurately predict which people will suffer from the condition later in life. While these findings were appropriately lauded as a medical breakthrough, the news has significant social implications as well.

4 Case in point: the life insurance industry. Life insurance is a virtual necessity in the U.K.—it is nearly impossible to make a long-term financial commitment, such as a mortgage, without it. And like any other

文化・社会

kind of insurance, it is based upon risk assessment. ¹⁶⁶⁸**Diagnostic tests** such as the one developed for Huntington's disease could give insurance providers a much greater level of power over the consumer, allowing them to adjust ¹⁶⁶⁹**premiums** in accordance with test results or even exclude applicants altogether. The National Consumer Council in England has argued that people may actually have to avoid taking genetic tests in order to prevent insurance companies from having the grounds to dismiss their applications. This could lead to an absurd situation whereby people are prepared to go undiagnosed so that they might be covered by insurance.

5 The issue of genetic prejudice has also ¹⁶⁷⁰**reared its head** across the Atlantic. Federal government agencies in the United States are banned from using genetic information as grounds to discriminate, but ¹⁶⁷¹**private-sector** entities are not bound by the same regulations. There is increasing pressure upon the U.S. Congress to ratify the Genetic Nondiscrimination in Health Insurance and Employment Act, which aims to extend such controls beyond the public sector. In the absence of such regulations, sophisticated levels of genetic testing may have the power to create a genetic ¹⁶⁷²**underclass**.

1662 ☐ **predisposition** [pri:dìspəzíʃən]	≒ tendency, weakness for, likelihood to develop *n.* <病気にかかりやすい>素質＜to ～＞, <…しやすい>傾向, 性質＜to...＞ *v.t.* predispose
1663 ☐ **overshadow** [òuvərʃǽdou]	≒ outweigh, nullify the good effects of, overpower, be more important than *v.t.* の影を薄くする, に影を投げかける

1664 ☐ **botanist** [bá(:)tənəst]	≒ a scientist who studies plants *n.* 植物学者 *n.* botany
1665 ☐ **trait** [treɪt]	≒ characteristic, quality *n.* 特性，特徴
1666 ☐ **pinpoint** [pínpɔ̀ɪnt]	≒ identify exactly *v.t.* を正確に定める；*adj.* 非常に正確な
1667 ☐ **susceptibility** [səsèptəbíləṭi]	≒ likeliness to contract or come down with, tendency to get, weakness for *n.* 感染しやすい体質，感受性，影響を受けやすい性質 *adj.* susceptible
1668 ☐ **diagnostic test**	≒ a test to discover and/or identify a disease 診断テスト
1669 ☐ **premium** [príːmiəm]	≒ the rate of an insurance payment *n.* 保険料，（保険の）掛け金，特別賞与，プレミア（割増金）
1670 ☐ **rear** *one's* **head**	≒ appear, develop, become a threat 現れる，頭角を現す，頭を上げる
1671 ☐ **private sector**	≒ non-government affiliated groups or individuals *n.* 民間部門，民間セクター
1672 ☐ **underclass** [ʌ́ndərklæ̀s]	≒ a low-ranking group, a group of people in a society with fewer privileges and resources than groups above them *n.* 下層階級

文化・社会

More to Learn

Abbreviations—省略語

Ave.	Avenue
Bldg.	Building
Blvd.	Boulevard
c/o	care of
Dr.	Drive / Doctor
PhD.	Doctor of Philosophy
Pkwy.	Parkway
P.O.	Post Office
Rd.	Road
Rte.	Route
Sq.	Square
apt.	apartment
rm.	room
w/w	wall-to-wall carpeting
e.g.	*exempli gratia* (= for example)
et al.	*et alli* (= and others)
	et alibi (= and elsewhere)
etc.	*et cetera* (= and so on)
i.e.	*id est* (= that is)
vs.	versus

Chapter 1 & 2

例文の日本語訳

Chapter 1
既出例文　　342
予想例文　　366

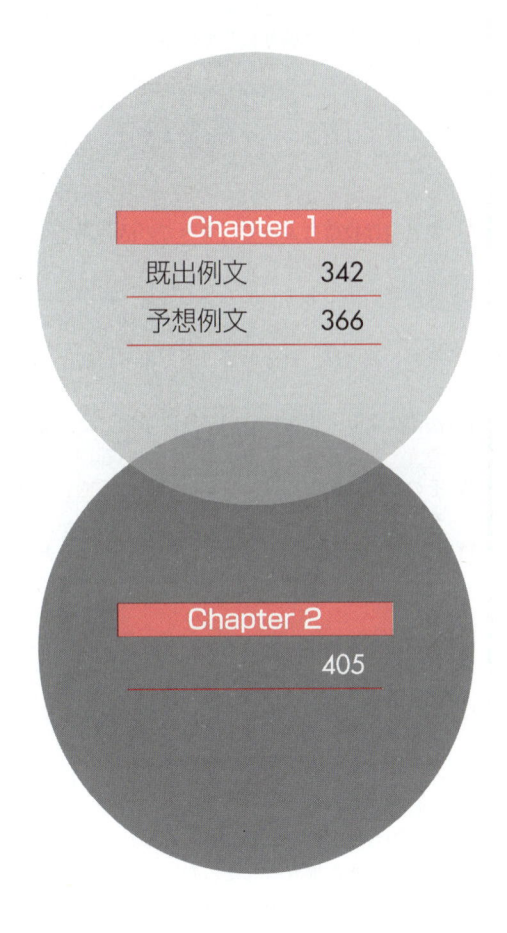

Chapter 2
405

短文の空所補充問題に出題される単熟語

既出例文—動詞

1. 土壇場になって，予想外の悪天候のため，ロケットの発射は中止せざるを得なかった。
2. 検察側が事件を立証できなかったとして，陪審は被告を無罪とした。
3. 会議が公式に休会になった後で，新たな提案についてさらに議論するため，参加者が数名部屋に残った。
4. うちのラジオ局はどのネットワークとも提携していない。私たちは独立した番組編成を大いに誇りにしている。
5. 話をする人たちが割り当てられた時間を超過することがないよう，タイムキーパーが雇われ，終了時刻になったらベルを鳴らすことになった。
6. その作家は自分のエッセイでよくロシア小説にそれとなく言及するが，そのことはロシア小説が彼の作品へ多大な影響を与えていることの表れである。
7. その若い起業家は，25歳になるまでに莫大な個人財産をためたいと思っている。
8. 委員会は投票によって，すべての活動面で性差別を禁止する条項を追加することによりその団体の憲章を改正することに決定した。
9. 披露宴の後であまりにも多くの食べ物が捨てられているのを見て，私はがく然とした。こんな無駄をなくす方法はないのだろうか。
10. その候補者は，自分の負けを，相手候補による自分に不利なキャンペーン広告のせいだと考えた。
11. 法律により，企業は会計年度終了ごとに，帳簿を独立した会計事務所に会計検査をしてもらうことが求められている。
12. その病院の医師団は，少年の病気に困惑し，外部の専門家を呼んで診断の助けをしてもらった。
13. バイヤーたちは私たちの革命的な製品に大きな興味を示していたが，高値にしり込みした。熟慮の結果，私たちはその値段を10パーセント下げることにした。
14. 次の休暇を豪華に過ごしましょう。トレードウィンド・リゾートは，プライベートビーチの白い砂浜での暖かいカリブ海の日光浴へご招待します。
15. 私の上司はいつもみんなの前で私の提案を笑いものにする。彼は私が女性だということだけで軽く見ているのだと思う。
16. その作家の最初の小説が成功したので，彼女は自信が増して奮い立ち，一連の受賞作を著した。
17. 君がやってくれたエンジン修理はひどいもので，おかげで車は1週間とたたないうちにまた壊れてしまった。
18. 戦闘地域からの報道記事は，軍当局によって厳しく検閲されている。

19 その外科医は許可なしに新しい外科的措置を行ったとして院内委員会から正式に非難された。
20 その企業は何らかの方法で規則の抜け道を見つけ、正式な締め切りの後にもかかわらず、契約の入札に加わった。
21 その女性は木の根元に立ち、愛猫を高い枝からなだめて降ろそうとしていた。
22 弁護士は依頼人が自白調書に署名を強いられたと主張した。
23 その消防士たちは火事で子どもたちを救ったことで市長に表彰され、メダルを授与された。
24 費用のかかる環境規制が多くなり、それらを遵守することを強いられ、その企業は利益を上げることがますます難しくなった。
25 10人から成るPTA特別委員会は、毎週土曜日に集まって、地元の学校に関する問題を話し合った。
26 私は彼女のやり方がとても嫌いですが、彼女が腕のいい経営者であることは認めます。
27 軍の上級将校数名が政府を倒そうと共謀しているところを発見された。
28 セクハラとは何であるのかを法的に決定するのは困難なことが多い。
29 大統領の車でのパレードが繁華街を通過する2時間前に、警察は通りのいくつかを遮断し、交通をしめ出した。
30 建物の地下室にある鉄パイプの古い部分は腐食していて水漏れを起こしたと、配管工は確認した。
31 私たちの例年の音楽祭は、地元のミュージシャンが2日間演奏した後、有名なカントリー歌手が登場すると最高潮に達した。
32 ジョンソン上院議員の新たな議案は軍の過剰な支出を削減し、それによって納税者の数百万ドルを節約することが狙いである。
33 ジョージ、あなたは人に責任を任せることを覚えないといけないわ。自分ですべてやることはできないのだから。
34 その新しい本の中で、元警察官は、警察署内で目にした腐敗を「許せない」として非難している。
35 警察はその銀行強盗事件に関連して、2人の男を尋問するめたに拘留した。
36 批評家はその映画のすべてが嫌で、筋はばかばかしく、演技はひどいと酷評した。
37 ヘビはえさをまるごと食べるものとして知られているが、実は食べ物に関しては好みがきわめてうるさい。
38 政府は地域社会の集会を通じて、有毒廃棄物投棄に関する地元住民の不安を払拭したいと願っている。
39 その記者は、いかなる場合でも情報の出所を明らかにしないという条件で、極

既出例文・動詞

秘の情報を得た。
40 その裕福な女性は**だまされて**,そのよそ者が,長いこと行方不明になっていた彼女の甥だと信じてしまっていた。
41 お客の数が**減る**につれ,経営陣はもっと人々を店にひきつけるような新しい戦略を急いで見つけようとした。
42 同僚からの支援**を得られ**なかったので,スティーブンは抗議を諦めざるをえなかった。
43 ロボットから変な音**がして**,やがて煙が出て,次には動かなくなった。
44 その政治家の演説は聞こえのいい言葉で**飾られていた**が,具体的な計画はほとんど含まれていなかった。
45 消防士たちは,すでに火に**包まれていた**建物に閉じ込められた人々を救おうと懸命に作業した。
46 プロのピアニストになるには,孤独な練習に膨大な時間をかける**必要がある**。だから,本当にピアニストになりたいのか,よく考えなさい。
47 その若い候補者は斬新なアイディアと,熱烈な話し振りで有権者**の心を捉えた**が,いったん当選すると,選挙公約を守らなかった。
48 あなたは家賃を数か月滞納しています。今月末までに支払わなければ,私たちとしても,部屋から**立ち退いて**いただかざるをえません。
49 「もし炭鉱を閉鎖するのが許可されたら,地元の失業問題**を悪化させる**だけで終わるだろう」と,鉱山労働者組合の代表は言った。
50 発掘をしている間,考古学者たちは,**発掘された**物がすべて間違いなく適切に確認され,記録されることを保証するように,細心の注意を払った。
51 我々はこの建築プロジェクトをこの財政年度末までに完成させる必要があるので,プロジェクト**を推進する**ために必要なことは何でもしなさい。
52 新しい本の中でその児童心理学者は親であることの喜び**を激賞した**が,同時に子育ては重大な社会責任であると警告した。
53 気候の変化に関する過去の記録から**推定して**,専門家たちは地球温暖化が進むものと予測している。
54 その研究者は,実験結果**をねつ造した**ことがわかり,研究所を解雇された。
55 アジアの一部では経済が**不振で**,政府もその回復策を見い出すことができないようであり,苦境に陥っている。
56 昨日は,宿題をやらなかった理由として**仮病を使った**ので,今日は先生にどんな理由を挙げたらよいか,その生徒は迷っていた。
57 2人の兄弟はどちらが家業を継ぐかで現在,**反目し合っている**。
58 今度の新入社員は立派な学歴にもかかわらず,その研究計画の責任者に任命されたとき**しくじった**ので,交替させられるはめになった。

59 両国が軍事同盟を結成したことによって，防衛力が高まり，軍事予算の削減につながった。
60 最近の脅威を考慮に入れ，現在警備担当者には，入り口で金属探知機が鳴った人であればだれをもボディチェックをする権限がある。
61 外国の病院でボランティアとして働いた楽しい経験から，私は医師になるという希望を強く持つようになった。
62 新しい科学技術は，太陽の力を利用し，それを毎日使うための電気に変換することを容易にした。
63 その老婆は一見したところ貧困のうちに死亡したが，死後ベッドの下に数千ドルをため込んでいるのが発見された。
64 キャンプ旅行の第2夜に寒波が入ってきたので，私たちは焚き火のまわりに身を寄せ合って暖をとった。
65 吹雪のため視界がひどく悪かったので，パイロットは近くの滑走路に緊急着陸することを決心した。
66 ヒマラヤの山の頂に近づくにつれ，深い雪と強い横なぐりの風で，登山家は大いに進行を妨げられた。
67 みなさん，ぜひ私にご投票ください。みんなで力を合わせれば，こうした変化を生むことができるのです。
68 犯していない罪のために12年間も間違えて投獄されていた男が，DNA鑑定で得られた証拠のおかげで釈放された。
69 私にはあなたの分析を支持したい気持ちがありますが，結論を出すにはもっと情報が必要です。
70 入院や治療で多額の医療費のかかりそうな人を特定するのに，遺伝子検査を使うことができる。
71 この新しく発見された恐竜について私たちはあまり知らないが，歯の形から肉食動物であったことが推定される。
72 聴衆の積極的な参加のおかげでそのセミナーは活気がみなぎり，大成功になった。
73 その建設計画の進行はすでに予定より遅れているのに，資材不足でさらに滞った。
74 その若い新入社員は，新企画のために部長のアイディアを盗んだのだろうと部長にほのめかされて，怒って会議を飛び出した。
75 和平会談が失敗した後，国連は反乱軍と政府を話し合いの場に戻そうと仲裁に入った。
76 その政治活動家は警察の圧力に脅されることを拒絶し，政府に対して抗議を続けた。

既出例文・動詞

77 血中アルコール濃度テストの結果，事故当時運転手は<u>酒に酔っていた</u>ことが判明したため，逮捕された。

78 航空機が行方不明になったと報道された後，不安を抱いた肉親からの電話がその航空会社<u>に殺到した</u>。

79 最初にもっと多額の投資をしておくことが，長い目で見ればもっと大きな利潤<u>につながる</u>とその銀行員は我々に保証した。

80 最近のある調査の結果では，英国人は民族料理を誇りに思う点で，他のヨーロッパ人よりはるかに<u>立ち遅れている</u>ことが示されている。

81 オルブライト博士は最新作の中で，彼が「核心的な精神的価値」と呼んでいるものの放棄が増加していることを<u>嘆いている</u>。

82 首相は新しい課税計画への支持<u>を得る</u>ために，できるだけのことをしている。

83 その川は森や野原をゆっくりと<u>曲がりくねって</u>海へと流れる。

84 物語を語る人のなだめるような声に，子どもたちはすっかり<u>魅了され</u>，身動きもせずに座っていた。

85 そのプロジェクトが論争に<u>はまり込んで</u>しまったので，意見の一致が得られるまで，私たちは資金供給を延期した。

86 予期せぬ贈り物で妻の機嫌<u>を和らげられる</u>と思ったが，私が突然に記念日の夕食を取りやめにした埋め合わせにはならなかった。

87 その申し出を受けるか拒否するかの最終決定をする前に，我々はそれ<u>についてじっくり考える</u>必要があるだろう。

88 空腹とのどの渇きで弱ってはいたが，道に迷ったそのハイカーは，何とか歩き続ける力<u>を奮い起こした</u>。

89 組合の指導者たちは，会社の現存する契約は労働法規に違反していると主張し，<u>破棄する</u>ことを要求した。

90 いじめが起こりやすくなるのは，ある人が<u>のけ者にされ</u>その集団の外に置かれるときである。

91 取締役たちはその社長<u>を追い出して</u>，外部の者を彼に代えることに賛成の票を投じた。

92 ウィルソン家の人々が数週間外国にいた後で帰国してみると，庭は雑草<u>で覆われていた</u>。

93 政府が行った調査によって，毒性の廃棄物がその工場周辺全体の土壌<u>に浸透している</u>ことが明らかになった。

94 予定の飛行機が欠航になり，重要な会議に出席できなくなったため，その重役はおおいに<u>困惑した</u>。

95 彼女の新しい学生への好奇心は，彼の父が世界的に有名なテニス選手だという噂によって<u>そそられた</u>のであった。

96 その店の支配人は，配達されることのなかった販売品目の代わりに割引券を提供することで，怒った客の気持ちを和らげようとした。
97 その会社の四半期の収益に関する悪い知らせが出た後で，株価は49%急落し，その年の最安値で終わった。
98 先延ばしにするのをやめなさい。この調査用紙を今日中に発送しないと，締め切りに間に合わないぞ。
99 詮索するつもりはありませんが，もしかしてあなたはランカスター在住のブリックウェル家とご関係がありませんか。
100 増加する暴力の恐怖を抑える目的で，政府は自動武器の所持を違法とする新しい法律を成立させた。
101 よく冷えた1杯のレモネードほど，夏の暑い月に喉の渇きを癒してくれるものはない。
102 暴徒は店先を荒らしたり，停めてある車をひっくり返したりしながら都心部を数ブロックほど暴れ回った。
103 休暇から帰宅すると，家が荒らされ，貴重品がみんななくなっていた。
104 私は新しい隣人と知り合いになろうとしたが，彼は私のお付き合いの申し出をすべて拒絶した。
105 相手側が譲歩したので，この話し合いを進めるつもりなら，あなた方はそれに報いる必要がある。
106 株式市場は下がっていたが，ジェームズはある程度損失を取り返そうと市場に留まっていた。
107 不注意なご主人へのアドバイス ― 奥さんの誕生日を忘れたのですか。それなら，花束を買ってきて名誉を回復してください。
108 そのアパートの火事から数週間，玄関は焼けたペンキの臭いを放っていた。
109 その古いホテルは，70周年を記念して全面的に改装され，まもなく市で一番のホテルという評判を取り戻した。
110 あなたの会社は私たちの契約期間のすべての旅費を私たちに返済してくれますか。
111 政府の役人が決してテロリストと交渉しないという意見を繰り返しても，人質の肉親は行詰まりに対して穏やかな解決を要求した。
112 同窓会は楽しかった。久しぶりに会って昔のことを思い出して話をするのはよかった。
113 「新しい税法がこの国の経済復興を遅くしている」とその怒った政治家は言った。「今すぐに撤回させるべきである」
114 石油産業の後押しを受けて，消費者団体は，新しいガソリン税を撤廃するよう政府に要求した。

既出例文・名詞

115 私は新しい考えを十分に受け入れ，批判にも巧みに対応する人物として，この候補者を推薦いたします。
116 外務大臣は，もし自分の国に貿易制裁が加えられれば自分の国も同様の制裁で報復するだろう，と言った。
117 その寝袋の素材は火のまわりを遅らせはするが，100％の不燃性ではないと使用説明書に警告してあった。
118 州の新しい条例に従わないならば，当局はあなたの会社の営業許可を取り消さざるを得ない。
119 新しく当選した国会議員は，長い間のライバルに勝利したことを喜んだ。
120 かかりつけの医師は，その病気の原因を突きとめられず，専門家の意見を求めざるを得なかった。
121 妻と私は，しばしば，だれが手紙をチェックするべきかとか，だれが目覚まし時計をセットすべきか，というようなつまらないことでけんかする。
122 衛生官たちは，危険な新型インフルエンザの流行の抑制に役立てようと，集団予防接種計画を設けた。
123 独裁政府は反対意見を抑圧する方法をいくつも持っており，多くの場合軍事力に頼る。
124 会社の規則では，機械の操縦者はすべてその職につく前に安全のための講習を受けることが規定されている。
125 「新プロジェクトの開発にいくら必要だと思う？」
「私たちの予測だと，1万ドルあれば十分だと思う」
126 その刑事は事件を再現した後で，その強盗事件には少なくとも3人がかかわっていると推測した。
127 その不誠実な投資アドバイザーは彼の顧客数名から老後の貯えをだまし取った。
128 その自転車競技の優勝者の勝利は，不法な麻薬使用の申し立てで汚点がついた。
129 飛行機トイレ内の煙感知器に無断で手を加えることは法律により罰せられる重大な犯罪行為です。
130 選挙運動への違法な献金が報道されたため，今日まで数々の業績を上げたにもかかわらず，その候補者の名声には傷がついてしまった。
131 その電子工学会社は深刻な財政困難に陥っていて，破産のがけっぷちをさまよっている。
132 バスケットボールのコーチは，チームの成績が悪いことの責任をとってシーズンの最終戦の後，チームのオーナーに辞任を申し出た。
133 勝利のパットを沈めた後でそのゴルファーは，空にこぶしを突き上げた。

134　突然の嵐による強風で，船は航路から外れてしまった。
135　自分が話す順番になったとき，自分の考えを伝える能力のなさに悩んだ。
136　その科学者の議論を呼んだ説は，他の研究者たちが彼の実験データを確認したとき，やっと立証された。
137　何年もレイチェルの同僚だったので，彼女の正直さと真面目さは，私が保証できる。
138　クラシック音楽への関心が薄れているため，交響楽の演奏会の切符の売り上げが減少している。
139　この会社は市場の占有率を落とすことなく，4年にわたる不況期を乗り切ったが，これは全社員の賞賛に値することである。
140　ハリケーンが陸地に近づいて来るにつれ，強い風と激しい雨が海岸近くの村落をめちゃめちゃに破壊する恐れが出てきた。

既出例文―名詞

141　その上院議員の議論のばからしさが，税制改革という議題について彼にまったく知識がないことを反映していた。
142　政敵からの巧みな中傷キャンペーンにもかかわらず，市長は再選された。
143　その新しいレストランはアールデコ調の室内装飾と洗練された雰囲気を備えているので，値段が手ごろなのに嬉しい驚きを感じた。
144　医者は，患者が手術中に起きていられるように，局所麻酔をすると説明した。
145　2人の市長候補は辛らつな批評や敵意に満ちた選挙広告の中で，互いに憎悪をむき出しにしていた。
146　自国の人権侵害に異議を唱えたかどで投獄されるのを恐れ，そのジャーナリストはスウェーデンへの政治亡命を求めた。
147　委員会の年長者たちは，すぐに指導体制を変えるべきだという提案をする新人の図々しさに憤慨した。
148　提案された消費税の引き上げに対する世論の反発が非常に大きかったので，政府は計画の見直しをせざるを得なかった。
149　この新しい翻訳ソフトウェアは，海外の客からの電子メールを理解するのに苦労しているビジネスマンには朗報になろう。
150　数人がけがをしたけんかに関与したので，両方の野球チームの選手が出場停止となった。
151　その建設会社が予定通りに橋を完成できなかったとき，市は契約違反でその会社を訴えた。

152 新しいディスカウント・ショッピングモールの成功は，その地域の他の店を破産の瀬戸際に追い込んだ。
153 フライトの後，グレアムは荷物の回転式コンベアーのところで30分待っていたが，彼のスーツケースが出てくる気配はなかった。
154 有罪（死刑）を宣告されたその男は，彼の最後の慈悲の請願を知事が棄却した後に処刑された。
155 けんかが突然始まると，サッカーの観衆の間に大きな騒ぎが起こった。
156 おとり捜査官によって警察の関与が明らかにされた後，警察はその密輸事件の共犯として告発された。
157 友人の事故のニュースはとてもショックだったので，スーザンが落ち着きを取り戻すのにはしばらくかかった。
158 暴動がいつ起こるか分からないので，どのような不測の事態に対しても備えておくように，軍の責任者は指令された。
159 「要するに，もし生産コストを劇的に減らすことができなければ，国内の工場をすべて閉鎖しなければならないということだ」と社長は言った。
160 離婚訴訟の判決で，裁判官は母親に夫妻の子どもたちの親権を与えた。
161 ロックバンドの新しいCD宣伝のためのコンサートは，5人のメンバーのうちの2人が酔っぱらってほとんど演奏できない状況で登場して，完全な失敗に終わった。
162 ハリケーンの後，洪水の跡に残った瓦礫を取り除くのに数週間かかった。
163 その少女の人前での力強い振る舞いは，私生活での彼女の内気な態度とはとても対照的だった。
164 その地域の石炭業の消滅は，地域経済を不況に追い込んだ。
165 万引きを厳しく罰するのは効果的な防止策でないかもしれない。自分が捕まると思っている人はほとんどいないからだ。
166 その女性は医者の命令も聞かずに残業を続け，健康を害してしまった。
167 最近空は大変込んでいるので，1機の飛行機が飛行計画からちょっと外れただけでも大変危険となりうる。
168 私たちは最近私たちのチームが努力をしていないというコーチの怒った痛烈な非難を何時間にも感じられるくらい聞いていた。
169 新しい体育館についての提案で唯一の欠点は，実施するのに金がかかることである。
170 木綿の生地から汚れを取り除く際のその化学物質の有効性を調べるために，実験室でのテストが行われた。
171 学生活動家たちは，怒りと抗議を表明して，新しい軍事独裁者の等身大の人形を燃やした。

172	その熟練した警察官は，10の犯罪容疑で訴えられたが，それには盗まれた銃の売買と公金の<u>着服</u>も含まれている。
173	安全保障理事会の緊急会議で，突然の侵攻は国連加入国の明らかな主権<u>侵害</u>だったということで合意した。
174	党の指導者たちの仲裁にもかかわらず，2つの政治陣営間の<u>敵意</u>は依然強い。
175	著者は最新刊の中で，犯罪率の高さは社会における家族の価値が<u>衰退</u>し続けていることが原因だとしている。
176	歴史的に有名なその地域にある新しい建築物は，内部はとても近代的であるが，通りから見ると<u>外観</u>はその地域の18世紀の様式を残している。
177	その販売促進運動は，市場調査のための十分な資金が調達されなかったために，<u>大失敗</u>に終わった。
178	下の階に降りて行って何も見つからなかったので，聞こえてきた奇妙な音は<u>想像の産物</u>だったと，自分に言い聞かせた。
179	私にそんなにいいことをたくさん言ってくれても無駄ですよ。<u>お世辞</u>は役には立ちませんよ。
180	今年のうちの野球チームはひどい。だから，先週，リーグでもっとも強いチームに勝ったことは単なる<u>まぐれ</u>であった。
181	夕方のニュース番組は救急隊員が浸水した家から家族を救い出す<u>映像</u>を流した。
182	その製造業者は，自社のコンピュータがハードディスクの<u>欠陥</u>でたびたび動かなくなったので，回収した。
183	何度も挫折があったが，締め切りが近づいていたので，プロジェクト・チームは<u>前進</u>し続けた。
184	<u>後になって考えてみると</u>，大学に行けという父の忠告に従わなかったことを後悔している。
185	その歌手が悲劇的な死を遂げた後で，ファンは，彼が射殺された場所に集まり，ろうそくを灯して，彼に<u>敬意</u>を表した。
186	新しい会社の株価が上がるという<u>予感</u>に基づいて，私はブローカーに電話して100株買った。
187	和平交渉は双方ともそれ以上の譲歩をしようとしなかったために，<u>行き詰まって</u>しまった。
188	その航空会社は客に早期に予約をさせる<u>刺激策</u>として，特別予約料金を提供している。
189	この財団は設立の<u>当初</u>からそれに値する大勢の大学生に金銭面の援助を提供している。

既出例文・名詞

190 先生はその生徒の期末試験の素晴らしい結果と，前の試験の低い点数の間の差異に衝撃を受けた。
191 その絵画のオークションでは，購入希望者は5万ドルから始めて1千ドル単位の増額で入札するよう要請されていた。
192 歴史的に見て，有権者は初めて立候補する人よりも再選をねらう現職者を好む傾向がある。
193 接近戦の選挙で，その候補者が勝ったとき，彼の支持者の間から歓喜の声とホッとした安堵の声が上がった。
194 交渉のこの重要な時点において，われわれは結束して要求をし続けることが必要である。
195 私の兄［弟］は物を修理する特技を持っている。家の物がいつ壊れても，彼はその直し方を知っている。
196 その女優は，彼女が違法な麻薬を使用したという誤った中傷記事を掲載したことで，その新聞社を名誉毀損で訴えた。
197 航空会社が利用客にサービスの質について意見を求めたとき，公衆はうんざりするほど数多くの不満で答えた。
198 その弁護士は，税法に，その企業が莫大な金額を節約できる抜け穴を見つけ出した。
199 選挙でのその政治家の大勝利は，不正を取り除くという彼の計画を支持するはっきりとした民意の現れであった。
200 実業界で出世したいなら，よき助言者，つまりキャリアのことで力になってくれる年配の重役を持つことが重要だ。
201 選手のほとんどはコーチの戦術に大きな疑念を抱いていたが，チームからはずされることを恐れて何も言わなかった。
202 ますます多くのデータが大衆の手に入るにつれて，新しいダムへの反対は勢いを増した。
203 その企業は技術的に優れたスポーツカーで最高級車市場に得意分野を確立した。
204 毎年この日には，大震災による市の破壊を悼んで記念祭が行なわれる。
205 マラリアにかかると，患者は熱や震えなどの症状を経験する。
206 金銭的援助は第三世界の国々の諸問題に対する万能薬ではない。彼らは自立することを学ばねばならない。
207 テロ攻撃の可能性があると警告を受けた後，司令官は基地周辺をパトロールする警護者の数を増やした。
208 容疑者は自分の話をもう一度話す機会を与えてほしいと懇願したが，彼の嘆願は無視された。

209 テレビで放送された洪水による被災者の窮状に同情して，全国の人々は食料，毛布，それに衣類を寄付した。
210 その子の不作法は，ほとんど両親の注意を引くためだけの手だった。
211 裁判所のその判決は，インターネット上での個人情報に関するそれ以後の法律にとって先例となった。
212 生物は最初から明確な型に分れていることを示唆して，その教授は進化の基本的な教えに異議を唱えた。
213 夏の間中，その地域の降雨量が通常よりかなり少なかったので，住民は節水するようにとの通告を受けた。
214 ショーンは何か良くないことが起こりそうな予感を感じていたが，果たせるかな，まさにその翌日，株式市場での貯えをすべて失ってしまった。
215 日本とのよりよい関係を促進するために，アジアの国の中には日本語の技能を入学の条件とすることを考えている大学もある。
216 事件への警察の調査の結果，その企業の重役の多くが市の職員を買収しようとしていたことが分かった。
217 インターネットの人気が上がって，主にウェブサイトを閲覧したり電子メールを送るために使用する顧客を狙った，手に入れやすい低価格のコンピュータが広く行き渡ることになった。
218 ジェフリーは何か悪いことが起こると他の人たちに罪を押し付ける傾向があった。だから，彼がその事故の責任すべてをとったときは私たちは驚いた。
219 先週末開催された会議に，銃所持が違法行為になるような新たな戦略を練るために，銃規制支持者が全国から集まった。
220 その祭典の準備委員会は悪天候に備えて広い屋内競技場を予約した。
221 事故現場のすぐ近くに住んでいる人たちは，こぼれた化学物質が除去されるまで，家から避難させられた。
222 サムはトップにのぼりつめるために同僚を踏みつけることに対して何の後ろめたさも持っていなかった。
223 不安定な市場環境の中で管理者たちは生産を増やすべきかそれとも減らすべきかをめぐって，ジレンマに陥っていた。
224 外で行われている夜間の道路工事は騒音がうるさくて，私たちはだれも眠れなかった。
225 販売部長はスタッフといい関係を築いているが，オープンなコミュニケーション方針をとれば，能率が上がると考えているのである。
226 定期的にビタミンCを多量に服用する一般的な根拠は，ビタミンCが身体の免疫機構を強化するというものだ。
227 人気のあるクリスマスキャロルを独創的に歌ったその歌手の歌い方は，聴衆

既出例文・形容詞

におおいに受けた。
228 私の過失ではなかったが，部署の悪い成績の<u>罪を負わされ</u>，私は仕事を失った。
229 従業員たちは，人員削減で一時解雇されたとき，6か月分の給料に相当する<u>解雇</u>手当を受け取った。
230 週末にまれに映画のセットから解放されると，その監督は山の静かな隠れ家に<u>慰め</u>を求め，創造力を充電したものだった。
231 党員は選挙運動中は<u>団結</u>を維持していたが，終わるといくつかの派閥に分裂した。
232 新しく選出された首相は，戦略的に重要な湾岸地域における自国の影響力の<u>範囲</u>を広げるつもりだと言った。
233 マーサは初めてのボーナスをもらうとすぐ買い物<u>騒ぎ</u>に出かけ，自分と家族全員のために贈り物を買った。
234 私の意見では，当局は過度の騒音公害に対してもっと厳しい<u>姿勢</u>をとるべきである。
235 組織は，あなたにこの仕事の専任分の給与を出すことはできないが，日々の出費をまかなうくらいの<u>俸給</u>は少しお出しします。
236 2歳のその子は母がキャンディを与えないと，ひどい<u>かんしゃく</u>を起こした。
237 勤務成績が悪かったという理由でその従業員を解雇したことは正当な理由があると認められたが，支配人はもっとしっかりとした訓練を彼に施さなかったことに刺すような<u>後悔の念</u>を覚えた。
238 その弁護士は建設会社に対し，今後も夜遅く騒音の出る機器の使用を続けるなら，地元住民が会社を訴える旨の<u>最後通告</u>を出した。
239 タイヤを切り裂き，窓ガラスを破るなどの<u>器物破壊行為</u>の増加への対処として，市長は中心街の辺りを巡回するために追加の警察官を任命するように要請した。
240 来年の大会の日取りは決めたが，1,500人の参加者を収容できる<u>開催地</u>は決まっていない。
241 政府からの思いがけないほどの大きな契約を受け，その製造業社は喜んだ。それは，その後数年間の財政的安定を約束する<u>予期せぬ幸運</u>であった。

既出例文―形容詞

242 新しい市長はスラム街を見て回り，彼のまわりに広がる<u>悲惨な</u>貧困状況にショックを受けた。

243 双方が妥協しようとしないので，貿易交渉の雰囲気は<u>辛らつさ</u>を増し，その結果，無期限の延期となった。

244 その少数党は<u>巧みな</u>政治工作によって，保健法案を通過させた。

245 その知事は公金悪用の<u>容疑</u>で調べを受けている。

246 大統領は説得力があり<u>歯切れの良い</u>演説者であるから，彼の教育改革に支持を取りつけるのに何の苦労もなかった。

247 ケビンは理事会と良い関係になろうとして，<u>抜け目なく</u>多くの理事がゴルフをするカントリー・クラブの会員になった。

248 定期検査で医師は患者の胃に腫瘍を見つけたが，運がよいことに，それは<u>良性</u>だった。

249 その男の不注意な運転のくせは<u>明らかに</u>他人の安全を無視していた。

250 その女優はテレビでのインタビューのあいだ，<u>何も包み隠すことなく</u>，彼女の私生活に関わる，もっとも知りたい質問にも答えていた。

251 この重役職に関しては，給与は経験<u>に応じて</u>決まる。すぐれた業績のある部長には応募を勧める。

252 その会社は弁護士に現在の法律事務所を辞めさせるのに，非常に<u>心を動かすような</u>2つの条件，つまりより高い給料とより短い就労時間を提示した。

253 現在わが社は市場で最大のシェアを持っているが，<u>自己満足</u>にならないようにしよう。今の成功に寄りかかることはできない。

254 私はいつも図書館で試験勉強をする。というのも，寮の雰囲気が勉強の上で<u>良い結果につながら</u>ないからである。

255 そのコンピュータのメーカーは，<u>欠陥のある</u>チップが見つかったので，一番新しい機種のパソコンを回収した。

256 現在の<u>人口統計</u>の傾向を見積もって考えると，先進国では出生率が下がり続けると予測できる。

257 ラジオのインタビューで自分のチームの何人かの選手を<u>笑い者にする</u>コメントをしたとして，その野球の監督は非難を受けた。

258 銀鉱が閉鎖されるとみんな町を出て行った。かつて賑やかだった地域社会も今ではまったく<u>閑散としている</u>。

259 来月，工場が閉鎖されることを知らされて，労働者たちは失望し<u>落胆して</u>その集会を後にした。

260 自転車に乗っていたその人はけがをしており，<u>緊急に</u>治療が必要だったが，

既出例文・形容詞

数マイル四方，病院はなかった。

261 そのスキャンダルに関連している人々のプライバシーを尊重してその記者は，控えめな質問を少ししただけだった。

262 その映画批評家は，アジアの映画の質について先ごろ自分がけなすような発言をしたことで詫びた。

263 反体制の学生グループが集まり，反政府の抗議運動を組織した。

264 本校の学生にはかつては素直で従順という評判があったが，現在ではいろいろと規律面の問題を起こしている。

265 新しい全国税計画議案はみじめにも廃案になったので，この問題は数年間放置されていたが，新しく当選した2人の政治家が再びそれを取り上げた。

266 投資をする前に，危険の低さと利回りの良さは互いに相容れないものだということを認識すべきだ。

267 警告：この映画には露骨な暴力シーンが含まれていますので，子どもには不適当です。

268 世界人口の急激な増加に直面して，未来の世代のために天然資源を保存するように，一層努めなければならない。

269 その犯罪には目撃者がいなかったが，髪の毛や指紋といった法廷で使える証拠がすぐに容疑者の逮捕につながった。

270 新型のコンピュータ・ウイルスが常に出現している中で，完全なコンピュータの安全を確保することは大変な仕事である。

271 提案された山岳探索は危険を伴うので心配される。そのため，もっとも強靭で経験豊富な登山家のみ参加を許される。

272 水漏れするボートから水を汲み出そうとするのは無駄と分かり，私たちは岸に向かって泳がなければならなかった。

273 亡命者たちは不運な状況に陥っていた。祖国に引き返すこともできなければ，亡命先の国にも留まれなかった。

274 多忙を極めたスケジュールにもかかわらず，その最高責任者は組み立てラインの従業員ひとりひとりに話しかける時間を定期的にとっていた。

275 死刑を肯定する人たちは，犯罪の中には死刑を正当化するほど凶悪なものもあると主張する。

276 その美術品収集家は，18世紀に作られたそのようなすばらしい花瓶が，蚤の市で完全な状態で売られているのを見つけて喜んだ。

277 洪水の水位は高くなりつつあったが，その町には差し迫った危険はなかった。

278 一時解雇が差し迫っているという噂は，会社の士気に重大な悪影響を与えた。

279 ゴミの総量を減らすために，政府がさらに多くのことをしてリサイクル対策

を強化することが絶対必要である。
280 請求書に関しての間違いは、不注意によるものだということを保証致します。不当な代金を要求するつもりはまったくございませんでした。
281 その候補者はライバルの個人的生活について扇情的な発言を行い、市政史において最もひどい中傷作戦を誘発することになった。
282 収賄スキャンダルへの関わりは、市長の評判に拭えない汚点を残し、やがて辞職へと追いやった。
283 連絡船はいつも過剰に客を乗せていた。いずれ事故が起こるのは必然であった。
284 その技師たちはまともな装備がなくても、その故障を直せる巧みな修理法を考えついた。
285 いつもの同じ提案にはうんざりだ。私たちに必要なのは、この問題に対する斬新な解決策である。
286 不動産業者は、購買契約に一度サインをしたら、それは解約不可能だと言って、私たちに忠告してくれた。サインをしたら後戻りはできないということだ。
287 調査官によると、美術館の安全システムが非常に甘かったため、泥棒たちは絵画を盗むことができた。
288 その野球選手の今までの悪行を考慮すると、たった1試合だけ出場させないというコーチの決定はまったく寛大なものだった。
289 カジノ事業は非常に利益が上がることが分かってきたので、そのカジノの持ち主は他の都市に事業を広げることにした。
290 フランクは安い給料で暮らしているので、友人たちと外食する余裕がなかなかなかった。
291 ブロードウェイでのそのショーをべた褒めしていた新聞の論評を読んで、私たちは見に行かなければと思ったが、並みの演技にかなりがっかりさせられた。
292 新しく採用されたそのソフトウェア・エンジニアは、コンピュータ室の床掃除というつまらない仕事をあてがわれた。
293 この病院は、臓器移植をめぐる無数の法的問題を扱うのに、弁護士の一団に頼っている。
294 航海も2時間になると、私は吐き気を感じ始め、胃のむかつきをおさえるために薬を飲まなければならなかった。
295 警告を聞いていなかったので、そのスキーヤーたちは手遅れになるまで雪崩の危険を知らないままでいた。
296 今朝の降雪は競技に最適の条件を提供するだろうと、スキーの役員たちは喜

既出例文・形容詞

んで報告した。

297 その宮殿の水晶のシャンデリアを飾った豪華な食堂は，費用がかかりすぎて火災後の再建は不可能だった。

298 聴衆は唖然とした。講演者がこんなひどいコメントをするのを聞いたことがなかったからである。

299 株主が大いに失望したことには，その企業の株価は過去1年でたった0.1%上昇しただけである。

300 森林警備隊員は徒歩旅行者たちに対して，すでに危険な状況にあるその山への登山は気象の変化によってさらに危険度が高まるだろう，と警告した。

301 あなたが言っていることはこの話し合いに関係がない。テーマから逸れないようにしてください。

302 もし君が僕をこんな豪華なレストランに連れてくると分かっていたら，もっときちんとした服装をしてきたのに。ここで上着とネクタイをつけていないのは僕だけだ。

303 重役は「もう時間がないし，この計画はあまりにも非現実的だ。この問題に対してはもっと現実的な方法をとる必要がある」と言った。

304 最終テストで良い成績がとれたからといって，この科目でAがとれると思うなんておこがましい。出席も同じくらい重要だ。

305 大きな岩石を機械の助けなしに長い距離を移動するには，ピラミッドをつくった人たちの桁外れの努力が必要だったに違いない。

306 社長の健康状態が悪化していることを考慮し，重役会のメンバーは彼に代わる人を探し始めることが賢明であると判断した。

307 その隠遁作家が公の場に姿を現したという噂が立ってから，テレビ報道陣が彼の居所を突きとめようと互いに競い合っている。

308 そのビクトリア朝風ホテルは博物館のようで，アンティーク家具や装飾品でいっぱいだった。

309 その著者は今度の小説については会見者と熱心に話し合ったが，最近の自身の離婚については何も語らなかった。

310 私の初歩的な医療知識をもってしても，友人の脚のけがはひどく，緊急の手当てが必要なことは明白だった。

311 メアリーはジョンが就職できると自信を持っていたが，面接後の彼の悲しそうな表情は，うまくいきそうもないと語っていた。

312 そのハリウッドの映画は次から次へと辛らつな批評を浴びたが，それでも，何百万という人が見にやってきた。

313 停戦が実施されていたにもかかわらず，まだ反乱軍に占拠された地域では散発的な暴力行為が報告された。

314 その人権団体は難民キャンプの劣悪な生活環境を厳しく批判する報告書を出した。
315 敵対勢力の強力な反対にもかかわらず，その国会議員は貧しい人々のための公営住宅の支援姿勢を崩さなかった。
316 新しいそのホラー映画に関するその映画批評家による「映画そのものがひどいものだ。見るべきではない」という論評は，簡潔で的を得たものであった。
317 「イ・オールデ・スイート・ショップで，たまらなく食欲をそそるように並べられたケーキと手作りのお菓子をどうぞ」
318 うそ発見器によるテストを拒否することは，時として罪を犯したことを認めたことと同等とみなされる。
319 重役会が水曜日の会合で合併案を承認するものとして，木曜日に集まって協定に署名するように仮の計画を立てておきましょう。
320 予想に反して，一般市民は新しい知事の演説に気のない拍手をしただけだった。
321 些細なことに聞こえるかもしれませんが，この2つの単語の間にはハイフンがいると思います。
322 携帯電話は10年前は珍しかったが，現在ではどこにでもあるものになった。
323 その少年が父の車を洗うと言ったのには隠れた動機があった。週末にそれを借りようと思っていたのだ。
324 その投資アドバイザーは他の投資家が見逃してしまう儲け株を選び取る，人並み外れた能力をもっていた。
325 楽しい最初の飛行の後，その女性は飛行に対する自分の恐れが根拠のないものだったと悟った。
326 固く決心したその重役は，仕事に就いたその日以来ずっと会社社長の地位を絶えず追い求めてきた。
327 そのクラブの新しいピアニストは非常に多才で，ジャズからクラシックまで何でも演奏できる。
328 残念なことに，代替エネルギー源に投資をするそちらの委員会の計画は現段階では実行可能ではない。我々には推進すべき資金がまったくない。
329 顧客がジャニスの明るい人柄に惹かれたので，彼女がセールスで成功するのに長くはかからなかった。
330 争っている当事者双方は停戦に同意しているが，状況は依然不安定で，闘いがいつまた始まるかわからない。
331 10代の多くはものすごい食欲がある。彼らは食べることを決してやめないようだ。

既出例文—副詞

332 その教授は，彼の研究とは逆の証拠を見せられた後も，自分の意見を変えることを<u>断固</u>拒否した。

333 ウォルドーフ・スミザース卿の意思は，彼の地所から生じる資産は４人の子どもに<u>公平</u>に分配されることであった。

334 これらの無人島に軍隊を派遣することによって，あなたの国は<u>非道にも</u>私たちと交わした協定を破った。

335 今のような経済的に厳しい時代に，収入内でやっていこうとすれば人々はますます<u>倹約して</u>生きなければならなくなる。

336 その教師がどんなに生徒の関心を引こうとしても，生徒たちは<u>無関心</u>に机に向かったままで，授業に参加しようとはしなかった。

337 美術館のオープニングに出席した他のゲストたちは<u>申し分なく</u>着飾っていたので，カジュアルなセーターとジーンズを着ていたクリスは場違いな感じだった。

338 新たな高額の広告キャンペーンにもかかわらず，その四半期の売り上げは<u>わずかに</u>増えたのみであった。

339 私のルームメートは<u>几帳面に</u>掃除をするので，部屋の彼女の側にはほこり1つない。

340 遠くで<u>不気味に</u>大きくなっている黒雲は，激しい嵐が発生していることを示していた。

341 警察官の質問に答える内容が矛盾だらけだったことからも，容疑者が嘘をついているのは<u>だれが見ても</u>明らかだった。

342 その映画は子どもの悲劇的な死というとても<u>痛ましい形で</u>終わったので，観衆は泣いた。

343 そのホテルのマネージャーは，私たちの予約に混乱があったことで<u>過度</u>に謝罪し，予約していたものより高級な部屋を私たちに提供してくれた。

344 その大きな遠洋定期船は，ゆったりと<u>静か</u>にその最後の航海に港から出て行った。

345 元首相の葬列は，ゆっくりと<u>厳粛</u>に通りを墓地へ向かって進んでいった。

346 犯罪現場には具体的な証拠が何一つなかったが，それにもかかわらず，その捜査官は<u>粘り強く</u>手がかりを探し続けた。

347 その会合で，ストライキの動議はみんなが賛成の挙手をして<u>満場一致</u>で採択された。

348 その教員組合は自分たちの職業の保証が脅かされるという理由から，人事に関する理事会の新しい提案に<u>激しく</u>反対した。

既出例文―熟語

349 以前は所得税改革で争っていた二大政党は，ついに歩み寄りの兆しを見せ始めた。

350 政府は，経営困難な金融機関を公的資金によって救済するという，物議をかもしている計画を，ついに断念した。

351 私は今週末，彼の手伝いには期待していない。今までにも何回も裏切られたから。

352 コーチの激励の言葉の後，我々のチームは選手権試合で優勝を勝ち取る準備は万全だった。

353 「そんな話をぼくが信じるなんて思うなよ，ジュリアン。うぶじゃあるまいし」
「だけど本当なんだよ！　家族のだれに聞いてもいいよ」

354 こんなに忙しかったことはないよ！　仕事に忙殺されて，いつ終わるのか見当もつかない。

355 宇宙飛行士たちが何か月にわたって，小さな宇宙ステーション内で生活することによるストレスにどのように耐えるのかを調べるため，専門家のチームが結成された。

356 安全を強化するため，その企業は新しいハイテク警報システムを取り付け，あと数人の警備員を雇った。

357 大統領は選挙の年までにはそのスキャンダルが忘れられることを望んでいたが，マスコミはこの話題を打ち切らないよう決意しているかのようだった。

358 監督者の主たる責任は，労働者の生産性を高めることと結果の数字を改善することに帰着する。

359 クリス，怒りを抑えたままではいけない。何で悩んでいるのか言ってごらん。

360 私たちはかなり長い時間働き，みな疲れていたので，終わりにして帰宅することにした。

361 私は角を曲がったときにトラックに衝突しそうになった。本当に危機一髪だった。

362 どうやってこの情報を得たの？　極秘のはずだけど。

363 その若者はいつも一攫千金を狙った計画を立てていたが，どれ1つうまくいかなかった。

364 私たちは情報通信技術の最先端でさらに競争力を強めるために，当社の研究努力を強化させています。

365 その問題は法的に込み入っているので，私たちは弁護士に契約書を作成して

もらうべきです。

366 私は一晩中寝ていなかったので，午前の授業で<u>うとうと</u>しないでいるのは大変だった。

367 その環境保護団体は公開の会合を開き，川沿いの新しい工場建設禁止に向けての支持<u>を獲得しようとした</u>。

368 脱税が見つかってしまったからには，あなたは<u>甘んじて罰を受け</u>なければならない。

369 何年にもわたる計画にもかかわらず，新しい複合ショッピング・センターを建設しようとするプロジェクトは，何人かの住民が土地を売るのを拒否したため最後の段階で<u>失敗した</u>。

370 取り調べを終えるために君が私に不愉快な質問をする必要があることはわかっている。<u>さっさと始めなさい</u>。私は何も隠すことはない。

371 その役員は新しい事業の長となる積極的な人物を求めていた。彼女は最終的に，サンドラ<u>がそれにぴったりだ</u>と判断して彼女にその職を与えた。

372 キャシー，それはいい考えだけど，上司に提出するまでには，もっと詳しい情報で<u>肉付けし</u>なくちゃ。

373 フレッドが今週4度目に宿題を提出しなかったとき，先生は<u>ひどく怒って</u>クラス全員の前でどなりつけた。

374 主な競争相手が製品を5％割引で売り始めたので，当社も<u>追随して</u>同様に値引きするしかなかった。

375 兄は車とぜいたくな休暇に遺産<u>を浪費して</u>しまい，今では一文無しである。

376 この計画が実行不可能であるのは，みんなが同意している。それは忘れて，もう一度<u>最初から</u>始めてはどうだろう。

377 ケビンはしばらく運に見放されていたが，旧友が就職の話で電話をくれて，ようやく<u>状況は好転した</u>。

378 宿題が見つからなかったというデイブの授業欠席の理由は信じ難かったが，教師は<u>善意に解釈して</u>，成績を下げなかった。

379 ケリーはボーイフレンドが自分の親友といちゃついているところを見たので，彼<u>を無視した</u>。

380 そのスポークスマンは話の中で会社が犯した多くの失敗<u>を巧妙に言い繕おう</u>とした。

381 ジョナサンの提案を受け入れるよう上司に言われたが，そのことは本当に<u>不本意だ</u>。いまだに私の提案の方がよほどいいと思う。

382 不幸にもテッドは有名になった後，成功に<u>うぬぼれて</u>，とても横柄に振る舞い始めた。

383 「ジェレミア<u>の優秀さは認める</u>べきだ。彼は職場でだれよりも働く量が少な

384	いのに，すべてうまく手柄を独占しているから」ジャックはお気に入りの馬にすべてを賭け，生涯すべての蓄えが<u>どうなるか分からない</u>中で，固唾をのんでレースを見守った。
385	あなたが私に言うのは，待て，待て，待て，だけ。いつも遅れてばかりで<u>うんざりだ</u>。
386	警察は逃亡した受刑者が国境に到着する前に彼<u>の行く手をはば</u>もうとした。
387	<u>あらゆるところを</u>探したが，車のカギが見つからなくて，タクシーで映画に行かなければならなかった。
388	ジュリーと私は大学時代から親友だった。新入生のオリエンテーションの初日に会ってすぐに<u>うまが合った</u>。
389	すごく疲れたので，今夜は早く<u>寝る</u>つもりだ。皿を洗うのは明日にしよう。
390	君の意見の論理は受け入れられない。ただ単に<u>筋が通って</u>いない。
391	私の友人の中にはその政治家の演説には説得力があると思った者もいたが，私はほとんどが<u>大ぶろしき</u>だと思った。
392	昨年度の優勝者がもう1つのタイトルを手にすることは<u>ありえ</u>なかった。決勝戦で惨敗したのだった。
393	<u>ぎりぎりで間に合う</u>ように駅に着いて，ドアが閉まる直前に列車に飛び乗った。
394	その提案にはいくつかの問題点があるが，来週の締め切りまでにそれらの問<u>題を解決できる</u>自信がある。
395	新しい仕事での成功をお祈りします。状況については<u>お知らせください</u>。
396	もし，君がその仕事<u>をおろそかにする</u>ようなら，その昇進はできないだろうよ。
397	その2つの保険会社は合併計画をほぼ完成させているが，正式発表がなされる前に完了すべき<u>未決事項</u>がまだいくつかある。
398	地震があったときに覚えておくべき大切なことは，落ち着いていることである。<u>冷静さを失って</u>はいけない。
399	日本市場で少しも<u>注目すべき進展が見られ</u>なかったため，その自動車メーカーは日本での業務を閉鎖せざるを得なかった。
400	開発業者たちがぜひその土地を購入したいと切望したので，土地の所有者たちはそれをもとの値段の3倍で売って<u>大もうけをした</u>。
401	そのバイオリニストは立派な音楽家ではあるが，どうしてもその弦楽四重奏団の他のメンバーの高い水準<u>には達し</u>ない。
402	スピーチをするようにと突然言われたので，まったくの<u>即興で</u>やらなければならなかった。準備をする時間があったらよかったのに。
403	今回はその未成年者の初犯であったので，判事は彼を<u>無罪放免</u>にすることに

既出例文・熟語

決定した。
404 その家族は固定資産税を払い続けられないので，その不動産を売りに出すことにした。
405 この中古車はとても状態のよい車だとセールスマンは言っているが，彼が正直なことを言っているのかどうか自信がない。
406 ローラはスペイン語を一言も話さないので，メキシコ人の友人の結婚披露宴ではいささか勝手が違った。
407 私の父は75歳だが，いまだに元気で，衰えたとは決して思っていない。
408 モニカは中古車を買うことでお金の節約になると信じていたが，結果的にはとても高い修理に法外な金を払うことになった。
409 ハンサムな俳優によるたばこの宣伝は，格好よく見せたいという若者の欲望につけこむものだと論じる人もいる。
410 ショーンは，実際には友だちの転職に賛成だったが，わざと同意しない振りをした。
411 その手品師はステージ上のものをすべて消してみせると言ったが，彼が本当にそのような難しいことをやってのけるだろうと思っていた人はほとんどいなかった。
412 職を見つけるのが大変なようなら，知らせてください。私がコネを利用すれば私の会社に雇ってもらえると思います。
413 数か月努力をしたが結果が得られなかったため，主任技師はプロジェクトを中止する時期だと気がついた。
414 その男のけがはひどかったが，医師たちは，適切な治療をすれば回復すると確信していた。
415 その年次総会で，株主たちは重役の給料について厳しい質問を浴びせて，取締役たちを窮地に追い込んだ。
416 その会社は実用的かどうかを調べるために，市内の交通の中でその電気トラックを試してみた。
417 最近時間外労働をすることが多い。この状態がいつまでも続かないといいのだが。
418 店の経営者に文句を言いに行くべきだよ。こんな質の悪い家具をつかまされるとは，一杯食わされたんだと思うね。
419 株式市場の長引く沈滞を乗り切れると楽観的に考えている投資家は多い。
420 前触れもなく会議で講演をして欲しいと頼まれたとき，メアリーはその急場に対処し，見事なスピーチを披露した。
421 僕はチャーリーが新しいアパートに引っ越す手伝いをさせられてしまった。
422 うちの娘の新しいボーイフレンドはなかなか真面目な男なので，娘にその影

響が表れることを私は期待している。

423 殺された被害者の財布も身の回り品も盗まれていなかったので，警察は盗みは動機ではないと判断した。

424 職場の管理者はある一定レベルの規律を保たなければならない。しかし，厳しすぎる管理者は部下を遠ざける危険がある。

425 そのコンピュータ販売員の高圧的な売り込み口上に非常に腹がたったので，私は別の店へ行った。

426 修理店で車を引き取ったとき，最初の見積もりのほとんど2倍のお金をしぶしぶ支払わなければならなかった。

427 離婚調停の一部として，ビルは彼が持つ家の権利を前妻に譲渡するよう裁判所に命じられた。

428 私は助手に対し昼食にあんなに長時間をかけないように何度も言ったが，どうしても分かってもらえないようだ。

429 その大型の電器店は旧式のセキュリティ・システムを使っていたし，静かな通りにあったので，強盗にとっては，まったくのいいカモであった。

430 うちの上司は得意客を失ったことで悩んでいたので，数日はその話題を回避しなければならなかった。

431 観衆の声援に後押しされ，地元の人気者は，マラソンの最後の数メートルのところで，国の代表選手になんとか追いついた。

432 もし他の星の周りを回る惑星があるなら，生物の存在しうる他の惑星があっても当然だ。

433 今日の会議で僕を支持してくれてありがとう。君の援護がなかったら，僕の提案は承認されなかっただろう。

434 ベンチに座っている老女が1人で寂しそうだったので，リンダは彼女の隣に座って話しかけた。

435 君はまったく世間知らずだね。車のセールスマンの言うことなんか，いちいち真に受けてはだめだよ。

436 経済の将来についての楽天的な予測は，過去の予測がどんなに不正確だったかを考えると，少し割引いて聞いたほうがいい。

437 僕が試しにやってみても構わないのなら，君のコンピュータは直せると思うよ。

438 君が仕事に不満なのはわかっている。しかし僕に当たり散らすのはやめてくれ。彼らが君を昇進の候補からはずしたのは僕のせいではない。

439 すまないけど，サリー，昼食時に仕事の話をするのは本当にいやなんだ。その話は事務所に戻ったらにしよう。

440 新聞社のその編集長は，その警察署についての批判の調子を和らげるように

予想例文

何人かの記者に圧力をかけた。

441 私たちは今でももっと大きな家に引っ越そう<u>という考えを持っている</u>が、それだけのお金があるかどうか確かでない。

442 ジムは飛行機を怖がっているから、私たちと一緒にハワイに行かせるには<u>強力に説得</u>しなければならないと思う。

443 この新しいソフトを使うと、大量のデータ<u>を調べる</u>ことなしに、マウスをクリックするだけで必要な情報を引き出すことができる。

444 ノーマンにはたばこをやめるように<u>いくら言っても無駄</u>だよ。君の言葉を聞くような男ではないから。

445 くたくたに疲れた１日の後で<u>緊張をほぐす</u>最善の方法は、ゆっくり熱い風呂に入ることである。

446 コンサートの前に練習する時間がなかったので、そのバンドは<u>即興で演奏して</u>、あとはうまく行くよう祈るしかなかった。

447 その企業が投資をした産業用ロボットは完全な失敗作品であることが分かった。そのため、その企業は損失としてそれら<u>を帳簿から消さ</u>ざるをえなかった。

448 最近のハッキング事件を捜査している連邦捜査局の捜査官たちは、ロサンゼルス地域の３人の容疑者<u>に的を絞った</u>。

予想例文

449 今にも負けるかもしれないという瀬戸際に見えたそのとき、敵の攻撃が<u>弱まり</u>、我々が勝利した。

450 私の母は、家の中でだれかが悪態をつくの<u>には我慢できない</u>。

451 登山家たちは、通り抜けることができないほど危険な<u>深い淵</u>にまもなく到達するという事実を忘れているように思えた。

452 大学近くのバーで、酔っ払った暴漢が、座ってビールを飲みながらただ話をしている学生たち<u>に話しかける</u>と、暴力沙汰が起こった。

453 公的に認められている大学の単位と学位を授与するためには、高等教育機関は<u>認定</u>を取得する手続きを経なければならない。

454 私は酢の<u>つんとする</u>においがとても不愉快なものであると思う。

455 彼はよく、自分の講演を活気づけるために、民話からの有名な<u>金言</u>を引用した。

456 大統領候補は立ち上がり、出席者<u>に向かって</u>断固とした態度で<u>演説をした</u>。

457 少年のときでさえ、彼は、スポーツ、音楽、学問に<u>熟達していて</u>、その才能と多才さで知られていた。

458	キリスト教価値観の忠実な信者として，彼は聖書の言葉の教えに従った。
459	驚いたことに，大火災の現場の隣りにあった家は燃え落ちなかった。
460, 461	私がいくら厳しく息子に不勉強であることを注意しようとも，彼は批判には動じないようである。
462	生涯の保守主義者であったその男性は，伝統的な生活様式にいかなる変化を加えることにも反対であった。
463, 464	グリングリッチ上院議員は彼の対抗馬の私生活を調べよと主張したが，ついには，知らず知らずのうちに自分の政治生命を絶つことになった。
465, 466	ボブは誰にでも愛想がよく，よい食事，素晴らしいワイン，そして高級車を好むことで知られていた。
467	空き巣狙いを追い払うため，その男は芝生のまん中に立っている高い柱に照明装置を取り付けた。
468	我々はかつて，世界というのはいくつかの共通利益を持つ国民国家の集合体であると考えたのだった。
469	会社を救うために広く経費節減をする必要が出てくると，社長はだれかをレイオフする決定をするのにいちいち悩んだ。
470	針治療が，慢性的な首の痛みを和らげるだけでなく，ついには事実上，それを完全に取り除いてくれたことが分かった。
471, 472	イエス・キリストは，よきクリスチャンというものは温厚で他人には利他的に振る舞うべきで，顔をたたかれたら，もう一方の頬を差し出すことすらしなさい，と説いた。
473, 474	その少年はいつも，有名になった父親に対しては感情の上で葛藤があったが，自分自身がビジネスマンとして成功した後でさえも，父親には礼儀正しく敬意を持って接した。
475	彼の病気の永久的な治療法はないが，市場に出ているある新薬が彼の状態を改善してくれるかもしれないと，医者は彼に言った。
476, 477	南アフリカ共和国で，アパルトヘイト以後の政府は憎しみによる犯罪者に恩赦を与えたが，そのもとでは，多くの犯罪者が，もしすべてを開示し謝罪するプログラムに参加することに同意するなら，罪が許されることになっていた。
478	情報提供者の匿名性を守るため，政府側の弁護士は，できるだけ早く裁判を進めることを望んだ。
479	スピーチを行う前に，大統領は敵対者に対し，レトリックを抑えて合理的な姿勢で問題を扱うようにと促した。
480	ワクチンは人間にある種のバクテリアと戦う抗体を作ってくれるが，それは目標と定めた病気にかかることから防いでくれるのだ。

481	その女性は正体不明のヘビにかまれたが，医者はその毒の解毒剤を持っていなかった。
482	あるバクテリアは実際に，病院で見られるような非常に衛生的で殺菌された状況で繁殖するよう進化してきている。
483, 484	その大学の経営陣は学生と教師両方の問題に無関心であるように見えただけでなく，将来の深刻な財政問題にもしばしば鈍い反応しかしなかった。
485	ヒトラーをなだめようと，多くの西洋諸国が努力したにもかかわらず，結果的に彼らは攻撃を受けることになった。
486	その財産の価値を慎重に評価してから，その購買の申し込みをした。
487, 488	テロリストを逮捕するための多くの努力が失敗に終わったが，アメリカ占領軍の担当官たちは，自分たちは勝利を収めるだろうと語った。
489	法の原則への熱心な献身の中で，トンプソン氏は，たびたびそれらの原則を乱用する者を激しく非難している。
490, 491	毎晩，12の鉄道の車両に石炭を積み込むという骨の折れる仕事をしながら，バドは自分を人間というより使役馬のように感じていると言っている。
492	マイケルはサリーに何度となく，公共の場所でなく，もっとプライベートな場所で不平は口にすべきだと強調した。
493	イラクでは，たくさんの兵器の隠し場所が見つかってきたにも関わらず，大量破壊兵器はまだ1つも見つかっていない。
494	私の友人の家は，優雅な建築と気の休まる室内備品の巧妙な融合となっている。
495	2人の考古学者がもう諦めようとしたそのとき，弱くなっていく光の中でかろうじて見えるアステカの貴重な人工物を発見した。
496	デービッド・カッパーフィールドは，巧妙な小細工を使うことで知られているが，それをいくつか使って全観衆を魅惑した。
497	判事は子どもの世話を怠ったとして，有罪となった犯人を激しく責めた。
498	アメリカにおける多くのマイノリティに対する残酷な仕打ちは，単なる謝罪と申し訳程度の仕事の提供によって和らげられるものではない。
499	メアリー・ジェニングスは，仕事がなかったわけではない。彼女は会議のコーディネーターとして，すべてをうまく組織化しスムーズに進めていた。
500	その若い男性は，株投資によって自分の遺産を増大させようとした。
501, 502	中華レストランでの伝統的な習慣の1つにフォーチュン・クッキーがあるが，それは吉，不吉の事件が起こることを示唆する。
503	一部には低い金利と消費者の高い信頼の後押しがあることによって，経済学者たちは翌年は経済状況の厳しさは少しはよくなるだろうと予測していた。

504, 505	マハティール首相は最初数十年の政権の間は高く評価されたが，副首相のアンワール・イブラヒムの悪魔扱いにおいてどんどん専制的になっていき，歴史上の彼の地位には汚点がついたようだ，と米紙は伝えた。
506, 507	その若い作家は，率直な資本主義に対する嫌悪感のため，ビジネスびいきのマスコミによって，不当にも，コミュニストの烙印を押されることになった。
508	最後の瞬間，スミス機長は，緊急着陸をしてなんとか大惨事を回避することができた。
509	ハワード・ヒューズは主に航空機産業への投資により，世界でもっとも裕福な人間になった。
510	ウラジミール・ナボコフは偉大な作家であると同時に，熱心な昆虫学者であった。
511, 512	トム・ハンクスのアカデミー主演男優賞連続受賞の結果，授賞式に出席していた数人のライバルたちはいかにももの欲しげな目つきを隠すことになった。
513	未処理の注文が山積していたため，客は新しいトヨタ車を手に入れるのに，6か月近く待たなければならなかった。
514	ハルは，何年にもわたって何かをしようとすると兄からいじめられたので，よく選んだ風刺たっぷりの言葉で仕返しをしてやろうと，とうとう決心した。
515	ジムはいつも女性をからかったり，しばしば甘い言葉で彼女たちの笑みを奪ったりしたため，学校中で一番の人気者になったようであった。
516	中国は軍事力増強を続けているが，その兵器技術は依然として，近代工業国の進んだ軍事力からはほど遠いものであることに変わりない，とポスト紙は伝えた。
517	その将来性のある若い俳優の最近の映画は明らかに失敗作であったが，彼はすぐに元に戻れる自信がある。
518	その少女はとても天真らんまんに見えたので，頭痛やら他の症状を装って，自分が病気だと，簡単に母親をだますことができた。
519, 520	彼の父は彼に，すべてにおいて節度を守ることが彼にとって義務であると言った。
521, 522	エドガーはいつも好戦的な態度を持っていたが，警察官を襲ったときは，彼は拘置判決を受けた。
523, 524	ヒロシは，上司のところに出頭させられたときはほとんどいつも，ひどく叱りつけられていたので，恐れおののきながらやっとのことで彼に話しかけることができるほどであった。
525, 526	その夫婦は子どもの死によってひどく希望を失っていたので，だれが何

予想例文

をしようとも，子どもを失ったこと<u>をあきらめる</u>助けとならなかった。

527, 528 私は，有名なオリエント・エクスプレスの1等車の上段<u>ベッド</u>を確保したが，列車が一晩中前に<u>揺れ</u>たり左右にもひどく揺れたりしたので眠れなかった。

529, 530 編集部員が，手遅れになる前に変更せよ，と社長<u>を攻めれば</u>攻めるほど，社長は彼らの提案を<u>馬鹿にする</u>のであった。

531 マンデラ大統領は，南アフリカのアパルトヘイト体制下で犯罪を犯したものすべてに広く温情<u>を示す</u>措置をとった。

532, 533 教授が，いつもどおりの<u>分かりにくく</u>一貫性のない調子でとりとめなく話す様子を，学生たちは本当に<u>当惑</u>して見つめた。

534, 535 控訴裁判所は，被告の前の有罪判決は公平な裁判を受ける権利を<u>侵害する</u> <u>偏った</u>証言に基づいたものと裁定した。

536, 537 広くひろまった批判と誤った非難の最中，私は事実によって私<u>の嫌疑が</u> <u>晴れる</u>ときがくる日まで単に<u>待つ</u>ことを心に決めた。

538, 539 多くのコードは<u>二項</u>対立の原理によって動いているが，それはコンピュータ・プログラム・コードの1と0のように，互いに基本的に対立関係を持つ2つの要素<u>を示している</u>。

540 彼は奇妙な発明の1つで金持ちになるまで，いつも家族の中の<u>厄介もの</u>と考えられていた。

541 だれかのせいで少しでも車のスピードを下げなければならないときはいつも，彼は警笛<u>をうるさく鳴らし</u>，悪態をつく。

542 私はお気に入りのシャツにインクをこぼしてしまった。そして残念ながら，それ<u>は漂白</u>できなかった。

543 アメリカと世界中のブッシュ政権の外交政策批判者は，イラク侵攻を，アメリカのモラルの清廉さに長期にわたる<u>暗い影を落とすもの</u>と非難している。

544 その芸術批評家は，最近絶賛されている画家の作品は，いい加減に絞り出した絵の具の<u>しみ</u>とほとんど変わらない，と述べた。

545 有名なウォーターゲート事件で，大統領が事件に関係しているというジョン・ディーンの告白が，犯罪の陰謀を隠そうとするニクソン体制の試み<u>を暴露</u>することになった。

546 車を運転する人は，引火して<u>爆発する</u>恐れがあるため，給油所のガソリンポンプのあたりで喫煙をすることはしないよう警告されている。

547, 548 北朝鮮は，将来の話合いを<u>牛耳る</u>ために，核兵器を持つ力があると宣言して国際社会<u>を脅かそう</u>としていると，一部の人々は考えている。

549, 550 北アメリカ大陸に移住した人々は，西に向かうにつれ多くの<u>実り豊かな</u>谷や川を見つけたが，最後には南部イリノイ州の肥沃な農地を<u>居住地</u>に定め

ることに決めた。

551, 552 私の同僚の何人かは，その少女は恥知らずなほどまでに遠慮がないと思ったが，私はそのような勇気に感心していた。

553, 554 彼は株式投資で損をしたことをあまり心配せず，最終的には完全に損得なしになるだろうとご機嫌に話している。

555 彼はプロのピアニストであったので，演奏活動をやめなくてはならないことは彼をひどく悲しませた。

556, 557 警察官に賄賂を渡したとして非難され，証言台の男は検事に対し，ひどい声でどなり始めた。

558 彼女は本当は昇給に値したが，上司に敢えてそのことを持ち出さなかった。

559, 560 彼は独りで暗闇の中に座り，何時間もたわいのないことに思えることをじっと考え込んでいたものだった。

561, 562 マーガレットはシャイで物静かな少女だったが，たぶんそのせいで，我々の課長の辛らつなしゃべり方の矢面に立たねばならなかったのだ。

563 彼は普通はぶっきらぼうで，時には耳障りなほどのしゃべり方をするが，彼をよく知っている人は，同時に，彼は親切で優しい面も持っていることを知っていた。

564 その車はガードレールを突破したが，運転手のけがは軽いものだった。なぜなら大きな茂みが衝突の衝撃を和らげたからであった。

565, 566 その心臓疾患の患者を検査すると，心臓から血液を運び出す大動脈の1つが肥大しており，破裂を防ぐために緊急手術が必要であることが分かった。

567 かつての力士が手術が必要となると，医者たちは彼の体の大きさでは複雑な手術になるだろうと言った。

568 人質を救出する試みは，2機のヘリコプターの操縦者が離陸のときにしくじってお互いに衝突したので，失敗に終わらざるをえなかった。

569 谷に春がやってくると，どこでも木々が花を咲かせたが，その様は花々がすべての葉と枝から萌え出るかのようであった。

570, 571 中世ヨーロッパの偉大なゴシック大聖堂は，飛び控え壁を利用したが，それは建物の支えとなる構造を強化するだけでなく，全体的なデザインを優雅に見せる役割も果たした。

572 彼女の初演技に少々の弱点はあったものの，大体において，それは印象的なパフォーマンスであった。

573, 574 福音書に今ある話の多くが，我々が今日読む形で書かれる前に，長いあいだ口承で広まったものだった。その結果，多くの学者が，その歴史的正確さに疑いを抱いている。

予想例文

575 1929年のアメリカ株式市場の大暴落は，アメリカと世界にとっての経済的大惨事であった。

576, 577 極めて多くの非常に優れた才能を持つ候補者が，我々の宣伝している2つのポジションに応募してきたので，我々としては，履歴書を送ってきた精彩に欠ける応募者は，ずばり無視することができた。

578 アブラハム・リンカーンは，率直さと優雅さをあわせ持つ希有の演説の才能を持った人であった。

579, 580 結婚して自分の子どもを設けた後でさえも，エリザベスは気まぐれで何をしでかすか予測し難く，しばしば，論理的によく考えた上というより，そのときの気分で振る舞っていた。

581 目撃者は，そのバスは突然コントロールを失って傾き，道路をはずれると崖の端でグラグラ揺れ，鋭い音を立てて止まったと言った。

582, 583 フラフープが市場に出回るやいなや，それはヒットし，売り上げはうなぎ上り，世界中の何百万という人々が購入するまでになった。

584 死というものは，心臓の鼓動が止まることよりむしろ，脳の機能の永久停止によって定義づけられる，とする人もいる。

585 グレゴリオ聖歌はたぶん，西洋の単旋律音楽の最もよく知られている例であろう。

586, 587 チャーター便がペルーの起伏の多い山岳地帯に墜落したとき，亡くなった乗客の遺体のほとんどが回収できなかった。

588, 589 いわゆる「男性優越主義者」の女性の権利に対する行動と態度が，世界中の人権団体を刺激し男女の平等を求めて戦う起爆剤となってきた。

590, 591 最初，私は，息子を誕生日にディズニーランドに連れていくのは費用がかかり過ぎると思ったが，私の両親が資金援助をしてくれたので，息子をそこに連れていくチャンスに飛びついた。

592, 593 まず，砂糖と香料を加えながらクリームと氷をどろどろするまでかき混ぜ，新鮮な手作りのアイスクリームをおたますくって子どもたちのボールに盛った。

594 多くの場面において，マイケル・ジョーダンは自分のチームの勝利を確実にするのに必要な点を稼いだ。

595 被告側の弁護士は，自分の依頼人に不利な陳述全体がつまるところ状況証拠にすぎない，と反論した。

596 彼らの握りこぶしは堅く握られ，表情は厳しかったが，その2人の敵同士はいやいやながら和睦に同意した。

597 最後のわずかな得点が決め手になり，サンアントニオ・スパーズは勝利をつかんだ。

598	彼らは新しいショッピングモールを建設する許可を得ることが困難であることが分かっていたので，市当局に影響力を持つ友人と接触を持った。
599	泥棒がその老婦人の財布を奪おうとしたところ，彼女は両手でしっかりと握りしめて絶対に放すまいとした。
600	彼の行動は無教育で粗野なものであったが，それが彼にある種のあどけない魅力というものを与えていた。
601	聖書では，世界の終わりがいつか起こるとされている。
602, 603	アメリカの歴史を通じ，多くの宗教的そして政治的な動機を持つコミューンが，似たような価値観を持ち結束した生活様式を望む人々のグループからできあがってきた。
604, 605	『The Bell Curve』（正規分布［釣鐘型］曲線）という本がしたように，知的能力は人種とお互いに関係がある，とした研究が，見えすいたいんちきであることが証明された。
606	アインシュタインは，思考の問題を想像的に用いることによって相対性理論を思いついた。
607, 608	演説者は簡潔に話すよう言われたが，彼女はおしゃべりな性格だったので，20分近くしゃべるのをやめられなかった。
609	ゲイリー・ヴァン・デン・ヒューベルは，スーザン・ランガーの1200ページの傑作を，『Mind: An Essay of Human Feeling』という一冊のテキストに要約した。
610	多くの市民が，ふつうの人の横柄な振る舞いは大目に見ないだろうが，それが映画スターやロック・ミュージシャンとなるとあまり気にしないようである。
611	トマト缶詰め工場で研究室技術士として訓練されたとき，私は顕微鏡のもとで，ある種のカビの形状を識別することができるようになった。
612	スペインの異端審問は，ローマカトリックの信仰に反すると思われるものは何でも非難し没収した。
613	約束されていた昇級の件をめぐって上司と懸案の対決をするために勇気を奮い起こすまで，彼には2日間かかった。
614	怠け者ではあったが，彼はいつも他人に対し愛想がよく，なおかつ親切であったため，人生ではうまくやっていた。
615	最近，ワールドビュー・コーポレーションは大きな企業合併を発表したが，それはいくつかのメディアと娯楽産業の巨大複合企業体を形成するものであった。
616	警察は，爆発があった場所の付近1街区を，片付け作業を行なう間，見物人がそこに集まるのを防ぐため，交通遮断した。

予想例文

617　ある理論が客観的事実と一致していない場合，それを修正する必要がある。
618　考えられる容疑者に関する重要な情報が報道関係者にもれたことで，大衆は警察がすぐに逮捕するだろうと推測するに至った。
619　自動車会社は来年度のラグジュアリー・カーの注文を削減している。なぜなら，委託販売しているラグジュアリー・カーが十分な早さで売れていないからである。
620　新しい会社社長はすべての従業員を招き彼らの不平不満を述べさせた。大幅な給料カットに対しては小さすぎる慰めでしかなかったが。
621　重罪で有罪になった人は，他の前科者とつき合うことは法的にはできない。
622　彼は自分は恥ずかしがり屋だと言っていたが，いつも派手な色のネクタイと奇妙な帽子をかぶって目立っていた。
623　十分な収入と，好きなことができる時間の余裕のある夫婦の方が，2人の関係においてより強く変わらぬ愛情を持てるようである。
624　どんな星座を見分けることになったとしても，彼の目に映るのは無秩序に散らばった星々にすぎなかった。
625, 626　医者たちは，その老婦人の冠状動脈がかなり収縮しているだけでなく，規則的な心臓鼓動をさせるためにはペースメーカーを埋め込む必要もあることを発見した。
627　私たちは，ほとんどの複雑な本文に，いろいろな意味の解釈をすることができる。
628　西山老教授は，自宅の庭で働いているときほど満足するときはないと感じている。そこでは彼は自然界の深遠なる秘密を見つめることができるからだ。
629, 630　ヴァン・ゴッホ作であるとされる絵画が本当に本物なのか，あるいは単なるまがい物なのか，という激しい討論が行なわれた。
631, 632　被告側の弁護士は，主な証人に対する検察側の偽証告発を調査するため，裁判の2日間継続を要求した。
633　公判中の被告は判事に，自分の犯した悪事のいずれをも深く悔いていると話した。
634　私たちは，相手側がこちらの強力な攻撃をストップさせる特別な戦略を考えているのを知っていたので，彼らの意表を突く別の攻撃を企てた。
635, 636　国連の安全保障理事会は，北朝鮮の核開発プログラムをめぐる一触即発の状況を取り除こうと緊急会議を開いた。
637　ドイツ，フランス，ロシアというイラク戦争に対抗する勢力がまとまり，国連の安全保障理事会のメンバーであるこの3か国がアメリカの政策に対する強力な反対勢力を構成した。
638　大学は，言語学の最新の研究に精通している客員講師を探していたので，ノ

639, 640 第一級殺人で有罪になった直後，その冷酷な犯人は彼を裁判にかけたやつらに復讐してやると誓った。

641 赤ん坊が高熱を出しけいれんし始めたとき，私たちは病院に連れていかなければならなかった。

642 西山教授は，次の授業までに読んでコメントするよう，アメリカの超越主義者の著作の印刷物をたくさん学生に配った。

643 職場の労働者にソフトボールのチームを結成するという機会があったとき，彼らは満場一致で私たちを仲間に入れることに同意した。

644 ブッシュ大統領は一連の東京での会議において，日本で同等の立場にある小泉首相に会った。

645 ウォーターゲート事件は，基本的にはニクソン政権による犯罪的陰謀を隠そうとする試みであった。

646 CIA と FBI の秘密活動は，国内，国外を問わずますます批評家からの批判にさらされてきている。

647 コメディアン，ロビン・ウィリアムズはとてもおもしろいことで有名で，共演者さえも，ときどきリハーサル中の彼のおふざけにゲラゲラ笑い出すほどである。

648 私はていねいにシャツを詰め込んだが，私のスーツケースへの入れ方はすべてのシャツに変なしわを作り出してしまった。

649 彼女はとても信じ込みやすかったので，だれの言うことでも信じたと思う。

650 上司ははっきりとは述べなかったが，私は彼のコメントから，私の仕事のすべては財務危機をどう扱うかにかかっていると推論した。

651, 652 グリーンピースは，今，主な工業国に，現在見られる世界の熱帯雨林の嘆かわしい破壊を抑制するよう圧力をかけようとしている。

653 世界の知られているところだけの石油とガスの供給をざっと調べてみても，今世紀中盤には，利用可能な化石燃料は，需要をはるかに下回ることが分かろう。

654, 655 何人かの学生が西山教授に要求される課外図書の量を減らしてくれるよう頼んだが，怠惰な学生だと言ってそっけなく叱りつけられるだけであった。

656 過去においては，気立てのよい若い女性というのは，人前での行動では上品で控え目であることを期待されていた。

657 多くの政治家は，政治的な成功のカギは，国民の前にニンジンをぶら下げておくことで，そうすれば彼らに全政策綱領をたやすく信じ込ませることができる，と思い込んでいる。

658, 659	学校関係者は，多くの中学生が，学校に行く途中だらだらして，見た人には無作法と映る言動で人々を困らせていることを懸念していた。
660, 661	証拠が不足しているにもかかわらず，ハーンズ警部はどこでどのように殺人が起こったかを突きとめることができた。
662	人質たちは，テロリストから解放された後になっても，完全に情報を報告させられるまで数日間拘束された。
663	全員が巧妙な詐欺に関係している，世界で最も悪賢い犯罪者の一味によってもくろまれたその見事な強盗事件に，警察は完全に一杯食わされた。
664	彼はきちんと育てられ，怒っているときやストレスがあるときでも上品に威厳を持って振る舞うよう教育された。
665	その会社は，健康保険，税金，年金に充てるため，いつも従業員の月給総額から約25%を控除していた。
666, 667	きちんとした礼儀作法に関することでは，私はいつも西山教授の完璧な判断に従う。
668, 669	何人かの批評家は，グリーンピースによるこれ以上極端なやり方は，地球を救うという最も重要な目的から大衆の注意をそらせ，その結果，彼らの努力の効果を損なうだろうと語った。
670	アンドレ・アガシはウィンブルドンで勝った最年長プレーヤーの1人だが，いまだに活躍している。それは一部にはベースライン上における彼の賢くて器用な戦術によるものだ。
671	研究の結果，よく使われる風邪薬の一般的な欠点は脱水症状を引き起こしたり加速させたりすることであることが分かった。
672	アメリカのクリスマスシーズンには，郵便業務がホリデイカードや小包でいっぱいになる。
673	その若い女性はエイリアンに誘拐されたという妄想を抱いている。
674, 675	議会は特別な検察官が最新のワシントンのスキャンダルを調査するよう再び求めたが，ホワイトハウスはすべてを秘密にしたままである。
676, 677	1時間もしないうちに，そのビル取り壊しチームは，市中心部のかなり広い土地を占有していた巨大なビルを倒すことに成功した。
678	私の兄は，軍隊にいたころ，一度だけ反抗して格下げになったことがあることを認めた。
679	年老いた西山教授はまたカギをどこかに置き忘れたので，我々は彼の研究室に，ドアのロックをこじ開けて入らなければならなかった。
680	日本は，アフガニスタンのタリバンとの戦争を助けるためオイルタンカーを配置することに同意したが，直接の軍事的かかわり合いは除外した。
681, 682	彼は，年10%の設備の減価償却費を補わなくてはならなかったが，こ

	の出費が彼の課税水準を下げるであろうことを知って満足できた。
683	名高いイギリス人科学者が，政府から卑劣な扱いを受けたとして意気消沈し最近自殺した。
684	最も進んだ法医学研究所は，人間の血のほんの小さな跡でさえも見つけ出すことができる。
685	警察は，最近の主要な殺人事件の容疑者を拘留していると言っている。
686	テロリストが引き起こした脅威と向き合っている者の最大の恐怖の1つは，主要な都市中心部で核兵器を爆発させる能力を彼らが手に入れるという不吉な可能性である。
687	子どものときでも，彼女は機敏で運動選手らしい体つきだった。
688	話し手が悪魔のような様子を目に浮かべてにらみつけると，部屋にいた者はみなこわばった。
689	哲学者，スーザン・ランガーは，理性と感情の間の伝統的な二分法に果敢に挑んできた。
690	その学生は頭が良かったが内気で従順であったため，自分の才能を最高にいかすことはできなかった。
691	学科長は，自分は教授たちのいざこざをなだめることで多くの時間をつぶしていると，私に言った。
692, 693	歴史上最も大きな科学上の嘘の1つは，人間の「ミッシング・リンク（失われた環）」の完全な骨がトルコで発掘されたという話が完全に作り話だと判明したときのことだ。
694, 695	ワクチンは，人間の血流に注入され抗体を作り出す働きをする伝染性のバクテリアを希釈したサンプルである。
696	彼はお人好しで人に警戒心を起こさせないように見えたが，実は個人的利益のために政治の動きを操作するのがうまかった。
697	ある有名な投資信託会社が最近，幹部数人を，疑惑を招く行為をしたとして解雇した。
698, 699	私は今週，私の銀行口座に大きな矛盾があることを発見した。誤りのクレジットカードの請求で300ドルの負債が記入されていたのだ。
700	私が日本の税関を通っているとき，出入国管理の係官は軽蔑のまなざしで私のことを見た。
701	我々は，かつて独立国民国家によって支配されていた伝統的な世界秩序が次第に崩壊しつつある様を見届けている，と信じている批評家もいる。
702	安い労働力は国のGNP（国民総生産）にとって大きな恩恵となるかもしれないが，労働者と経営側の間の大きな経済的不均衡を必ず生むことになる。
703, 704	イランは核兵器開発に携わっているという非難に反論しただけでなく，

予想例文

これらの疑惑のもととなっている証拠<u>を明らかにする</u>約束もした。

705 中世には，医学の先駆的な学生は，処刑された犯罪者の死体<u>を解剖した</u>が，それは墓地から盗んでこなければならなかった。人間の体を切り開くことに対するタブーがあったためである。

706, 707 学者たちは，最古の人類の<u>広まり</u>はアフリカで始まり，それからアジアやヨーロッパ大陸に<u>分散した</u>ということを認識している。

708, 709 モラリストたちは，人気映画に勇ましいものとして描かれた<u>放蕩的な</u>ライフスタイルが若い世代の価値観<u>を堕落させ</u>ている，とよく主張する。

710, 711 カリフォルニアのリコール選挙では，女性団体が，最近の性的な不品行の申し立てにより，さまざまな派閥を説得してアーノルド・シュワルツネッガー<u>の支持</u>を<u>やめさせよう</u>とした。

712 乱視は眼球の水晶体に欠陥があるため，視覚に<u>ゆがみ</u>が生じることをいう。

713 私たちは，1人のみすぼらしい老人が酔っぱらって<u>排水溝</u>に横たわっているのを見つけた。

714 私がソールズベリー・ステーキにすると言うと，彼女は「私も<u>同じもの</u>にするわ」と言った。

715 科学者としての彼にマイナスであったことは，彼は自分の信念において非常に<u>独善的で</u>，問題と解決を柔軟な気持ちで見られないことであった。

716 彼は数年前に失業したとき，政府の<u>失業手当</u>に頼るしかなかった。

717 彼は鏡を覗き込むときはいつも，年をとってきた顔が自分にとって<u>破滅</u>の顔のように映るのである。

718 シーグフリードは，末の息子を<u>溺愛していた</u>が，今になって子どものとき彼を甘やかしてだめにするという大きな間違いをしたことを理解した。

719 彼は貯金を株式市場に投入したが，1年もたたないうちに，そのほとんどが<u>無駄</u>になった。

720, 721 徐々に経済が<u>下降</u>していくこの時期に，多くの投資家は，より不安定な株<u>を放棄し</u>，債券に投資している。

722 絶えまなく降る冷たい雨が何日間か続き，家は冷たく<u>すきま風が入り</u>，少し憂うつな感じであった。

723, 724 私たちは石油を求めて何週間もその辺りを<u>掘り</u>続けたがうまくいかなかった。そのとき突然，石油が地面の数カ所から同時に<u>噴き出し</u>始めた。

725, 726 クラスメイトがみすぼらしい服を見て私を嘲笑したとき，私はいつか彼らが<u>貧窮して</u> <u>前言を取り消さ</u>なければならなくなると予言した。

727, 728 この土手付近で<u>弱くなって</u>いる小さな水の流れは，力強い山からの流れで始まっているが，数カ所で<u>分岐し</u>，そのたびに流れはますます弱くなって最後には海に注いでいるのである。

729	ブッシュ政権の国務長官，コリン・パウエル氏は，アメリカ軍で最も高い<u>地位</u>に達した。
730, 731	先月，私たちは新しいタイプの博物館を訪れた。そこは，館長の<u>折衷主義</u>の趣味を反映して，世界中の<u>種々雑多な</u>芸術品が展示してあった。
732	並はずれた業績にもかかわらず，彼は依然として，<u>仰々しい</u>賛辞に当惑している。
733, 734	謎に満ちた一連の殺人を調べている捜査官は，新しい目撃者が殺人の動機<u>を解明して</u>くれることを願ったが，彼らの尋問は<u>失敗に終わった</u>だけであった。
735, 736	アブラハム・リンカーンはアメリカの奴隷<u>を解放し</u>，彼らの個人の自由の<u>抑圧</u>に終止符を打つことを誓った。
737	16世紀前半に，フェルディナンド・マゼランは地球を一周する旅に<u>出航した</u>。
738	英語と日本語の大きな違いの1つは，<u>挿入される</u>形容詞節と前置詞句の位置である。
739	フェミニズム運動は，次第に，平等の権利を勝ち取る闘いにおいて，多くの女性<u>に権利を与える</u>ことに成功してきている。
740	私はいつも，西山教授の超然とした態度を，うらやむよりも，<u>負けない</u>ように努力しようとしてきた。
741	新しい首相は，長期の景気後退に立ち向かうため，厳しい財政政策<u>を制定した</u>。
742	偉大な哲学者であるスーザン・ランガー教授は，凝り性の学者であったが，彼女の著作は驚くべきほど多岐にわたる学問の分野と巨大な知識<u>を包括して</u>いる。
743	ハイカーたちは重い荷物とひどい凍雨<u>で動きを妨げられて</u>いたが，素晴らしい粘り強さでもって森から抜け出した。
744	ハーバード大学は，毎年何百万ドルという<u>寄付</u>を受け取る。
745	子どもたちだけがサーカスの演技に夢中になったのではなく，大人たちも同じようにその出し物に<u>夢中になっている</u>ようであった。
746	今までにない新しい病気を研究している医者たちは，休眠状態であった遺伝子が突然活発になり，患者の神経システムを攻撃し始める<u>謎</u>を説明することができなかった。
747, 748	政府のトップの高官たちが企業の取引スキャンダルに<u>巻き込まれた</u>のが明らかになると，民衆は<u>不正行為</u>があったものと考えた。
749	人々の中には，宇宙から<u>生命体</u>が我々の惑星を訪れた，と信じる人もいる。
750	有名な女優が文書偽造罪で逮捕されたとき，彼女の弁護士は，彼女は単に警

予想例文

察のわなの犠牲者であると反論した。

751 松本氏がスピーチコンテストの準備をさせているときに，彼は学生たちに，言葉をゆっくり，はっきり発音するように切に求めた。

752 エッセイを終わらせるとき，主題となる部分を際立たせるには，偉大な作家の簡潔なエピグラムを引用するのが，しばしば非常に効果的である。

753, 754 我々はついに庭中に穴を掘り庭をだめにしているモグラを根こそぎにする専門家を雇わざるをえなくなった。

755, 756 高校時代，私の成績は一定でなかったが，最高学年のとき，私はついに猛烈に勉強することに決めた。

757 西山老教授の物忘れは相当なものだが，唯一彼の学識だけが，それを超えている。

758 私の父は，最も辛かったのは一番の親友の葬式で追悼の辞を述べなくてはいけないときであったと，私に言った。

759 衣類乾燥機を使うよりもむしろ，私はしばしば，洗濯物を外に干して蒸発させて乾かす。

760, 761 謝意を表す国民によって，身分の低い農民がその土地の最高ポストまで出世すると，国中で行われた楽しい祝賀に多くの国民が参加した。

762 試合の間，得点が取れずいらだちが高まったが，なんとか落ち着きを保ち，最後には得点した。

763 ある国に政治的圧力を加えるために，アメリカは，その国の関税を免除する「最恵国」という地位を取り消すという脅しに出ることができる。

764 国連は，近隣諸国に対する戦争行為をやめるよう最後通牒を発することによって，いわゆる「ならず者国家」に圧力をかけようとした。

765 自分の外の世界にはほとんど興味を持たない自己満足的な多くの学生にうんざりして，鈴木氏は，もっと将来のことを深く考えるように彼らに熱心に勧めた。

766 アヤトラ・ホメイニは，パーレビ国王政権の反体制勢力であったが，追放から復帰し1979年にイスラム革命を率いた。

767, 768 学者たちは，いつ初期の人間の最初のアフリカ脱出が始まったのかは分からないとするが，それが人間の遺伝子の分化，そして近代の人間の進化へのはずみとなったことは分かるとしている。

769 歴史を通して繰り返されてきたパターンで，独裁者はある少数グループをスケープゴートに選んできたが，彼らは粛正あるいは故郷からの追放の犠牲者となっている。

770 「マッカーシズム」の名で知られるアメリカの歴史の暗黒時代には，複数のアメリカの一般市民が強制的に共産主義者であると認めさせられ，嫌疑をか

けられた者からはお金が没収され，多くの生活が破壊された。

771, 772 ノーベル賞委員会は2人を熱狂的に賞賛したが，彼らが「磁気共鳴映像法」(MRI)を開発したとしてほめたたえたのだった。それは，医者が体に有害なX線を使ったり体にメスを入れる手術をしたりしなくても，体の中を見ることを可能にしたのである。

773 医者はその男性に，彼の潰瘍は胃から出る胃酸が原因であると話した。

774 そのボクサーは，オリンピックの金メダルをかけた試合で，相手に対し満場一致で勝利票を与えられ，とても喜んだ。

775, 776 クリントン大統領の社会自由主義と財政保守主義のコンビネーションは，選挙民のさまざまな派閥を利用することを可能にしたが，それは，伝統的な民主党同盟の一部を無視しても，選挙では勝利する結果となった。

777 西山教授のような，非のうちどころのない判断をする人でさえも，時として誤りを犯すことを避けられない。

778 時を経るにつれ，ティモシーの話はますますこじつけっぽくなって，私たちに話したことの多くは，完全ないんちきだということが分かった。

779 彼はいつも少しばかり卑屈な性質を持っていたが，彼が露骨に上司にへつらっているのを見るのは屈辱的なことであった。

780 専門家は，その新しい医療法は理論的には実行可能だと同意したが，実践となると効果は疑わしいと多くの者が思った。

781 その詩人は自然愛好家で，森に入るとほとんど没我の状態になることができたが，それは至福と人間を超越した至高の生き方であった。

782 オサマ・ビン・ラディンを隠れ家から捜し出すことは，最初考えられていたよりもずっと難しいことが分かった。

783, 784 ロシア大使は，国連安全保障理事会の他の国々が自分の国の提案に従うことを強く望むと言った。

785 彼女はまだ経験が浅い若い教師であったが，だれも彼女の熱意を疑う者はいなかった。

786 その学校の校長は，学校のマスコットを盗もうとしたとして，数人の少年を厳しく叱った。

787 化学実験室で，何時間もかけて実験溶液の不純物をろ過して取り除いたのに，私はそれを衣服全体にこぼしてしまった。

788 彼が悪質なディーラーに賄賂を贈ってポーカーを操作していた，と聞いたのは本当に残念であったが，彼がそのことを友人に大っぴらに吹聴していたことは，まさに信じがたいと言うほかない。

789 小さい子どもであったときも，ジャズ・アーティストのチャールズ・ミンガスは驚くべき音楽の才能の閃きを見せた。

予想例文

790 彼らはテントの下でパーティを開くことにしたが，それは強風に耐えるにはあまりに<u>弱い</u>ことが分かった。

791 イギリス人の詩人，マイナ・ロイは，詩で知られているのと同じように，伝統的な価値観<u>を軽視している</u>ことでよく知られている。

792, 793 株式相場が，不安定な経済状況によって<u>変動している</u>ので，投資からの<u>配当金</u>や利息に頼って生活している引退した人々の多くは，厳しい時期を迎えている。

794 男性からのどんなにささやかな注目もその若い女性<u>を当惑させた</u>ため，彼女はほとんど口をきけなかった。

795 ニューオーリンズ市の郊外にあり，かつて南部プランテーションと呼ばれたその広大な自作農場は，<u>入口の間</u>と応接間を改装するために，公開を中断した。

796 ひどい自動車事故で，車の運転手は右足を複雑<u>骨折</u>した。しかし，後部座席に乗っていた人は奇跡的にかすり傷一つなく逃れたのだった。

797 私たちは，友人がさらされている情け容赦のないプレッシャーのために，<u>ぼろ布</u>のように疲れ果ててしまったのでは，と心配だった。

798 私たちは母に，そんな些細なことで<u>いらいらする</u>理由は何もない，と言い続けたのだが，彼女はそうしないではいられなかった。

799 彼はいい給料を取るだけでなく，素晴らしい<u>付加的</u>利益も得ている。

800 「ばかにされた女性の<u>怒り</u>ほど恐いものはない」という格言は，多くの現代女性によって，女性蔑視のコメントとして考えられている。

801 物理学では，「<u>融合</u>」は2つの原子核が合体し，巨大なエネルギーを生み出すことである。

802 私の母は，孫たちがやってくるというときはいつも<u>大騒ぎ</u>をした。

803 彼は愉快なほどに旧式であった，<u>女性に親切</u>で太っ腹で。だが，ときおり悪ふざけができないほどに，堅苦しいやつではなかった。

804 私たちの職場の最も<u>おしゃべりな</u>2人が仕事を休んだときは，まるで墓場のように静かであった。

805 <u>けばけばしい</u>色の飾りと騒々しい音にあふれたパチンコ店ほど，伝統的な日本人の好みから外れているものはあるまい。

806, 807 国連の救援部隊が飢饉に陥ったアフリカの国に到着するまでには，何百万という避難民が，飢えのために顔は<u>げっそりやせて</u>お腹は<u>膨張している</u>のが見られた。

808 面接担当者は，まるで彼の性格<u>を測定する</u>かのように志願者をじっと見つめた。

809, 810 西山老教授は，<u>温厚</u>な人として知られているが，ときには研究室で<u>うた</u>

た寝をするのが好きで、その間、学生たちはドアの外で忍耐強く待ち続ける。

811 彼は給料は少なかったが、質素な生活をしていたため、やっていくには十分であった。

812 技師たちは、スチールベルトを巻きつけ、塔が倒れるのを防ごうとした。

813 教授会で、私は、先月出席した国際言語会議での基調演説の要点を繰り返すように頼まれた。

814 相撲の試合では、力士が勝利のあとに喜びのポーズをとることは、良い態度とは見なされない。

815 経済状況はまったく新規ビジネスにとって助けとならず、多くの新しい会社が破たんした。

816 その少女は自動車事故でひどいけがを負い、すべて彼女の夢は煙りのように消えてしまった。

817 彼女は夜にたらふく食べては吐き出していたことを認めたが、これは「過食症」と呼ばれる症状である。

818, 819 政治的にはアウトサイダーであったジミー・カーターは、草の根運動を通してアメリカ合衆国大統領になったが、それは一般の人々が大切にしている、根強いキリスト教的価値観から人気を得たからであった。

820 放蕩息子に恨みを抱くどころか、彼の父は彼を強く抱き締めると、彼のために豪華なごちそうを用意させた。

821 大学祭のとき、悪魔の出現と我々が思ったものは、実は西山教授が悪魔の恰好をして現れたものであった。

822 イルカやジュゴンのような水生のほ乳類は、一生のほとんどを水中で過ごすが、ときどき水面まで上ってきて空気を吸わなければならない。

823 サイモンの態度はいつもは問題なかったが、ビールを数本がぶがぶ飲んだときは、いつもビーチまでよろよろと歩いていき、日光浴をするのだった。

824, 825 政党は何週間も細かな点をめぐって言い争ったが、ついには何とか同意にこぎつけた。

826 銀行口座に従業員の賞与を振り込むのを待たず、社長は会議を召集し、その場で賞与を配ることに決めた。

827 数年前は、我が社はどんな商取り引きでも獲得するのに大変な思いをしていたが、最近はどんどんお金をもうけている。

828 その子どもたちは不運に見える。通りをぶらぶらしながらまったく知らない人に小遣いをせびること以外、1日中何もすることがないようである。

829 隣の州に引っ越すとき、彼は持ち物を運ぶのに大きなトレーラーを雇わなければならなかった。

予想例文

830 地震が交通のラッシュアワーの最中に襲い，救急隊にとって凄まじい<u>大混乱</u>を引き起こした。

831 ジャックがジルと出会ったとき，彼らはそりが合うだけでなく，すぐに，お互いに<u>ぞっこん</u>になってしまった。

832, 833 大統領は法を破った者をみな等しく例外なしに起訴する約束をしたが，彼の息子が賄賂で逮捕されたときは，<u>言葉を濁し</u>，息子の場合は<u>酌量すべき</u>情状があると主張した。

834 その映画はチケット売り場では1番であった。なぜならそれは<u>とても楽しい</u>し，いつかは古典の1つとなるであろうと，みなが認めていたからだ。

835 5時頃に，西山教授は研究室を出ると，家に<u>向かう</u>。

836 もし君がゴージャスな女性を結婚相手として待っているのなら，<u>期待して</u>はいけないよ。

837 テロリストたちは食料も水もない洞穴に捕らえられたので，そんなに長くは<u>持ちこたえ</u>られないだろうと我々は考えた。

838 <u>ホログラフィーによる</u>映像は，3次元の物体の幻影を作り出す方法である。

839 高価な宝石を身にまとい，グッチのバッグを腕からぶら下げて，彼女はまるで自分が<u>注目の人</u>であるかのように振る舞った。

840 驚いたことに，生まれつきエイズに対する<u>免疫</u>を持っているらしい人間が少数発見されている。

841 昔のような影響力は失ったと言うが，西山老教授は相変わらず学生たちに知識<u>を伝えている</u>。

842 アメリカの法律制度は，犯罪で起訴されたどんな人間でも，彼または彼女の社会的に同等である<u>偏見のない</u>陪審員団による裁判を受ける権利があることを，保証している。

843 クリントン大統領の<u>弾劾</u>は失敗に終わったが，そのことは，彼の政権時代の晩年の数年間は，彼の影響力に深刻な打撃を与えたのであった。

844 世界で最も力のある軍隊といえども，国全体に敵の占領軍を受け入れる<u>ことを強いる</u>ことはできない。

845 偉大なマジシャンは<u>いつの間にか</u>移動し，観客が気づかないうちに，突然ステージの反対側の端に立っていた。

846 シンプソン氏は，彼の娘に，将来のことを<u>性急</u>に決める必要はなく，慎重に熟考した上で大学を選ぶようにと言った。

847 O. J. シンプソンの弁護団は，人種的偏見が依頼人の公平な裁判を受ける権利を<u>侵害した</u>と反論した。

848 ちょっと<u>信じがたい</u>話だが，ニュースメディアでは，新しい奇跡の薬を，私たちを苦しめるすべてのものの万能薬として大きく宣伝している。

849, 850　政府は，核技術の盗みの<u>共謀</u>に<u>関係している</u>とされる秘密結社を捜索している。

851　彼は，しばしば学部長にさえ生意気に口答えする<u>直情的な</u>若者である。

852　<u>簡潔に言えば</u>，アインシュタインの相対性理論は，ニュートンが唱えた万有引力の法則の普遍性に疑問を投げかけたという理由で，現代物理学における突破口となったのであった。

853, 854　その上院議員は，彼の再選が<u>確実だ</u>ということを聞くと，<u>大得意</u>であった。

855　現代のメディアは，下がるだけ下がった知的レベルの低い<u>馬鹿げた</u>ものだが，古典文学作品の代用となり始めしまったことを，多くの教育者が悔やんでいる。

856　ウイルスは生物と<u>無生物</u>両方の性質を見せる。

857　世界中のリーダーたちが集まって，厳かなケネディ大統領の<u>就任式</u>に出席した。

858　<u>お香</u>をたくことは，1960年代のヒッピーの間で一時期大流行した。

859　私たちは窓に打ち付ける<u>絶えまない</u>雨の音で，一晩中目を覚ましていた。

860　科学者たちは，地上の生命の<u>初期の</u>誕生について，「原始のスープ」のような状態で始まり，その中で次第に進化していったと言及している。

861　レーザー外科技術の発明のおかげで，しばしば大きく<u>切開</u>することなく，体の中に最小限手を入れるだけで手術をすることが可能になった。

862, 863　息子が群集<u>を扇動して</u>暴動に導いたとして訴えられると，市長は国で最高の<u>弁護士</u>を雇って彼につけた。

864　アルバート・アインシュタインでさえも量子力学の大きな新発見には懐疑的であった。なぜなら，原子構造が単なる偶然によって特徴づけられるという考え方は<u>想像もつかない</u>と，言っていたからである。

865　小さな交易所として始まったものが，次から次へと小さな町<u>を編入して</u>，巨大都市に成長した。

866　アメリカの法律のもとでは，個人は法廷で自分の配偶者<u>を告発</u>しなくてもよい。

867, 868　その実験の指示は，別々のペトリ皿で2種類のバクテリア<u>を</u>6時間<u>培養</u>し，それから一緒にして数時間たったら混ざりあって<u>合体させる</u>というものであった。

869　私の叔父は，第二次世界大戦でドイツと戦ったときに，しばしば敵の陣地に短い間<u>侵入</u>したものだ，と私に語った。

870　戦争と経済対策の失敗を何年も繰り返したので，多くのアフリカの国々は貧窮したが，その結果，何千という<u>貧乏で</u>家のない避難民を生み出すことにな

予想例文

871　その有名な映画スターは，空港のセキュリティ担当官が，隠し持っているかもしれない武器を調べるため，ボディチェックを受けなければならない，と彼女に伝えると，大いに憤慨した。

872　全体主義的な政府はしばしば，国家の教育システムを子どもたちを洗脳することに利用する。

873　彼は怠惰な性格にもかかわらず，ひょうきんで教師たちから気に入られていた。

874, 875　私たちはホプキン氏が学科長の座を受け入れてくれるよう説得できる自信があったが，彼が断ると，私たちはかなり的外れな話をしていたのだと気づいた。

876, 877　彼は，カレンに夢中になるまでは堅く独身を守り通してきたが，彼女の穏やかで控えめな性格に攻略されたのだった。

878, 879　イラクにおけるサダム・フセイン政権の崩壊後，その国はイスラム反体制分子による侵入をある程度経験した。

880　敵は連合軍に多大な損失を負わせたにもかかわらず，彼らが勝利を勝ち取るまで屈せずに戦い続けることは明らかであった。

881　少年の行動はしばしば図々しく無鉄砲だったので，彼は部屋に入っていくだけで父親を激怒させた。

882　彼のより洗練された同僚に似ず，ジムは非常に純真だったので，企業間の競争や無情な野心の世界ではうまくやっていくことができなかった。

883　彼はマリファナをふかしたことは認めるが，吸い込まなかったと主張した。

884　ルソーは，人間は本質的に悪ではなく，社会によってそのようになるのだ，という考えを信奉していた。

885　ヘンリー8世は，食べ物，酒，女性に飽くことを知らない欲望を示した。

886　私たちの先生はときどき不可解な表情で私たちを見たものだった。

887　その有名な作家は，ある評論家が論評の中で，彼の作品は基本的には退屈である，とほのめかしているのを読んで激怒した。

888, 889　女子学生が不作法で横柄であるというだけでなく，10時の門限を破るのが多すぎることがわかり，女子寄宿学校を改革するのに新しい校長が任命された。

890　何年も経ってから，警察は，かつて解決不能と宣言した事件を何とかして解決した。

891　多くの企業が事実上破産していると分かったとき，あまねく豊かであった古き良き時代は去ったのであった。

892　その国の指導者は，反抗勢力は単に，その国の地方において混乱状態を扇動

893 彼の両親は，世界のより恵まれない状態にいる人々に深い理解を示すよう，彼に教え込んだのだった。

894, 895 その教授は，学生の論文はまったく内容がないとこぼしていた。深みに欠けるだけでなく，ちょっとした脚注にした方がいいような筋違いの事柄で基本的に構成されているとして。

896 マルセル・マルソーは世界で最も偉大なマイム役者と考えられているが，彼は言葉を使わずに，人間の漠然とした感情を表現できるのだ。

897 敵のミサイルを迎撃することを目的とした防衛システムは，いまだに完全からはほど遠い。

898 私の弟と妹が口論すると，ほかの者はだれも一言も口をはさむことができなかった。

899 警察は12時間に渡って容疑者を尋問し，ついに彼は犯罪を認めた。

900 批評家たちは，力のある国が，力の弱い国々の支配に介入する権利を持つかどうかをめぐって，意見が2つに分かれた。

901 心臓専門医として，グラムフェルド博士は非常に複雑な手術を行うよう，たびたび要請された。

902 マングースとヘビの戦いを見ているとき，私はマングースがヘビを襲うよう訓練されていたのか，それとも本質的に敵意を持つものなのか，考えをめぐらした。

903 家の外へ出たくなって，私たちは涼しい夕べの空気の中を散歩し，少し元気が出た気がした。

904 フォート・ノックスの金庫は，アメリカの準備金を保管しているのだが，難攻不落であると信じている者もいるが，専門家は破れない安全システムなどないことを知っている。

905 リチャード・ニクソンの大統領としての遺産は，ウォーターゲート事件で取り返しがつかないほどにダメージを受けた。

906, 907 古代の文化でさえも，乾燥または半乾燥地帯を耕地にするため，灌漑設備を作ることを知っていた。

908 牛牧場の周りにある電気仕掛けのフェンスは，そこに触れた牛に痛みを伴う衝撃を与えるので，脱走を防ぐことができる。

909 私の祖父はいつも，家族のもめごとを扱うのに公平で思慮分別を欠いたことがなかった。

910 最高齢公式記録保持者が122歳で亡くなった。

911 現在核兵器開発を進めている国は，それらを抑止力として正当化しているが，それは，そう言って彼らをこきおろしているすでに核を持っている国が，冷

予想例文

912 基調演説者はひどかった。演説がけだるく単調であるだけでなく，内容も漫然としたつながりのないモノローグのようであった。

913 緑色の草木と咲き誇る種々の野の花に囲まれて，穏やかなそよ風のもと，湖面に広がる銀色のさざ波が浜に打ち寄せていた。

914 だれ一人として知事の素晴らしい才能を疑う者はいないが，ときおり思わぬ判断の間違いを犯すので，率直に言うと彼の仕事ぶりには一貫性がない。

915 今日，人間の潜在能力の限界を本当に推測することはだれにもできないと信じる科学者もいる。

916 裕福なビジネスマンの娘として，彼女は，その育ちを反映したスタイルで，ぜいたくに暮らした。

917 その有名なコーチが有名大学のヘッドコーチにならないかという申し出を受けたとき，彼がふさわしいと思うように指導するという完全な自由を与えてくれるよう主張した。

918 石油採掘所で数週間働くと，男たちは町に行き，うっぷんを晴らすためにばか騒ぎをするが，決してだれかに危害を加えるようなことはしなかった。

919 ときどき，私は無気力な学生に向かってどなることがあるが，彼らを侮辱するわけではなく，単に学ぶことの喜びに目覚めさせてあげたいのだ。

920 スターリンは，彼の反対者を，彼の権力を脅かすようになる前に，単に粛清してしまうのがベストだと考えるタイプのリーダーであった。

921 サルトルは現代世界の多くの思想家が「アンニュイ」に苦しんでいると説明したが，それは，意味を欠く世界に対する深い無関心，または倦怠感である。

922 数年前，私の妹は家の裏庭に捨てられていた一腹の5匹の子ネコのために数軒の家を探さなくてはならなかった。

923 ビルは昇進を見送られてだまされたと考え，そのことにとても腹を立てた。

924 数人の高齢者が警察を呼んで，街角でうろつき見知らぬ人に失礼なことを言って時間をつぶしている頑健な男たちのことを，抗議して訴えた。

925 彼はいつも前向きに考えるこつを心得ていた。物事が絶望的なように見えるときでも，良くなっていると感じていた。

926 コロラド州のデンバー付近の景観は，本当に素晴らしい。特に冬，雪をかぶった山々がいつも高くそびえ立っているときが。

927 知事は自分の仕事を守る戦いで負けつつあると感じたので，彼は対立候補の選挙運動を個人的な不品行を中傷的に責め立てることによって脱線させようと試みた。

928 知事のリコールが政治状態を混乱に陥れたが，事態は変化しなくてはならな

い，という人々からのメッセージは明確であった。

929 ミルズ教授はしばしば雄弁であったが，学生たちは，彼が言葉数を減らせば彼の講義はもっと分かりやすくなるのにと感じた。

930 アブラハム・リンカーンはつまらない農場の仕事をしながら貧困の中で育ったが，彼はおそらくアメリカのもっとも偉大な大統領として，世界の歴史の中で注目を集めた。

931 人肉をも食べた連続殺人犯，ジェフリー・ダーマーの発見は，人間が悪意に満ちた行為や忌しい行為を行えるということを明らかにしたのだった。

932 悪性の腫瘍があることが発見されると，その老人は健康保険もなく乏しい貯金だけで，治療費をどう払えるか見当がつかなかった。

933 私は学生たちに，それぞれの卒業論文をその明晰さ，深さ，独創性で評価し，他からとった情報を言い換えただけのものは評価を下げると伝えた。

934, 935　競技担当職員はトラックから少し離れたところを線で区切り，そこに疾走する車から少なくとも10ヤードは見物人を遠ざけるため，フェンスを立てた。

936 その大統領は政治家であるだけでなく，どんなときにも適切な格言を引用することのできる学識のある人物であった。

937 元合衆国大統領のジミー・カーターは数多くの国際論争の仲裁で非常に活躍してきた。

938 そのフランス外人部隊はロマンティックに描写されているものの，実は金額が妥当であればだれとでも，どこでも，喜んで戦うという傭兵隊であった。

939 私たちは，彼の経済改革戦略は単に無謀であるだけでなく，完全にしくじると最初から考えていた。

940 韓国は北朝鮮の核開発プログラムによって高まった緊張感を和らげようとベストを尽くしているが，その問題はアメリカ，日本，他の国々の敵意を引き起こしているのだ。

941 数年前，マレーシアの首相，モハメド・マハティール氏は，世界の通貨市場におけるリンギットの変動制を一時停止し，1ドル3.8リンギットに固定するという発表をした。

942 少女がそのような服装で家に帰ると，母親は屈辱感を覚え，娘に向かって不適切な服装だと言ってどなった。

943 会議は途中で議題を放り出してしまったかのように，混乱状態で終わった。

944 彼はちょっと俗物で，自分を洗練されている人間だと思い，普通の人の平凡な世界には侮蔑以外の何も感じることがなかった。

945 スージーの無言の抗議は，もう私とは会わないということを示していた。

946 アルカリ溶解は，ときどき酸の作用を無効にするのに用いられる。

予想例文

947 我々は海外からの書類をいくつか証明する必要があったが，公証人が絶対必要と言われた。

948 会社で駆け出しのわりに彼は生意気で自信過剰に見えたが，言ったことは何でも実績で実証するつもりであった。

949, 950 大試合でのティムの勝手なプレーは実に迷惑以外の何ものでもなかったが，最終結果におけるその影響は無視できないものがあった。

951 その若い大統領候補は，対抗者がよく批判されているような遠回しなしゃべり方は避けるようにアドバイスされた。

952 太陽が沈んだ後でさえ，夕闇の光が，暗闇が完全にそれを消すまで渓谷の壁に1時間近くも漂っていた。

953 コンピュータは，市場に出回るとほどなく時代遅れのものとなるように見える。

954 最初，私たちは隣人たちは単に親切にしてくれているだけだと思ったが，時が経つにつれ，でしゃばりになり，ついに横柄に思えるようになってしまった。

955, 956 私も万策尽きた気分だったが，旅団の士気を保たねばならなかったので，戦い続けるよう部下を駆り立てた。

957 オフィスの新人の女性はすでにオフィス業務の流れのすべてを習得してしまっていて，確かに有能である。

958 新しい会社に勤めてたった1か月ばかりたったころ，上司は私の仕事がどんな義務を伴っているか，正確に思い出すようにと私を呼びつけて叱った。

959, 960 前の独裁者は2003年の4月から逃走中で，8か月間身柄拘束から逃げおおせることができた。

961 ちょうどのどまで出かかっている言葉を思い出せないときのイライラといったらない！

962 多くのラグジュアリー・カーの窓は外からは不透明に見えるが，内側からは透けて見えるようになっている。

963 光学器具のセールスマンとして，ニューヨークからロサンゼルスのフライトで検眼士の隣に座ったことは好都合であると感じた。

964 私たちの町の最も裕福な男性は高校卒業後，大学に進学せず，その代わりに自分でビジネスを始める道を選んだ。

965 カルロス神父は20年前にローマカトリックの司祭に任命されて以来，神の目から見て神聖であるよう服従，慈愛，純潔の誓いを守ってきた。

966 医者は，彼は非常に頑健で生きることへのすさまじいまでの意志により，砂漠での10日間の厳しい試練を耐え抜いた，と言った。

967 メトロノームは一定の周期で2点間を往復するので，音楽のリズムを取るのに利用することができる。

968	私は有名なショー・ビジネスの名士をたたえる祝宴に招待されたとき，<u>場違いだ</u>と強く感じた。
969	ヨーヨー・マは，バッハのチェロ協奏曲の素晴らしい演奏で，総立ちの<u>大喝采</u>を浴びた。
970	最近の演技がますます<u>度を越して</u>いるように思えるため，その若い男のシリアスな役者としての評判は疑問視されている。
971	1週間ずっと空は曇って雨が降りそうだったが，今日，目を覚ますと，まだ空は<u>雲に覆われて</u>いた。
972	私たちは，銀行口座から<u>借り越しをして</u>しまったと分かったとき，しばらく本当に切り詰めないといけないと決めた。
973	ヒギンズ氏は，銀行への住宅ローンの<u>支払いが遅れた</u>とき，彼は二度と滞納してはいけないと勧告を受けた。
974	私は，ふだん料理が素晴らしいレストランに同僚を連れていったが，どういうわけだかその晩は，料理はかろうじて<u>食べられる</u>といったところだった。
975	スタントン夫人は心臓発作で危機一髪だったが，その後，数か月は<u>青白く</u>弱々しく見えた。
976	人生で何をしようとも，幸福が<u>最高</u>だ。
977	その上院議員が賄賂で有罪とされたとき，報道機関は彼を新聞上でけなし，いわゆる彼の友だちとされる一部の人たちからも，<u>のけ者</u>のように扱われた。
978	経営側によくある特徴は，会社あるいは大学でも低い地位の者に<u>責任を押し付ける</u>傾向があるということだ。
979, 980	彼の容態がどんなに<u>痛ましい</u>ものになろうとも，表面上は彼は<u>陽気で</u>楽観的な様子を保っていた。
981	その社会のバイタリティは，古い問題を解くのに新しい考えを持つ想像力豊かな人間が極端に<u>不足</u>していることによって，脅かされている。
982	ライティングの授業で最近人気があるテクニックは<u>仲間</u>による批評である。
983	オルダス・ハックスレーは<u>知覚</u>に幻覚作用を及ぼすドラッグの影響について有名な本を書いた。
984	王の豪華な住居の周り中に，<u>多年生の</u>花と，花を咲かせる木々が植えられた。
985	そのように<u>おざなりな</u>やり方で学問を扱い続けると，2年生が始まる前に，彼は成績不良で退学することになるだろう。
986, 987	警察は，もっとも熟練した警察官でさえ彼の告白と彼自身の行動に対する<u>未熟な</u>態度にショックを受けるほどの<u>悪らつな</u>行為に対して，ある男を逮捕した。

予想例文

988, 989 デビッドソン警部は、銀行強盗の犯人たちを捕まえたと確信したが、裁判での証拠は彼らの容疑を完全に晴らしてしまった。

990 古代ギリシャの哲学的、科学的遺産は、西洋の知性の歴史全体に浸透している。

991 その少年の母親は、彼の妹に嫌がらせをしているのを見て注意した。

992 嘆願書には1万を超える人々の署名が寄せられたが、街の端で操業している危険な原子炉を市長に閉鎖させることを期待したものであった。

993 化石は、有機生命体が粘土に覆われ、それによって石になる、つまり石化して生じるのだ。

994 彼はクラシック、ジャズ、ポピュラー音楽の作曲家として分類されることに腹を立てていた。彼にとってそれはみな音楽というものに変わりはないからだった。

995 私の祖父は外出するとき、だれかが彼の持ち物を盗まないように、いつも部屋にカギをかけていた。

996 彼はとても利口な政治家なので、彼の財力についてはっきり言わせるのはほとんど不可能である。

997 何年も貧窮に見舞われた役者としてがんばって過ごした後、彼はついにアカデミー賞を勝ち取って成功の頂点にたどりついた。

998 初期の探検家たちが太平洋を Pacific Ocean と名づけたのは、少々間違っていた。彼らがそれを穏やかで静かな海と思っていたからだ。

999, 1000 小学生のとき、私は毎日、合衆国国旗と「それが表している共和国に対して」忠誠を誓うように求められた。

1001 私たちはみな、TESOL の年次総会に出席したかったのだが、すべての席は私たちがそこに到着する前にいっぱいになっていた。

1002 最初、市場において石油の不足があるように見えたが、数か国がこの状況に素早くつけ込もうとした後、すぐに過多になり価格は急落した。

1003 現代の彫刻家は、大理石やブロンズよりも加工しやすい材料を求め、プラスチックや粘土、その他のびっくりするような物質を使い、3次元の形を創り出す。

1004 エジプトのピラミッドの多くは、泥棒たちによってすでに荒らされてから何世紀もしてやっと発掘されたのだった。

1005 違法に暴利をむさぼる者が、単に戦利品として使うためだけにゴリラの密猟を続けていれば、この素晴らしい種は絶滅してしまう可能性がある。

1006 まだ13歳ほどの幼い少女が、はじめてのバレエでそれほどの落ち着きと優雅さをもって演じたことにみな感銘を受けた。

1007 その大学の学長はおそらく私がそれまで会った中で最も尊大な人間の1人で

あったが，いつも世の中で最も重要な人間の1人であるかのように振る舞っていた。

1008 論理的な話し合いで神の存在を支持しようとする彼の努力において，トマス・アクィナスは第一原因の原則を前提としていた。

1009 コブラの毒はとても強力なので，数分程度で人間を死に至らしめることができる。

1010 何層にも重なった葉を通して，私たちは，体勢を整えて今にも飛びかかろうとしているヤマネコを見つけた。

1011 あの少年たちは非常にいたずらで，いたずらがうまくいけば，それより楽しいことなんてないのだ。

1012, 1013 滑りやすくて危険な山道で，私たちの車は突然スリップして尻を振り始め，危うく傾いてコントロールが利かなくなるところであった。

1014 コンピュータによるレーザー手術は，従来のメスを用いる外科医よりはるかに正確な手術を行える。

1015 ジェニファーがRCAとの長期にわたるレコード契約にサインしたことでいくつかの不利益が生じたが，その1つは，将来他の会社と取引をすることを除外することであった。

1016 最近のアメリカの政策は自己防衛という正当な原則として，先制攻撃の考えを擁護してきた。

1017 彼の論議は2＋2＝5のような誤りの前提のもとにあった。

1018 ジャニスはレオナルドとの結婚に同意したとき，どこでどのように結婚式を行なうかについては，自分が決める権利を持つことを明らかにした。

1019, 1020 彼は生涯のほとんどを大都市の中心で過ごしたが，牧歌的な田舎の生活様式という彼の素朴なイメージを失うことはなかった。

1021 彼女は生涯にわたり過食という性癖と戦ってきた。

1022 彼は，快適な家と少しばかりのぜいたくなものを彼と彼の家族のために手に入れようと，生涯がんばって働いた。

1023 その教師は，すべての生徒に自分の可能性を呼び起こさせようと最善を尽くした。

1024 トゥイーディ氏が医者を訪ねると，彼にガンが見つかったが，この種の腫瘍は予後が良い，と医者は言った。

1025 アイザック・アシモフは，サイエンス・フィクションとポピュラー・サイエンス史上最も多作な作家の1人として認められている。

1026, 1027 単なる著作権事務員として仕事をしていたが，アルバート・アインシュタインは1905年に彼の特殊相対性理論で頭角を現した。しかし1916年の一般相対性理論の出版後，世界中での彼の地位は絶対的なものとなった。

予想例文

1028 焼いていたステーキの1つが燃えている炭の中に落ちたとき，彼は大きなフォークを使ってそれを取り出した。

1029 古代ローマ人はしばしば，神託を伝える人（祭司）に頼った。彼らは未来を予言することができると信じていたのだ。

1030 真実か誤りかの見解は，しばしば陳述の形で表される。

1031 私の祖母はよく，純粋に論理的な「正しさ」よりも，行動の社会的礼節の方に関心があった。

1032 エドワーズ氏は能力のある人で，よく働く専門技術者だが，彼の執筆となるととても単調で，わずかな想像力がある人ならだれでもぐっすりと眠ってしまうほどだ。

1033 元ヘビー級ボクシング・チャンピオンであるマイク・タイソンは，挑発されたかどうかに関係なく襲撃を加えることがあったので，何度も逮捕されている。

1034 最近の研究で，飼いネコも，獲物を探しながら近所の道や裏庭をうろつく，すぐれた殺傷能力を持った生き物であることが分かった。

1035 『3匹の子ブタ』の話の中の大きな悪いオオカミのことはほとんどだれでも知っているが，彼は「はあはあブッと息を吐いてお前たちの家を吹き飛ばしてしまうぞ」と言ってブタたちを脅かすのだった。

1036 その学校の校長は，とてもだまされやすかったので，生徒たちは時々彼をからかうのがおもしろいと思っていた。

1037 自分の暗室で白黒写真をプリントすることで嫌なことの1つは，薬品の鼻を刺すようなにおいである。

1038 ナチス・ドイツ時代のホロコーストは，ユダヤ人を国から除こうとするヒトラーの試みであった。

1039 現代言語教育の会議のコーディネーターとして，私は200を超える質問を受けた。

1040 マーク・トウェイン作とされる1つの警句に，「たばこをやめるのは簡単である。なぜなら実際もう何回もやめているからだ」というのがある。

1041 キュリー夫人とピエール・キュリーは放射線の研究業績によりノーベル賞をとった。

1042 円の半径は非常に多くの数学計算で，重要な数値である。

1043 量子論から派生する問題は，まだ完全に研究し尽くされてはいない。

1044 中国の代表は，知的所有権に関しての条項修正に他の国が同意するなら，中国もその条約を批准するのに同意するつもりだと言った。

1045 その男性の精神分析医は，父親へのうっ積した強い憎しみをコントロールするのに助けを求めるよう促した。

1046 フォード自動車会社は先週，2003年12月以前に購入されたすべての新車に500ドルの払い戻しを提供すると発表した。
1047 陪審への最終弁論で，被告側の弁護人は検察側の議論に徹底的に反論した。
1048 ガリレオは太陽を中心とした太陽系説を支持する陳述を撤回するよう強制された。
1049 教師は学生の1人に，クラスの学生に読んでくるように言ったテキストの基本的な意味を要約するよう求めた。
1050 ひどい洪水の後，ミシシッピ川の水がみなが家に帰れるほどに引くまでに，1か月以上かかった。
1051 数人の分析家の計算によると，イラクの戦争と復興にかかるお金は結果的には3,500億ドルを超えるだろうと言われている。
1052 日本政府は，海洋を干拓するのに何兆円もお金を使った。
1053 私の叔父の1人は，第二次世界大戦のときにアメリカ軍のために偵察飛行をドイツ上空で行なった。
1054 安田教授は，しばしば，終戦直後の東京大学での学生時代の話を詳しく語った。
1055 盗みでその少年を逮捕する代わりに，被害にあった店のオーナーは，盗んだ品物の価値に値する労働をすることによって，彼のしたことを正すチャンスを与えることを申し出た。
1056 手術後元気になるまで，私の兄は6か月近くかかった。
1057 第二次世界大戦時の日系アメリカ人に対する恥ずべき扱いを償うのに，アメリカ政府は何十年も経ってからとりかかった。
1058 頼んだ本が20ページ欠けて届いたので，私はその会社に手紙を書き，返金を要求した。
1059 メアリーは，白血病から回復したが，2年間快方に向かったあと，明らかに逆戻りし始めた。
1060 いったん会社の経営側に嫌われると，彼は外を見ることのできる窓が1つもない地下のオフィスに追いやられた。
1061 その老人は発作で亡くなるまで会社を経営したが，精神的にはっきり考えたり話したりすることができなくなっても権力を譲ることを拒んだ。
1062 6月に私は税務署から正しい額の市民税を送金していないという通知を受けた。
1063 精神病患者はしばしば，自分のやったことの何にも良心の呵責を感じることができない。
1064 気前よい報酬に加え，その仕事は，従業員に特別な刺激となるよう多くの魅力的な特典を備えていた。

予想例文

1065 アメリカの南北戦争においては，南部であれ北部であれ，裏切り者はしばしば絞首刑になったり銃殺されたりした。

1066, 1067 最初，その19世紀の農家の家に引っ越したとき，私たちは家族の娯楽室を長く広げ，キッチンを改造しようと決めた。

1068 日本当局は北朝鮮に拉致され誘拐された日本人を帰国させたいと思っている。

1069 8時間にわたる血みどろの戦いの後，敵の部隊はついに撃退された。

1070 クローン技術は，ある有機体のDNAを複製し，生存可能な複製品を創り出すプロセスである。

1071 多くの真面目なイスラム教徒はイスラム教テロリストの行動を非難されるべきことと見ている。

1072 フロイトは，精神疾患は人間の自然な本能を抑圧する社会的抑制の結果であると信じていた。

1073 その学生たちは全員，学校の構内で喫煙をしたので，厳しく叱責された。

1074 学部長は，各自のコースで問題の学生を扱う適切な解決法を見つけ損なったとして，数人の教師を退けた。

1075 第二次世界大戦中に看護婦として，彼の母親は，目撃せざるをえなかった恐ろしいことによってしばしば気分が悪くなった，と私たちに話した。

1076 彼の評判は，人によっていろいろであった。

1077 心に障害を持つ患者は施設から逃げ出そうとしたため，肉体的に拘束されなければならなかった。

1078 裁判における転機は，検察側の主要な証人の1人が被告に対する以前の告訴を取り消したときに，やってきた。

1079 マイク・タイソンはリングでは常に攻撃的なファイターであり，打たれても決して後退することはない。

1080 セスティーナは手の込んだ古く12世紀フランス詩の形式であるが，最終行の言葉は反復のパターンに従っている。

1081 アブラハム・リンカーンの暗殺から時が経つにつれ，世界は彼を生前よりいっそう崇敬するようになってきた。

1082 精神医学の診断は，その男性は社会に復帰しても安全だと当局者を確信させたが，1週間以内に元の反社会的な行動に逆戻りしてしまった。

1083 『サバイバル』のようなテレビ番組では，人は危険なスタントをしてみたり，うじ虫で覆われたチーズのようなひどく不快なものを食べたりする。

1084 地震の後，至る所で混乱が起こり，略奪が横行した。

1085 私は両親の間で広がる不和を癒す助けになれることを考えたが，楽観してはいなかった。

1086 エリックがその会社に雇われたとき，どんな状況のもとであっても会社の伝統に波風を立てようとしてはいけないと言われた。
1087 その老人は，いろいろな種類のテクノロジーに投資して財産を蓄えることができた。
1088 丸一昼夜の時間の長さは，地球がその地軸の周りを1周するのにかかる時間を表している。
1089 景気後退の間は試練であったが，景気は，ついに上向きになりつつある。
1090 いったん，敵の軍が前線を突き進んでくると，我々の軍は自信を失い，すぐに敗走した。
1091 遅れているフライトを待って空港で一晩を過ごすと，彼のスーツとシャツは完全にしわくちゃに見えた。
1092 彼はとてもよくやっているように見えたが，脱税や虚偽の会計報告のような他の違法行為に関与したことで，法律に触れ始めた。
1093 私は，秋のかすかなそよ風が窓の外の葉をかさかさといわせていたので，真夜中に目を覚ました。
1094 ジンギス・カンはとても冷酷であるとの定評があったが，多くの点で，彼は征服した土地に安定と秩序をもたらした。
1095 素晴らしい話し手というのは，しばしば，自分の話の最も大事なポイントを最後までとっておくものである。
1096 キースとエイミーは，ブルックス神父に，エイミーの両親が結婚式を行ったのと同じチャペルで特別なセレモニーを挙げて，彼らの結婚式に神の恵みを与えてほしいと，頼んだ。
1097 何百万という粛正でも，ヨセフ・スターリンの血への渇望を満足させることはできなかった。
1098 1年近く前庭で車の手入れをし続けると，地面にオイルがすっかり染み込んでしまったので，ジムはそこにまた芝生を生やすために表土を運び込まなければならなかった。
1099 小犬たちは，母犬が心配そうに見ていたが，芝生の上ではね回っていた。
1100 会社の電源がショートしてしまったとき，私たちはどこに問題があるのかをつきとめるため，電気系統の配線図を探さなければならなかった。
1101 中世に，黒死病がネズミによって広まる災いになったが，何百万というヨーロッパ人が亡くなった。
1102 レポートの期限が迫ってくるにつれ，委員会のメンバーはプロジェクトを争って仕上げようとしていた。
1103 私の友人は世界を見るため海軍に入隊したということだが，半年間彼のやったことといえば，船のデッキのペンキをこすり落とし何度も塗り直すという

予想例文

作業であった。

1104 私の上司のお気に入りの言葉は「君が好意を示すなら，私もそれに応えよう（魚心あれば水心）」であった。

1105 イゴールは若いときのほとんどを少年犯罪者保護施設で過ごしたが，茶色の紙袋全体に「報復」という言葉を書きなぐっていた。

1106 私たちはビーチに立って，カニが水のなかに急いで入っていくのを見つめていた。

1107 アメリカ人作家，ヘンリー・デービッド・ソーローは，ウォールデン池の隣接する林の中の人里離れた小屋で生活を送った。

1108 我々が大統領の執務室に到着するまでには，彼は怒りで煮えくり返っていた。

1109, 1110 アメリカは「るつぼ」と呼ばれるが，それは，多くの移民のグループが，かつては分離されていたものまでも，次第に主流の国民に同化しつつあるからである。

1111 事故のあと，その男性は，もはや，意味の通る文を作ることができなかった。

1112, 1113 確かに彼はその王宮の召し使いとして従属的であることを求められたが，ときには過度にへつらっているように思えた。

1114 アメリカの南北戦争の理由の1つは，アフリカ系アメリカ人を奴隷の身分から解放することであった。

1115 その子どもは回復してきているようであったのに，ひどい感染症が始まって，危篤状態になった。

1116 ボーイスカウトの一隊が背中にリュックを背負い森の中を出発した。

1117, 1118 その行動は世界中から広く批判を浴びたが，アメリカ政府は疑わしいとするテロリスト・キャンプを砲撃するのは，単に便宜の問題であると反論した。

1119, 1120 世界中で彼は警察や軍隊に追われていたが，30年以上にわたってそれから逃げおおせるほど抜け目がなかった。

1121, 1122 我々は霧に包まれた風景の中を歩いていた，危険がすぐそこまで迫っていることを知りながら…。

1123 ジョディ・フォスターは子どもの頃から映画スターだが，彼女は人目につくことを避けている。

1124 1970年代，一時的なガソリン不足が急速にその値段を上げ，多くの人々が，夜にちんぴらにホースでガソリンを抜き取られないように鍵つきのガスキャップを車につけた。

1125 その男性の妻は，彼女が侮辱されたときに手をこまねいているだけで夫が何もしなかったので，非常に腹を立てた。

1126 その知事は，人々が最も好む政策に自信を持てないときはいつも，どっちつ

かずの態度をとり，風向きを見極めるまでそうしていたものだ。
1127 調査の材料が少ないと，結果をわい曲することがある。
1128, 1129 彼女は巨大なブティックに入り，目の前にあるずらりと並んだイブニングドレスをざっと眺めていった。
1130 その子馬は，明るい10月の太陽のもとで，毛並みがつややかで美しかった。
1131 そのボーイスカウトの集団は，毎年夏にカヌーの探検を行うが，土と砂の中を何マイルもやっとの思いで進みながら，浅瀬でカヌーを運ぶのに多くの時間を使ってしまった。
1132 それは単なる噂であったが，いい人の評判も，そのような中傷で崩されうるものである。
1133 そのコーチはときどき選手にいらいらすると，注意を引くため彼らの後頭部をたたいたものだった。
1134 政治候補者はふつう，他の候補者の批判は本当は彼らの名声を汚すための運動であると主張するものだ。
1135 証人たちは，その警察官が突然，まるで罪のない通りがかりの人に対して銃を発砲して，自制心を失ったようだったと言った。
1136 その公園の付近にいるサルはとても人に慣れているので，旅行者にこっそりと近付いて，できるものなら何でもひったくって逃げていくのだった。
1137 彼の言葉は形式的に礼儀正しかったが，声の調子は横柄で意地悪であった。
1138 彼は，ある日はあなたにとても親切にしてくれても，次の日にははっきりと冷たくあしらうような人間だ。
1139 イヌワシは雲の中に舞い上がると消えて見えなくなった。
1140 1990年代のバブル崩壊以来，日本の多くの大手銀行の支払い能力は疑問視されてきている。
1141 ヒリアード夫人は事故でひどく動転していたので，だれも彼女をなだめるようなことを言ったりしたりすることができなかった。
1142 報道機関はまもなく，政府最高レベルが関係しているらしい政治スキャンダルにまつわる汚い詳細を入手した。
1143 モンタナ州は，とても人口が希薄なので，人が住んでいるところはおろか，1人の人間も見ずに何マイルも旅することができる。
1144 彼女は母親の命令に従うと約束したが，声は悪意に満ちていた。
1145 その子どもが誤って錆びたカンで動脈を切ってしまったとき，彼の手首から血が噴き出した。
1146 マイクロソフト社の敵は，そのソフトウェア会社がそのインターネット・ブラウザで競争から彼らを締め出そうとしていると主張した。
1147 私たちのこの前の休暇の請求書を受け取ったとき，私はその総額に本当に呆

然とした。
1148 子どものときでさえも、私の甥は才能ある歌手として、大勢のものから抜きん出ていた。
1149 多くの教育者たちは、学力が劣る生徒を特別なクラスに入れることは彼らに汚名を着せることになるのでは、と懸念している。
1150 1960年代と70年代の初期、ビートルズが、多くの人々を魅了し、旋風を巻き起こしたが、いわゆる「ビートルマニア」が、事実上、十代の若者すべてを巻き込むほどにまでなった。
1151 インドからイギリスへのボート上で密航者が発見された。
1152 陸軍士官学校は、その厳格な規律と教育水準の高さでアメリカ中に知られていた。
1153 1971年のアッティカ刑務所の有名な反乱は、刑務所員とニューヨーク州警察官と州兵により暴力的に鎮圧されたが、33人の囚人と10人の人質の犠牲を出すことになった。
1154 2か月にわたるほとんどやむことのない雨の後、モンスーンはやっとおさまったが、村は洪水の被害で荒廃していた。
1155 多くの豊かな国は、ある好みの国内産農産物を助成するが、このやり方はしばしば発展途上国を怒らせる慣習である。
1156 1950年代のマッカーシー時代に、多くの才能ある芸術家や映画制作者が、破壊活動を行っているとしてブラックリストにのせられた。
1157 高齢者の患者は、患っているけがや病気で亡くなることは少なく、代わりに肺炎にかかって、死ぬことがよくある。
1158 5つ星の将軍が突然ホワイトハウスに召喚されたとき、だれも彼が昇進するのかクビになるのか分からなかった。
1159 前国王についてイランの国民をそれほどまでに怒らせた1つのことは、国王の壮麗な宮殿であった。
1160 株式市場は、通常の経済指数のほとんどが、第3四半期になっても強気を示していることから沸き立った。
1161 彼は少年時代のみじめな貧乏状態を乗り越えようと一生懸命に働いた。
1162, 1163 私たちは沼をボートに乗って進んでいった、頭のすぐ上の枝や水面のすぐ下にどんな生き物が潜んでいるか知りもせずに。
1164 ちょうど先週、ジョンは、過去数か月の彼の販売記録をめぐって首が危うい、ただ耐えて待つだけだ、と言われた。
1165 学者たちは、芸術の均整美は自然の対称性を真似ていると指摘している。
1166 そのダンス・グループは、コンサートに向けて、動きが完全に揃うのを確実にしようと、2週間1日6時間も練習をした。

1167 高橋教授は優秀な講師であり学者であったが，彼はよく同僚や学生との関係においては機転がきかず鈍感であった。
1168 彼は5年間その小説に取り組んできたが，ついにそれは形を成し始めた。
1169 西山老教授が部屋に入ると，そこにいたみなが彼に話してほしいと言った。
1170 投票所のドアは数時間前に閉鎖されたが，投票を数え上げるのに，ほとんど丸1日かかるだろう。
1171 嵐が家の窓とドアを揺らしたが，やがて，だんだんとおさまり始め，最後にはかすかな霧雨になった。
1172 彼の先輩たちは，ふつうの習慣からの彼の奇妙な逸脱についてあざ笑っていたが，彼は，たびたび，問題を解決するのに創造的で効果的な方法を発見したのだった。
1173 私は自分の書いたエッセイのあまりの稚拙さにぎょっとして，それを破り捨て，もう一度はじめからやり直した。
1174 その仕事はつまらなくてきついが，彼は，最後には，若い学生たちにとって有用でユニークなテキストを作れるのではないかと考えていた。
1175 世界で最も肥沃な農地は温暖な気候帯にあるということは，一般的に真実である。
1176, 1177 その子馬は柵にきちんとつながっていると思っていたが，突然ゲートに向かって駆け出し，全速力で逃げ出した。
1178 容疑者たちが警察に強く打たれたとき，彼らは犯していない犯罪を自白したものだった。
1179 父は，私がパーティ用に適当に選んだ服に気づくとすぐに，「なんと素晴らしい服だ！」と，皮肉たっぷりにささやいた。
1180 私の母は倹約家でやりくり上手であり，いつも本当に必要なときはお金を持っているようであった。
1181 大きな民衆の抗議が，政府の危険戦闘区域に軍隊を送り込むという計画をくじくことになった。
1182 私たちは，たくさんの支出があり，今月はすべての勘定を払うことができなかったので，なんとか切り抜けるために一時的なローンを組まなければならなかった。
1183 景気後退の時期，多くの日本人家族は倹約をする必要があると感じた。
1184 ギリシャを旅行したとき，食事はまあまあであったが，素晴らしいというわけではないと思った。
1185 その地域の地質調査を仕上げるためには，地形図を見る必要がある。
1186 西山老教授が通常の時間，空間の境界というものを超越してきたのは明らかだ。

予想例文

1187 大統領のスピーチを書き取るのは，彼の多くの文法上，語彙上の間違いのために，何時間もかかってしまった。
1188, 1189 その少年は，よく遅刻して早く引き上げたが，この違反が上司に対する直接的な侮辱となったとき，彼は解雇された。
1190 名声は一時，人生は短し。
1191 彼の数学の間違いが，解いていた問題の数の1つのうち，2つの桁の数字を入れ替えてしまったために起こったことがわかるまで，何時間もかかってしまった。
1192 会議における彼の発言は，十分的確であったが，ありふれた文句と品のない冗談でいっぱいだった。
1193 祭で全体が興奮しているなか，パレードが見えてくると群集の中から突然大きな騒ぎが起こった。
1194 中東における最近の不穏な時期の中，ブッシュ政権の平和への「ロードマップ」は，暴力に拍車がかかる状況の中でほとんど無実化しているように見える。
1195 芸能界における同僚からの小馬鹿にした扱いを何年も受けたのち，彼は映画・テレビ評論家になって形勢を逆転させることができ大いに喜んだ。
1196 私のネコはよく，一度に何日間か家を留守にしてしまうが，遅かれ早かれまた姿を現す。
1197 彼のけんか腰のスピーチは，政府の政策に対する臆することない拒否であった。
1198 私の家では，母は息子たちがシャツを着ないで食卓につくことは無作法だ，と考えていた。
1199 何回かの指し手の後，チェスの名人は相手プレーヤーに敗北を認めるかどうかかたずねたが，挑戦者は不屈にも，ゲームの続行を主張した。
1200 スタントン氏の妻はいつも彼をあごで使っていた。
1201 毎晩，私はキャンパスのとなりにある湖の端に座り，沈む太陽に波がうねるのを見つめたのだった。
1202 陸軍，海軍，海兵，空軍そして州兵といった軍隊は，アメリカ軍の単位部門を形成している。
1203 私たちは男の子たちをできるだけ外で遊ぶようにさせるが，彼らが手に負えなくなって隣人に迷惑をかければ，家の中に入らせて，静かにゲームでもして遊ぶようにさせている。
1204 そのレーシング・カードライバーたちが，そのひどい事故にあっても完全に無傷であったことは，信じられないことであった。
1205 私たちはみな，その教授の見苦しい装いは妻にとっては気恥ずかしいのでは

ないかと考えた。
1206 明白な事実の前に自分の立場が危うくなったときでも，彼は自分の意見を1点たりとも変えることを拒んだものである。
1207 デービッドは，ついに，彼女が彼に対する感情で何週間も揺らいでいたということを理由に，彼女を見捨てた。
1208 過去10年の間に，東京の大きな電車の駅で生活する浮浪者はますます増えたようだ。
1209 何年も勇敢に戦ったにもかかわらず，ネイティブ・アメリカンの将軍，ジェロニモはついに敗北した。
1210 化粧品会社と美容院は，潜在顧客に内在している虚栄心を利用したがっている。
1211 テロリストは，もし当局が彼らの要求に応えることを拒んだら，人口の大中心地を粉微塵にしてやると脅した。
1212 アメリカ英語のつづりには，イギリス英語と異なった非常に多くの変形がある。
1213 世界は，まもなくその若いボクサーが自慢の腕前に応えられるかどうかを見ることになる。
1214 最近の追悼式には，何千という人々が集まり，その時代の最も素晴らしい俳優の1人であったグレゴリー・ペックに敬意を表した。
1215 彼はしばしば，罪のない見物人に怒りをぶつけることがあった。
1216 その婦人はとてもおしゃべりで，「ハロー」というただ一言が彼女のボキャブラリーにはないようだ。
1217 アル・ゴアがアメリカの大統領選でついに勝ちそうに見えたちょうどそのとき，最後の最後のフロリダの逆転選挙で，再び負けてしまった。
1218 西山老教授は，アメリカの知性の歴史に非常に精通している。
1219 共和党の大統領は，けん銃販売の規制を求める議案であれば何でも拒否すると，いつも脅しをかける。
1220 彼女は子どもの頃から病弱で，生まれた家からほとんど離れたことがなかったので，本や映画を通して自分のことのように感じ，エキサイティングな人生を過ごした。
1221 スピーチコンテストの12人の最終出場者は，1等をめぐって競い合うだろう，それは500ドルの証券と素敵なトロフィーがついてくるのだ。
1222 軍の新兵訓練キャンプにはたいてい過酷な運動がつきものだ。
1223 その精神異常の殺人者は，ひどい手紙を書き，それを電話帳から適当に選んだ人の宛先に送りつけたのだった。
1224 彼女はいつも，少女のときも，活発で陽気だったので，たくさんの友人がい

予想例文

るのも不思議ではない。
1225 多くの人が戦闘を拒んだベトナム戦争の時代と比べると，第一次世界大戦と第二次世界大戦は，多くの若い人が軍役の1つに自分の意志で参加した。
1226 1950年代には，マリリン・モンローのような官能的な若手女優が，10年後に人気が出たツィギーのような鉛筆のように細いモデルよりも，一般的に好まれていた。
1227 その少女の母親は彼女に，彼女の服装は外に身につけて行くにはあまりに下品であると言った。
1228 その男はとても太っていたので，アヒルのようによたよた歩いた。
1229 私の妹は家族の中で，すぐにけちをつけて場をしらけさせる人として知られていた。
1230 開発中の新しいヘリコプターは，とても静かで羽根のブンブンいう音がほとんど聞こえないくらいだ。
1231 踊りを信仰の基本とするイスラム秘儀者は「踊り回る修業僧」と呼ばれる。
1232 その新しい高層オフィスビルは，弱り切った経済を考慮すると厄介ものになるだろうと多くの人は予測した。
1233 彼は必要とあらばその見知らぬ男と戦うつもりだったが，その男が手斧を振り回しながら彼の家に向かって走ってきたとき，彼は気持ちを変えた。
1234 討論は激しくなり，相手が答え始めるたびごとに，ジョージがたじろぐのがよく分かった。
1235 彼はときどき，彼の古いアルバムを引っぱり出して，彼の妻がまだ生きていたときの自分の若き日々の写真を物思いに沈んだ様子で眺めたものだった。
1236 ジョイント企画が終わりに近づくころには，参加者はお互いにひどく争うようになり，すべてをすんなりと終えるようなことはできなかった。
1237 その若者は上司の政策の知恵に挑もうとして激怒を招いた。
1238 ヨーロッパやアメリカでは，クリスマスの時期には，玄関のドアにリースをかけるのが習慣である。
1239 シーズン最大のゲーム直前に，スター選手が練習中にひざをひねって2週間プレーできなくなってしまった。
1240 イエスは弟子たちに，彼を手本とし，彼の教えをできる限り広めるという情熱を吹き込んだ。
1241 人生への彼の情熱は感心すべきものだが，彼はしばしば自分の幸福の追求においては無責任で自己中心的である。

長文問題に出題される単熟語

医学

1 タイミングがすべて

1 私たちの肉体はバランスを維持するよう，驚くほど巧妙に作られているようだ。体を冷ますためには汗をかくし，血圧が下がれば心臓が¹²⁴²激しく鼓動する。しかし，¹²⁴³あいにく私たちの自然のままの状態は一定ではない。血圧から脳の働きまで，すべてが太陽，月，それに季節の回転と共にリズム的に変動することを研究者たちは分かり始めている。そして，彼らの¹²⁴⁴見識のおかげで，心臓病やガンといった死亡率の高いよく知られた病気¹²⁴⁵を防ぐための新しい戦略が生まれつつある。

2 たいていの医師は医大在学中に，¹²⁴⁶慢性病のある人々は一定のペースで薬を飲むべきであると教わる。「だれもがそう教わっていますが，それは病気を治療するにはひどいやり方なのです」と，医師のリチャード・マーチンは言う。例えば，¹²⁴⁷喘息患者が最も発作を起こしやすいのは，¹²⁴⁸粘液の分泌量が増加し，空気の通路が狭まり，¹²⁴⁹炎症性の細胞が過重に働く夜中である。ところが，たいていの患者は昼も夜も一定の水準の薬品を血液中に入れて¹²⁵⁰おこうとする。最近の研究で研究者たちは午後の中ごろに¹²⁵¹ステロイドや¹²⁵²気管支拡張剤を多量に投与するのは，数回小さく分けて投与するのと同じ程度に安全で，しかもその方が夜間の発作を抑えるにはもっとよいことを発見した。

3 医師のウィリアム・ハルシェスキーは，ガン治療薬の多くは1日の特定の時間帯に限って使えば，毒性が少ないことを示した。彼の診療所やその他の所で，携帯用注入ポンプを使って強弱をつけたガン治療を受けている患者は，継続的な注入を受けている者より心臓，胃，それに¹²⁵³骨髄の損傷が少なかった。

4 日々のリズムがガン治療に影響を与えうるただ1つのリズムであるわけではない。ハルシェスキーは乳ガンで¹²⁵⁴手術を受けた41人の女性の記録を分析し，¹²⁵⁵生理の周期の中ごろに手術された者は他の時期に受けた者より10年生存率が高いことを発見した。

5 この治療法はたいていの新しい治療法と異なり，それが取って代わった（古い）治療法より出費がかさむわけではない。時間はしょせん，無料なのだから。

2 若さの泉を探究する科学者たち

1 老いを研究する学者である ¹²⁵⁶老人学者たちは，老いの謎を解き明かそうと努力を続けている。彼らは通常の ¹²⁵⁷消耗の他に，肉体の破壊につながる主たるメカニズムとして，¹²⁵⁸遺伝的なもの１つと，化学的なもの２つの計３つを確認している。

2 一般的に私たちを構成している細胞は，¹²⁵⁹有限の ¹²⁶⁰寿命を持つようにプログラムされているように思える。人間のものであれ，虫けらのものであれ，すべての細胞は一定の回数しか再生ができない。その後では細胞の ¹²⁶¹新陳代謝の機能が ¹²⁶²衰え始め，¹²⁶³細胞膜が弱まり，そして細胞は（そしてついには私たちも）死滅する。何がこの細胞の予定表を進行させているのかは，まだ科学者にも分かっていない。それを克服する道が見つかるまでは，人間の生命は 120 年程度に限定されると思える。

3 不幸なことに，２種類の化学的反応が作用し合って，私たちの現実の寿命を理論上の限界より大幅に下回らせている。最初のものは ¹²⁶⁴フリーラジカル酸化作用と呼ばれている。肉体は発電所と同じように，燃料（食物）を燃やして，エネルギーを出すときに老廃物を生み出す。これらの老廃物は遊離基酸素と呼ばれるもので，それは接触するほとんどすべての生物学的物質と結合する，高い反応度を持つ酸素 ¹²⁶⁵分子である。遊離基が ¹²⁶⁶タンパク質や粘膜に付着すれば，それが ¹²⁶⁷組織や内臓器官を弱める。DNA に付着すれば，ガンの元となる ¹²⁶⁸突然変異を生むことにもなる。破壊の２つ目のメカニズムは糖タンパク質化と呼ばれるもので，それは ¹²⁶⁹血流中の糖分がタンパクを覆い，互いにくっつき合い，それが通常は固定しないはずの個所に固定する経過のことである。これが次には関節を硬くし，¹²⁷⁰動脈を塞ぎ，その他多くの不調の元となる。これは元来 ¹²⁷¹糖尿病と関連づけられていたが，現在では老化に大きな役割を果たすと考えられており，研究者たちはそれを防ぐ薬品の開発を望んでいる。

4 何年にも及ぶ研究にもかかわらず，特定の疾病を治すことを目的としない治療法で，寿命そのものを延ばすものは，¹²⁷²カロリー制限と ¹²⁷³ホルモン補充治療の２つしか確認されていない。老人学者たちは動物を使って，ビタミンとミネラルは適切な水準に保ちながら，餌の消費を正常値の約 30％減らすことで寿命が 40〜50％延びうることを示した。しかし，このような食餌 ¹²⁷⁴療法を続けるには，たいていの人にはおそらく不可能なほど，大きな意志力を働かせる必要があるだろう。研究者が求め続けているのは，人々が好きな食べ物を食べてもなお，カロリ

一制限の効果が得られるような薬品である。しかし，それはおそらく少なくともまだ20年は先のことであろう。

5 これに対して，ホルモン補充治療はそれよりはるかに容易で，生活の質の面からも，はるかに有効である。例えば，女性ホルモンの[1275]エストロゲンのように，自然に徐々に減っていく量を補うためのホルモン補充治療はしわを減らし，歯を健全に保つのはもちろん，さまざまな病苦を防ぐ上で役立つことが，最近の研究から分かっている。ホルモン補充治療は，平均で8年程度[1276]寿命を延ばしており，心臓病の危険要素の高い女性の間では最大の効果がある。エストロゲンを摂取している男性についての研究でも，心臓病の危険性の著しい減少が見られている。しかし，たいていの男性にとっては，[1277]女性化による影響の方がプラス面の可能性[1278]より大きな比重を占めている。

3 反撃を開始した微生物

1 60年前，細菌による病気を迎え撃つ武器としてのペニシリンの画期的発見によって，[1279]多数の[1280]伝染病が一掃されないまでも防ぐことができるようになり，黄金時代が到来した。[1283]その後の年月に開発されたますます多くの強力な[1282]抗生物質の[1281]蓄積により，[1284]肺炎，[1285]腸チフス，その他の病気が薬品の入手可能な世界の広い地域で治癒可能となった。（ところが）これらの同じ抗生物質を過剰使用や乱用した結果，現在では上記およびその他の病気で薬品に抵抗力のある型が盛り返しつつあり，公衆衛生に世界的規模の脅威を与えている。

2 医学の進歩にもかかわらず，世界保健機構（WHO）によれば伝染病は依然世界第1位の死因で，この20年間だけで30[1286]種以上の新しい伝染病が出現したと同機構は述べている。皮肉にも病院そのものが，これらの薬品に抵抗力のある[1287]細菌の多くにとっての最も一般的な培養場所になっている。有害なバクテリアが完全に死滅しないときは，それらは遺伝子上の突然変異を遂げ，増殖し，一層強くなって盛り返す。最近では，入手できるうちで最も強力と考えられていたバンコマイシンでさえニューヨーク市内で発見された強力型のバクテリアの蔓延を防げなかった。

3 抵抗力は地域によって大いに異なるが，研究が明らかにするところでは，バクテリアの型の中には現在ペニシリンに対して最高で55％，もっと強力なメチシリンに対しては最高30％の抵抗力をつけているものもある。感染力のあるせきの病気である[1288]結核にも薬品に抵抗力のある変種が現われ，最高40％の事例では

抗生物質による初期の治療にも死滅しない能力を示している。

4 どうしてこのようなことになったのか。その原因は次のようにいくつかある。すなわち，バクテリアを原因としない ¹²⁹⁰ウィルス感染症，その他の ¹²⁹¹疾患に対し医師が不必要に抗生物質を ¹²⁸⁹処方したこと，患者が ¹²⁹²服用量を守らなかったり，抗生物質による治療を途中でやめてしまったこと，それに，家畜用の餌の補給物に抗生物質を使用したため，その肉や乳が人間用の食物連鎖の中に入ったこと，などである。ありふれた4種のバクテリアは，動物から人間に移された後，現在では抵抗力のある変種を生み出している。

5 これら薬品に抵抗力のあるバクテリアの変種は海外旅行の増加の中で，急速に世界的規模で広まっている。その結果，先進諸国は止めることのできない病気の危険に対して発展途上国とほとんど同じ程度に ¹²⁹³弱い状態にある。ところがこうした共通の脅威にもかかわらず，国境を超えて問題の全体像を監視する，あるいはこれら ¹²⁹⁵強力微生物の拡大を防ぐ上で役立ちうる方法について医師，患者，¹²⁹⁴畜産業者などを教育するための組織的な運動を策定する，といった足並みそろえた努力は現在までのところほとんど見られない。

6 国内および国際的な保健団体は，抗生物質の適正な使用法について医学界を教育するため，地球規模での人知を結集する手助けをすべきである。すでに先頭を切って，新しい抗生物質の開発を進める一方で，特定のバクテリア変種の抵抗力についてのデータや情報を公開し始めたところもある。

4 いびきを治す

1 「笑えば人はともに笑う。いびきをかくとだれも一緒に寝てくれなくなる」と英国の作家アンソニー・バージェスは書いている。しかし慢性のいびきという問題を抱えている成人の25%にとって，独りで寝ることは，よく ¹²⁹⁶笑いものにされるこの病気に起因するかもしれない深刻な健康への害に比べれば大したことはないのである。

2 いびきという状態は，患者の気道での呼吸障害によって起こる。のどの後部にある気道に空気が到達すると，軟 ¹²⁹⁷口蓋と舌が接するあたりにある収縮する組織によって道をふさがれてしまう。口蓋垂として知られるたるんだ肉は軟口蓋からぶら下がっているのである。これらの体の部分がお互いにぶつかり合って震えると，あの特徴的な「う～ん」という音や，¹²⁹⁸ゼイゼイいう音が作り出されるの

である。

3 この空気の遮断が起こる原因にはいくつかの要素が考えられる。アルコールの摂取，¹²⁹⁹睡眠薬の服用，そして単なる熟睡により，舌やのどの筋肉が緊張しなくなるということがある。筋肉がゆるむと，舌が気管の方へと後ろ側へ落ち込んでしまったり，のどの筋肉が内側へ¹³⁰⁰収縮することになってしまうのである。別の原因としては，例えば¹³⁰¹扁桃腺や¹³⁰²アデノイドのようにのどの組織が異常に大きくなることや，のどが¹³⁰³肥満によって過度に肉付きがよくなることがある。時には，口蓋や口蓋垂が異常に長く，それらが気管の方に下がりすぎていることもあるし，あるいは，風邪や¹³⁰⁶花粉症やアレルギーによって¹³⁰⁵鼻の中の空気の通り道に¹³⁰⁴障害があるのかもしれない。

4 ひどい場合では，「睡眠時無呼吸」が起こることもある。睡眠時無呼吸は，完全に妨害された呼吸によってしばしば大きないびきが中断されるときに起こる。患者は，1時間に最高7回ぐらいまで，1回につき10秒ほど呼吸を止めてしまうのである。睡眠時無呼吸の患者は，決してリラックスできないし，また熟睡による恩恵も受けられない。短期的に見れば，睡眠時無呼吸は昼間の眠さや仕事能率の低下につながりうるし，長期的に見れば，高血圧や心臓肥大につながる。

5 アメリカの特許庁には，300以上のいびき対策の道具が登録されているが，1つとして効果が完全なものはない。重症の場合には，外科手術も施されてきたが，¹³⁰⁷体にメスを入れるものであり，費用もかさむ。しかしながら，最近スコット・E・ブリーツキー博士がたいていの患者のいびきを根絶できるという新しい技術を開発した。ブリーツキーの注射によるいびき形成外科は，軟口蓋にテトラデシル硫酸¹³⁰⁸ナトリウムを注射するのである。この薬品は，のどの奥の組織を硬直させる瘢痕（はんこん）組織を形成するのを手助けし，いびきを起こす口蓋の¹³⁰⁹震えを抑える。

6 今までにこの技術を施された27人の患者のうち，まだいびきで悩んでいると答えたのはたった2人である。¹³¹⁰副作用としては，2～3日続く咽頭炎に似たわずかな不快を感じたが，仕事には支障がなかったと患者たちは報告している。口蓋に注射をするとは痛そうに聞こえるが，最も神経質な患者でも不快感は1から10までの段階の中で3とつけただけである。それに，静かで安らかな眠りを得られるチャンスのために，短時間の少しの痛みを我慢できない人がいるだろうか。

5 血液の代用品

1 血液以上に大切なものはない。それが十分にあるかないかは生死を分けるからだ。たいてい病院は血液が不足している。17世紀以来，医師たちは，動物の血液から油やミルクに至るまであらゆるものを不運な患者に ¹³¹¹注入して，血液の代わりになるものを実験してきた。しかし，つい最近になるまで，安全で効果的な代用品は ¹³¹²見つかっていなかった。

2 1999年5月，アメリカのある病院で医師たちがある患者に対して革命的な新しい治療法を試みた。この患者は，不思議なことに ¹³¹³免疫システムが ¹³¹⁴赤血球を攻撃し始めたのだった。この患者の赤血球減少に対処する方法が分からないまま，医師たちはこの危機的なほどの ¹³¹⁵貧血の若い女性への望みを失いかけていた。もうこれでだめなら最後だという気持ちで，¹³¹⁶集中治療室長のジョージ・ジアコッペ医師は，効果的な血液代用品を開発しようとしている会社と連絡をとった。患者が死に近づく中，ジアコッペ医師は当局から許可を得て，高度に精製された牛の血液から実験的に作られた血液代用品であるヘモピュアというものを患者に輸血し始めた。成功する可能性は低かった。その血液代用品はまだ ¹³¹⁷臨床試験の段階にあり，この段階をパスした代用品は1つもなかったのである。驚くべきことに，この代用品は効いたのである。ヘモピュアは，免疫システムから攻撃を受けることなく，非常に不足している酸素を患者の貧血性の細胞に運んだのである。数時間後，彼女は上体を起こして，医師たちと話をしていたのである。

3 もし今，保健当局が血液代用品の使用にゴーサインを出すなら，ちょうどよい時期であろう。¹³¹⁸エイズや ¹³¹⁹狂牛病のような病気からの感染を恐れ，献血ができる人についての規制が着実に強くなっている。その結果，血液は足りなくなっている。さらに，代用品には通常の輸血よりもいくつかの利点が見込まれている。代用品は人間の血液ほど急速に ¹³²⁰だめになることはないし，また冷蔵の必要もない。医師たちは，提供者と患者の血液型の不一致という致命的なミスを犯すのではないかと心配することもない。そして，重要なことだが，血液代用品は人間のウィルスに感染する可能性がより少ない。

4 かつて，新しい血液供給の需要があれば，アメリカの保健規制を担当する主要機関であるFDAによる代用品の認可は早まるのではないかと考えられていた。しかし，FDAの長官であるアブドゥ・アレヤッシは，迅速な認可は必ずしも望ましいものではないと言っている。現在検討が進められている血液代用品も完璧に

血液の代わりを果たすことはできない。それらの代用品は赤血球よりはるかに効果的に酸素を運ぶが，病気と闘うという白血球の保護的な役割を果たすことはない。代用品中の酸素を運ぶ粒子は赤血球よりもずっと小さい。そのため，それらは ¹³²¹つまった動脈をすり抜けることができる ― これは本当に利点である。しかし，これと同じ性質が副作用を引き起こすのではないかと研究者たちは心配している。彼らはまた，代用品の輸血を ¹³²²受けた人の血圧が上昇するというはっきりとした傾向を心配している。「これらの製品には害があるかもしれないが，これらと比較するものがない」とアレヤッシは言っている。彼は，ジアコッペ医師の患者のようなケースでは，何百人もの患者を対象とする長期で ¹³²³綿密な臨床試験の代わりは務まらないと言っている。

コンピュータ

1 コンピュータウィルス制作者

1 コンピュータウィルス制作者とはコンピュータシステム ¹³²⁵を破壊し，多額の損害を与える ¹³²⁴デジタルペストを作り出す人のことである。これまでウィルスについて書かれたものは数多く存在しているが，制作者自身については最近になるまでほとんど何も知られていなかった。コンピュータのセキュリティの専門家であるサラ・ゴードンは，ウィルス制作者の心理に関する大規模な研究を行った。その結果は驚くべきものである。ウィルス制作に必要な技術は ¹³²⁶ハッキングほど高いものではまったくないため，多くの場合，彼らは非常に若い。中には10歳，11歳という例もある。そのため，彼らは非合法な技術の ¹³²⁸階層の中では下 ¹³²⁷位にいることになる。これらの ¹³²⁹悪意ある ¹³³⁰神童たちは年齢が上がるにつれ，通例，ウィルス制作の域を超え，階層の上位へと向かって，他の技術を追求するようになる。

2 また，中には知らず知らずのうちにウィルス制作の世界に足を踏み入れてしまう人がいることをゴードンは発見した。おそらくウィルスやそのコンピュータへの影響を調べる中で，¹³³¹自己増殖するプログラムコードに取り組んでいるうちに，¹³³²善意で行なっていたそのプログラマーが新しいウィルス ¹³³³を放出してしまう可能性がある。しかし，やはり制作者の多くは自分たちが作り出す大混乱を綿密に計画している。それは ¹³³⁴悪評を得ようとする場合もあれば，政治的，個人的メッセージを出す場合もある。破壊を目的としているウィルス制作者は新しい技術を利用する場合が多く，たいていは既存のウィルスを更新する形で行っている。それゆえ，将来のウィルスの発生はさらに複雑で ¹³³⁵破壊的なものになるという

予測が可能なのだ。

3 社会はどう対応すべきであろう。ゴードンによれば，対応は犯罪者の年齢によるという。彼女の調査で，成人したウィルス制作者には，罰の恐怖によって思いとどまらせることが最も効果的だということがわかった。「成人にとって重要なのは法律ではなく，その法律により起訴される可能性があることを認識させることなのです」とゴードンは言う。逆に，年少者は法的手段を恐れる可能性はない。教育がより効果的な ¹³³⁶対抗策である。また，コンピュータやインターネットでのマナーのある行動の仕方を子どもたちに教えることは，社会が持つ道徳的な義務であるとゴードンは述べている。

2 インターネット上での詐欺師

1 大学の構内での ¹³³⁷盗用は新しいことでも何でもない。しかし，この古来からの問題の ¹³³⁸新しい展開として，インターネットを利用して既製の ¹³³⁹学期末レポートを販売する会社も出ている。

2 こうしたインターネットを利用した学識が簡単に手に入ることに業を煮やした教育者たちは，このハイテクによる学期末論文工場 ¹³⁴⁰に宣戦布告をしている。大学側に支持されているテキサス州の新しい法律の下では，インターネットで論文販売をした会社は 500 ドルの罰金の対象になる。別の例では，ボストン大学は詐欺および ¹³⁴²脅迫 ¹³⁴¹容疑で 8 つのインターネット上の会社を訴えている。

3 教育者たちはこうした努力を ¹³⁴³学問の高潔さの名のもとに弁護している。しかし，学生による不正使用でなく，論文を作る側に怒りをぶつけるのは見当違いである。教育者たちは ¹³⁴⁴姿の見えない ¹³⁴⁵オンライン上の学問の世界を取り締まろうとしている一方，大学生の重大な犯罪行為である盗用の責任を大目に見ている。

4 ウェブ・サイトでは，幅広い科目について学期末論文が提供されているし，インターネット上での研究の公表，および販売は不正行為にはならない。また，作成済みの学期末論文は，キャンパスを本拠地としている起業家や，学生向けの刊行物に案内広告を出している通信販売の会社を通じて，¹³⁴⁶オフラインでも簡単に手に入る。教育者たちがアメリカ中のオンライン上の学期末論文制作工場を閉鎖することが仮にできたとしても，インターネットのサイトの 40% がアメリカの外に本拠地を持っており，それらのサイトにそうした工場が加わるのを止めることはできない。

5 インターネットによる学期末論文制作工場を告訴するとなると，重大な憲法上の問題が生じる。最高裁は昨年，1347インターネット上のポルノから子どもたちを守ることを目的としたある連邦法を違憲とした。インターネット上の盗用1349をなくすために言論の自由を制限しようとする企てに対し，裁判所がもっと1348寛容な判断を示すだろうと考える根拠はどこにもない。

6 盗用を止める最も賢明な道は，安易な道を探している学生に的を絞ることである。学生がインターネットや通信販売のカタログから資料1350を無断利用したものであっても，既製の学期末論文を見つけ出すのは簡単であると教授たちは言う。特に独創的な論題を与え，自分で評価をしている教授たちから見れば，既製論文は要点はずれで表面的なものが目立つという。

7 インターネットの有無にかかわらず，教育制度の裏をかこうとする学生は常に存在している。偽りの研究1351をまことしやかに使おうとする人でなく，それを作る側に焦点を合わせることにより，学問の面同様，倫理面においても，学生たちが高水準の価値ある教訓を学ぶ道は閉ざされることになる。

3　新しい競売の舞台

1 わずか2，3年前には，株式市場アナリストたちは，どうやってインターネットでお金を稼ぐことができるだろうかと思っていた。確かに，何百万という人たちが1352ログオンしていたが，点滅する1354バナー広告が付いた無数の無料のサイトで，比較的少ない現金しか1353やりとりされていなかった。しかしそれ以来，ネットは究極の世界的市場となり，主だった会社の株価は1355最高レベルまで高騰してきている。最も急成長しているものの中には，オンライン競売者があり，売り手に少額の1356手数料を課して買い手に無料のアクセスを提供する。その開拓者でありリーダーであるイーベイは，日に1,500以上の部門で200万以上の物件を載せ，それに400万人の登録したユーザーがインターネットで入札する。

2 イーベイで品物1357に入札するのは，少々の違いはあるが，伝統的な競売で入札するのに似ている。まず入札者は，部門をクリックするか，例えば「エルビス・プレスリーのサイン入りの写真」のような商品を検索する。もしそのような品物が競売にかけられていたら，それに例えば50ドルなどの秘密の最高価格で入札できる。もし他の誰かが20ドルで入札すると，サイトは20ドル50セントといった，指定された最小限の増額で最初の入札者の代わりに1358対抗買い注文を入れる。競売が終わったとき，まだ最高額の入札者だったら，電子メールで売主に

連絡し，発送の手配をしてから代金を送る。すべてがうまくいったら，間もなくサイン入りのエルビスの写真が壁に掛かる。そして売るのも同様に簡単だ。オンライン競売ハウスに店を構えて，釣りの擬似餌からフェラーリまで，何でも提供できる。

3 危険はないだろうか，オンライン競売は怪しげな妙薬のセールスマンと同等では，と思うかもしれない。確かに危険はあるが，満足した客は [1360]<u>詐欺の被害者</u>の数をはるかに [1359]<u>上回る</u>。そしてイーベイは，買いたい人たちがブルックリン・ブリッジに入札する前に，過去の取引に関するコメントを読んで，売り手の評判を判断することができる意見システムを提供している。他の安全策には，入札に成功した人たちが，買った品物が配達されるまで安全な口座に支払いを置かせる第三者預託システムがある。毎日数千の取引がされるので，すべての取り引きを取り締まるのは不可能だが，イーベイは，競売の最後の瞬間に飛び込んで最低の増額でより高い入札をする「入札ロボット」と呼ばれる精巧なソフト・プログラムなどのさらにひどい濫用に [1361]<u>断固たる処置を取る</u>ように努めている。

4 詐欺の可能性はさて置いて，多くの入札者は自分自身が競売に取りつかれているということに気づく。祖母の飾り戸棚を飾っていた骨董品のガラスの花瓶を探して，何日も，何週間も，何年も蚤の市や中古品割引店を探し回る代わりに，競売サイトで一瞬のうちに1つ，いや1ダースも発見できるのだ。まもなくあなたの飾り戸棚は骨董品のガラス製品で膨れ上がり，銀行預金が減っているだろう。しかし失望しないように。それ [1362]<u>を補給する</u>方法がある。それは，競売サイトの売り手になることである。

科学・テクノロジー

1　女性の平和維持軍を軽く見てはいけない

1 もし，あなたが動物界の中で犯罪を犯す階層を探しているのなら，高等 [1363]<u>霊長類</u>の雄から先を探す必要はない。ゴリラの雄は乳を与えている雌と交尾するために，他の雄を父とする子どもを殺して平然としているし，ライバル関係にあるチンパンジーのグループは，自分たちの [1364]<u>縄張り</u>を守ったり雌の群れを大きくするために，血なまぐさい境界線争いをするし，人間の男性は振り返ることもできないほどの昔からの犯罪の歴史を持っている。しかし，最近の研究によれば，ボノボという大型類人猿の一種では雄はこのような [1365]<u>野蛮行為</u>はまったく行わないことが分かった。ボノボの社会は行動面での枠が設定され，治安が大体におい

て保たれ，違反者は即座に罰せられる社会なのである。このような秩序が保たれている理由は単純で，つまりボノボの間では法を施行しているのが雌だからである。

2 雌のチンパンジー（ボノボと同じ系統に属している）は，その場限りの群れしか形成しないが，雌のボノボは生涯にわたる関係を確立し，互いの付き合いにほとんどの時間を過ごす。[1366]攻撃的性格を持った雄から見れば，このような強力な雌同士の仲間意識は[1367]面倒ということになる。もし，成熟したボノボの雄が雌に好まれざる関心を示した場合，その雌が緊急時の鳴き声さえ出せば，報復のための雌のグループがすぐに現場に駆けつける。餌場で果物の[1368]密かな蓄えを保存しようとしているような態度の悪い雄も同じように威嚇され，追い払われる。雄同士にだけ攻撃性を限定している雄でさえ，自分たちの行動が何のプラスにもならないことを知っている。このような[1369]雄の闘争の唯一の目的は雌との交尾権を獲得する点にあるが，ボノボの雌は一番強い雄にも対抗できるほどにたくましいから，そうしたけんかの結果は何の意味も持たないからだ。

3 このような雌の主導による[1370]平和主義が，どのように発達してきたのかは明らかではないが，その答えは食べ物にあるように考えられる。チンパンジーは豊かな人間と同じように肉と成熟した果実しか食べないが，ゴリラは葉や茎といった粗末な食事でやっていける。ボノボはどちらの食べ物にも適応しており，これは手に入るものは何でも食べながら1か所に留まって生き延び，程度の差はあれ永続性のある群れを形成することができるという[1371]利点を生む。このような[1372]生涯にわたる定住は，本質的に闘争的な雄にはあまり有益ではないが，雌にとっては[1373]横柄な雄から自分たちを自由にしてくれる連合を形成できる機会を提供してくれることになる。

4 人間から見てここから学べる文化的教訓は明らかである。女性団体は長い間，戦争から家庭内の虐待に至る人間の抱える最も執拗な問題の多くは，まず[1374]殴り合った後で初めて[1375]和解することで問題解決をしようとする男性の性癖から直接に起こっていると論じてきた。この霊長類（ボノボ）の成功は，両性の間での権力の分かち合いが政治的にも意味あるものであることを暗示している。

2 天文学と現実

1 天文学は時として真実性に欠けることがある。現実にそうなのである。

科学・テクノロジー

2 ハッブル宇宙望遠鏡から送られてくる爆発を続ける天体，^1376 星雲状のガス雲，それに ^1377 かすんだ繭状のものから生まれつつある星などのあの鮮やかな映像はすべて，多かれ少なかれコンピュータによって画質改良が加えられている。つまり画像は処理され，^1378 磨きをかけられ，エアブラシを当てられ，ハリウッドの多くのスターたちと同じように化粧を施されているのである。

3 人々はときおり裏庭に据えた普通の望遠鏡を覗いては裏切られた思いを抱く。彼らには緑や紫色に輝く巨大なガス雲などは見えないのだ。土星はほとんど白黒にしか見えない。だが実際にはこれは幻覚なのだろうか。

4 興味深いことに，ガリレオが彼の ^1379 粗末な望遠鏡を初めて覗いて月面の山や木星の周りにある衛星を見たとき，人々は彼に見えているのは目の錯覚だと思った。彼の望遠鏡は（事実でない）まがい物を作り出しているのだ，と人々は言った。つまり，肉眼で見えないものはすべて，現実には本物ではなかったのである。

5 今日では，レンズを通して見えるものの真実性を疑う者はいない。実際，我々の多くは，世の中がもっとよく見えるようにと，レンズを眼球の上に浮かせたり鼻先に ^1380 乗せたりして歩き回っている。それに，我々が心の中に思い描く映像は脳によって余すところなく処理されているのを我々は知っている。脳こそが ^1381 網膜に映る逆さまの像を正しい向きに変え，盲点を補い，視野の中にある ^1382 血管とか浮遊物のような，いわゆる「ノイズ」を消してくれていることも。脳は動きに合わせて調節をし，色を「修正」し，事物をまともな位置関係に置いてもくれる。

6 ハッブル関係の科学者がやっているのは，彼らなりのやり方で，これとまったく同じことをすることなのである。天文学者は，宇宙線の痕跡のような，映像内の「ノイズ」を取り除き，ゆがみを修正しなければならない。ハッブルの映像は白黒である。それが異なる色彩に異なる反応をする感光フィルターで処理される。天文学者たちがそれらを元の形に1つにまとめ上げるのである。それもまた人間の目の働きとかなり似ている ― 色彩に敏感な細胞が像を処理し，それを脳が再構築するのである。

7 というわけで，ハッブルからの像はどことなく真実性がない，と論ずるわけにはいかない。しょせん，^1383 無処理，無修正の像などは存在しないのである。さらに言えば，視覚，聴覚，触覚，味覚，嗅覚のいずれであれ，無処理の ^1384 感覚知覚といったものも存在しない。（だから）ことの真実を説明することは難しい。

確かにハッブルの像は処理され，修正され，人工的に着色され，全体的に ¹³⁸⁵多彩化されている。しかしそれとても我々が自分の2つの目で見る像以上に鮮明化されているということはないのである。

3 他の惑星上の生物

1 他の惑星上に生物を探すのは，それ自体非常に興味ある探求ではあるが，現実には非常な困難を伴う探求である。しかし，その基になる論理はきわめて単純で，地球という惑星上で40億から45億年前の昔に，化学物質から成り立っている ¹³⁸⁶原生液の中から生命が生み出されたのなら，宇宙の少なくとももう1つ別の惑星にそれが起こってもしかるべきではなかったか，というものである。天文学者たちは地球と同じような惑星は，宇宙中に何億と存在していると計算している。

2 宇宙開発が進んでもまだ他のところに生命は見つかっていない。火星は乾燥していて ¹³⁸⁷不毛であり，金星は荒れ狂う ¹³⁸⁸地獄のような場所であり，木星は気体の球である。生命が発生し，そして存続するために必須と考えられていた厳密な条件を考えれば，生命が地球以外の他のところに生まれたことがあったかについて懐疑的な科学者たちには ¹³⁸⁹十分な言い分があった。小さすぎる惑星は，大気を保有することがまったくできない。熱すぎたり冷たすぎたりするものには液状の水がない。そして，水がなければ，日光を化学エネルギーに変換する ¹³⁹⁰光合成という化学的過程は不可能である。酸素を含む大気がなければ，細胞が他の化学物質からエネルギーを奪うことを可能にする化学的作用も通常では起こりえない。

3 しかし，我々の住む惑星についての新事実から，科学者たちは生命についてあまりにも ¹³⁹¹狭い考え方をしていたのではないかと考え始めている。¹³⁹²微生物が ¹³⁹⁴火山の噴火口，温泉，¹³⁹⁵間欠泉など，かつては不可能と考えられていた環境の下で ¹³⁹³繁殖しているのが発見されている。南極大陸の表面下，深いところにある岩石や冷たい水域，それにコロンビア川流域の ¹³⁹⁶地下水には，火星その他の惑星上での生命の発生を示す ¹³⁹⁷地球的なモデルが含まれているかもしれない。そして，まだ大いに論争の余地はあるにしても，火星から得られた興味深い証拠からすれば，後に死滅してしまったにしても，ある程度類似した形の生物がそこに実際に生まれていたかもしれないというヒントは少なくともある。

4 ¹³⁹⁸過酷な環境下でも生物が生存している証拠は近年，高度に精密な ¹³⁹⁹遺伝子

配列技術によって，実験室内の条件では生育させることのできない[1400]微生物を確認できるようになるにつれ増加し始めた。深海に潜る潜水艦は，[1401]地熱による熱のエネルギーで新陳代謝を続けている有機体を見つけた。地質学者はコロンビア川流域を地下2マイル掘削した結果，[1405]玄武岩と地下水との[1404]化学反応によって生み出される[1403]水素をエネルギー源として使い，[1402]繁殖する有機体を発見した。

5 研究者の中には，これらの微生物の多くは，おそらく地球上で一番古い生命体である「原始有機体」と呼ばれる，特異で今まで知られていなかった種類の生命体に属していると論じる者もある。もし，彼らの言うとおりであれば，生命には，暖かくて好都合な原生液が絶対に必要だったのではなく，極端で過酷な環境下でも生育することができたかもしれない。そうであれば，原始有機体のような微生物は，水が液体の状態で存在しているその表面下の，極端な環境の中でも生存可能となるし──そうすれば，火星に生物は存在しうるということにもなる。

4　小さいものによるすごさ

1 エイムズ研究センター（NASAの一部門）のプロジェクト主任であるアル・グローバスは，「ごく小さな宇宙船内の高性能なコンピュータ」を製造するための彼のビジョンを説明する。彼の言っているのは非常に小さなもので，数千[1406]ナノメートル（1メートルの何10億分の1）程度のものである。グローバスが言っているのは，他の惑星に飛んで行って生産的な仕事をする顕微鏡的宇宙船である。「たった1つだけ飛ばすのではなく，何百万個も飛ばすのです」と彼は言う。

2 これがナノ［微小］テクノロジーの基本的な考えである。簡単に言えば，ナノテックとは個々の原子や分子から物を作る科学で，[1407]小型化の究極を約束するものである。科学技術は何十年にもわたり，ますます小さなトランジスタを搭載したますます小さなマイクロチップで動く，ますます小さな機械を設計するという形で「上から下への」小型化を追求してきた。ナノテックの技術者は，逆に「下から上へ」の方法がよいと信じている。原子と分子を使えば，[1408]客の要望に合わせて大きな物，とてつもなく強度な材料，デザイナーネーム入りの食べ物，それに小型のロボットなども作れると彼らは言う。もし，ナノテックの技術者たちが，彼らの[1409]考えていることの何分の1かでも実現させれば，人類の未来に対する意義は大変なもので，インターネットはテレビに余分につけたチャンネル程度に色あせたものに見えてしまう。

3 アメリカの有名な物理学者リチャード・ファインマンは，ナノテックの基本的概念を 1959 年，[1410]非公式の談話の中で語った。しかし，ナノテックの中心的な提唱者は，エリック・ドレックスラーというあまり名の知られていないエンジニア上がりの夢想家だった。ドレックスラーは 1970 年代の中頃，まだマサチューセッツ工科大学の在学生だったときに，[1411]遺伝子工学という新しい分野の本を読んでいて，ナノテックについての最初の考えを抱いた。生物学者たちが DNA を構成している分子の操作の仕方をようやく知り始めていた頃，ドレックスラーは原子から[1412]無機質のメカニズムが作られたっていいのではないかと思っていたのである。

4 この考えはドレックスラーにとって[1413]強迫観念となった。そうだ，再生能力を備えた機械を作ろうと彼はやがて決意した。1 つの機械が 2 つになり，2 つが 4 つに，次には 8 つに…と無限に増えていくような。それに，単純な原料を使ってナノテック的に特定の物品を作る能力を加えれば，そこから考えられる成果は想像もできないほどに豊かな世界しかないと彼は考えた。「組立て工」とドレックスラーが呼んでいる微小ロボットを使えば，空腹の人たちのためには無限の食料を，家のない人たちには無数の家屋[1414]をつぎつぎと作り出すことができるだろうし，人の血管内を巡って細胞を修復させ，それによって病気や老化を止めることができるだろうと。そうすれば，やがて人間は科学空想作家たちがナノボットと[1415]呼んでいる微小ロボットが世の中のすべての仕事をこなしている間，手をこまねいてのんびりしていることができるかもしれないのである。

5 これにはもちろん[1416]マイナス面もありうる。再生能力を持った機械は，理論的には周囲の物を食い尽くして再生し，さらに 2 倍の物を食い尽くして再生し，次にまたそれを繰り返し，ついには[1417]物質界全体を食い尽くしてしまうことで，手に負えなくなることも考えられる。

6 ナノテックを疑問視する人が依然[1418]主流を占める中で，ドレックスラーは徐々に[1419]同調者を増やし続けている。自然界にある第一の建築材である原子を利用するようになれば，すべてが今までとは一変する歴史の転換期の 1 つになるだろう。そして，ドレックスラーは十分な研究と資金的援助があれば，15 年以内にナノテックの広範な応用が見られるだろうと力説している。

5　機械翻訳

1 1950 年代に，ロシア語で書かれた技術文書の英訳に対する冷戦時代の需要が押

科学・テクノロジー

し寄せ、それは多くのコンピュータ科学者に機械が正確な自動翻訳をするように設計できるという、胸がわくわくするような考えを抱かせる ¹⁴²⁰役割を果たした。今日、いくつかのソフトウェア・プログラムが、この ¹⁴²¹偉業をやってのけたと主張している。でも、この主張はどれほど現実的なのだろうか。

2 30年前、米国政府からの契約のもとで、シストランという会社が機械による翻訳の分野を開拓した。¹⁴²²原型は「直接システム」で、それぞれの語句を ¹⁴²³辞書で調べて、対象となる言語でそれに相当するものに置き換えることで、直訳をした。この技術は、アメリカの数学者ノーバート・ウィーナーによって進められた短絡的な類推に負うところが大きい。コンピュータは戦時中、敵の暗号を解読するのを助けるために使われた。¹⁴²⁴暗号解読は、セットになったシンボルを変換するものだ。言語の翻訳も同様であり得る。しかし学者たちが実際に機械 ¹⁴²⁵を作動させると、結果はそう素晴らしいものではなかった。

3 機械による翻訳（MT）の大きな ¹⁴²⁶障害は、語順である。最新の製品は、文の中でどの単語がどんな機能を果たしているかを判断するための文法の規則を組み入れることで、これを克服しようとしている。このプログラムは、「構文解析ツリー」という、文の中のそれぞれの単語の文法的機能を示す ¹⁴²⁷図式を作る。その結果は、対象となる言語における文法的組み合わせを定義するもう1つの一連の規則の助けを借りて、その言語に移し替えられる。

4 その最新の結果はどうかというと、それはだれにたずねるかによるだろう。その製品の翻訳に対する批判に直面して、MTの販売元は、「¹⁴²⁹細かいことを言うな。犬が少しでも話せるとは驚くべきことだ」というような、「話をする犬」の例 ¹⁴²⁸を持ち出しがちである。そして公正を期して言えば、まったくの誤訳は思ったよりずっと少ないのだ。

5 MTの本当の限界は、文法の複雑さより、コンピュータには常識がないということと関係がある。言語は曖昧さでいっぱいで、正しい ¹⁴³⁰構文法がそれを解決するのにはあまり役立たない。「バンク」はお金を預ける所か、それとも河川の縁だろうか。5歳の子どもはその違いを理解できるが、コンピュータにそうさせるのは別問題だ。

6 言い換えれば、意味論がMTの鍵であり、意味論は言語学の範囲をはるかに越えたものだ。それは、実社会の知識を必要とするからである。事実、語彙を狭い、特化した領域に制限することにより、ほとんどどのシステムを使っても完全に近

い翻訳をすることができる。例えば，カナダのラジオ局は，ソフトウェアを使って，天気¹⁴³¹ニュースを英語からフランス語に訳す。わずか数百語の辞書でもって，このプログラムは，90％以上の正確さを達成する。

7 現在MT業界でなされている主な試みは，いろいろある意味の中から，どれを話者が意図しているのかを判断できるようにしている人間の知識¹⁴³³を複製することを可能にする，意味の¹⁴³²精巧な分類法を開発することだ。もちろんこれは事実上¹⁴³⁴人工知能への挑戦に等しい。つまり，考えるコンピュータ，ないしはそれと区別できないほど人の思考に近いコンピュータを製造することである。

6　すべての遺伝子の母

1 ¹⁴³⁵聖書にあるアダムとイブの話は，長い間，多くの人から作り話と片付けられていたが，現在，¹⁴³⁶遺伝学者や人類の起源を調査する人々の注目を集めている。最近の¹⁴³⁷ヒトゲノム研究によれば，現在の人類は，その先祖を10人のアダムと18人のイブにさかのぼることができる。彼らはすべて，先史時代のアフリカに住んでいたある小さな集団から発生したものである。さらに，その28人全員はおよそ20万年前に生きていた1人の女性，おおもとのイブにさかのぼることができる。

2 ジョージア州アトランタのエモリー大学医学部のダグラス・C・ウォーリス博士は，母親から娘に遺伝する¹⁴³⁸ミトコンドリアDNAを基準にして，¹⁴³⁹前述の18人のイブから始まる人類の系統図を開発した。一方，スタンフォード大学のピーター・A・アンダーヒル博士とピーター・J・オフナー博士は，父から息子に遺伝する¹⁴⁴⁰Y染色体を基準にして，10人のアダムから始まる，似たような系統図を作った。

3 最初のイブが生まれた，人類の祖先となった集団は，約2,000人で構成されていたと，遺伝学者は信じている。はじめのイブからしばらくたった，およそ14万4,000年前，この集団は分化を始めた。それらのうちのいくつかの集団はアフリカに残り，その他の集団はヨーロッパ，アジア，その他の世界の各地へ広がっていった。ウォーリス博士の発見によれば，アメリカ先住民のほとんどすべては，ミトコンドリアの¹⁴⁴¹系統で博士がA，B，C，Dと名付けたものに属するのに対し，ヨーロッパ人は，H～KとT～Xという2つの異なる系統に属する。予想通り，A～Dの系統はアジアでも見つかっており，このことは，アメリカ大陸は，最後の氷河期にシベリアから陸地続きだったところを渡ってきたアジア人が住み

科学・テクノロジー

着いたものだという広く受け入れられている理論を確証するものである。

4 しかし，1998年，ウォーリス博士と彼の研究仲間は，ヨーロッパにはあるが，アジアには見られない珍しいX系統を北米のアメリカ先住民族に発見した。このことは，先史時代の人類の移動が，もともと考えられていたものよりも複雑で，ルートももっと多かったことを示唆している。

5 このアフリカ起源説にこれまで反論がなかったわけではない。研究者の中には，遺伝学者の仮説や発見の不備を指摘し，別の理論として，現代人は約200万年前にアフリカで発生し，1つの種族として進化したという ¹⁴⁴²多地域進化論を支持しているものもいる。アフリカで進化した種族は，その後，長い時間をかけてアフリカから広がり，それぞれの地域でもとから住んでいたネアンデルタール人やその他の ¹⁴⁴⁴古代人と ¹⁴⁴³融合した。研究者たちは，最近発見された化石は，古い集団が，ポルトガルからオーストラリアまでも広がる地域のより新しい現代人の集団と融合した証拠であると指摘している。

6 しかしながら，両陣営とも，それまで科学の世界では ¹⁴⁴⁵絶対の真理であった人種間の厳密な境界線が崩れているという点では意見が一致しつつある。研究によれば，遺伝子レベルで「人種」の存在を示すものはない。その結果，人類の起源は同一の先祖であるという聖書の説明は架空の話ではなくなった。アンダーヒル博士は言う。「我々はみなY染色体レベルではアフリカ人であり，我々はみな本当に兄弟なのである」

7 羽の進化

1 羽の存在が必ずしも鳥と他の動物を区別してきたわけではないかもしれない。事実，歴史上初めての羽は必ずしも動物が空を飛ぶ時代 ¹⁴⁴⁶の幕開けを意味するものではなかった。そしてこの点が対立する2つの ¹⁴⁴⁷古生物学者グループの間に大論争を引き起こしている。そのうちの1つは，羽ははじめは二足歩行の ¹⁴⁴⁸肉食恐竜の小さな1グループで進化したと主張している。ロサンゼルス自然史博物館のルイス・チアッペは，羽の ¹⁴⁴⁹原型となるものは，もともと，つがいとなる相手をひきつけたり体温を保ったりなど，飛行とは異なる目的を果たしていたと信じている。¹⁴⁵⁰航空力学の分析用コンピュータ・シミュレーションによると，羽毛に覆われた，翼に似た手足のような ¹⁴⁵¹付属器官があるが飛ばない恐竜は，翼 ¹⁴⁵²をはばたかせると，より速く走れて，よりすばやく方向転換をすることができ，¹⁴⁵³獲物を捕らえたり ¹⁴⁵⁴捕食動物から逃れたりすることができたであろう

ことが分かる。もちろん，この理論は羽のある恐竜は現代の鳥の遠い先祖であることが前提である。

2 また，古生物学者の中にはこの「地上から空中へ」という理論に反論している者がおり，羽は「木から下った」進化をした可能性の方が大きいと言っている。2つ目の理論の提唱者たちは，現在の羽の進化と飛ぶ力は同時に発生したと考えている。ある人たちは，木で生活した小型のは虫類が ¹⁴⁵⁵短い突起物を進化させ，その結果，皮膚の上の気流を円滑にして，すばやくジャンプをして天敵から逃げることができるようになったと確信している。それらの突起物から長めの ¹⁴⁵⁶繊維が発達したは虫類はより速く，より遠くへ跳べるようになった。ルイジアナ州立大学の進化生物学者であるドミニク・ホンバーガーは，これらの羽の ¹⁴⁵⁷先駆けとなったものは，現代の羽が持っている役割すべてを果たしていたわけではないが，生き残る上で圧倒的な有利さを与えたと主張する。

3 古生物学者の間での羽に関する議論はまだある。羽がどのように進化したのかを明確にするため，化石記録の分析のみに頼っている人たちもいれば，現代の鳥だけに注意を向けている人もいる。前者のグループは， ¹⁴⁵⁸化石化した遺物に共通する特徴を分析することで，いろいろな生物体の進化の関連性を探している。この分野は「分岐学」と呼ばれている。彼らは，体全体の構造，骨の数や形，皮膚の種類などの共通する特徴の分析結果に基づいて進化の系図を作成している。後者のグループの科学者は，調査を化石記録に限定するのは愚かしいと考えている。このグループは，古代に存在した鳥の ¹⁴⁵⁹前身における羽の進化の様子の手がかりを得るために，現代の鳥の特徴を研究している。

4 化石を中心にするグループとそれほど制約を受けないグループの間での論争は激化している。分岐学の陣営に属するチアッペは，彼の対抗グループを「¹⁴⁶⁰直感的に自分たちに都合がよいと感じるものに頭を使ったり探し求めたりする，説得力のない学派」と呼んでいる。「直感的に都合がよいものなど何もない。化石記録の中にそれを見つけるまでは」と彼は言う。その彼の対抗グループは，化石記録ではあまりにむらが多く，一体何が起きたのかがはっきりとわからないと言っている。この状況を複雑にしているのが，現在知られている最も古い鳥の化石である有名な ¹⁴⁶¹始祖鳥には既に羽があったらしいという事実である。

5 もし羽が何か別のものから進化したのであれば，どのようにして，またなぜそうなったのかを示す決定的な証拠を化石記録で出す必要がある。どちらの学派の古生物学者も，始祖鳥以前の鳥の化石の発見を今か今かと待っている。そして，そ

の発見が自分たちそれぞれの考えが正しいことを証明し、この論争を ¹⁴⁶²完全に終わらせてほしいと願っている。

経済・ビジネス

1 アメリカおよび地球に対する中国の挑戦

1 この数十年，世界人口の5%もないアメリカが，世界の資源の3分の1以上を消費していることに注目している論者は多かった。しかし，現在ではこれはそうではなくなっている。いくつかの分野で，中国がアメリカを追い越しているからである。例えば，中国は現在，アメリカより穀物と赤肉を多量に消費し，より多くの ¹⁴⁶³肥料を使い，より多くの鉄鋼を生産している。中国の人口はアメリカの4.6倍であるから，地球資源に対する ¹⁴⁶⁴1人当たりの需要はまだ（アメリカより）はるかに少ない。極端な例で言えば，平均的アメリカ人は平均的中国人の25倍の石油を消費している。

2 ¹⁴⁶⁵1人当たりの消費はまだわずかではあるが，中国は好況の経済と引き換えにすでに環境面で高い犠牲を払っている。例えば，石炭に大きく依存しているために，かつて東欧で見られたのに近い空気汚染になっている。

3 アメリカよりはるかに大きな人口を有する中国が，アメリカで発展してきた消費者経済の再現を図ろうとしている今，アメリカ方式では環境面で維持不可能であることがはっきりしてきている。アメリカにその経済体系が環境的に維持不可能であることを最終的に認識させるのは，皮肉にも中国であるかもしれない。

4 ¹⁴⁶⁶要は莫大な人口を抱えた中国が，¹⁴⁶⁷今日まで追求されてきたどの発展経路をたどるにしても，長くそれに従うことはとてもできないだろうということである。中国は新しい ¹⁴⁶⁸進路を策定しなければならないのである。紙と ¹⁴⁶⁹火薬を発明した国（中国）は，今や西洋 ¹⁴⁷⁰を跳び越え，環境面で維持可能な経済を建設する方法を示す機会を持つことになった。もし，それを果たせば，中国は世界の他の国々が賞賛し，模倣するための輝かしい先例となることができよう。もし，それができなければ，我々みんながその代価を払うことになろう。

2 名前に何がある？

1 先日，サンフランシスコ ¹⁴⁷¹市交通局は，いくつかの地下鉄の駅に名前をつける

権利を売却するとを検討中だと発表した。もしサンフランシスコ交通局がそうするなら，新しい会社が，サンフランシスコ中の公の交通機関の駅に，彼らの会社名をつけてもらうための何百万ドルを払うために ¹⁴⁷²行列するだろう。やはり，たくさんの人々が見るであろう非常に混雑した場所に会社名をつけることは，大きな宣伝となるように見える。

2 しかしながら，これらの会社が知らないかもしれないことは，これらの会社名が株式市場に与える影響である。株式市場は迷信や神話であふれている。毎日の市場の値動きは，経済的な ¹⁴⁷³要因より恐怖感に関係があるのである。市場は前兆や徴候に反応するのである。そして，ある会社が大金を払って電光看板に自社名を出した場合，歴史的に見て売りのサインなのである。

3 最悪のケースが，ナショナルホッケーリーグのセントルイス・ブルースである。2000年，このチームは，サビス・コミュニケーションズというインターネット企業に競技場の命名権を売り，現金とサビス社の株を手に入れた。サビス社の株はそれ以来80％値下がりし，セントルイス・ブルースは，何百万ドルも損をした。近い将来株が ¹⁴⁷⁴持ち直さなければ，ブルースは選手やコーチに給料が払えなくなるのは言うまでもなく，スタジアムの維持もできなくなるかもしれない。

4 ブルースの経験は珍しいものではない。実際，これら一連の出来事はよくあることなのである。それなら，なぜ会社は何かに ¹⁴⁷⁵会社名を冠することを続けるのだろうか。おそらくきっかけは，¹⁴⁷⁶うまくいかなかった市場計画か，もしくは自分たちの会社名が大きな電光看板にあるのを見たいという代表取締役たちの意味のない欲求を映し出しているだけなのかもしれない。いずれにしても，結局痛い目を見るのは投資家たちの株である。会社名を大衆化することは，会社の価値を上げるとは限らないのである。実際，¹⁴⁷⁷反対のことがよく起きるのである。もし，市場調査課が，このような，企業がスポンサーになることについて研究すれば，将来はこういった冒険的なことには ¹⁴⁷⁸二の足を踏むだろう。

3 オフショア・プライベート・バンキング

1 一般的に「バンキング（銀行業務）」という用語はいわゆる ¹⁴⁸¹小口取引銀行の ¹⁴⁷⁹当座預金口座や ¹⁴⁸⁰普通預金口座での毎日のお金の運用を指し示す場合が多い。しかし，バンキングには，「プライベートバンキング」として知られる隙間的な領域が存在する。これは，High Net Worth Individual（HNWI）という，100万ドル以上に相当する ¹⁴⁸²投資対象財産を持った人のみを対象にしたものであ

る。

2 プライベートバンキング市場は、さらに2つの領域に¹⁴⁸³<u>分割</u>することができる。それは、個人が自分のお金を国外で管理する¹⁴⁸⁴<u>オフショア</u>領域と、国内で管理する¹⁴⁸⁵<u>オンショア</u>領域である。人々はスイスやバミューダといういわゆるオフショアセンターにある銀行口座に魅力を感じている。そこには、銀行の秘密厳守や規則の緩やかな海外の管轄で可能な節税のチャンスがあるからだ。

3 多くのアナリストがプライベートバンキングは全体としてこれからも急速な割合で成長し続けることに同意しているが、同時に彼らはオフショア領域が近年謳歌した成長を保つことは疑わしいと言っている。過去数年の間で、オンショアプライベートバンキングのサービスの質はかなり向上した。理由の一部は、政情がより安定したことと¹⁴⁸⁶<u>通貨の乱高下</u>が少なくなったことである。さらに、オフショア¹⁴⁸⁷<u>税金回避地</u>は世界中の規制当局からの非難の的となっており、それが、いくつかの有名なオフショアセンターに対してのより強い規制を生む結果となっている。

4 オフショア領域は何をすべきであろうか。多くのオフショアセンターは、これらの税金回避地が¹⁴⁸⁹<u>マネーロンダリング</u>の¹⁴⁸⁸<u>温床</u>になっているという懸念を軽減する目的で、報告要件を強化することで行動を起こし始めた。しかし、その過程の中、オフショアのプライベート銀行がオンショア銀行との競争の上で持っていた最大の利点は間違いなく弱まるだろう。オフショア銀行がどの程度現在の¹⁴⁹⁰<u>顧客</u>を満足させながら同時に新たな富裕階級を引きつけられるかは、自身の運命のみならず、彼らが基盤を置いている国の将来の財政状況を決定づけることになるだろう。

4　眠ることのない会社

1 飛行機便の予約をしようと、夜11時過ぎにロンドンから英国航空に電話をすると、アメリカなまりの返事が返ってくる。「まるで、ニューヨークにいる人のように聞こえますね」とこちらが言うと、「それは実際ニューヨークからですので」という返事が来る。科学技術を使って、¹⁴⁹¹<u>標準時間帯</u>の違いをうまく利用する会社が増えているが、英国航空はそうした会社の1つなのである。地球の回転のおかげで、ぱっちり目が覚めているアメリカ人の代役がいるのに、英国で夜半まで交換手を起こしておく必要はないというわけである。

2 それによる利点はよく知られている。3つの時間帯を持つ世界を作る先駆けとなった金融市場は，地球規模での24時間営業に慣れている。他の業界も同じ方向に進んでいる。そうすることを促進している1つの力は生産性である。¹⁴⁹²交替で働く3つのチームが行う仕事の取引きや研究計画を総合すれば，何日も節約できる。もう1つは技術である。客から遠く離れた場所で組み立て，電話で売ることができるサービスがますます増えている中で，技術を持った従業員が安く手に入るところで生産するのはますます容易になるからである。保険金の支払い要求やクレジットカードの記録などの大量の書類整理は，仕事の数より教育を受けた労働者の数の多い発展途上国で行えばよい。

3 それによる問題もよく知られている。一貫作業をしている¹⁴⁹³旧来型の生産会社は，交替で行う作業には注意深い管理が必要であるのを知っている。夕方からの勤務組は，夜勤組が苦労して解決しなければならない困った状況を後に残すこともあり，またその夜勤組は昼間の勤務組にもっとひどい状況¹⁴⁹⁴を残すこともありうるからである。

4 さらに悪いことに，平均的な炭鉱や製紙工場の場合には，夜勤の人は昼勤務の人と¹⁴⁹⁵道を隔ててすぐ近くに住んでいるのに対し，¹⁴⁹⁶債券の売買に携わっている東京のチームはニューヨークの¹⁴⁹⁷連中と顔を合わせることはまずないかもしれないし，シンガポールのアナリストたちは1日の終わりと次の日のはじめの間にわずかに交わす電話の会話でしか，ロンドンのアナリストを知らないかもしれない。最低限，会社は国際チームには何が期待されているかを分からせ，また旧来の同じ現場で働くチームが持っていた仲間意識に取って代わるものを見つけさせる必要がある。

5 客もまた，世界規模での交替勤務制の障壁となる可能性がある。違う時間帯に住んでいる人々は，違う冗談に笑い，違う言い回しに¹⁴⁹⁸腹を立てるものだ。大銀行の中には，客は遠くの国の人間に話しかけるより，プッシュボタンを押し，録音された声を聞く方を好むものだということを知っているところもある。

5　ブランドを求めるアジアの大実業家たち

1 シンガポールの中心的商店街であるオーチャード・ロードを歩くと，店で大声で売られているぜいたくなブランド品に取り囲まれる。香港でもそうであるし，アジアの伝統的な買い物天国を外れた所でさえそうであるが，これは第一には，その地域の中産階級の良いものを身につけようという意志によるものである。アジ

ア人が求めているレッテルは¹⁴⁹⁹常に西洋ものて，このためアジアは西洋のトップブランドにとって第一の成長市場になっている。現在，ぜいたく品の総売り上げの3分の1はアジア向けて，10年以内にはアジアが世界市場の半分を占めるだろうと予測する者もある。

2 しかし，そのときまでには，アジアは今彼らが欲しがっているブランドの多くを自分のものにしているかもしれない。アジアの小売業者および卸売商の多くは，本国の市場で西洋の品¹⁵⁰⁰の販売権を与えているだけでは飽き足らなくなっている強力な国際グループの一部になりつつある。そうしたアジアのグループの中には，目下売り込んでいるブランドものの代わりに，自社製品を製造したいと考えていたり，またブランドを¹⁵⁰¹そっくり買収したいと考えているところもある。例えば，衣料および食料部門のブランドものの¹⁵⁰²品揃えを強力に広げているオン・ベン・センの例を見てみよう。彼はアジアだけでなく，オーストラリアや英国で40以上のアメリカのトップブランドの代理店となっている。オンは最近，ダナ・キャランが創設したファッションブランドであるDKNYと合弁企業を作ったが，これによって日本およびその他のアジアの地域に一連のブティックができることになる。

3 ブランドを扱っている他の¹⁵⁰³大物たちは，¹⁵⁰⁴高級志向のブランドものをあまりに広げすぎ，結果的に市場を冷やしてしまうことを心配している。そこて，彼らは中流の商品を加えて彼ら独自のアジアブランドを作ろうとしている。香港の小売業者は中流向けであることが多いが，西洋風の名前をつけて地元のファッションブランドを作ろうとしている。例えば，香港に本社を持つジョルダーノ社は，自社ブランドの廉価でカジュアルな衣類をアジア中に販売するチェーン店を作るのに成功した。

4 アジアは世界的規模の独自のブランドを作り出すことができるだろうか。日本人はやってのけたが，それは主として自動車，カメラ，それにテレビなどの技術製品においてであった。日本の「生活様式」ものの中には，ケンゾーのように世界の舞台に登場したものもあるが，概して言えばホンダ，キヤノン，あるいはソニーなどよりはるかに知名度は低い。だとすれば，アジアの会社はどうすれば，生活様式のブランドを世界規模の製品に変える魔法の¹⁵⁰⁵妙薬をつけ加えることができるのであろうか。ブランドにはある種の地理的¹⁵⁰⁶誇張が含まれる — ¹⁵⁰⁷気取った服はフランス製，最高品質の革製品はイタリア，そして最高級の時計はスイス製といった具合に。アジアで追い求められている西洋のファッションブランドが魅力を発揮するには，それが代表している生活様式を含めて，はっきりとは

定義できないさまざまな性質が必要なのである。成功のためのピッタリ合った要素の組み合わせを見つけ出すことは容易ではない。

6　グローバル化についての考察

1 メディアはグローバル化[1508]を賞賛することも非難することも好きである。ニューヨークタイムズ紙のトム・フリードマンはこれを「富と技術革新が開花したものであり，それに類するものはこれまで例がない」と表現している。一方，有名な辛口批評家のデービッド・コートンは，これを「市場の[1509]暴虐で，まるでガンのようにその範囲を地球全体にまで広げている」と言っている。しかし，その[1510]賛否にかかわらず，グローバル化の誇大広告はやはり単なる誇大広告でしかない。確かに，これまで合併や買収，国際貿易の拡大への傾向はあったが，国際貿易がアメリカの国民所得に占める割合は10％にすぎないし，その数字がさらに大きくなる様子はない。

2 世界規模の企業は[1511]収益逓減の法則と呼ばれる経済上の原則に取り組まなければならない。この法則は企業の規模には上限があり，その限界を超えると，複雑さや非効率さ，機能停止などが利益を阻害するようになるというものである。例えば，銀行業界では，合併や買収が[1512]新聞紙上をにぎわしている一方で，連邦準備制度理事会の調査によると，銀行の規模が一定の大きさ（資産約1億ドル）に達すると，それ以上拡大してもコストの面で有利にはならないことが分かった。中には，巨大銀行が，規模の不経済を招いていると示唆するデータまである。金融市場センターが後援する別の研究によると，限られた地域の中で貸し付けを行っている銀行の方が，全国レベルで事業を行っているような銀行よりも2倍収益性があることが分かった。国や世界規模での合併が報道されてはいるものの，地方銀行，信用金庫，[1513]小規模融資基金などの動向の方が活発なのである。

3 地域密着型農業の世界規模での急速な成長にも同じような力が働いている。以前，農業経営者は，消費者に販売される農業生産物の価格1ドルにつき50セントを受け取っていた。企業経営農業の現代では，消費者が払う金額1ドルにつきたった9セントしか農業経営者のものにならない。生産物そのものとはほとんど関係がない販売業者が67セントを受け取っている。しかし，生産者が消費者とより近いところにいれば，両者にとって利益となる。消費者はより新鮮で質の高いものを手頃な価格で購入することができるし，農業経営者は生産物に対しより高い収益を得ることができる。何と言っても，世界は広く，そのため，世界的な企業は商品を広範囲の地域に配送しなければならず，そのことが，最終的な利益

自然・環境

[1514]を削っている。石油価格がこの4年間で[1515]4倍になっており，輸送費はばかにならない。

4 世界規模の生産企業は地域の好みに特化した商品を生産しようと努力しているが，世界規模の企業はこの競争において不利な状況にある。地方の企業は小売店や消費者とコミュニケーションをより取りやすく，また，タイミングよく配達ができるため，地域の市場に合った品物を企画したり，生産するのにより適している。小さな会社でも情報技術を利用して，経営や経理，通信，出版などの業務を遂行することができるし，また，インターネットがあれば，小さな会社や自宅でのビジネスでも大企業と競うことが可能である。

5 この傾向は必ずしもグローバル化に[1516]凶運をもたらすものではない。というのも，実際に，すべての商品を地域ごとに生産することは不可能であるからだ。世界規模での貿易は，今日のように，多くの経済活動の中で小さな割合を占めながら，今後も残るであろう。

自然・環境

1 オゾンの菌類

1 [1517]フロンガスなどの気体は，もともと冷蔵庫の部品やエアコンで使用するために開発されたものであるが，しばしば[1519]オゾン層[1518]減少の原因だとされている。しかし，オゾン[1520]を浸食している気体の多くは，実際には人間が作ったものではない。最近になるまで，これらの物質の出所は科学者たちには謎であった。しかし，[1521]予備調査の結果，森林によく見られるある[1522]菌類が，オゾン減少を引き起こす地球大気中の気体の少なくとも一部の生成に関与していることが示唆されている。その菌類は樹木の根元に育つ。その場所で菌類は土から[1523]窒素と[1524]リンを集め，これらの[1525]生きてゆく上で必要な栄養素を樹木と共有している。代わりに，菌類は自分を養ってくれる樹木から[1526]炭水化物を受け取っている。

2 温暖な熱帯雨林には菌類が生息しているが，樹木と菌類の関係が森林の健康状態を保つのに役立っている。しかし，同じことはオゾン層にはあてはまらないかもしれない。菌類1グラムが1日に排出する気体はわずか百万分の2～3グラムだが，それは，菌類が育つ世界中の森林の土壌中の有機物質の15％にもなる。菌類が排出する気体の中には臭化メチル（オゾン破壊要因の10％を占めると考えられている）と[1527]塩化メチル（オゾン破壊のさらに15％を占めるとされる）が

ある。大気中の臭化メチルの一部が農業や人間の他の活動から排出されていることは長く科学者の間で知られていたが，大気中の臭化メチルの少なくとも4分の1は出所が突きとめられずにいる。その探索はまもなく終わるかもしれない。

■3 オゾンを破壊する気体の大部分が本当に菌類によるものなのかどうかを確認するため，さらなる検査が進行中である。さらに，変化を見せている世界の気候が菌類の活動にどのような変化をもたらすのかを，科学者たちは知りたいと考えている。いずれにしても，一見したところ無害な森林の菌類は今，¹⁵²⁸<u>まったく新しい見方をされている</u>。

2 民間による保護

■1 環境破壊に対する一般の意識の高まりを反映して，そのことを心配している人々は自国の自然遺産を守るために¹⁵²⁹<u>自腹を切っている</u>。多くの人々が，自費や友人と資金を貯めて，¹⁵³¹<u>伐採</u>や開発用に¹⁵³⁰<u>指定されている</u>土地の一区画を買っている。

■2 同様に，一般の人たちは，結成された数多くの¹⁵³³<u>土地保護トラスト</u>に寄付することで，¹⁵³²<u>危険な状態の土地</u>の購入を助けている。アメリカに拠点があるネイチャー・コンサーバンシーは，アメリカで最大かつ最も資金力がある環境保護団体であり，年間¹⁵³⁴<u>取引高</u>が4億5,000万ドルで，同様の6つの団体の取引高を合わせたくらいの額になる。土地保護を目的とするトラストのほとんどは「回転資金」戦略を採用している。これは，土地を買い，¹⁵³⁵<u>約款</u>をつけて，再びそれを売るというものである。約款は地所の開発を禁止しており，その土地の持ち主が変わっても，その禁止は永久的に有効である。約款は土地¹⁵³⁶<u>を保護する</u>上で最も効果的な方法であると考えられているため，自然保護の方法として最も急速に人気が出ている。

■3 オーストラリアでは，オーストラリアン・ブッシュ・ヘリテージ・ファンドが，先ごろ，クィーンズランドで開発するかどうかで¹⁵³⁷<u>議論になっている地域</u>の1つにある5万9,000ヘクタールの牧畜場を買い上げたことで，話題を呼んだ。最高経営責任者ダグ・ヒューマンは，保護トラストは現在でも成長する可能性を持っていると信じており，その考えは最近の多額の寄付金によって裏づけられている。彼は「我々はまだこの分野に対する地域社会の理解や関心について，その¹⁵³⁸<u>氷山の一角</u>に引っかき傷すらつけていないということは間違いない」と述べている。

自然・環境

4 ブッシュ・ヘリテージ・ファンドの成り立ちは，環境団体の間では伝説に近いものとなっている。タスマニア出身の活動家が 1990 年にトラストを立ち上げ，伐採が予定されていたタスマニアの個人所有の原始林を買い上げる上での [1539]頭金 のために，環境活動の賞金としてもらった5万ドルを使った。それ以来，その基金はさらに 13 の土地を買い上げ，同様の目的を持つ数多くの個人や団体を援助してきた。ヒューマンは，民間のトラストが [1540]増えている のは，政府にはオーストラリアの自然遺産をきちんと保護する意志も財源もないという確信が一般の間に広がっているからだと断言している。

3 ブルー革命

1 最初の農業革命によって，農作物の栽培と動物の飼育がもたらされた。現在，もう1つの革命が [1541]展開中である。すでに世界中の食卓にのぼる魚の5匹に1匹は [1542]養魚場 からとれたものであるが，その割合は増えていくと予測されている。この「ブルー革命」は，地上における [1543]緑の革命 の場合と同じように，より高い効率とより安定した供給を約束するものである。

2 多種類の人気の高い魚の総量が大幅に減る中で，[1544]水産養殖 が [1545]普及して くるのは明らかである。しかし，緑の革命に暗い側面があったのと同じように，ブルー革命にもそれはある。汚染，病気，種類の多様性の喪失，淡水その他の希少資源の不足の深刻化などが起こるかもしれないからである。それでも何らかの手は打たれなければならない。

3 この危機に対する1つの解決策は，養殖する魚の種類を限定することである。多種類の天然魚を享受するのではなく，たくさんのティラピアを食べるつもりになるべきである。水産界のニワトリともいうべきティラピアは，ほとんどどんな餌でも食べ，成長が早く，信じられないほどの過密状態にも耐えるアフリカ産の中型魚である。科学者たちは現在，農作物や動物の場合に大きな効果を上げたえり抜きの品種改良技術を使って，良質なティラピアの改良をしている。

4 しかし，発展途上国の低技術しかない養魚場では，現在でも西側からの融資返済に充てるための [1546]現金を稼ぐ ため，エビやサケといった高級魚を飼育しなければならないことが多い。地元の市場で売ることのできるような安い魚は，大規模な養殖 [1547]に向か ないことが多く，かといって西側の人々の [1548]好みに合った 魚は，いくら多く養殖できたとしても，飢える地域の人々を養うこともできない。これらの高級魚は食物連鎖の中でも上位に近い種で，養魚場の中でも高タンパク

の餌が必要であるが，それは通常，¹⁵⁴⁹すり身にした海の魚である。タラやサケを養殖すれば，「海洋の負担が取り除ける」と言われている水産養殖についての神話は，まったくの偽りである。

5 集約的な水産養殖にはそれなりのマイナス面もある。人工池は深刻な淡水の不足を招きかねない。過密に詰められた魚かごからは直接水路に汚物が流れるので，ひどい水質汚染が起こりうる。そして，単一種だけを多数まとめれば，病気の危険が増大する — これは農業の場合と共通したもう1つの問題である。

6 それから，病気や汚染問題が解決できたとしても，そうした多くの養魚場をどこに作ったらよいのだろうか。タイのエビ養殖用の池に使われている面積の半分近くは，かつては¹⁵⁵⁰水田であったし，中国では¹⁵⁵¹耕地の水産養殖への転用を現実にすでに禁止している。

7 北アメリカの大草原を農業地にしたために，広範囲にわたる生態系が¹⁵⁵²台なしになってしまった。しかし，それに代わるトウモロコシ畑によって，世界で最も生産性の高い¹⁵⁵³穀倉地帯の1つになった。我々は沿岸水域で同じような¹⁵⁵⁴転換を正当化できるのであろうか。我々は体験を生かし，もっとバランスのとれた発展を企てることができるのであろうか。無計画な開発が目まぐるしく始まらないうちに，我々はすばやく決断する必要がある。

4　結果を評価する

1 決定は政策担当者たちにとって，必ずしも簡単ではない。財政的拘束と，矛盾する政治的利害関係と，そして多くの場合不十分ではないとしても限られた評価と査定データに直面して，彼らはしばしば¹⁵⁵⁵成功が望めない状態に陥ることになる。

2 ¹⁵⁵⁶適切な事例はテリコ・ダム計画だ。1967年にアメリカ連邦議会はリトル・テネシー・リバー沿いにおけるダムの建設を全員一致で可決した。民衆は二重に恩恵を受けるはずだった。建設は，大いに必要とされていた地元の雇用を生み出し，完成すると民衆は安い電力を得，干害に際して水を得るはずだった。6年後，ダムが75％完成したところで，スネイル・ダーターという絶滅危機種法に載っている魚の一種が，¹⁵⁵⁷近くで発見された。環境保全論者は，ダムが種としての魚の生存を脅かすとして，建設を止めるように要請した。政策担当者たちは反目し合った。ほとんど終わっているダムの建設を続けて奉仕する民衆に安い電力を供

給するか，それともすでに危機に瀕している魚を救うために建設を止めるのか。5年間にわたって論争が¹⁵⁵⁸<u>続いた</u>。1979年に票割れで，議会はダムを建設することを決定した。

3 米国国境外の政策担当者たちも，同様に¹⁵⁵⁹<u>苦境</u>にある。大体80万の小さなダム，4万の大きなダム，そして300の主要なダムが，世界の電力の5分の1を賄っている。不幸にしてこの電力は，¹⁵⁶⁰<u>台帳</u>にはじめに記載されたようには安く供給されていない。河川の状態を監視する学者の組織である国際河川ネットワークによると，カリフォルニア州の大きさに等しいおよそ40万平方キロの肥沃な土地が，ダムの後方で水浸しになり，世界の淡水魚の20%が絶滅の危機に瀕しているかすでに絶滅しており，ダムを建設するために，3,000万から6,000万の人たちが家を立退かされた。内陸と岸の浸食という¹⁵⁶¹<u>陸水学上の影響</u>と，大規模なダム建設の結果，今は干上がってしまった氾濫原沿いの森林伐採により，将来ひどい土地の品質低下が起こるだろうという事実を考えると，こうした数字は氷山の一角にすぎない。

4 かつてダム建設のリーダーだった米国は，1994年にダム建設の一時停止を宣言し，皮肉なことには，米国でかつてダム建設担当だった政府機関が，今は環境調整庁としての権限を持っている。しかし毎年およそ260の新設という規模でダム建設は続いている。¹⁵⁶²<u>商業的に可能</u>で，環境に優しい他の手段が開発されるまで，こうした国々の政策担当者たちは，難しいジレンマに直面するだろう。

5 『The Closing Circle（何が環境の危機を招いたか）』の著者であり環境問題活動家であるバリー・コモナーは，最小限の干渉の原則を提唱して，もし人類が種の運命を決める自然自らの淘汰の過程に干渉すれば，世界の生態系が均衡を失うだろうと警告した。だから，自分自身を公共政策担当者¹⁵⁶³<u>の立場に置き</u>なさい。ダム建設がスネイル・ダーターの生存以上のものを脅かすことを承知で，あなたはどんな決定をするだろうか。その結果をどう評価するだろうか。

文化・社会

1 交通への新たな取り組み

1 どこでもいいから大都市エリアの道路地図を開いてみると，そのほとんどに¹⁵⁶⁴<u>同心円</u>がいくつか並んでいるのを見ることになるだろう。バイパスを表すこれらの線は木の年輪の¹⁵⁶⁵<u>形</u>に似ており，道路が年輪と同じように発達したこと

の証拠である。その発達とは，都市エリアが外へと膨張していったということである。世界中の都市の当局は，その形状に ¹⁵⁶⁶ふさわしく環状道路と呼ばれる道路を建設して，より大量の車両交通に対応しようとしている。交通専門技術者は環状道路が渋滞を解決する確実な方法だと考えているため，それらのバイパスは，そこを通るトラックや自動車と同様，あちこちに存在するようになった。

②多くの政府が，交通渋滞を和らげる効果的方策としてバイパスを推進している一方で，バイパスの増加を止めようという市民の動きは時として政治的な混乱を生んでいる。メルボルンの都市計画者は，人々がこれ以上アスファルトが増えないようにと反対しているため，¹⁵⁶⁷障害にぶつかっている。オーストラリアの反環状道路団体（ARRO）は新たなバイパスがメルボルンでの道路の ¹⁵⁶⁹渋滞 ¹⁵⁶⁸を増進し，公害を悪化させ，¹⁵⁷¹中心部が空洞化し ¹⁵⁷⁰外に雑然と拡大する車依存都市を生み出すことになると確信している。

③反環状道路団体は地方自治体の首長にハセルト市長の持つ考え方を反映してほしいと考えている。ハセルト市はベルギーの都市で，人口は7万人弱だが，毎日20万人が通勤してくる。増大する債務と渋滞で ¹⁵⁷²のろのろした車の往来という事態に直面し，ハセルト市長は市の周りを走る予定であった3番目の環状道路の建設計画を中止した。それに関連して，市長は2本ある市の環状道路のうち1つを閉鎖し，それを歩行者用通路と自転車通路のある緑地帯にした。市長はまたバスサービスの質を向上し本数を増やすと同時に，乗車料金をすべて無料とした。ある情報筋によると，1年以内で，公共交通機関の利用は800％という非常に高い数値に上昇し，商人にとってはビジネスがより ¹⁵⁷³活発になり，交通事故と犠牲者の数が減少した。

④もちろん，賞を得たハセルト市の混雑や公害への対処方法がどこでもうまくいくというわけではない。しかし，交通専門技術者にも気づいている人がいるように，バイパスは回避できるのである。

2 仕事中に眠る？

①大人たちが行なう様々な活動の中で昼寝が高い位置を占めたことはない。ふつう昼寝は，成人になる途中のどこかで，コーヒー・ブレイクや冷水器へ通う回数に追い越されてしまうものだ。ところが現在，その昼寝が企業文化 ¹⁵⁷⁴に徐々に受け入れられつつある。最近の研究からうかがえるのは，従業員たちは昔に比べてより多くの時間を会社で過ごすようになっていることと，恒常的に睡眠 ¹⁵⁷⁵不足

の者が半数に達していることである。コーヒー・ブレイクは [1576]一時的気休めにしかなっていないことを会社側は認識し始めている。そして従業員に本当に必要なのは，昼寝のための部屋だ，と結論づけようとしているのである。

② ハーバード・メディカル・スクールの心理学教授マーチン・モア・イデはしばしば，昼寝制度を取り入れるよう会社側に勧告する。「最初の反応はほとんどいつも決まって，否定的なものです」と彼は言う。それでもモア・イデは続けて，一時的な記憶喪失，免疫体系の [1577]衰弱，注意力の喪失など，睡眠不足による生産力低下の影響についての研究結果を挙げる。すると最後には，彼の勧めを受けた企業の3分の2が従業員に昼寝のための休みを取るように勧めるようになった。

③ コーネル大学の心理学者で，大企業に「生産力アップのための睡眠」のセミナーを開いているジームズ・マースは，昼寝の必要性は目覚めた8時間後あたりが特に強いと言う。「そのときが注意力が大きく [1578]低下するときです。15～20分仮眠することで創造力や問題解決力を取り戻せるのです」と彼は説明する。

④ 企業側は今，昼寝によって収支決算に [1579]目に見える形のプラスがあることに気づきはじめている。仮眠室を作ってから，従業員用のソーダやコーヒーへの出費が30％減った会社もある。だが会社の中には，自分たちのところの仮眠室を人に見せることに慎重なところもある。「リラックス用の部屋」と呼ぶところもあるが，仮眠のことは話題にしたがらないところがほとんどである。人々に誤解された印象を与えることを懸念しているのである。

⑤ 『The Art of Napping（仮眠術）』というユーモラスなガイドブックを書いたウィリアム・アンソニーは，こうしたためらいの態度は当然だと考えている。アンソニーは自分たちの体験を公にするよう，人々に働きかけたいと思っている。それまでは仮眠は静かな革命に留まるだろう，と彼は言う。

③ 有意義な休暇

① 「ボランティア活動」という言葉で [1581]資金集めの目的で通りのゴミを拾ったり缶集めをしたりするイメージ [1580]を呼び起こすとすれば，考えを変えた方がいい。ボランティア活動は，わずかな計画性と広い心さえあれば，会社から [1582]人道的な目的のための休暇とも，価値ある文化的体験ともすることもできる。たとえ厳しい仕事でも，休暇を現地で過ごすのはその国を知る素晴らしい方法である。その気持ちがあり ― 自分で金も支払う ― ボランティアにとっては，アジアでの働

き口の¹⁵⁸³範囲は広く，また，多種多様である。その選択肢としては，例えば，バングラデシュの勤労奉仕キャンプ，韓国の建設現場，タイの¹⁵⁸⁴考古学的発掘などである。

2 もしもボランティア休暇と聞いて，のんきに休日を過ごすよりはましな選択肢だというぐらいに思うなら，注意した方がいい。というのも，真剣な気持ちや現実的な期待を持たない人は，辛いこと¹⁵⁸⁵になりかねないからである。アメリカのキリスト教団体で，建設事業の手配を世界的規模で行っている「ハビタート・フォー・ヒューマニティ」のデービッド・ミニックは，「軽はずみな気持ちでこうしたボランティア休暇に臨まないよう人々に警告したいと思います」と言っている。「期待を抑えることも大切です。建設現場で10日間貢献しても，長い過程のほんの一部が見られるにすぎません。1週間で世界が救えるなどと思わないことです」

3 とはいえ，仕事に¹⁵⁸⁶没頭することは一緒に働く現地の労働者たちの慣習を知る絶好の機会になる。それから，ガイドブックなどは持っていかないことである。「ただ気ままな旅行者のふりをしたい人にとっては，これは筋違いのものなのです」と，ボランティア活動の機会を幅広く提供している「アースウォッチ」のブルー・マグルーダーは言っている。

4 国際規模の勤労奉仕キャンプの多くは，社会保障と地域社会開発を中心に据えている地元団体が運営している。ボランティアをする人は通常，¹⁵⁸⁸水道といった近代設備のない¹⁵⁸⁷過酷な状況に置かれ，寝袋も持参するように言われる。

4 水晶玉を管理する

1 サリーの心霊ギャラリーは，未来のことを探すような場所には見えない。その店舗はガソリン・スタンドの裏の小さなレンガ作りの建物の中にあって，外からは¹⁵⁸⁹超自然的な様子はうかがえない。お客になろうとするみなさん，安心してください。サリーはメリーランド州セシル郡当局から占いの免許をもらっているのだから。

2 消費者が通常は自分で用心することになっている時代にあって，セシル郡は¹⁵⁹⁰だまされやすい人たちを守ろうとする数少ない場所の1つだ。ここで占いをしようとする人は，「¹⁵⁹¹手相占い師，¹⁵⁹²占い師，および¹⁵⁹³易者の免許証」が要る。郡書記官が占い師になろうとする人の過去に「倫理的に¹⁵⁹⁴卑劣な犯罪」が

文化・社会

ないかを調べて，それで納得したら，250ドルの免許料を徴収する。

3 しかし ¹⁵⁹⁶占い師志望者に ¹⁵⁹⁵資格証明書を出す試みは，この業界の性格を変えたようには見えない。占い業は安い費用で営むことができ，占い師になりたい人の適性は調べにくいので，この職業には必要以上に怪しい人たちが寄ってくる。カリフォルニア法廷の判決が地域の占い業禁止を覆したとき，ハンティントン・ビーチの町は，地元の警察官の言葉では，「人々に ¹⁵⁹⁷いくつかの規則に従わせる」ために作成された4ページの免許法でもって答えた。予見できたことではあったが，これは数年後に1人の占い師が客から15万ドル以上 ¹⁵⁹⁸をだまし取るのを防げなかった。この話の教訓は？ 買い手が気をつけるべきだということになる。

4 不用心な人たちを守るためにできることに限りがあるなら，こうした政策を全面的に放棄したらどうだろうか。実は，そうした動きは消費者にとって有利に働くかもしれない。この特派員の非科学的な調査では，占い料金は規制されたセシル郡の方が他の所より高かったことを示している。ここの ¹⁵⁹⁹賢人たちが将来の規制解除から利益を得るかどうかは，¹⁶⁰⁰だれにもわからない。いや，だれかに分かっているかもしれない。恐らくサリーとその仲間はすでに未来を見ているはずだ。

5 新しい青銅時代

1 ¹⁶⁰²従来からの知恵に挑戦する ¹⁶⁰¹という点では，年商40億ドルの屋内日焼け産業の ¹⁶⁰³図々しさにかなう商売はほとんどない。健康団体や政府機関からの非難にもかかわらず，全国の5万軒の日焼けサロンを代表する業界団体は，マスメディアによる宣伝で対抗している。「新しい研究で，ほどよい日焼けでガンが予防できることがわかりました」と，¹⁶⁰⁴新聞発表で述べている。

2 しかし，業界は次のようなPR面でのちょっとした障害に直面している。つまり，第一線の専門家の中で，その主張を受け入れている者は1人もいないのだ。彼らは1人残らず，太陽および日焼け用ランプからの紫外線が皮膚ガンを起こしかねないと言って，日焼け用ブースに近づかないよう消費者に警告している。科学者たちは総体的には，アメリカ ¹⁶⁰⁶皮膚病学会に ¹⁶⁰⁵支持されている「安全な日焼けなどはない」という見解を受け入れている。

3 業界一のある団体の理事長ジョセフ・レヴィが，今年から毎月広告を出し始める

きっかけとなったのは，まさにこのような（日焼けに関する）^1607悲観的な発言であった。「我々は長い年月にわたって，医学界から受けてきたまったくのマイナスの条件づけを解消させようとしているのです」とレヴィは言う。しかし，批判的な人たちは業界が証明されていない理論を利用したり，現在の研究を誇張したりして，自分たちの言い分を通そうとしていると主張している。例えば，この団体の広告や新聞発表では「もし，もっと多くの人々が定期的に日焼けをしたら，毎年3万人のガンによる死亡が避けられるかもしれない」とほのめかす研究を強調している。その研究は，実は日のよく当たる地域で暮らしている人の間では，^1609結腸ガンや乳ガンの発生率が低いので，日光に当たればそのような恐ろしいガンは防げるかもしれない^1608と仮定している書評用の論文なのである。しかし，^1610伝染病学者たちは食物や運動量といった他の重要要素も温暖地と寒冷地では異なるので，日光をガンの一治療法として公式に認めることはまずできないと言う。

4 健康団体からの間断ない攻撃も影響を与えているのかもしれない。10年前，室内での日焼けは最も成長の速い産業の1つであったが，その成長は1986年から1988年の間が54%であったのに比べ，今年は4%以下に下がってしまった。だが，レヴィは21世紀は日焼け産業にとって「^1611青銅時代」となることを確信している。

6　カード破産

1 破産への道はプラスティックで舗装されている。今年，個人の破産を申し立てたアメリカ人の数は，今までの最高で，100万人にわずかに^1612届かなかった。破産の中には，高額の医療費や人員削減によるものもあるが，大部分はクレジットカードによる借金に関連していた。昨年^1613クレジットカードでの買い物を促す勧誘は約27億件あった。カードを発行する側は，飛行機を多く利用する人への^1614マイレージサービス，現金の払い戻し，初回の借り入れ時の低金利率などの動機づけによって，消費者が借り入れをするのを奨励する。無料で財政相談を行っている全国規模の^1616非営利団体で，シンシナチにある消費者信用相談センター（CCCS）の常務取締役のバーニー・カイザーは「大勢の人たちがクレジットカード^1615に頼って生活をするようになっています。クレジットカードの支払いをクレジットカードで行っている人さえいます。収入を補うのにクレジットカードを使っているのです」と述べている。クレジットカードは所有者を^1617気前のよい気持ちにさせるが，現実は大いに違う。

文化・社会

2 破産はもともと不可抗力の事情による負債から，人々を救済するためのものであったと CCCS の教育部長マット・ジェラルドは言う。しかし，今や破産はあまりにも普通のこととなってしまったため，かつての恥辱の感覚は大方なくなってしまった。カイザーは「実際に二度も申し立てを行った人が大勢います」と言う。

3 心理学者のオリビア・メランは多くの人の場合，使い過ぎの原因は子ども時代にあるという。[1618]甘すぎる両親をまねるとか，逆にかまってくれなかった両親による[1619]むなしさを充たそうとして，情緒面の欲求を充足させようとするのだという。離散家庭や消費重視を抱えた現代アメリカ文化の中で，人々は連帯感を失い，孤立した気持ちになっている。しかし，メランによれば，資力以上に使い込む人は買い物をしても，愛され，大事にされ，あるいは求められているとは感じないと言う。彼らは買い物によって，欲求の度合いをますます強めていくのである。

4 信用失墜は長期にわたる影響を持ちうる。雇用主，家主，保険会社になる可能性がある個人や会社は，10 年にわたって破産の事実が保存されている過去の信用記録を調べることができる。「もし，ある人がローンを申し込んだ場合，申込用紙には過去に破産[1620]を申告したことがあるかどうかをたずねる質問項目があります」とジェラルドは言っている。その質問に正直に答えない場合には，申込者は詐欺行為を行ったことになる。銀行は毎日，ますます多くの詐欺による損失を調べつつある。

7　警察教師

1 法によるしつけの威力を学校へも広げよう[1621]との企てから，シンガポール警察は先生たちを選んで特別志願名誉[1622]警察官（VSC）という，校内に管轄権を持つ教師兼警察官にすることを開始した。この計画は 1997 年，数校の学校で[1623]試験的に導入されたものであるが，このほどその詳細が[1624]少年犯罪を減少させるためのセミナーで明らかにされた。

2 任命された者は，[1626]学校の規律を取り締まることによって非行[1625]に対応するのが任務となろう。彼らは警察の用いる方法で訓練を受け，警察の制服を着用し，問題児に対処することによって教室内の秩序維持に努める。これらの新特別志願警察官は校外の警察の仕事に参加することは考えられていないが，校内ではある程度の警察力を行使する権利を持つことになろう。

3 特別志願警察隊は1946年，正規のシンガポール警察隊を増補する目的で結成されたもので，現在，1,600名の隊員を有している。[1627]新入隊員は警察学校で基礎訓練を受けるが，それには小銃を扱う訓練，[1628]武器を持たない戦闘技術，基礎的法律知識講座などが含まれる。

4 [1629]内務大臣のウォン・カン・セン氏によれば，この計画は学校教師に権威を与えるためのもう1つの方法であったという。「さらに権力を与えられたことで彼らは，教師としてだけでなく，警察官としても見られるようになるだろう」と語った。

5 このニュースはそのほとんどが教師であった500名ほどの聴衆に物議をかもした。何に関する権力をどの程度教師兼警察官が持つことになるのかについて，懸念を表明する者もあった。最高補佐官で警察の長官でもあるベネディクト・チェオン氏はそれに応えて，「学校が直面[1630]しそうなシナリオについては議論」の必要が残っていると語った。

6 ウォン氏は，警察と学校のつながりは強化されるだろうと言った。学生に対応できなくなったときにだけ校長が警察に連絡を取っていた以前とは違い，今後警察はもっと積極的に行動し，特に[1631]微罪を重ねている学生[1632]を監視するようになろう。「警察はそうした学生を選定し，巡視し，学校の校長と教師だけでなく，警察もその子が[1633]真面目な生活を続けることに関心がある点を明確にしたい」と，同氏は語った。

8 ニュースの中身

1 10年ほど前まで，アメリカの新聞は何が「ニュース」なのかについて，はっきりした考えを持っていた。ニュースとは主要国の首相や大統領が記者会見で発表する事であり，政策や外交や[1634]内閣改造であり，経済の統計や[1635]企業合併や金融市場だった。しかしここ12年ほどの間に，アメリカの新聞はそういう概念から離れて，よりゆるやかな，[1636]特集記事中心の，[1637]時代の流れに沿ったものへと大きな変化を遂げてきた。

2 マックス・フランケルは，1986年から1994年までニューヨークタイムズの編集長として君臨し，それゆえ報道の[1638]話題を決定するのに関わった人だが，第1面に堅くない記事を，という考えを広めた人である。フランケルは，新聞を読んでもらえるものにしたかった。カントリーミュージックやミニスカートについて

の記事は，興味を引くだけでなく，重要な動向を反映していると，彼は主張した。すなわち，おそらく，多くの読者は ¹⁶⁴⁰軍縮会談 よりも ¹⁶³⁹スカートの裾の線 に関心を持っていたのである。

3 フランケルのもと，タイムズは冷戦後の世界の ¹⁶⁴¹外交問題 を取り扱う，新しく，注目せずにはいられないような方法を探し始めた。政治は以前ほど重要視されなくなっているので，特派員は外国の政府よりむしろ外国の「人々」についてもっと書くべきだ，と編集者たちは感じていた。特派員たちは，首都にいて大臣と語る時間を減らし，地方で農場経営者や主婦と話をする時間を増やすよう要求された。社会の流れにより注意が向けられるようになったのだ。実際，フランケルは「時に，最も重要なニュースというのは，たった1日で起こるものではない」と強調していた。

4 他の新聞，特にワシントンポストとロサンゼルスタイムズは，似たような方針をとった。彼らはみな科学や医学の報道を強化した。やがて，健康やフィットネス（例えば，ビタミンCは風邪を防ぐのか，ウェイトリフティングはランニングと同じくらい ¹⁶⁴²体重を落とすのに役立つか）についての記事が第1面に持ってこられたとき，だれも驚かなくなった。ウォールストリートジャーナルは，企業疑惑報道という新境地を開拓し，その先頭に立った。そして，じきにすべての大手新聞社が，政治家同様，¹⁶⁴⁴法人の幹部 にも ¹⁶⁴³調査報道記者 を割り当てた。

5 しかし，批評家たちは，新聞が ¹⁶⁴⁵読みやすく なるにつれて，多少 ¹⁶⁴⁶不可欠な物ではなく なってきていると不満を漏らしている。ビタミンCについての記事は面白いかもしれないが，もし見逃してしまっても困らないのである。第1面がたくさんの面白い人々の記事 ¹⁶⁴⁷でいっぱいになった ので，もし何かが起こったとしても，本当に大切なものは何かが分かりづらくなっていた。さらに人々の情報源の選択肢としてインターネットがテレビに加わると，若い人の多くは簡単に新聞を完全に ¹⁶⁴⁸はねつけた 。

6 問題は解決されていない。新聞社の幹部たちは，¹⁶⁵⁰堅いニュース の ¹⁶⁴⁹報道 を減らせば新聞の必要性は減ると大変心配しているが，インターネットやケーブルテレビのニュースが24時間存在する世界にあっては，最新の出来事を人々に一番に知らせるという点ではまったく相手にならないのである。彼らは他のアプローチを採らなくてはならない。

9 黄金のチャンス？

1 1999年春，インゴ・ポトリクスという名前のスイスの科学者が，世界の飢餓や病気と闘う上で強力な武器となる「ゴールデンライス」の開発に彼のチームが成功したと発表した。ポトリクスと彼の [1651]共同研究者の主任であるピーター・ベイヤーは，ラッパスイセンから [1652]ベータカロチンを作る遺伝子を取り出し，アグロバクテリウムツメファシエンスとして知られる [1653]細菌のDNA構造に挿入した。形を変えた細菌は米の [1654]胚に入っていき，入っていく過程で米の内乳にベータカロチンを作り出す遺伝子を運んだのである。新種の米に黄金色を与えているベータカロチンはふつう精米にはなく，また，体がビタミンAを作る上で極めて重要な成分である。ポトリクスの夢は，毎年 [1656]ビタミンA不足で100万人の子どもが死に，さらに35万人が目が見えなくなる国々でゴールデンライスを [1655]主要作物として使用することである。

2 予想通り，みんながゴールデンライスを賞賛しているわけではない。英国の医学学術雑誌『ランセット』の編集長であるリチャード・ホートン博士によれば，「世界の飢餓のために技術によって急場しのぎの食糧対策を行うことは，われわれの時代の科学界最大の論争というだけでなく，新世紀における最も営利的で悪意に満ちた [1657]無駄な努力である」という。[1658]遺伝子組み換え食品の議論は多くの人がよく知っている。一方の側には「緑の革命」を推進する科学者と農業関係のビジネスをする人たちがいる。彼らは害虫に強いものから収穫量の多いものまでいろいろな特徴がDNAに組み込まれた様々な遺伝子組み換え穀物の集中農業を奨励している。反対側には，別の科学者と環境保護団体がおり，最高レベルの注意を喚起している。彼らは，遺伝子操作の長期の成果はまだ分かっておらず，また，このように広まっている，我々の [1659]食糧の遺伝子構造への干渉の結末が有害だと，この先分かるかもしれないと警告している。

3 ゴールデンライスに反対する人たちが挙げる別の問題点は，ポトリクスが作ったものが安全で制御が可能な形の遺伝子組み換えであったとしても，それはまだビタミンA不足問題の答えにはならないという点である。明確にしなければならない問題は他にも数多くある。ただ単に新しい穀物を用意しても，必要としている人たちにそれが届く保証はないと述べている批評家がいる。実際，[1660]栄養失調の子どもの4分の3近くは食糧が余っていると自慢している国々に住んでいるのだ。環境団体グリーンピースの広報担当者はこう述べている。「飢餓や栄養失調の本当の原因は貧困や非効果的な食糧配分，政治的意欲の欠如である」

文化・社会

4 ゴールデンライスや他の遺伝子組み換え食品が世界の飢餓問題に最も効果的な解決方法を提供するかどうかはまだ分からない。しかし，我々に¹⁶⁶¹選り好みができるのだろうか。この論争が複雑になる中でも，栄養失調の惨劇は衰えることなく広まっている。遺伝子組み換え食品に反対する人たちは，これからも重要な問題を挙げ続けるだろう。しかし，発展途上国の飢えている子どもにとって，これらの問題はほとんど関係がないのである。昔の格言が示すとおり，「食糧があるとたくさんの問題が起こる。食糧がないと問題は1つしかない」

10 遺伝子格差

1 近年，遺伝学の分野の進歩はめざましい。ますます複雑化する遺伝子間の相互関係を観察する能力や病気の¹⁶⁶²傾向を調べる並外れて正確なテスト方法を開発する能力により，今では，ある人に対し，将来発症する健康上の問題点を症状が出る何年も前に警告をすることができる。しかし，それらの知識は非常に将来有望ではあるが，遺伝子検査は，将来の進歩¹⁶⁶³に暗い影を落とし，場合によっては進歩を妨げるような悪影響も潜在的に抱えている。

2 遺伝学はオーストリアの¹⁶⁶⁴植物学者グレゴール・メンデルから始まると一般的に考えられている。彼は，親細胞の遺伝子の組み合わせから，身体的¹⁶⁶⁵特徴の遺伝の法則を発見した。遺伝学が進歩するに伴い，親から子孫へと伝えられる情報は単に身体的な類似性を支配するだけではないことを研究者たちは発見した。実際，遺伝情報は，免疫制御やある種の病気や障害に¹⁶⁶⁷かかりやすいかどうか¹⁶⁶⁶を特定する上で一定の役割を果たしている。このことは治る人にとっては非常に大きな医学の進歩である。しかし，ある人に治療法のない病気が発見された場合，問題が起こる。

3 2000年10月，イギリス政府のある委員会がまさにこの点を問題にした声明を発表した。ハンチントン病として知られる脳の致命的状態を調べる遺伝子検査について調査を行い，委員会は，現在ではどの人が後にハンチントン病にかかるかを正確に予測することができると発表した。これらの調査結果は，医学においては飛躍的な進歩として称賛されるにふさわしいことではあるが，このニュースは社会的にも非常に大きな意味を持っている。

4 生命保険業界がその好例である。生命保険はイギリスでは不可欠といって差し支えない。それがなければ，住宅ローンなどの長期の財政的約定は不可能である。生命保険は，他の種類の保険と同様，危険度合いの査定が基本となっている。ハ

ンチントン病検査のような ¹⁶⁶⁸診断テストがあると，保険会社が消費者よりも非常に優位な立場になってしまい，検査結果に応じて会社が ¹⁶⁶⁹保険料を調整したり，場合によっては加入希望者を完全に拒否することが可能になる。保険会社が加入希望者を拒否する理由を持たないためにに，人々が遺伝子検査の受診を避けなければならなくなるかもしれないとイギリスの消費者委員会は述べている。そうなると，保険に入れるようにと，人々が診断検査を受けないままでいるというばかげた状態が生まれる可能性がある。

5 遺伝子に関する偏見という問題は大西洋の向こう側でも ¹⁶⁷⁰起きている。アメリカ合衆国連邦政府の機関は遺伝子情報が根拠となる差別をしてはならないのだが，¹⁶⁷¹民間部門はその同じ規則に拘束されないのである。合衆国議会に対して，上記の拘束が公共部門以外にも及ぶことを目的とした「健康保険と雇用における遺伝子的無差別規定」を批准するように圧力がかかっている。そのような規制なしでは，精巧な遺伝子検査が遺伝子上の ¹⁶⁷²下層階級を生み出す力を持つかもしれない。

INDEX

A

a case in point	309
abate	90
abide	90
abject	52
abode	106
abort	8
abrasively	107
absurdity	34
abyss	90
academic integrity	255
accost	90
accreditation	90
acquit	8
acrid	91
acrimonious	52
adage	91
adamantly	69
address	91
adenoids	244
adept	91
adherent	91
adjacent	91
adjourn	8
admonish	92
adroit	52
adversary	34
adverse	92
advocate	92
aerodynamics	281
affability	92
affiliate	8
affinity	92
affix	93
affront	218
aforementioned	278
aggregate	93
aggressive bent	260
agonize	93
AIDS	248
alleged	52
allegiance	184
alleviate	93
allot	8
allude	9
altruistic	93
amass	9
ambiance	34
ambivalent	94
ameliorate	94
amenable	147
amend	9
amnesty	94
amorphous	255
amplify	312
anemic	248
anesthetic	34
animosity	34
anonymity	95
antagonist	95
antibiotic	240
antibody	95
antidote	95
antiseptic	95
anybody's guess	320
apathetic	96
appall	9
appease	96
appendage	281
appraise	96
apprehend	96
aptly	312
aquaculture	306
arable land	307
archaeological	317
Archaeopteryx	282
archaic	278
ardent	97
arduous	97
arena	97
arid	168
armament	97
arms-control talks	332
around the corner	206
array	207
arsenal	239
artery	236
artful	97
articulate	52
artifact	97
artifice	98
artificial intelligence	275

as it turns out	231
ascertain	125
ascribe	9
assail	98
assault	102
assimilate	204
assuage	98
asthmatic	231
astute	53
asylum	35
at loose ends	98
at odds	72
at-risk land	303
attorney	160
audacity	35
audit	9
augment	98
auspicious	98
austere	99
authentic	120
autocratic	99
aversion	99
avert	99
aviation	100
avid	100

B

back to back	100
backlash	35
backlog	100
bacterium	335
badger	100
baffle	10
bail out ~	72
balk	10
band-aid	315
bank on ~	72
banner ad	257
banter	101
barbarism	260
baron	294
basalt	268
bask	10
be a far cry from ~	101
be back on track	101
be born yesterday	72

be geared up	72
be in for ~	317
be tolerant of ~	255
be up to one's ears	73
bear up	73
beef up ~	73
beguile	101
behoove	101
belittle	10
belligerent	102
beloved	307
benign	53
bequeath	291
berate	102
bereave	102
berth	103
besiege	103
bestow	103
beta carotene	335
bewilderment	103
biased	104
Biblical	277
bid for ~	258
bide one's time	104
binary	104
black sheep	105
blare	105
blatant	53
bleach	105
blemish	99
blight	105
blockage	244
blood vessel	264
bloodstream	236
blotch	105
blow over	73
blow the lid off ~	105
blow up	106
bluff	106
boil down to ~	73
bolster	10
bolt	216
bond	291
bone marrow	232
boon	35
botanist	339

botch	11
bottle up ~	73
bottom line	284
bountiful	106
brand	99
brawl	35
brazen	106
breach	35
breadbasket	307
break even	107
break one's heart	107
bribe	107
brigade	177
bring up ~	107
brink	36
brisk	313
bronchodilator	232
Bronze Age	323
brood	108
brunt	108
brusque	108
buffer	108
bulge	109
bulk	109
bulletin	275
bungle	109
buoyant	142
burgeon	109
burrow	141
business merger	331
buttress	109
by and large	110
by word of mouth	110
bystander	173

C

cabinet shuffle	331
cache	261
calamity	110
caliber	110
call it a day	74
call the shots	106
callow	182
caloric	236
candid	53
candor	111

capricious	111
carbohydrate	301
careen	111
caricature	295
carnivorous	281
carousel	36
catch on	111
catch prey	281
catnap	151
caustic	108
censor	11
censure	11
cessation	111
CFC	300
change hands	257
chant	112
chap	292
charge a commission	258
chart a course	284
chartered	112
chauvinist	112
checking account	288
chemical reaction	268
cherish	153
chip away at ~	298
chip in	113
chloride	301
choosy	336
chronic condition	231
churn	113
churn out ~	271
chutzpah	322
cinch	113
circumstantial	113
circumvent	11
clemency	36
clench	113
clientele	289
clinch	114
clinical trial	248
clogged artery	248
clogged with ~	333
close call	74
clout	114
clutch	114
coalesce	161

448

coarse	114	conspire	12
coax	11	constancy	118
coerce	11	constabulary	328
cohesive	115	constellation	119
collaborator	335	constitute	13
collusion	158	constrict	119
colon	323	construe	119
come by ~	74	contemplate	119
come to blows	261	contentious	120
come to pass	114	contingency	37
come to terms	261	continuance	120
commend	12	contour	312
commensurate	53	contract	244
commercially viable	310	contrite	120
commit a minor offense	329	contrive	120
commotion	36	convene	121
commune	115	conventional wisdom	322
compelling	53	converge	121
competency	115	conversant	121
complacent	54	convict	122
complicity	36	convulse	122
comply	12	cook up ~	74
composure	37	copious	122
comprise	12	cordon	13
con	320	corporate executive	332
concede	12	corporate titling	286
conceive	115	corrode	13
concentric circle	312	count in ~	122
concisely	115	counter	328
condense	116	counterbid	258
condone	116	countermeasure	252
conducive	54	counterpart	123
confer an advantage	261	covenant	304
configuration	116	cover up ~	123
confiscate	116	coverage	333
confrontation	116	covert	123
congenial	117	covetous	100
congestion	312	crack down on ~	258
conglomerate	117	crack up (~)	123
congregate	117	crease	123
congruity	117	credential	319
conjecture	117	credit offer	325
consignment	118	credulous	123
consolation	118	crib	255
consort	118	cripple	251
conspicuous	118	crude	263

crunch	124
crux	37
culminate	13
culprit	94
curb	124
currency volatility	288
cursory	124
curtail	13
curtly	124
custody	37
custom build	271
cutting edge	74
cyberporn	255

D

dainty	125
dangle	125
dawdle	125
dead center	312
dearth	125
debacle	37
debase	134
debilitate	315
debit	132
debrief	125
debris	37
debunk	133
deceased	112
deception	126
decode	274
decorous	126
deduct	126
defective	54
defer	126
deferential	94
deflect	127
deft	127
defuse	121
defy	145
dehydration	127
delegate	14
deluge	127
delusion	128
delve	128
demeanor	38
demise	38
demographic	54
demolition	128
demote	128
demure	163
den	129
denote	104
denounce	14
depletion	300
deplorable	124
deploy	129
depreciation	129
deprive	315
derisive	54
dermatology	322
desolate	55
despicable	129
despondent	55
destitute	137
detain	14
detect	129
detention	130
deteriorate	235
determinant	286
deterrent	38
detest	14
detonate	130
detract	127
detriment	38
devastating	252
deviation	38
devour	14
dexterous	130
diabetes	236
diabolic	130
diagnostic test	339
diagram	274
diatribe	38
dichotomy	130
diffident	131
diffuse	131
dig into *one's* pocket	303
dig up ~	131
digital pest	251
dilute	131
dip	315
dire	55

disarming	132
discharge	132
discreet	55
discrepancy	132
disdain	132
disintegration	133
disparaging	55
disparity	133
dispel	15
dispensable	333
disperse	134
dispute	133
dissect	133
dissemination	134
dissident	56
dissipated	134
dissuade	134
distend	151
distortion	135
ditch	135
ditto	135
diverge	137
divest	136
dividend	148
divulge	15
docile	56
dogmatic	135
dole	135
doom	135
dormant	56
dosage	241
dote	136
down payment	304
down the drain	136
down the line	107
downbeat message	322
downside	271
downtrend	136
drafty	136
draw a blank	138
draw up ~	74
drawback	39
drift off	75
drill	136
drum up ~	75
dub	271
dubious	110
dupe	15
duplicate	275
dusty cocoon	263
dwindle	15

E

earmark	303
eat away ~	300
eat *one's* words	137
ebb	137
echelon	137
eclectic	137
efficacy	39
effigy	39
effusive	138
elaborate	275
elated	159
elicit	15
elixir	295
elongate	197
elucidate	138
elude	177
elusive	247
emanate	15
emancipate	138
embark	138
embed	139
embellish	16
embezzlement	39
embryo	336
eminence	189
empower	139
emulate	139
enact	139
encompass	139
encroachment	39
encumber	139
endorse	134
endowment	140
engross	140
engulf	16
enigma	140
enmesh	140
enmity	39
ensue	310

entail	16
enthrall	16
entity	140
entrapment	141
enunciate	141
envision	271
epidemiologist	323
epigram	141
equitably	69
eradicate	141
erosion	40
erratic	141
erudition	141
espouse	322
estrogen	237
eulogy	142
evade	206
evaporation	142
evict	16
evoke	317
exacerbate	16
exalt	142
exasperation	142
excavate	17
exclusive	56
exculpate	182
exempt	143
exert	143
exhort	143
exile	143
exodus	144
exonerate	104
expediency	205
expedite	17
explicit	57
exponential	57
expulsion	144
extenuating	155
extol	17
extort	144
extraneous	166
extrapolate	17
exuberant	145
exude	145
exult	145

F

fabricate	17
facade	40
face the music	75
faction	145
fall through	75
fallible	146
falter	18
far-fetched	146
fawn	146
feasible	146
feat	273
feature-oriented	332
feign	18
felicity	146
feminizing effect	237
fend off ~	255
ferret out ~	146
fertilizer	284
fervently	147
fervor	147
feud	18
fiasco	40
figment	40
figure into ~	273
filament	281
filch	147
file for ~	326
filter out ~	147
finite	235
fire away	75
fire up	274
fish farm	306
fishtail	187
fit the bill	75
fix	147
flagrantly	69
flap	281
flare	148
flattery	40
flawless	126
flesh out ~	76
flimsy	148
flounder	18
flout	148
fluctuate	148

fluke	41
fluster	148
flutter	245
fly off the handle	76
follow suit	76
foodstuff	336
footage	41
foreboding	98
foreign affairs	332
forensic	57
forerunner	281
forge	18
formidable	57
fortify	109
fortune-teller	319
fossilized remains	282
foul play	140
foyer	149
fracture	149
franchise	294
fraudulent	131
fraught	57
frazzle	149
free-radical oxidation	235
frequent-flier miles	325
fret	149
fringe	149
frisk	18
fritter away ~	76
from scratch	76
frugally	69
fuel	19
fundraising	317
fungus	300
fury	149
fusion	150
fuss	150
futile	57

G

gallant	150
galvanize	112
garrulous	150
gauche	125
gaudy	150
gauge	151
gaunt	151
gene-sequencing technique	268
genetic	235
genetic engineering	271
genetically modified food	336
geneticist	277
genial	151
geothermal	268
germ	240
gerontologist	234
get a break	76
get by	151
geyser	267
gird	151
gist	152
give ~ the benefit of the doubt	77
give ~ the cold shoulder	77
glitch	41
gloat	152
gloss over ~	77
go against the grain	77
go awry	286
go broke	152
go to *one's* head	77
go up in smoke	152
gorge	152
gospel	278
grass roots	153
gratifying	129
green revolution	306
ground-up	307
grudge	153
guise	153
gullible	319
gulp	153
gunpowder	284
gush	136
guzzle	153

H

hacking	251
haggle	154
hammer out ~	154
hand it to ~	77
hand out ~	154
hand over fist	154

hang in the balance	78
hang out	154
hapless	58
hard news	333
harness	19
harsh	317
haul	154
have a strong case	267
have had it up to here with ~	78
havoc	155
hay fever	245
head off ~	78
head over heels	155
headway	41
hectic	58
hedge	155
heinous	58
hemline	332
herald	280
here to stay	306
hierarchy	251
high and low	78
hilarious	155
hindsight	41
hit it off	78
hit the books	141
hit the road	155
hit the sack	78
hoard	19
hold *one's* breath	156
hold out	156
hold water	79
holographic	156
homage	41
Home Affairs Minister	329
hormone	237
hot air	79
hot stuff	156
hotbed	289
hotspot	304
huddle	19
human genome	277
hunch	41
hydrogen	268
hydrological effect	310

I

idyllic	188
immaculate	58
immersion	317
imminent	58
immune system	248
immunity	156
impair	19
impart	157
impartial	157
impasse	42
impassively	69
impeachment	157
impeccably	70
impede	19
impel	157
impending	58
imperative	59
imperceptibly	157
impervious	92
impetuous	157
impetus	144
impinge	158
implant	119
implausibly	158
implicate	158
implore	20
impulsive	158
in a bid to *do*	328
in a nutshell	158
in tatters	307
in the bag	159
in the cards	79
in the nick of time	79
in the shoes of ~	310
inadvertent	59
inane	159
inanimate	159
inauguration	159
incarcerate	20
incendiary	59
incense	159
incentive	42
inception	42
incessant	160
incipient	160

incision	160
incite	160
incline	20
inconceivable	161
incongruity	42
incorporate	161
increment	42
incriminate	161
incubate	161
incumbent	42
incur	20
incursion	161
indelible	59
in-depth	249
indigent	162
indignant	162
indoctrinate	162
indolent	162
induce	162
ineptly	162
inevitable	59
infatuated	163
infectious disease	239
infer	20
inferno	266
infiltration	163
inflammatory	232
inflict	163
infringe	104
infuriate	163
infuse	21
ingenious	59
ingenuous	164
inhale	164
inherently	164
inhibit	21
inhospitable	268
inject	131
innovative	60
inorganic machine	271
insatiable	164
inscrutable	164
insight	231
insinuate	21
insipid	164
insolent	165
insoluble	165
insolvent	165
instigate	165
instill	165
insubstantial	166
insurgent	163
intangible	166
intensive-care unit	248
interbreed	278
intercede	21
intercept	166
interject	166
interrogate	167
intervene	167
intimidate	21
intoxicate	21
intricacy	167
intrinsically	167
intuitively	282
inundate	22
invariably	294
invasive	245
investable asset	288
investigative reporter	332
invigorate	167
invincible	167
invoke	274
iron out ~	79
irreparably	168
irrevocable	60
irrigation	168

J

jazz up ~	264
jolt	168
jovial	181
jubilation	43
judicious	168
jump at ~	113
jump through the [a few] hoops	320
juncture	43
just down the road	291
justify	22
juvenile delinquency	328

K

keep ~ in check	329
keep *one* on the straight and narrow	329
keep ~ posted	79
kick the bucket	168
knack	43

L

lackluster	110
ladle	113
lag	22
lambaste	169
lament	22
land-conservation trust	303
languid	169
lap	169
lapse	169
largesse	325
latent	169
laud	145
lavishly	169
lax	60
lay it on	205
leapfrog	284
ledger	310
leeway	170
lenient	60
let off steam	170
lethargic	170
let ~ slide	80
lexicon	274
libel	43
life expectancy	237
life span	235
lifelong homesteading	261
likely scenario	329
line up	286
lineage	278
liquidate	170
listlessness	170
litany	43
litter	171
live off ~	325
livestock breeder	241
livid	171
log	303
log on	257
loiter	171
look at ~ in a new light	301
look up	171
loom	171
loophole	43
loose end	80
loquacious	115
lose ground	171
lose *one's* head	80
loud and clear	172
lucid	172
lucrative	60
lurch	103
lurk	213

M

macho combat	261
mad cow disease	248
make a dent in ~	80
make a killing	80
make a splash	172
make it into ~	307
malady	241
malevolent	172
malignant	173
malnourished	336
mandate	44
marginally	70
mark down ~	173
mark off ~	173
marshal	22
maxim	173
meager	61
meander	22
measure up to ~	80
mediation	173
mediocre	61
membrane	235
menial	61
menstrual cycle	232
mentor	44
mercenary	174
mesmerize	23
metabolic	235

meticulously	70
microbe	267
microloan	298
microorganism	268
miniaturization	270
mire	23
miscellaneous	137
misgiving	44
miss the boat	174
mitigate	174
mitochondrial DNA	278
moderation	101
molecule	235
mollify	23
momentum	44
money laundering	289
moratorium	174
mortify	174
mucus	231
muddle	175
mull	23
multiregional	278
mundane	175
municipal	286
muster	23
mutation	236
mute	175
myriad	61

N

nanometer	270
nasal airways	244
nauseous	61
nebulous	263
negate	175
negligible	176
new twist	254
niche	44
nitrogen	300
nonprofit organization	325
notary	175
notoriety	252
novice	175
no-win situation	309
nuisance	176
nullify	23

O

obesity	244
oblique	176
obliterate	176
oblivious	61
obscure	103
observance	45
obsession	271
obsolete	176
obtrusive	177
obtusely	96
off line	255
off the cuff	81
off the hook	81
offhand talk	271
offshore	288
old-fangled	291
ominously	70
on *one's* last legs	177
on the ball	177
on the block	81
on the carpet	177
on the level	81
on the run	177
on the tip of *one's* tongue	178
once and for all	282
on-line scholarship	255
onset	45
onshore	288
opaque	178
opportune	178
opt	178
optimum	62
opulent	62
ordain	178
ordeal	179
oscillate	179
ostracize	24
oust	24
out of *one's* element	81
out of place	179
outnumber	258
outrageous	62
outright	294
outweigh	237
ovation	179

over the hill	81
over the top	179
overbearing	261
overcast	179
overdraw	180
overdue	180
overindulgent	325
overrun	24
overshadow	338
ozone layer	300

P

pacifism	261
palatable	180
palate	243
paleontologist	281
pallid	180
palm reader	319
paltry	62
panacea	45
paramount	180
pariah	180
parochial	267
pass off ~	255
pass the buck	181
patently	70
pathetic	181
paucity	181
pay through the nose	82
peer	181
per capita consumption	284
per capita demand	284
perception	181
perch	263
perennial	182
perfunctory	182
perilous	62
perimeter	45
perjury	120
permeate	24
pernicious	182
perpetrator	182
pertinent	63
perturb	24
pervade	183
pester	183
petition	183
petrify	183
philanthropic recess	317
phosphorus	300
photosynthesis	267
physical world	271
picky	274
pigeonhole	183
pilfer	183
pilot program	328
pin down ~	184
pinnacle	184
pinpoint	339
pique	25
placate	25
placid	184
plagiarism	254
play on ~	82
play the devil's advocate	82
plea	45
pledge	184
plenary	184
plethora	185
pliable	185
plight	45
ploy	46
pluck	106
plummet	25
plunder	185
pneumonia	240
poach	185
poignantly	70
poise	185
pompous	186
portfolio	294
posh	63
posit	323
postulate	186
potent	186
pounce	186
pound	231
pragmatic	63
prank	186
precarious	187
precedent	46
precept	46

precipitation	46
precision	187
preclusion	187
precursor	282
predator	281
predecessor	282
predicament	310
predisposition	338
predominate	271
preemptive	187
preliminary test	300
premise	187
premium	339
premonition	46
prerequisite	47
prerogative	188
prescription	240
press release	322
presumptuous	63
prevail	96
primate	260
primordial	266
pristine	188
private sector	339
pro or con	298
probe	47
proclivity	188
procrastinate	25
procure	188
prod	188
prodigious	63
profusely	71
prognosis	189
proliferation	47
prolific	189
prominence	189
prong	189
propagate	268
propensity	47
prophesy	190
proponent	47
proposition	190
propriety	190
prosaic	190
protein	236
prototype model	273
provision	48
provocation	190
prowl	191
proximity	48
prudent	64
pry	25
puff	191
pull off ~	82
pull *one's* leg	191
pull strings	82
pull the plug on ~	82
pull through	83
pungent	191
purge (*oneself* of ~)	191
put A through A's paces	83
put in ~	83
put ~ on the spot	83

Q

quadruple	298
qualm	48
quandary	48
quell	25
quench	26
query	191
quip	192

R

racket	48
racketeering	255
radiation	192
radius	192
raise the hard cash	307
ramification	192
rampage	26
rampant	165
ransack	26
rapport	48
ratify	192
rationale	49
raw deal	83
reach out	192
readable	332
rear *one's* head	339
rebate	193
rebound	286

rebuff	26
rebuke	124
rebut	193
recant	193
recapitulate	193
recede	193
recipient	249
reciprocate	26
reckoning	194
reclaim	194
reclusive	64
reconcile	102
reconnaissance	194
recount	194
recoup	26
recruit	328
rectify	194
recuperate	195
red blood cells	248
redeem	27
redress	195
reek	27
refund	195
refurbish	27
regimen	237
regress	195
reimburse	27
reiterate	27
relegate	195
relinquish	196
reminisce	28
remit	196
remorse	196
remuneration	196
rendition	49
renegade	196
renovate	197
repatriate	197
repeal	28
repel	197
replenish	258
replete	64
replicate	197
reprehensible	197
repression	198
reprimand	198
repudiate	198
repulse	198
repute	198
rescind	28
respond	28
restrain	199
retail bank	288
retaliate	28
retard	29
reticent	64
retina	264
retract	199
retreat	199
retrogradation	199
revere	199
revert	199
revoke	29
revolting	200
rice paddy	307
ride out ~	83
rife	200
rift	200
rip-off victim	258
rise to the occasion	83
roadblock	312
rock the boat	200
roll up ~	200
rope ~ into ...	84
rotation	201
rough ride	201
rout	201
rub off on ~	84
rudimentary	64
rueful	65
rule out ~	84
rumple	201
run afoul of ~	201
run the risk of ~	84
rung	251
running water	317
rupture	109
rustle	201
ruthless	202

S

safeguard	304

sage	320	sink in	85
sales pitch	84	siphon	206
salient	202	sit on *one's* hands	207
sanctify	202	sit on the fence	207
satiate	202	sitting duck	85
satirize	243	skew	207
saturate	202	skim	207
savings account	288	skirt around ~	85
savor	29	slap	93
scamper	202	sleek	207
scapegoat	49	sleep-inducing drugs	244
scathing	65	slog	208
schematic	203	sluggish	313
school discipline	328	slur	208
scoff	103	smack	208
scores of ~	239	smear	208
scourge	203	snag	274
scramble	203	snap	208
scrape	203	snatch	209
scratch *one's* back	203	snide	209
scribble	203	snowball	111
scuttle	204	snub	209
secluded	204	soar	209
seethe	204	sodium	245
segmentation	288	solace	49
segregate	204	solicit	29
self-replicating	252	solidarity	49
semantically	204	solvency	209
sense perception	264	somberly	71
serenely	71	soothe	209
servile	205	soothsayer	319
servitude	205	sordid	209
set in	205	sparsely	210
set out	205	spectrum	317
set the agenda	332	spell doom	298
severance	49	spell trouble	260
shed pounds	332	sphere	50
shell	205	spite	210
shell out ~	84	spoil	248
shrewd	206	sporadic	65
shroud	206	sprawl	312
shun	206	spree	50
shy of ~	325	spruce up (~)	263
side effect	245	spur on ~	85
sign over ~	85	spurious	115
sinister	251	spurn	333

spurt	210
squabble	29
squalid	65
squeeze out ~	210
stagger	210
stance	50
stand out	210
stand to reason	85
staple crop	336
steadfast	65
steal the headlines	298
stem	29
sterile	266
steroid	232
stick up for ~	86
stifle	30
stigma	211
stipend	50
stipulate	30
stir	211
stowaway	211
strain	240
stratosphere	258
strike up ~	86
stringent	211
strive	232
stubby	281
subdue	211
subsequent	240
subside	211
subsidize	212
subterranean	267
subversive	212
succinct	65
succumb	212
sue A for B	254
suffice	30
summon	212
sumptuous	213
superbug	241
supernatural	319
suppression	138
surge	213
surgery	232
surmise	30
surmount	213

susceptibility	339
swamp	213
swanky	295
sweat it out	213
swell	304
swindle	30
symmetry	214
synchronize	214
syntax	274

T

tactless	214
taint	31
take a crack at ~	86
take it out on ~	86
take offense	292
take shape	214
take the floor	214
take ~ at face value	86
take ~ with a grain of salt	86
talk shop	87
tally	215
tamper	31
tangible	315
tantalizing	66
tantamount	66
tantrum	50
taper off	215
tarnish	31
taunt	215
tax haven	289
tear up ~	215
tedious	215
teeter	31
temperate	215
tenaciously	71
tender	31
tentative	66
tepid	66
term paper	254
terrestrial	267
tether	216
the law of diminishing returns	298
the opposite is the case	286
the tip of the iceberg	304
think twice	286

thrashing	216
threads	216
thrifty	216
thrive	267
thrust	31
thwart	216
tide over ~	216
tighten *one's* belt	217
time zone	291
tissue	236
to date	284
tolerable	217
tone down ~	87
tonsils	244
topographic	217
topple over ~	128
tout	297
toy with ~	87
trade-off	307
trait	339
transcend	217
transcribe	217
transfusion	247
transgression	218
transient	218
transpose	218
trend-driven	332
trepidation	102
trifling	108
trite	218
trivial	66
tuberculosis	240
tumult	218
turbulent	219
turf	260
turn the tables	219
turn up	219
turnover	303
turpitude	319
twinge	50
twist *one's* arm	87
typhoid fever	240
tyranny	297

U

ubiquitous	67
ulterior	67
ultimatum	51
unabashed	219
unanimously	71
unarmed combat	328
uncanny	67
uncouth	219
undaunted	219
under *one's* thumb	220
under wraps	128
underclass	339
undulate	220
unfold	306
unfounded	67
unitary	220
unleash	252
unprocessed	264
unrelenting	67
unruly	220
unscathed	220
unseemly	221
untenable	221
unwittingly	92
up-market	295

V

vacillate	221
vagrant	221
valiantly	221
vandalism	51
vanity	221
vaporize	222
variant	222
vaunted	222
veer	32
vehemently	71
venerable	222
vent	222
venue	51
verbose	223
verge	223
versatile	67
versed	223
veto	223
vex	32
viable	68

vibrant	68
vicariously	223
vicinity	309
vie	224
vigorous	224
vile	224
vindicate	32
viral illness	240
vital nutrient	300
vitamin A deficiency	336
vivacious	224
void	326
volatile	68
volcanic vent	267
volition	224
voluptuous	225
voracious	68
vouch	32
vow	122
vulgar	225
vulnerable	241

W

waddle	225
wade through ~	87
wage war against ~	254
wane	32
ward off ~	231
waste *one's* breath	87
wear and tear	234
weather	32
well-meaning	252
wet blanket	225
wheeze	243
when it comes to ~	322
whim	111
whir	225
whirl	225
white elephant	226
whiz kid	252
wield	226
wild goose chase	336
win converts	271
wince	226
wind down	88
windfall	51
wing it	88
wistfully	226
work in shifts	291
work *one's* way into ~	315
workhorse	97
would-be seer	319
wrap up ~	226
wrath	226
wreak	33
wreath	227
wrench	227
write off ~	88

Y

Y chromosome	278

Z

zeal	227
zero in on ~	88
zest	227